CHINA AND THE WORLD TRADING SYSTEM
Entering the New Millennium

China, the world's sixth largest economy, has recently joined the rules-based international trading system. What are the implications of this accession? Leading scholars and practitioners from the United States, Europe, China, Australia and Japan argue that China's membership will affect the WTO's decision-making, dispute resolution and rules-based structures. It will also spur legal and economic reform, have far-reaching social, political and distributional consequences in China, facilitate a new role for China in international geo-political affairs, and alter the shape, structure and content of the international trading system as a whole. This book will be of interest to international trade lawyers and economists as well as scholars of China and international relations.

DEBORAH Z. CASS teaches international economic law at the London School of Economics.

BRETT G. WILLIAMS is lecturer in the Faculty of Law at the University of Sydney.

GEORGE BARKER is director of the Centre for Law and Economics at the Australian National University.

CHINA AND THE WORLD TRADING SYSTEM

Entering the New Millennium

Edited by

DEBORAH Z. CASS,
BRETT G. WILLIAMS
AND GEORGE BARKER

CAMBRIDGE
UNIVERSITY PRESS

PUBLISHED BY THE PRESS SYNDICATE OF THE UNIVERSITY OF CAMBRIDGE
The Pitt Building, Trumpington Street, Cambridge, United Kingdom

CAMBRIDGE UNIVERSITY PRESS
The Edinburgh Building, Cambridge, CB2 2RU, UK
40 West 20th Street, New York, NY 10011-4211, USA
477 Williamstown Road, Port Melbourne, VIC 3207, Australia
Ruiz de Alarcón 13, 28014 Madrid, Spain
Dock House, The Waterfront, Cape Town 8001, South Africa

http://www.cambridge.org

First published 2003

Printed in the United Kingdom at the University Press, Cambridge

Typeface Adobe Minion 10.5/13.5 pt   *System* LaTeX 2_ε [TB]

A catalogue record for this book is available from the British Library

ISBN 0 521 81821 4 hardback

CONTENTS

FIGURES

TABLES

CONTRIBUTORS

Ichiro Araki is director of research at the Research Institute of Economy, Trade and Industry (RIETI) in Japan, and was formerly at Japan's Ministry of International Trade and Industry (MITI). From 1995 to 1998, he was a legal affairs officer at the Legal Affairs Division of the World Trade Organization. He has published various articles on international trade law issues in Japanese and in English including: 'GATT/WTO and managing international trade relations' (coauthored with Gabrielle Marceau), in Jin-Young Chung (ed.), *Global Governance – The Role of International Institutions in the Changing World* (The Sejong Institute, 1997), and 'National experiences in state trading: comments', in Thomas Cottier and Petros C. Mavroidis (eds.), *State Trading in the Twenty-first Century* (University of Michigan Press, 1998).

Christopher Arup is a professor of law at Victoria University in Melbourne, Australia. He is author of *The New World Trade Organization Agreements* (Cambridge, 2000) and coeditor of the Cambridge University Press series, Studies in Law and Society.

Raj Bhala is the associate dean for international and comparative legal studies at The George Washington University Law School in Washington, D.C. He holds the Patricia Roberts Harris Research Chair of Law. He is the author of *International Trade Law: Theory and Practice*, a leading casebook in the field, as well as over a dozen law review articles on trade. He earned a law degree from Harvard, Master's degrees from Oxford and LSE while on a Marshall Scholarship, and a Bachelor's degree from Duke University while on an A. B. Duke Scholarship.

Deborah Z. Cass, LL.B (Melb.) 1989, LL.M (Harv.) 1995, teaches international economic law at the London School of Economics and Political Science. She was a chief investigator on the China and the WTO project funded by the Australian Research Council, upon which this book is based.

Ian Dickson was, at the time of writing, in the China Economic and Trade Section of the Department of Foreign Affairs and Trade, Australia. He is now located at the Australian Department of Treasury. Prior to these positions, he worked on Chinese economic issues at the Office of National Assessments in Canberra, Australia, and completed a Master's thesis on the international integration of China's steel industry while at the University of Adelaide.

Jeffrey L. Gertler is senior counsellor in the Legal Affairs Division of the WTO, Geneva. He served as secretary to the GATT Working Party on China's Status as a Contracting Party from 1988 to 1995 and then to the Working Party on China's Accession to the WTO from 1995 until its conclusion in 2001.

Angela Gregory, Bachelor of Asian Studies, LL.B. (Hons) (ANU), Grad. Dip. Leg. Prac. Legal Practitioner (ACT and High Court), is a solicitor at Deacons, Canberra, Australia. Her research and professional interests span commercial, governmental and international areas of law.

Elena Ianchovichina is an economist at the World Bank.

John H. Jackson joined the Georgetown University Law Center faculty in 1998, after a distinguished career as professor of law at the University of Michigan. He is the editor-in-chief of the *Journal of International Economic Law* and the director of the Institute of International Economic Law at Georgetown University Law Center.

Ravi P. Kewalram has undergraduate and postgraduate qualifications in economics, law and international relations.

Qingjiang Kong was educated in China and is currently associate professor at Hangzhou Institute of Commerce. He has published articles in leading journals on law and China studies, such as *International and Comparative Law Quarterly, Journal of International Economic Law, Journal of World Trade, Heidelberg Journal of International Law, Journal of World Intellectual Property* and *Issues & Studies*.

Michael Lennard is Senior Lecturer in Law, University of Sydney, Australia.

Ian Macintosh is an executive officer in the Services Trade and Negotiations Section, Department of Foreign Affairs and Trade, Australia.

Will Martin is lead economist, Development Research Group, Trade, at the World Bank.

Sylvia Ostry is distinguished research fellow, Munk Centre for International Studies, University of Toronto. Formerly deputy minister of trade and ambassador for multilateral negotiations in the Uruguay Round, she has written many books and articles on trade policy and the WTO.

Hamish Redd, BA/LL.B. (Hons) (Melb), legal practitioner of the Supreme Court of the Australian Capital Territory, is at the Australian Human Rights and Equal Opportunity Commission. He is also involved with the Australia–China Human Rights Technical Co-operation Programme and is a candidate for a Master of Laws at the University of Sydney.

Ligang Song is a fellow and director of the China Economy and Business Program in the Asia Pacific School of Economics and Management at the Australian National University. His primary research interests include applied international trade studies, transition economics, the Chinese economy and regional economic integration.

Daniel Stewart, BEc LL.B. GradDip (ANU), LL.M. (UVa), is a lecturer at the Australian National University, teaching and researching in intellectual property as well as completing a dissertation on judicial review of public and private organizations.

Antony S. Taubman is at the Australian Centre for Intellectual Property in Agriculture, Faculty of Law, Australian National University, and recently was director, WTO Intellectual Property Section, Department of Foreign Affairs and Trade, Canberra.

Alice E. S. Tay is Challis Professor of Jurisprudence, University of Sydney and President, Australian Human Rights and Equal Opportunity Commission. She is the author and editor, and coauthor and coeditor (with the late Eugene Kamenka and Günther Doeker-Mach), of 20 books and over 120 articles. Her work is focused on socialist legal systems and legal culture (including the former Soviet Union, the People's Republic of China and Vietnam), comparative law, legal theory and philosophy, jurisprudence and human rights.

Graeme Thomson is an international trade and market access consultant. He was formerly senior trade official and principal adviser at the Department of Foreign Affairs and Trade, Canberra, Australia and was chief negotiator for Australia during China's accession to the WTO 1994–2001.

Brett Gerard Williams LL.B., BEc., Ph.D. (Adelaide), barrister and solicitor of the Supreme Court of South Australia and the High Court of Australia, is a lecturer in the Faculty of Law at the University of Sydney. He is also an affiliate at the Adelaide University Centre for International Economic Studies, a research affiliate at the Australian National University Centre for Law and Economics, and a consulting principal at Law and Economics Consulting Group.

Mark Williams is an assistant professor of law at Hong Kong Polytechnic University. He was EU visiting professor of law at Fudan University, Shanghai 1998–9. He has lived in Hong Kong since 1995 and specializes in Hong Kong and Chinese commercial law. He holds an LL.B. from the University of Bristol, an LL.M. from the University of London (King's College) and is admitted as a solicitor in both England and Hong Kong.

Richard Wu LL.B., PCLL (Hku), BSc. (Econ.), LL.M. (London), MBA (Warwick), LL.B., LL.M. (Peking), formerly partner of Messrs Johnston Stokes and Master, the largest law firm in Hong Kong, is associate dean, Faculty of Law, University of Hong Kong. His research interests include financial regulation, e-commerce and internet laws.

Dene Yeaman is a senior associate with the international law firm Sidley Austin Brown & Wood, and is based in the firm's Hong Kong and Shanghai offices. His practice focuses on foreign direct investment into the People's Republic of China as well as a wide range of PRC commercial and transactional matters. He has worked on structuring various foreign-investment projects in the distribution and logistics sectors in China. He is a graduate of the Australian National University.

PREFACE

This book arose from a research project funded by the Australian Research Council and the Australian Department of Foreign Affairs and Trade (DFAT). The idea for the project first emerged in 1997 in discussions between Deborah Cass and Geoff Raby, former head of the Trade Negotiations Division at DFAT, and subsequently Australian ambassador to the World Trade Organization; and Graeme Thomson, formerly principal adviser in the DFAT Trade Negotiations Division, who oversaw much of Australia's role in the accession negotiations. The success of the project owes a great debt to the inspiration of Geoff Raby, and to the generosity of Graeme Thomson, who was always willing to share the wisdom of his vast experience in trade relations, and his understanding and appreciation of the unique questions arising from the Chinese accession. Invaluable advice and assistance was also received from other DFAT personnel during the project, including Toni Harmer, Ian Macintosh, Klea Maniatis, John Stroop and Antony Taubman in Canberra, Philippa Kelly in Beijing, and Rick Wells in Geneva.

The three-year project, which ran from 1998 to 2001, produced a series of results, in the form of seminars, working papers, essays, a website, a major conference and ultimately this publication. It was instrumental in bringing together, sometimes for the first time, interested parties from business, government and academia, to discuss the crucial issue of China's accession to the World Trade Organization. In March 2001 an international conference was held in Canberra, Australia, as a culmination of the project. Keynote speakers included the leading GATT/WTO scholar, Professor John Jackson, from Georgetown University; Professor Raj Bhala, from George Washington University; Dr Sylvia Ostry, former Canadian trade representative, distinguished research fellow at the University of Toronto and now member of the WTO Director General's Expert Advisory Group; and Mr Jeffrey Gertler, senior counsellor in the Legal Affairs Division of the

WTO, who acted for thirteen years as secretary to the WTO Working Party on China's Accession. The essays in this collection arose from this conference.

The original application for project funding was made by Deborah Cass and Ian McEwin in 1997, who began the research by holding a series of seminars in 1998. In 1999, while Deborah Cass was on leave in the United States, research assistance was provided by Jian Fu, Brett Williams and Fabio Spadi and administrative assistance by Kate Booth. Between them, Jian Fu and Brett Williams conducted research in Australia, Geneva, and China.

Ian McEwin left the project in 2000 and was succeeded by George Barker, director of the Centre for Law and Economics at the Law Faculty of the Australian National University, and a director of Legal and Economics Consulting Group (LECG). Brett Williams continued as principal research officer and was assisted during this time by Faye Liu, Tanya Canny, Scott Ralston and Wang Qiang. In addition, during 2000, Brett Williams identified most of the conference speakers who comprise the authors of this collection.

Warm thanks are due to Wendy Forster at the ANU Law Faculty for administrative assistance in relation to the project, for her extraordinary efforts in organizing the major conference (assisted by Annett Schmiedel), and for assistance with preparation of this manuscript; Amanda Tinnams at the Law Department of the London School of Economics and Political Science; Adam Birnbaum for excellent proofreading; and Bernadette Logue at LECG. Anne Thies worked superbly on research and preparation of the manuscript in its final stages.

Thanks are also due to Finola O'Sullivan at Cambridge University Press, who has been enthusiastic and creative in supporting the publication, to Jennie Rubio, Treena Hall and Jackie Warren at Cambridge University Press, and to Katy Cooper for meticulous copy-editing.

We would like to thank the Faculty of Law of Peking University for hosting Brett Williams as a visiting scholar in June–July 2000. For advice and assistance we are indebted to many people and organizations, including Peter Drysdale, Ligang Song, Malcolm Bosworth and Yang Yongzheng of the ANU Asia Pacific School of Economics and Management; Des Pearson and Daen Dorazio of the Australian Department of Industry, Science and Resources; Danny Moulis and Geoff Budd (then) of Freehills Lawyers; for interviews, the permanent missions to the WTO in Geneva of the United States, the European Union, Japan, the PRC and the Chinese territory of Taiwan; Mr Tang Xiaobing of UNCTAD, and Peter Milthorp and Cato Adrian of the WTO Accessions Division; in Beijing, officers from the Centre for International Agricultural Trade and the Centre for Chinese Agricultural Policy, both at the Chinese Academy of Agricultural Sciences, the Chinese Academy of International Trade and Economic Co-operation, the Legislative Affairs Office of the State Council, the Rural Industries Research Centre, the Department of Treaties and Law of the Ministry of Foreign Trade and Economic Co-operation, the US Embassy in Beijing and News Corporation.

We would also like to thank all those who presented papers at the March 2001 conference and those who chaired and commented.

Deborah Cass and George Barker would like particularly to thank Brett Williams for his tireless efforts between 1998 and 2001; Hilary Charlesworth for encouraging the initial project application; Ian McEwin for assistance in guiding the project in its early stages; the ANU Law Faculty for providing infrastructure support over the life of the project; and the London School of Economics Law Department, Baker McKenzie (Hong Kong office), the Australian Competition and Consumer Commission, Freehills Lawyers and the Canadian High Commission in Australia for financial assistance with the Canberra conference. Deborah Cass also thanks Gerry Simpson for his constant support and encouragement.

Brett Williams thanks Jeremy Webber, dean of the Faculty of Law of University of Sydney, for encouraging his continued participation in this project. He particularly wishes to thank his wife Annett, and his mother Bonnie, both of whom provided encouragement whilst (like China and the WTO) navigating significant challenges between 1999 and 2002.

On 11 December 2001, three years after beginning our research, China joined the World Trade Organization. It is a great privilege to have been amongst the first to study this momentous event. We present the fruits of that study in the confidence that the book will shed some light on a range of fascinating issues for future study by lawyers, trade specialists, industry, diplomats and the international community generally.

ACKNOWLEDGEMENTS

Earlier versions of these chapters were published as follows:

Christopher Arup (chapter 13). Previously 'Lawyers for China: the impact of membership of the World Trade Organization on legal services and law in China' (2001) 4 *Journal of World Intellectual Property* 741–65, Werner Publishing Company Ltd.

Jeffrey Gertler (chapter 4). 'China's WTO Accession: the final countdown', Joint Development Research Centre / World Bank project.

Qingjiang Kong (chapter 9). Previously 'Enforcement of WTO Agreements in China: illusion or reality?'(2001) 35(6) *Journal of World Trade* 1181–214, Kluwer Law International.

Michael Lennard (chapter 21). Previously 'Navigating by the stars: interpreting the WTO agreements' (2002) 5(1) *Journal of International Economic Law* 17–81, Cambridge University Press.

Will Martin and Elena Ianchovichina (chapter 7). Previously 'Trade liberalization in China's WTO accession' (2001) 16(4) *Journal of Economic Integration* 421–45, Sejong University, Seoul.

Alice E. S. Tay and Hamish Redd (chapter 10). Previously 'China: trade, law and human rights' (2002) 7 *International Trade and Business Law Annual* 301–24, Cavendish Publishing (Australia) Pty Ltd.

Disclaimer

ABBREVIATIONS AND ACRONYMS

Abbreviations

Protocol

Protocol on the Accession of The People's Republic of China, 10 November 2001, Doha, (published in Ministerial Decision of 10 November 2001, 'Accession of the People's Republic of China', WT/L/432, dated 23 December 2001). Available at http://www.wto.org/english/thewto_e/acc_e/completeacc_e.htm.

WP Report

Report of the Working Party on the Accession of China, WTO/ACC/CHN/49, 1 October 2001. Available at http://www.wto.org/english/thewto_e/acc_e/completeacc_e.htm.

Doha Declaration

Doha Ministerial Declaration, adopted on 14 November 2001 (WT/MIN(01)DEC/1, dated 20 November 2001).

Paris Convention

Paris Convention for the Protection of Industrial Property of 1883, as revised.

UPOV Convention

International Convention for the Protection of New Varieties of Plants, done 2 December 1961. UPOV 1961/72 means the treaty amended by the Act of 10 November 1972; UPOV 1978 refers to the Act of 23 October 1978; UPOV 1991 refers to the Act of 19 March 1991.

Vienna Convention

Vienna Convention on the Law of Treaties, done at Vienna, 23 May 1969, in force 27 January 1980, 1155 UNTS 331; (1969) 8 ILM 679.

| WTO Agreement | Marrakesh Agreement Establishing the World Trade Organization, done at Marrakesh, 15 April 1994, in force 1 January 1995, (1994) 33 *ILM* 1144. |

Acronyms

AAMA	American Apparel Manufacturers Association
AICs	administrations for industry and commerce
ALL	Administrative Litigation Law of the PRC
APEC	Asia Pacific Economic Co-operation forum
AQSIQ	the PRC State General Administration for Quality Supervision and Inspection and Quarantine
ASEAN	Association of Southeast Asian Nations
ATC	the WTO Agreement on Textiles and Clothing
BMAIC	Beijing Municipal Administration for Industry and Commerce
BZC	bonded zone trading companies
CAAC	Civil Aviation Administration of China
CBI	Caribbean Basin Initiative
CCB	China Construction Bank
CCF	China-China-Foreign joint venture enterprises
CCP	Chinese Communist Party
CEECs	central and eastern European countries
CIQ-SA	the former State Administration for Entry–Exit Inspection and Quarantine of China
CITA	the USA's Committee for Implementation of Textile Agreements
CITIC	China International Trust and Investment Corporation
CNAC	China National Aviation Corporation
CPA	chartered public accountant
CPC	UN Central Product Classification Categories
CPL	Criminal Procedure Law of the PRC
CSBTS	the former China State Bureau of Technical Supervision
DSB	Dispute Settlement Body
DSR	Dispute Settlement Reports
DSU	WTO Understanding on Dispute Settlement

ECJ	European Court of Justice
ELVIS	the USA's Electronic Visa Information System
EU	European Union
FDI	Foreign Direct Investment
FIE	foreign-invested enterprise
FSU	Former Soviet Union
FTC	foreign trade corporations
GATS	General Agreement on Trade in Services
GATT	General Agreement on Tariffs and Trade
GEDA	Guangzhou Economic and Technological Development Area
GI	geographical indication
HS	Harmonized System
IBRD	International Bank for Reconstruction and Development
ICB	Industrial and Commercial Bank of China
ICP	internet content providers
ICSID Convention	International Convention on the Settlement of Investment Disputes between States and Nationals of Other States
IFF Regulations	Administrative Regulations on Foreign Investment in the International Freight Forwarding Industry
IFFEFI Regulations	the Regulations on the Examination and Approval of International Freight Forwarding Enterprises with Foreign Investment
IIPA	International Intellectual Property Alliance
IMF	International Monetary Fund
IPR	intellectual property right
ISP	internet service providers
ITO	International Trade Organization
JVCE	Joint Venture Commercial Enterprises
MEI	the former PRC Ministry of Electronic Industries (now part of MII)
MFA	Multi-Fibre Arrangement
MFN	most favoured nation
MII	the PRC Ministry of Information Industry
MMF	man-made fibre

MNC	multinational corporation
MOC	the PRC Ministry of Communication
MOFTEC	the PRC Ministry of Foreign Trade and Economic Co-operation
MOR	the PRC Ministry of Railways
MOU	Memorandum of Understanding
MPS	the PRC Ministry of Public Security
MPT	the former PRC Ministry of Posts and Telecommunications (now part of MII)
NAFTA	North American Free Trade Agreement
NGO	non-governmental organization
NME	non-market economy
NPC	National Peoples' Congress of the PRC
NTB	non-tariff barrier
NV	normal value
OECD	Organization for Economic Co-operation and Development
PCT	Patent Co-operation Treaty
PNTR	permanent normal trading relations
RMB	renmimbi, the PRC currency
SABIC	Shanghai Administrative Bureau of Industry and Commerce
SAIC	the PRC State Administration of Industry and Commerce
SC	Standing Committee of the National Peoples' Congress of the PRC
SCER	State Commission for Economic Restructuring
SCIO	the PRC State Council Information Office
SCM	the WTO Agreement on Subsidies and Countervailing Measures
SDPC	State Development Planning Commission
SEMC	the PRC State Encryption Management Commission
SETC	the PRC State Economic and Trade Commission
SEZ	special economic zone
SOE	state-owned enterprise
SPS Agreement	the WTO Agreement on Sanitary and Phytosanitary Measures
State Council	State Council of the PRC

STIB	China's State Textile Industry Bureau
TBT Agreement	the WTO Agreement on Technical Barriers to Trade
TPRM	Trade Policy Review Mechanism
TRAB	Trademark Review and Adjudication Board
TRIMs	Agreement on Trade-Related Investment Measures
TRIPs	Agreement on Trade-Related Aspects of Intellectual Property Rights
TRQ	tariff-rate quota
TVE	township and village enterprises
UPOV	Union for the Protection of New Varieties of Plants
USO	universal service obligation
USTR	United States trade representative
VAT	value added tax
WFOE	wholly foreign-owned enterprise
WIPO	World Intellectual Property Organization
WTO	World Trade Organization

Introduction

China and the reshaping of the World Trade Organization

DEBORAH Z. CASS, BRETT G. WILLIAMS AND
GEORGE BARKER

A brief history

11 December 2001 marks a key date in the calendar of world trade. On
that day, the sixth-largest economy in the world, representing a population
of some 1.3 billion people, and reflecting a unique political and economic
system consisting of a hybridization of Marxism and free-market principles, joined the rules-based international trading system, by acceding to
the World Trade Organization (WTO). Even in the shadow of the momentous events of 11 September that year, China's entry to the WTO sealed a
critical moment in international trade, and indeed in international law and
relations of the new millennium.

China's entry to the WTO was generally greeted with approval as an event
whose time had come, and yet also with a little disbelief. A brief history will
explain why. In 1948, the Bretton Woods Agreement set out to establish a
tripartite international economic structure consisting of the International
Monetary Fund (IMF), the International Bank for Reconstruction and
Development (IBRD or World Bank) and the International Trade Organization (ITO). The ITO subsequently failed to come into existence owing to
US Congressional disapproval. China signed on as one of only twenty-three
original Contracting Parties to the provisional framework agreement for
trade liberalization, the General Agreement on Tariffs and Trade (GATT).
However, after the defeat of the Kuomintang nationalist forces by Chinese
communist forces in 1949, the nationalist government in Taiwan withdrew
from the GATT. Thereafter China remained officially outside the multilateral trading system for over forty years. From 1986 the People's Republic of
China sought, unsuccessfully, to revive its dormant position by becoming a

founding member of the World Trade Organization, the new international trade body to be established as part of the Uruguay Round package of agreements. However, negotiations to include China faltered, and in 1995, at the conclusion of the Uruguay Round, a new deal was sealed, the WTO was established and China, once again, remained on the outside.

China's lack of membership of the GATT did not preclude it from becoming an active member of the international trading community. Especially since the introduction of an open door policy in the late 1970s, and the appointment of Deng Xiaoping as paramount leader in 1986, China has pursued a vigorous trade policy. In the last twenty years it has undertaken economic reform aimed at freeing up its imports and exports and encouraging foreign investment. In short, China has undergone extensive political change, and conducted major reform of its legal system, both of which contributed to it increasing its slice of the international trade pie.

But China was still excluded from the international trading system. Until China entered the WTO in 2001 it had been limited in its ability to participate on the same terms as Member States in the negotiation of new standards relevant to trade; it was precluded from resolving international trade disputes under the judicialized process of the WTO, and, unlike most other states, it was subjected to the annual ritual of scrutiny by the US Congress in order to gain most favoured nation (MFN) status in the United States.

Nevertheless, despite its formal exclusion from the WTO, China and its trading partners have sought ways to facilitate its involvement in the organization, at two levels. Bilateral agreements for increased market access were concluded with forty-four countries. Simultaneous with the bilaterals, multilateral negotiations were conducted under the auspices of the GATT Working Party and then the WTO Working Party on China's Accession, which was required to negotiate the terms under which China's accession would occur. These terms were ultimately included in the Schedules of Commitments on goods and services, which, along with the Working Party Report, were annexed to the Protocol on the Accession of the People's Republic of China to the WTO. The accession process has thus acted as a continual spur for China's legal, administrative and judicial system reform.

In 1999 the major bilaterals were finally coming to a close, and the Working Party was moving towards its final stages, when international events intruded. US forces accidentally bombed the Chinese Embassy in Belgrade killing a number of people, and a Chinese national working in a US defence establishment was accused of spying. Negotiations were briefly suspended. However, in November 1999 the US bilateral was finally concluded, with the European Union following soon afterwards in May 2000. By September 2001 the issues in dispute had reduced to a few narrow but controversial matters. However, after the attack on the World Trade Center in New York on 11 September, and a brief day adjournment of the Working Party which followed, these outstanding matters were quickly resolved and the WTO announced that the conditions of membership were now satisfied.

Finally, in November 2001 the stage was set for China's accession. Many hoped it would coincide with the launch of a new round of trade liberalization at the Doha (Qatar) Ministerial, a goal that was deemed particularly desirable after the failure of the Seattle Ministerial in 1999, and the World Trade Center attack. Pressure from the latter events led to a widespread view that improvements in international security were, in part, dependent not just upon international economic growth but upon a fairer distribution of the benefits of that growth. Increased market access by industrialized countries to developing-country products, especially in agriculture and textiles; links between trade and the environment; implementation of Uruguay Round commitments; and resolution of intellectual property rights over pharmaceuticals deemed necessary for public health: these were some of the issues discussed at the Ministerial. China's accession was incorporated into an agenda for a nascent round, an agenda that was to be christened by some as the development round. After three days of discussions in Doha, a new series of trade liberalization negotiations were launched and China's long-awaited entry to the World Trade Organization was approved on 10 November 2001. A day later China signalled that the Standing Committee of the People's Congress had approved the terms of the accession. Following GATT rules, thirty days later, on 11 December 2001, China became the 143rd member of the World Trade Organization. In February 2002 China instituted its first complaint at the WTO against the European Union in relation to food-safety regulations.

Structure of the book and key arguments

The aim of this collection of essays is to address the implications of China's entry to the WTO. In chapter 2 Sylvia Ostry, a respected and artful observer of the international trading system, criticizes commentators, academics and trade officials for their failure to consider the effect of China's entry on the WTO system. She derides economists for their 'breathless' calibration of the pace of Chinese liberalization while ignoring this wider issue of the effect of accession on the international trading system. This collection of essays addresses some of those critical, unanswered questions by examining four key areas affected by China's accession: the accession process; the WTO in its rule-making and dispute settlement capacities; the domestic economy in China, and the international trading system as a whole. Based on papers given at a conference held at the Australian National University in March 2001,[1] this collection is the first to conduct a global examination of these four related areas in order to trace the evolving contours of an international trade system with China as a member.

The book is divided into a number of parts, each of which discuss a different aspect of China's entry to the WTO: the international trading system generally (Part I), the accession of China (Part II), China's internal economy (Part III), and the WTO (Parts IV–VII respectively on goods, services, TRIPs and dispute settlement). The underlying thesis of the collection is that China's accession has untested potential to alter the shape, structure and content of the international trading system as a whole and to facilitate a new role for China in international geo-political affairs. It will also spur dramatic legal and economic reform in China and effect changes to the WTO's decision-making, dispute settlement and rules-based structures. Each chapter speculates on the nature of one or more of these changes and gauges their impact. Like a weathervane on the field of international trade, the collection, as a whole, directs the reader to a number of directions those effects might take.

Several themes emerge from the work. First, the WTO, its rules, institutions, policies and processes, will be modified by China's accession. Secondly, the domestic effects of accession in China will be positive for China's long-term economic growth but raise significant political, social and distributional challenges. Thirdly, the accession package negotiated between China and WTO Member States represents a substantial commitment by China to the disciplines of the international trading system. And fourthly, the broad landscape of the international trading system – which has changed dramatically in the last twenty-five years, and is currently

[1] The conference was a culmination of a research project funded jointly by the Australian Research Council in partnership with the Australian Department of Foreign Affairs and Trade and located at the Australian National University.

undergoing a period of unsettled renegotiation – will be further altered by China's entry to the WTO and its concomitant need to forge a new role for itself in international relations. The remainder of this chapter introduces these themes, all of which can be found woven through each Part of the book, not necessarily corresponding in any linear fashion to the Part headings, but nevertheless informing all aspects of the discussion.

The implications of China's entry to the WTO

The world trading system

Part I examines the impact China's accession will have upon the overall architecture of the world trading system. It suggests that China's entry to the WTO has the potential to have a significant impact upon the world trading system precisely because it occurs at a time when many of the old verities of geo-politics and law, and law and diplomacy, are being questioned. The emergence of unconventional security threats, the (re)assertion of unilateralism to protect state security, and an increased emphasis on religious difference have all occurred at a time in which conventional wisdom had it that the demise of state communism, the contraction of absolute state sovereignty, the pluralization of the centres of legal and state authority and growth of transnational networks would lead, inevitably, to a new ordering of the international system, of which the World Trade Organization would be a key part.

However, a clutch of factors have buffeted these assumptions, and with it the international trade system. In an atmosphere of heightened strategic uncertainty China's entry to the WTO carries additional weight. The announcement in Febuary 2002 by Chinese Premier Jiang Zemin after meeting with US President George W. Bush that China and the United States now have 'more rather than less shared interests, and more rather than less common responsibility for world peace'[2] was an indication of the increasing importance placed by both states upon their new closeness, forged in part by mutual trade interests. In addition to new security threats, structural changes to the world economy continue apace in the form of changes in technologies, information transmission, communication and transport. Consumerism is rising; financial markets are expanding; multisourcing by

---

[2] John Gittings, 'Terror is ingredient binding U.S. and China', *The Guardian*, 22 February 2002, available at www.guardian.co.uk/archive/.

corporations is on the increase and there is an increased focus on environmental considerations as an integral part of economic calculations. Issues of food safety have achieved international notoriety (BSE, GMOs) and human rights awareness has increased at the same time as abuse continues.

In order to respond to these changes a new vocabulary, to which international trade is a great contributor, has been invented. Terms such as globalization, constitutionalization, even deterritorialization, have become commonplace. Deborah Cass examines the constitutionalization of the international trade system and argues that China's entry to the WTO has the potential to influence the phenomenon, whether constitutionalization is conceived of as expanding the trade 'rights' recognized by international trade, strengthening its institutions, or creating a new *demos* or community to legitimize the system.

Even prior to the current uncertainties of international political economy, the landscape of international trade was unsettled. Sylvia Ostry vividly portrays the scene China confronts entering the world trading system in 2001 instead of at the conclusion of the Uruguay Round in 1995. Instead of the North–South bargain that characterized Uruguay, in which developing states won increased market access in agriculture and textiles in exchange for inclusion of 'new' issues such as services and intellectual property, Ostry notes that the international community is facing a more precarious dynamic between North and South in which even the launching of a new round in Doha is perceived as successful simply because it averted complete failure such as that which occurred at the Seattle Ministerial in 1999. She argues that the old-fashioned notions of market access have expanded since Uruguay, from requiring states to simply remove border barriers to a focus on domestic regulatory policy. States, including China, are more frequently obliged to shift from an emphasis on negative regulation to positive regulation, in relation to, for example, intellectual property protection. Similarly, China, like all Member States, is facing an international context for free trade in which formerly domestic issues, such as environment and food-safety regulation, are examined for their trade restrictive impact.

On a similar theme, John H. Jackson's chapter argues that China may begin to exercise a role as diplomatic leader at the WTO, especially if it participates in the resolution of a number of key policy questions currently facing the organization. These include the extent to which the WTO is a member-driven organization, the role of consensus decision-making, and questions of participation, transparency and involvement of civil society.

Similarly, Ostry believes that China may forge a new position for itself by becoming vocal on matters including the use of *amicus* briefs in dispute settlement proceedings or 'participatory legalism' as it has been labelled. Moreover, she suggests China could play a critical role in relation to issues such as creation of a policy forum to discuss the intersection between international trade rules and legitimate domestic policy intervention, and the role of non-state actors in international trade. In short, both the landscape of international trade, and China's role within it, stands to shift in the context of China's accession to the WTO.

The accession

Part II examines the accession process and outcomes in detail. Jeffrey Gertler, secretary to the Working Party on the Accession of China to the WTO, gives a fascinating bird's-eye account of the 'longest and most arduous' accession negotiation in GATT/WTO history. The primary theme that emerges is that the accession package negotiated between China and other Member States of the WTO represents a significant commitment by China to the disciplines of international trade.

Graeme Thomson, who led Australia's negotiation with China, outlines the broad parameters of the package and comments on the 'tremendous' nature and range of China's various commitments. Apart from improvements in transparency, judicial review and uniform administration of trading rules, China has committed itself to massive liberalization of tariffs to about 80 per cent of goods[3] (for detail see Appendix to Thomson's chapter, and chapter 4, by Gertler). China has also agreed to: a reduction of industrial product non-tariff measures and elimination of all quotas, tendering and import licensing by 2005; participation in the WTO Information Technology Agreement; improved market access in the services sector, substantially deregulating both the conditions of entry and the scope of operation for businesses in China in sectors such as telecommunications, insurance, banking, accountancy, legal services, education and architecture; improvements in conformity-assessment procedures for technical barriers and sanitary and phytosanitary measures; and improved trading rights generally.

[3] For a summary of the services negotiation, see Brett G. Williams and Deborah Z. Cass, 'Legal implications for regulation of trade in services of China's accession to the WTO', in Ligang Song (ed.), *Dilemmas of China's Growth in the 21st Century* (Asia Pacific Press, Canberra, 2002), pp. 73–119.

Thus in respect of all the key foundational principals of the WTO – non-discrimination, liberalization, transparency and predictability, and removals of distortions to trade – China's accession is impressive. Gertler writes that 'the breadth and depth of the cuts [to tariff barriers and non-tariff barriers] are there for all to see'. In relation to service liberalization, he says the willingness of China to open up services is 'undeniable', noting that China 'made a more comprehensive set of initial commitments than those offered by most developed countries during the Uruguay Round'. To sum up, both authors, experienced observers of the accession process, conclude that China's willingness substantially to commit itself to the world trade system is clearly present in the final package negotiated.

China's internal arrangements

The third theme of the book concerns the way in which the accession to the WTO will affect China in its domestic sphere. Various chapters, principally in Part III, but also in other Parts of the book, examine the internal effects of WTO membership in relation to aspects of the Chinese economy, legal system and rights culture. It is anticipated that China's accession will be positive for its long-term economic growth but, like all complex institutional changes, controversy remains as to the precise nature of its effects.

The complexity and controversy over the domestic effects of WTO membership are, in part, simply due to the unique nature of the Chinese state. As Thomson points out, China is a difficult country to generalize about, having the characteristics of a developing country and yet also possessing massive industrial and agricultural potential as well as significant technological and intellectual property capability. Moreover, as Gertler puts it, although all accessions are unique, China's accession 'is in a class of its own'.

In particular sectors, changes wrought by WTO membership will be relatively swift and highly visible. In relation to service liberalization one of the key areas is telecommunications. Ian Macintosh provides a detailed analysis of the relationship between China's regulation of the telecommunications industry and commitments under GATS, focusing on mobile services, internet service providers and telecommunications regulation generally. Similarly, Dene Yeaman sets out the radical overhaul of retailing, wholesaling and logistics to which China has committed itself in its services commitments. He describes the way that many of these commitments have already been implemented in Chinese law. Access to foreign legal-services provision is also to be widened. In a state in which there is only a limited tradition of using lawyers to settle disputes, Christopher Arup argues that China's entry to the WTO will lead to an increase in formal and legalized dispute settlement and will pressure China to remove restrictions on foreign legal firms doing business in China. Arup, Alice Tay, Angela Gregory and Mark Williams all point out the gap between law-in-practice and the law-in-theory, and argue that WTO membership has the potential to bring about major changes in attitudes to traditional methods of decision-making and of doing business, but all also question whether China has the personnel and culture necessary to make a western-style legal and regulatory system work. On the specific subject of trademark counterfeiting, Angela Gregory observes that significant change can only be expected in the context of gradual change of the operation of the Chinese legal system.

Alice Tay and Hamish Redd consider linkages between trade and human rights. They remind us that China has almost no history of government under law and that the developing nature of the legal system means that many protections taken for granted in the West are either absent or impractical within China. They assess the mixed evidence of a move towards the rule of law, noting the influence that WTO membership could potentially have.

Of course, the impact of WTO membership will flow not only directly from China's new legal obligations. Some possible transformations in China may come more as a result of the more liberal environment that WTO accession will bring, rather than as direct results of implementing WTO obligations. For example, financial services face an uncertain future. Richard Wu discusses the pressure to allow banks and other financial institutions to become 'one-stop shops', able to compete with the range of services offered by overseas institutions. Like Mark Williams, he questions whether China has the experience and expertise available to staff the regulatory institutions that the new environment will require. In a chapter on competition law and policy, another field marked for change, Williams argues that new pressure will be placed on China's embryonic competition law to regulate the growing internal market, to eliminate the practices of administrative monopoly and internal local protection and to protect fledgling Chinese companies from elimination by larger and more experienced overseas companies. Some of these aims are potentially in conflict, but, as Williams reminds us, conflicting aims are not unusual in competition law and policy internationally.

In relation to goods, China's textile sector also stands to make considerable gains from accession, although these may take some time to emerge. Ian Dickson points out that, in relation to textiles exports, the initial benefits of WTO membership for China will not be great, although over the longer term they will improve. He suggests that a complex of factors including a reform process under the WTO Agreement on Textiles and Clothing that is based on existing quota growth rates, an implementation backlog and availability of various safeguards to other WTO members will impede immediate export gains to China's textile industry.

Membership of the WTO will also lead to significant alteration to some of the basic institutions of Chinese inter-state trade in goods. Ichiro Araki's chapter provides a succinct and insightful account of the negotiating history of technical barriers to trade arrangements, showing how China's two-tier inspection system for domestic and imported products will eventually be abolished. In yet other respects, China's commitments, although controversial during the negotiation of the accession, may have little or no effect. For example, Gertler observes that the 8.5 per cent cap on subsidies agreed to by China, in a departure from WTO rules for developing countries, will probably not have any detrimental effects domestically since it still represents a lower figure than total project budget outlays.

Two of the discussions on intellectual property in Part VI contain rather different analyses of the impact of the TRIPs Agreement on China. Angela Gregory emphasizes some of the differences between China and other countries in which trademark law operates effectively. By contrast, Antony Taubman emphasizes the similarities between the organic development of intellectual property law in China and in other countries. He challenges the commonly accepted view of China and other developing countries as being burdened by the imposition of western standards. Instead, Taubman argues that intellectual property law is being increasingly utilized in China and that substantial gains to China will result.

WTO accession will, however, have long-lasting effects on basic constitutional questions in China. The decentralization of law to China's sub-national entities is examined by Ravi Kewalram. He argues that as an essentially unitary state China will be obliged to take reasonable measures to bring WTO-inconsistent measures at the sub-national level into conformity with its WTO obligations, including removal of the offending measure. Implementation and enforcement of international agreements may change as a result of WTO practice. Qinjiang Kong also elaborates this difficult problem and argues that a host of factors will affect implementation, including: the absence of competence on the part of Chinese courts to correct an inconsistency between two normative rules at different levels; a legal culture in which rule *by* law rather than rule *of* law is emphasized: interest-group pressure; rising nationalism; the role of Taiwan; and institutional defects such as lack of transparency, a wide variety of law-making bodies, bureaucratic discretion, judicial inadequacy and corruption. Kong provides a meticulous description of the Chinese legal system, and Chinese practice in relation to transformation or incorporation of its international legal obligations, arguing that much ambiguity attends Chinese practice, and that attempts privately to enforce China's WTO obligations may occur.

Elena Ianchovichina and Will Martin provide a macroeconomic analysis of the economic implications for China of the liberalization of trade that will follow upon entry into the WTO with a prognosis that is largely favourable so far as China is concerned. They believe that the bulk of the benefit of membership will accrue to China. Some economies that currently provide China's cheap labour markets, such as India and Indonesia, which have until now benefited from economic growth in China, will face increased competition from a China that is a member of the world trading system and may suffer losses as a result. Similarly, Gertler suggests membership will 'allow China to lock in the accumulated benefits of the trade reform process that the Chinese government has undertaken to date, and provide a platform from which China can sustain its reform process into the future'. Others, however, are more dubious.

Raj Bhala examines accession from the perspective of labour surplus and Marxist models in relation to transition from agrarian to industrial economies. From this perspective he concludes that the WTO terms of entry will give rise to major structural changes to the domestic economy with concomitant serious adjustment problems, and that China's planners must know this. Bhala speculates then on why the government proceeded with entry to the WTO and concludes that the politicians and bureaucrats simply felt that there was no alternative. Ligang Song argues that certain areas of the Chinese economy, such as agriculture and financial services, and certain regions, such as the poorer inland provinces, are largely unreconstructed and will face the greatest challenges from China's accelerated integration into world markets. Considerable income and regional disparities can therefore be expected and social and economic policy will have to address these threats to stability.

In short, domestically China will experience considerable change in a variety of sectors, the timing of which varies greatly. The overall outcome remains uncertain. As Chou En Lai reportedly answered to a question about the significance of the French Revolution, 'It is still too early to tell.'[4]

The WTO, its institutions, rules, policies and procedures

China's entry to the WTO does not just have implications for China's internal arrangements. Parts IV–VII, and chapters throughout the collection, discuss the ways in which the WTO, its institutions, rules, policies and processes are likely to be transformed as a result of China's accession.

Dispute settlement will undoubtedly be affected by China's membership. Jackson speculates about whether China's entry will burden WTO dispute settlement by bringing a 'flood' of claims against China. Ostry argues that the 'endogenous legalization' of the WTO may be undermined by China's accession because, in the short term, China will be unable to comply with the transparency requirements of the covered agreements and Protocol. In particular, she argues that the evidentiary requirements of the WTO articulated in various Dispute Settlement Body (DSB) decisions will be difficult to meet in relation to disputes brought against China regarding, for example, its services sector, state trading enterprises or non-performing bank loans.

Other Member States may find that application of the Appellate Body's increasingly sophisticated jurisprudence of interpretation will lead to restitution of some matters in China's favour. Michael Lennard applies principles of interpretation referred to at the DSB (including *in dubio mitius, abus de droit, lex specialis*, acquiescence and estoppel) to a hypothetical case study concerning the standard of methodology for judging price comparability in anti-dumping cases and argues that states seeking to impose anti-dumping duties on China will have the burden of proving, to an objective standard, that Chinese prices are not set under market-economy conditions.

Institutionally the WTO structure may be affected in other ways as well. Gertler refers to the changes in the work of the committee system of the WTO, and the appearance of new faces in the Secretariat. Ostry argues that China's entry may divide the institution by creating a two-track system. Here she raises the spectre of companies, fearful of retaliation by China,

---

[4] Quoted in Simon Schama, *Citizens* (London, 1989), xiii.

failing to bring matters to the attention of home states. According to this scenario, whereas most states operate within a judicialized system, China alone would remain within the system, but beyond the reach of dispute settlement. In her view, China may become only partially integrated into the WTO and so, in the words of the chapter title, China's membership may be both 'to be and not to be'.

Daniel Stewart and Brett Williams discuss the forthcoming review of the TRIPs Agreement and the difference that China's membership is likely to make to it. Chinese policy-makers have particular interest in many of the biotechnology issues that are due for examination by the TRIPs review. They face a trade off between making foreign innovations available to Chinese enterprises that need them and encouraging the development of a local biotechnology industry for which China has considerable potential. Stewart and Williams speculate as to what China's position will be on some of the biotechnology issues arising for review.

The chapter is also a reminder that China's interest in the WTO is not only in implementing the rules but also in assisting in formulating them. Similarly, Macintosh's chapter on telecommunications, in drawing attention to some of the uncertainties in the application of the GATS rules to internet services and to developing technology, makes it obvious that China will have a significant role in any further elaboration of the GATS rules. Again, Dickson's portrayal of the importance to China of the liberalization in the textiles sector makes it clear that China has a significant interest at stake in the interpretation of the rules on safeguards and in any further development of those rules.

Indeed, particular WTO rules will be subject to change following China's accession. The accession process has already, for example, exposed the inadequacy of some rules. Jackson comments on the deficiencies of WTO rules on state trading enterprises highlighted by China's accession.[5] Thomson warns that the modification of WTO safeguard rules in the accession package, as a result of US pressure, may weaken WTO disciplines. Finally, in respect of rules changes, the relationship between rules and the accession is a two-way one. Araki comments that the accession negotiations regarding China's maintenance of a two-tier inspection system for domestic and imported products (in possible contravention of the Agreement on

[5] See the analysis of state trading in China and WTO Project Working Paper #1, Brett G. Williams and Deborah Z. Cass, 'China's accession to GATT and the control of imports of goods by state trading enterprises in China' at http://law.anu.edu.au/china-wto/index.html.

Technical Barriers to Trade) tracked closely developments in the *Korea–Beef* case.[6]

A number of the individual chapters illustrate the enormous change in the philosophy of the Chinese government toward a greater emphasis on the ability of the invisible hand of the market to achieve the best outcomes. However, while the Chinese have been embracing what they used to call 'western economics', China joins the World Trade Organization just as the western world is seized by doubts about the desirability of relying entirely on the market. Now, of course, China will have to be regarded as a key player in the evolution of the principles of the system and it will be interesting to see whether China's accession to the organization augments or diminishes the role of economics-based argument in negotiations and dispute settlement.[7]

In sum, China's accession has enormous potential to affect the rules, policies and institutions of the WTO.

Conclusion

The essays here present the first comprehensive discussion of the nature of implications for international trade of China's membership of the WTO and suggest that, in addition to specific effects within China and particular changes to the WTO, the broader contours of the international trading system, as a whole, will be modified by Chinese accession. In a reflection of the relevance of the key themes of the book, as we write this Introduction, an Atlantic trade war is brewing between the United States and the European Union, resulting from US inability to compete with steel produced in, amongst other countries, China. In response to domestic demand for increased protection, on 5 March 2002 the United States announced it was to impose safeguard measures consisting of tariff barriers of up to 30 per cent on steel imports to combat what it refers to as 'subsidised' steel imports from the Far East. In turn, an irate British trade secretary announced that she would urge the European Union to institute a complaint at the WTO, as well as to take safeguard action to protect British steel interests. China

---

[6] WTO Panel Report on *Korea – Measures Affecting Imports of Fresh, Chilled and Frozen Beef*, WT/DS161/R, WT/DS169/R, adopted 10 January 2001, and WTO Appellate Body Report, WT/DS161/AB/R, WT/DS169/AB/R, adopted 10 January 2001.

[7] See further discussion in Brett Gerard Williams, 'The influence and lack of influence of principles in the negotiation for China's accession to the World Trade Organization' (2001) 33(3&4) *George Washington International Law Review* 791–847, esp. 813–14.

will be adversely affected by the US safeguard measures. Moreover, it may perceive that it has received less favourable treatment than the European Union and Australia, both of which have been allocated tariff quotas exempt from the extra 30 per cent tariff.

One can expect, therefore, that this dispute will be mediated through discussion of the key themes that have emerged from this book. The complex relationship between external and internal economic and legal structures regulating production and export of steel in China and in the United States will be one focus. WTO rules governing safeguards against import surges, including the principle at the heart of the Chinese accession negotiation, non-discrimination, is another. The international trade system in a broader sense is a third. If China joins in this dispute, all four key forces in international trade negotiations – the United States, European Union, Canada and Japan (collectively known as the 'quad') – will be implicated here and the dispute may even determine the US government's negotiating authority in the Doha Round. The international trade system, the accession, China's internal arrangements and WTO rules are all at stake.

As the drama unfolds, the discussion in this book may shed a little light on the debate by thinking about the implications of China's entry to the WTO. At a time when trade protectionism and unilateralism threaten to re-emerge, and the demand for a more equitable distribution of the benefits of globalization is loud, China's role in the volatile landscape of international trade may be one of the keys to the construction of a binding and equitable system of international trade law.

PART I

The world trading system

1

The impact of China's accession on the WTO

JOHN H. JACKSON

Introduction

As of 11 December 2001, China became a full member of the World Trade Organization (WTO), after traversing a long and, some would say, tortured, fifteen-year accession path. I believe that this accession is the most significant activity in the WTO's seven-year life so far. The significance has many dimensions, and the ramifications are profound and extensive. For this chapter,[1] I do not write as an expert on China, but only reflect contributions made about China by many renowned experts as well as by the other excellent chapters presented in this volume.

Of the many dimensions of the impact of China's accession, at least three stand out, namely: (1) the all-important and potentially profound impact of accession on China, its trade and economic policy, its governmental structure and its society; (2) the impact of the accession of China on the WTO itself; and (3) the impact of this event and subsequent Chinese activities on China's relationship to the rest of the world, and the consequent effect on geo-political structures and alignments generally. This chapter will focus only on the second of these dimensions, but clearly these different dimensions are intimately related to each other, as other chapters in this volume demonstrate.

This chapter is divided into two major substantive parts, followed by some conclusions. The first part outlines the landscape of our explorations, noting the global context of the WTO and trading relations generally, with which China will be participating more fully. The second part turns to the special task of this chapter, and notes six different subjects (*inter alia*) that

---

[1] First presented as a paper at the conference on 'China and the World Trade Organization', 16–17 March 2001, Australian National University Faculty of Law, Canberra, Australia.

need to be appreciated about China's impact on the WTO. Finally, I briefly conclude with a few broad generalizations.

The global landscape of accession to the WTO

The policy foundations of the world trading system and the WTO

The first basic subject, and the starting point of the landscape addressed here, is the importance of markets and their effective and efficient operation. Although there can be sceptical queries and challenges to the centrality of markets as an economic organizing principle, the last few decades appear to have justified reliance on these principles in contrast to alternative modes of economic organization. The evidence appears strong in the light of past and recent history that markets can create and distribute a degree of wealth undreamed of in previous eras.

However, while markets have great advantages, there are also disadvantages. There are clearly losers in the free-market game. The firm belief, which seems empirically justified, is that the benefits are in excess of the costs. In other words, the benefits on those advantaged are more numerous than the penalties on those disadvantaged. But there is something poignant about the welfare of the losers, as evidenced during some of the recent backlash against globalization.

Another important subject that has arisen in the last three or four decades is globalization. This phenomenon has intrinsically changed the structure of international trade and international economic relations. There are those who assert that globalization is not a new phenomenon, and that the turn of the previous century saw a tremendous amount of globalization and free movement of various economic activities. There are, in fact, some major differences about today's situation. Certain technological breakthroughs in the last decades have had an immeasurable effect in shrinking the world. These technological phenomena are enormously influential upon us, on at least two counts. One is the dramatic drop in costs and time of transportation, and the second is the dramatic drop in costs and time of communication. Transportation and communication used to be natural barriers to trade. As those barriers dropped dramatically in the last three or four decades, the world began to experience a free-trade context that presented all sorts of new pressures and adjustments. Markets that have these technical advantages must be able to cope with the effects of this new phenomenon, such as the enormous increase in international interdependence and the speed with which economic situations can have an impact across borders.

Markets and institutions

My third proposition is taken directly from economists, and particularly some articulate, Nobel Prize-winning economists of the last three or four decades, namely Douglass North and Ronald Coase.[2] The proposition is that markets will not work without appropriate institutions. By institutions, I mean human institutions, a great many of which are law or rule-oriented institutions. Rule-oriented human institutions are critical and, without them, markets will fail. Evidence of that was shown in the Asian financial crisis, and more recently in situations such as major bankruptcies. Not all institutions must be governmental institutions, but in reality many of them are.

The fourth proposition of this policy framework series is that the WTO is *the* current principal institution for the global market, for globalization and for interdependence. The challenge for the WTO is to manage the problems that will inevitably emerge from the context of the markets currently in place in the world. So the question becomes, can the WTO, as an institution, cope with that enormous challenge? There are considerable worries about whether the WTO is ready for it. It is not the only institution on the landscape; there are others – the World Intellectual Property Organization, the World Health Organization, and the Food and Agriculture Organization and, on the financial side, there are the IMF and the World Bank. Then, of course, there are regional and bilateral institutions. But the WTO is front and centre at present, and there are advantages as well as disadvantages to that position. People fear the role of the WTO because they fear a concentration of power. They are also suspicious of any institution that seems (*seems* is the appropriate word) to be making decisions that hurt people's pocketbooks.

A fifth proposition is that an important necessity of the institutions that I have alluded to is *rule-orientation*. In 'econo-speak', rather than 'legalese', what is at stake is the so-called 'risk premium'. That is, with a certain amount

---

[2] See Douglass C. North, *Institutions, Institutional Change, and Economic Performance* (New York, 1990); Ronald H. Coase, *The Firm, the Market, and the Law* (Chicago, 1988).

of rule stability, there can be a reduction in the risk involved in the billions of decisions made every day by millions of entrepreneurs in a market-oriented system. It is that reduction in risk that will facilitate better allocation of resources and a better world economy, and prevent unscrupulous actors from taking advantage of market failures.

China's membership in the WTO

China's membership in the WTO presents a series of challenges, including a conceptual challenge to the institution. It is a challenge for international trade that is quite profound and affects dozens of issues and principles, many of which were thought to be reasonably settled. The issue of most favoured nation status (now known as permanent normal trade relations) was thought to be decided, and yet for China, selective safeguard questions are again controversial. Maybe it was thought that anti-dumping – the scandal of trade policy – was resolved, but challenges are still emerging from both sides of that issue. One can enumerate a whole list of other unsettled issues, including the institutions, structure and future of the WTO.

There are also significant *non*-economic, or non-trade-related, challenges of China's accession. One of the most succinct inventories in that regard is in a speech by US Senator Max Baucus, delivered on 27 February 2001, which mentioned the large number of issues at play – arms sales, the Taiwan situation, the UN human rights programme and resolution, missile defence at both theatre (Taiwan) level and at the US national level, Taiwan and US/Japan security, developments in the Korean peninsula, non-proliferation questions, the Export Administration Act, developments in APEC, particularly the autumn Shanghai meeting and the potential Bush visit.[3]

That list (plus the impact of the events of 11 September 2001) begins to paint a complex picture, with China's accession emerging as a very important subject, and it is not only a question of trade or economics.

The potential impacts of China's membership on the WTO

I agree with those (including other authors in this volume) who say that the WTO is facing a large number of problems, and many of those problems

---

[3] Max Baucus, 'The contours of a bipartisan China policy', speech given at the Nixon Center, Washington, D.C., 27 February 2001, available at http://www.senate.gov/~baucus/td52.html. See also Max Baucus, 'Re-assessing U.S.–China policy' (2001) 21(1) *SAIS Review* 303–6.

do parallel the magnitude of some of the problems of China's entry. There are a number of needed reforms of the WTO. Many who have spent time in Geneva might agree with the following analogy to the United States government, in Washington D.C. In the United States, many speak about an 'inside the beltway' phenomenon[4] that suggests a particular mentality among decision-makers that is not always tuned in to the constituents who are going about their daily lives and struggling with all the facets accompanying those decisions. But there is also an 'inside the beltway' mentality in Geneva (there *is* virtually a beltway there, but there is a lake interrupting part of it). There is an attitude toward the WTO that many often find disconcerting. Those inside the Geneva 'beltway' seem to cling to a series of principles that have not really been given very much inspection. It is not that these principles are particularly bad in all respects; it is just that they have not been examined and there is a tendency not to want to examine them.

One of those principles, or 'mantras', is that the WTO is a 'member-driven organization'. This principle can be quite destructive and undermining of the organization, and has often kept the organization on a very short leash. The checks and balances in the WTO Charter,[5] as well as the outrageously low level of funding, are just two of the many aspects of this issue. Another mantra that I point to as one of the most potentially problematic is the *consensus* principle. The consensus principle has enormous value to it, but it also has the potential to lead to paralysis. It seems to me that one can currently see some of the paralysis that results when an organization has over 140 members. Some of these problems already existed with 70 members, but now they are becoming exacerbated. A few nations are using the consensus system to 'ransom' the organization to achieve certain alternative goals. They want to be paid for restraining themselves from the breaking of consensus in certain situations. Thus, there is a need for some rethinking of the practicality of this principle.

In an article I published in 1998, I explored the concept of consensus in the context of what I called the 'emerging problems of the dispute settlement system'.[6] In so far as there is, in fact, paralysis, or the inability

---

[4] John H. Jackson, 'The WTO "constitution" and proposed reforms: seven "mantras" revisited' (2001) 4 *Journal of International Economic Law* 67–78.

[5] The phrase 'WTO Charter' refers to the Agreement Establishing the World Trade Organization, actually part of a larger treaty resulting from the Uruguay Round negotiations. See Agreement Establishing the World Trade Organization (1994) 33 *ILM* 13, 15.

[6] John H. Jackson, 'Dispute settlement and the WTO: emerging problems' (1998) 1 *Journal of International Economic Law* 329–51.

to achieve some of the reforms that are necessary to move ahead, there is a tendency to throw things at the dispute settlement system that may not belong there. The fact that the dispute settlement system has been working well makes it susceptible to this tendency. Among other things, the dispute settlement jurisprudence is extraordinarily interesting, rich, deep and detailed; more so, perhaps, than any other similar institution at an international law level in the history of the world. This jurisprudence is not about minor technical problems such as postal union rules; it is about big cataclysmic issues that affect important issues such as whether or not governments and prime ministers fall. But the dispute settlement system can only shoulder so much, and it may not be able to handle the effects of the paralysis of the decision-making and diplomatic processes.

China's impact on the WTO has at least six different facets. These run together and they are not in separate boxes with sharp partitions, but these six facets are used as the structure of the rest of this chapter.

First of all, there is the accession process itself. What has China's accession process perhaps already done to the WTO? Second, and related to that, are the particular rules and relationships of the Accession Protocol to the WTO rules. We know there are deviations from the norms in China's case, and clearly there will therefore be some potential impact on the WTO. Thirdly, there is the question of China's implementation of its obligations. A fourth dimension is the dispute settlement system and its impact on the China/WTO relationship and vice versa. Fifth is the question of China and its diplomacy in the WTO; that is, China as a leader of diplomacy with the accompanying coalitions, attitudes towards decision-making, allocation of decision-making as a matter of allocating power between the international and national levels, and the question of sovereignty. Finally, the sixth dimension describes the institutional problems for the WTO. For example, there are something like 150 or 200 items on various lists of suggested reforms for the WTO dispute settlement system. Many of those are minor fine-tuning, but there are also some major issues. This final dimension includes the needed reforms of the non-dispute settlement side of the WTO. The broad question is: what is going to be China's role in these various reforms?

Fundamental to all of these impacts or dimensions is the perception, shared by virtually all knowledgeable observers, that the WTO cannot be truly effective without embracing China as a member, bringing with it the largest population in the world, and the potential to become the largest economy in the world.

The impact of China's accession process

It is difficult to know what is appropriate in China's accession process. This is one reason why the situation is so important – precisely because it is so unique. There have been problems before in bringing non-market economies into the WTO and the GATT before it. There were some makeshift arrangements with Hungary, Poland and some of the other non-market economies. These arrangements were not entirely satisfactory to all parties involved, but the concerns were mostly small and could be accommodated, and one could brush over some of the tough conceptual problems. It is clear that the rules on state trading in the WTO are woefully inadequate. They do not prevent abuse by a country acceding on terms of so-called 'equality', but which, because of its economic system, has the opportunity to undermine some of the important rules of the WTO system. For example, the country might use state trading in a way that would operate like a tariff in some circumstances, or look like a quota in other circumstances. So it is obvious that the accession process itself has important implications for the WTO as an institution.

However, the China accession process has arguably been constructive. There are some worries about the way in which the United States has gone about the accession process, and the US negotiations with the Chinese have been curious in a sense. As one person close to the process in Washington has said, '[United States Trade Representative Charlene] Barshefsky was able to have a negotiation in which she demanded a lot and gave up nothing, and what a wonderful success that was.' Well, it is a success in a sense, but there must also be something in it for the Chinese.

Protocol rules and special measures

That anecdote leads to a second point. One can parse through the rules that are implied by China's accession protocol, and see some of the differences from previous accession protocols. I cannot analyse all of these differences in this short article as there are dozens, but I can single out a few. One of the things that has been significant is the problem of state trading. It could be, for instance, that the WTO will attempt to accommodate an economy that is substantially different from the WTO prototype model. That attempt is welcome. But it may actually create some new rules about state trading. Indeed, it may be necessary to reconsider the kind of state trading that persists in some of the *existing* member countries, and whether there needs to be more attention paid to those.

There is also the subsidies question. It is an enormous question, and many definitions will evolve throughout the process of accommodating China into the system. China's government-owned, or state-operated or owned, enterprises are a big challenge to the system, and it is hard to believe that this will not shape some of the thinking about subsidies. Some of those people who are dealing with questions such as countervailing duties at the national level are going to find themselves challenged, to put it mildly. There are obviously going to be some big problems in those areas and one can predict that in a couple of years some of the definitions in the subsidies code will have to be revised, if that is manageable. That is, of course, unless paralysis prevents this from happening.

Safeguards also raise an interesting point. There is much criticism of various parts of the so-called 'product-specific' safeguards clause. The question is whether the safeguards have been selective. Have they gone counter to MFN (PNTR)? That seems to be the real question here, although China is accepting that there will be a safeguard that will apply solely to it. That kind of selectivity can be constructive, it seems to me, and it is part of the trade off in trying to assimilate a society and a market structure that is really quite different from, and could abuse, an equal partnership, or a totally harmonized partnership role in the WTO. The hope is that the use of specific safeguards will be constrained by parameters of procedural transparency. Selective safeguards are something that has been discussed with the Chinese for almost fifteen years. The original position of the Chinese was an absolute 'no' to what they deemed 'second-class citizen' status in the WTO; but China has become more constructive and thoughtful on this matter, realizing that there are adjustments on both sides that have been made and will continue to be made.

The adjustments are going to be enormous. Those adjustments, at times, are going to challenge the stability of Chinese society, and the Chinese leadership is already keenly aware of this. On the West's part, there is a need for sympathy and understanding about that.

China's implementation of the obligations

China's implementation of WTO obligations is partly an adjustment problem. It is also partly a problem of the central government's power *vis-à-vis*
local governments. Implementation could have a significant impact on the
WTO in this respect. For example, the tendency is to think that compliance
is something that, if non-existent in a government's relationship with the
WTO, is the government's fault. But there are capacity questions involved
in compliance, and the WTO will have to incorporate those capacity issues
into its thinking. There are examples of that in the intellectual property
area in the WTO, for instance.

China's effect on the WTO dispute settlement system

The fourth dimension of China's impact on the WTO is its effect on the
dispute settlement system. Here, one of the questions is, is this going to
amount to a 'case flood'? Will WTO member countries bring cases against
China in droves very quickly after accession? Many doubt that that is going
to happen. In transitional periods, it will be very hard to establish a violation
case, so the transition clauses are going to be crucial in preventing too much
of a rush to litigation. Could there be non-violation cases? Probably not.
There have only been between five and eight non-violation cases in the
history of the GATT and the WTO.[7] The WTO language in the Dispute
Settlement Understanding[8] is quite startlingly different for non-violation
cases. So, one could doubt that there will be many of those cases, and in any
event, it can be hoped that members will show some restraint in bringing
them. In the longer term, will there be a flood of cases brought against
China? China is a large economy, and large economies face large numbers
of cases. The United States has brought and been defended in more than
half of all the WTO cases brought so far.[9] The European Union dispute
settlement participation is almost as great. Large trading entities already
face a big caseload. China can thus expect a caseload commensurate to

---

[7] John Jackson, William Davey and Alan Sykes, *Legal Problems of International Economic Relations*
(St Paul, Minn., 1995), p. 362.

[8] Agreement Establishing the World Trade Organization, Annex 2, Understanding on Rules and
Procedures Governing the Settlement of Disputes.

[9] See Young Duk Park and Georg C. Umbricht, 'WTO dispute settlement 1995–2000: a statistical
analysis' (2001) 4 *Journal of International Economic Law* 213–30.

its size. What are the implications for China? The answer is that it will be a two-way street. China will have to get used to 'lawyering', as they are very aware. Chinese officials manifest an eagerness to learn the rules of the dispute settlement process, and thus, perhaps if they are given a little breathing space for a couple of years, they will have an adequate number of capable people to handle these problems.

China as a diplomatic leader

The fifth dimension of China's effect on the WTO looks at China as a diplomatic leader. What kind of role will it play in diplomacy? It is really asking for trouble to try to predict its role exactly. People who have expertise on this subject tend to think that China on the whole (based on its historical record, and its participation in other international organizations) will be a 'good citizen'. Of course, it will have its own national interests as a very important bottom line, just as the United States or Europe do. But who says the United States and the European Union are always very good citizens? In relation to China's handling of treaty obligations, China's record is not perfect, but it is also not any worse than that of any of the other WTO members. These academics do not foresee a severe impact arising from that; instead, they see that there will be other kinds of diplomacy, in coalition-making affected by certain kinds of regionalism and sovereignty claims.

One must look at China as a leader of diplomacy, with a potential for coalition-seeking. One must recognize their attitudes towards decision-making as a matter of allocating power between the international and national levels, and face the question of sovereignty. When speaking about sovereignty, the question often is: where is the best place to make a decision? Is it Geneva? Is it Washington? Is it Sacramento? Is it Berkeley? Or is it in a neighbourhood of Berkeley? That is the broad context that involves many different questions, including the capacity of China's institutions to handle certain kinds of decisions. The questions of the appropriate allocation of decision-making competence and China's institutional capacity to handle certain kinds of decisions constitute the broad context in which China's role in the WTO must be assessed. These questions are embedded very much in the *Eu – Beef Hormones* case, for example.[10] Food safety, after

---

[10] Appellate Body Report, *European Communities – Measures Affecting Meat and Meat Products (Hormones)*, WT/DS26 and 48/AB/R, adopted 13 February 1998.

all, is important to national governments, and is not always based only on scientific evidence, but on societal attitudes as well. It was a question very evident in the *Shrimp/Turtle* case[11] and, indeed, virtually every case has had some aspect of sovereignty embedded within it. There are many other issues that could be involved in this subject, with the interesting potential to have an impact on some of the specific institutions.

For example, the Appellate Body is an institution that could feel such an impact. The Appellate Body now has a seven-member roster. There is a notion (which some of us hope will not be that strong) that certain nations tend to think that they should have one of those Appellate Body seats reserved for them – the United States, European Union and Japan, for example. I would guess that China would assert their 'right' to a seat as well. That takes care of four out of seven seats. What is the rest of the world supposed to do? One solution is to increase the number of seats on the roster, and perhaps that will be one of the results of China's impact on the WTO dispute settlement system.

China's role in addressing needed WTO institutional reforms

A final dimension of China's impact on the WTO is its potential role in the institutional reforms of the WTO. There are a series of areas in need of reform outside of the dispute settlement area. For example, some of the aforementioned 'mantras' need addressing. The consensus rule, the member-driven organization problem, transparency questions, participation questions, and the handling of civil society and NGO questions are all on many people's agendas for reform. In the context of the Uruguay Round texts, there is the problem of how to fill the gaps and resolve the ambiguities without always going to the dispute settlement system. There need to be *negotiated* settlements in some of those situations and thus there is a need for a procedure for those. Negotiations cannot be held hostage to a consensus breaker who has another agenda in mind.

In addition, one must consider how China will view an international co-ordinating body, particularly an economic one. Is China going to be very national-sovereignty oriented, and try to block any attempts at further, even modest, influence of the international organization on its country? Or is it

---

[11] Appellate Body Report, *United States – Import Prohibition of Certain Shrimp and Shrimp Products,* WT/DS58/AB/R, adopted 6 November 1998.

going to agree that there has to be reform in order for this organization to be more effective.

On the dispute settlement side, there clearly are some reforms needed, in which, again, China will play a role. Perhaps China would be more interested than other countries in developing a significant *mediation* phase between the consultation and the panel process, which some strongly endorse. Questions remain about the transparency of hearings. What should be done about the *amicus* brief question?

Concluding thoughts

Helpful in concluding this chapter is the juxtaposition of two authors' statements about the world, specifically Tip O'Neill's book, which says 'All politics is local',[12] and an article by Peter Drucker in *Foreign Affairs*, which says 'All economics is international.'[13] There is obviously some tension there, a sort of 'governance tension'. If all economics is international, but politics drives the decision-making and politics is local, there is a problem. So, how do we overcome that dilemma? Some additional questions will hopefully encourage discussion on these matters. The first question is: has China, in the protocol process, been pushed too far – too far for its own good, given the adjustment that it is facing, and too far for the West's own good in developing a more constructive relationship with China? The second question is: at present, given not only the economic issues, but the non-economic and non-trade issues mentioned above, who needs China in the WTO more: China, or the rest of us?

---

[12] See Thomas P. O'Neill and Gery Hymel, *All Politics is Local* (New York, 1994). 'Tip' O'Neill was the speaker of the House of Representatives.

[13] See Peter F. Drucker, 'Trade lessons from the world economy' (1994) 73(1) *Foreign Affairs* 99.

2

WTO membership for China: to be and not to be – is that the answer?

SYLVIA OSTRY

Introduction

The negotiations for China's accession to the WTO took almost fifteen years, but, as the saying goes, timing is everything. If China had joined the GATT, the negotiations would have been far easier since GATT-ese market access was mainly about border barriers, but since the Uruguay Round not only does the concept of market access embrace domestic regulatory policies but also both substantive and procedural legal issues. The barriers to access for service providers stem from laws, regulations, administrative actions that impede cross-border trade and factor flows. Implicit in this shift embodied in the GATS is a move away from GATT *negative* regulation – what governments must *not* do – to *positive* regulation – what governments *must* do. This aspect is now apparent in the telecommunications reference paper that sets out a common framework for the regulation of competition in basic telecommunications and is likely to be adopted in other sectors.[1] In the case of intellectual property the move to positive regulation is more dramatic, since the negotiations covered not only standards for domestic laws but also detailed provisions for procedures to enforce individual (corporate) property rights. But the Uruguay Round also dealt with *social* regulation, which has grown so rapidly in the OECD countries since the 1970s that it has been termed 'regulatory inflation'.[2] In the area of social regulation (covering environment, food safety and so on) the positive regulatory approach is procedural rather than substantive and the model is the western, especially American, administrative procedures model, of which more later.

---

[1] At http://www.itu.int/newsarchive/press/WTPF98/WTORefpaper.html.
[2] Organization for Economic Co-operation and Development, *Report on Regulatory Reform, Volume II: Thematic Studies* (Paris, 1997), p. 197.

The WTO rules thus involve commitments for many member countries of what is in effect systemic redesign. Further, and in my view most importantly, the overarching governing principle of the WTO trading system is the western system of law, especially its American version, and the WTO houses a supranational juridical system for settlement of disputes, a system that is becoming increasingly litigious.

But the transformation of the system is not the only aspect of timing worth noting. The political economy of post-Uruguay trade policy has also been transformed. The Uruguay Round was a North–South 'grand bargain', with GATT-ese market access (especially in agriculture and labour-intensive industries such as textiles and clothing) in exchange for the so-called new issues – trade in services and intellectual property involving investment in structural transformation often with uncertain long-term returns. It turned out to be a bum deal in the view of many southern countries and has left a wide North–South divide. That divide has been widening further with the demand for the 'trade and' (environment and labour) issues by the North, largely in response to the new global actors, the NGOs. However, not all the NGOs are the ones to be seen marching on CNN. Some are technical/legal groups possessing a highly valuable strategic asset – policy knowledge – and a number act as a virtual secretariat for the South. In post-Seattle Geneva, a seemingly paralysed North has been confronted by an increasingly proactive South. The credibility and effectiveness of the WTO is under serious challenge. The launch of a new round at Doha can be regarded as a major success simply by averting another failure. India, which had led the southern opposition to a round, was defeated at the end, but the outcome of the negotiations is far from clear, to say the least. The North–South debate will continue, especially over the so-called implementation issues. The political declaration on pharmaceuticals was hailed as a victory for both the NGOs and the developing countries. But, of course, the political declaration will kick off a difficult and prolonged negotiation over TRIPs (trade-related intellectual property). Since Chinese accession was announced at Doha, the role of China in the new negotiations will be significant – especially in the light of India's 'defeat' at Doha. Recent protectionist actions by the Americans, especially in agriculture, have seriously exacerbated the already difficult negotiating environment. Will China act as a facilitator or a blocker?

Since Chinese accession will arguably be among the most significant events in the history of the world trading system and is bound to have a profound impact on the system, surely both the WTO and the major trading countries have undertaken a careful analysis of the subject? Rather than provide a straight answer, let me recount a story. A few months ago I was at a conference at the University of Minnesota and asked a senior WTO official how many people in the Secretariat were analysing the impact of China on the operations of the WTO. He grinned (assuming I knew the answer), and said two people in the legal division were working 'round the clock' on technical accession matters. OK, I said, surely you have some studies from Brussels or Washington or... Nothing, he said, his grin fading. There are plenty of studies by business groups on the benefits of opening up a market of over a billion consumers, and many models estimating the impact of Chinese liberalization on China and the World. These are GATT-ese type studies, of course, and provide carefully calibrated numbers. (Many of the econometric studies are nearly breathless in admiration for the amazing extent and pace of Chinese liberalization and the bonanza of welfare gains, albeit with some costs for industries within China and many in Asia.) But studies on the WTO system? Alas, no.

I want to break ranks with my fellow economists (except for the growing institutional school) and look at Chinese accession through a legal template. I will then put forward a few, necessarily speculative, implications of Chinese accession for the future of the WTO.

China and transparency[3]

The WTO is a highly legalized system and I would argue there is a built-in tendency for further legalization. It can, for example, be observed in the growing evidentiary content of all disputes: panels are now in effect preparing reports less for the parties than for the Appellate Body. The requirement for ever-increasing amounts of detailed information has only just begun. Imagine what disputes in China's services sector or food safety and risk assessment would entail in terms of evidence; or what about a dispute on subsidies in China's SOEs (state-owned enterprises), privatized or not, which could include a demand for information on non-performing bank loans or non-existent 'services' of subsidiaries or cross-subsidization

---

[3] Much of this discussion is from Sylvia Ostry, 'China and the WTO: the transparency issues' (1998) 3(1) *UCLA Journal of International Law and Foreign Affairs* 1–22. See also Mark A. Groombridge and Claude Barfield, *Tiger by the Tail: China and the World Trade Organization* (Washington, D.C., 1999).

in telecommunications services or technology transfer conditions for foreign investors? But this aspect of so-called transparency is by no means the only problem. Far more important over the long term is the fundamental aspect of transparency as a pillar of the GATT and now the WTO, a pillar as important as non-discrimination in the origins of the system. This needs some explanation.

The drafting of the Charter of the International Trade Organization (ITO), which was to have been a part of the Bretton Woods institutional architecture, coincided with a new development in the American legal system, the establishment of the Administrative Procedures Act (APA) in 1946. The APA stemmed from the expansion of the role of government as a result of the New Deal and the war. It was, in effect, designed to constrain the discretionary power of bureaucrats. When the ITO became defunct, the main elements of the APA that had been included in the Charter became Article X of the GATT, entitled 'Publication and Administration of Trade Regulations'. No founding member objected, probably because all industrialized countries had adopted similar legislation as a result of the expanded role of government, and all therefore required the establishment of norms to control *what bureaucrats do and how they do it*. However, it is important to underline that the US approach was different in several respects in placing more emphasis on independent regulatory agencies with quasi-judicial or quasi-legislative functions; an emphasis on the right of notice and comment; freedom of information; and judicial review. The US approach (more adversarial and fact-intensive than the European) was reflected in Article X, although it is weaker than the APA in speaking of the desirability rather than the necessity of independent tribunals and judicial review, probably as a result of compromise in the negotiating process. In any case it was hardly a major item in the negotiations because the GATT's focus was on border barriers that are obviously 'transparent'.

The Tokyo Round nudged transparency and legalization a bit further, but a sea-change was introduced by the Uruguay Round. So, for example, transparency (the word actually appears in the TRIPs Agreement) now requires the publication of laws, regulations and the mode of administration in services as well as detailed enforcement procedures in the TRIPs Agreement. The Accession Protocol of China, of course, reflects these changes, including requirements on the administration of the trade regime and sections on transparency and judicial review.

Can China deliver on these requirements? The short answer would be not yet – and it is not clear when. Thus, 'transparency' covers publication of relevant laws and regulations; right of comment before implementation; enforcement only of those laws and regulations published; creation of a single inquiry point with a time limit for response. Unfortunately, while Beijing may be able to publish all central government laws, it is widely agreed that many (an unknown number) relevant state laws will not (cannot) be covered, and nor will the unpublished 'normative documents', a leftover from the old regime, still in use by local and state officials. More broadly, the multilayered complexity of the evolving Chinese legal system – including several administrative laws – make it impossible to conform to WTO transparency. The Chinese laws at present lack specified procedures to constrain bureaucratic discretion and include no mandatory right of comment. Finally, the requirement for judicial review, which has been watered down in recent negotiations, faces the basic problem that there is no separation of powers in the Chinese Constitution and that therefore there is no concept of an independent judiciary. Indeed, the CCP has the final say on judicial appointments. As several Chinese legal experts have noted, the Chinese tradition regards law as an instrument to maintain social discipline or promote policy or sovereign rights – rule *by* law not rule *of* law. While that is certainly changing, the instrumentalist approach to law is still widely prevalent.

The concept of instrumentalism is deep-seated. Thus, the pervasiveness of local protectionism stems from the decentralization of the economic reform process launched in the 1980s. There was no view of *systemic* reform but somewhat ad hoc *pragmatic evolution*. The same approach applies to legal reform. Law is an instrument of policy: there is a large and growing body of legal rules for domestic and foreign transactions and government administration. There is, however, no legal *system*, no protection against arbitrary and unpredictable government decisions.

But many, including economists and corporations, would say: so what? There will be an endogenous demand for the rule of law from Chinese business and lawyers as it becomes clear that the costs of relation-based corporate governance, the norm in China, rises astronomically with the rapid spread of economic liberalization. So *guanxi*, or the Chinese tradition of doing business according to personal networks and relationships, is a wasting asset and the rule of law is far less costly and more effective. Thus it is not the demand from the WTO but the demand from business itself that will make the rule of law the governance norm in China. This issue is now the subject of debate among institutional economists – it is all very interesting, but *guanxi* is still prevalent, foreign corporations are actively engaged in forging relation-based networks, and during the transition from one to the other there seems to be what some have described as chaos. There is also growing evidence that corruption and red tape, namely lack of transparency and the rule of law, have a significant negative impact on foreign direct investment and on economic growth.[4] So while obviously the transition will be lengthy, the need for some clearly delineated time-certain road map would be of crucial importance both for sustained economic liberalization and sustained growth in China – and also for the WTO. This brings me to the question of impact.

Impact of Chinese accession on the WTO

In the light of the complexity and difficulty of the profound institutional change required if China is to abide by its WTO 'transparency' commitments, it is worth noting that in the accession negotiations the United States, which had demanded a sixteen-year transition, settled for eight years. In an article in *Fortune* magazine, Senior Minister Lee Kuan Yew of Singapore notes the amazing transformation of China since 1978, but argues that to change the 'mindset' of the Chinese rulers will require replacement by a new generation mainly educated abroad. He estimates this will take '20 to 30 years'.[5] So maybe the WTO members know something that has escaped the notice of Lee Kuan Yew?

Seen through the prism of the legal template highlighted in this chapter, I would argue that the most significant impact of Chinese accession on the WTO will be on the dispute settlement mechanism. I have already noted the endogenous legalization process at work and its increasingly evidentiary-intensive nature, which could create serious problems of access to reliable information in China. Additionally, it is also worth noting that the pressure from the United States and North American NGOs for the right to present *amicus curiae* briefs is unlikely to abate. Indeed, a new rallying cry has

---

[4] See Shang-Jin Wei, 'Local corruption and global capital flows', *Brookings Paper on Economic Activity* 2 (Washington D.C., 2000), pp. 303–46. See also Comment and Discussion, especially Andrei Shleifer on the new institutional economics, ibid., pp. 347–51.

[5] Lee Kuan Yew, 'To be rich is glorious', *Fortune*, 13 November 2000, p. 334.

been provided: 'participatory legalism'.[6] Moreover, there is now a major drive by some academic lawyers and NGOs to promote the primacy of customary international law over international trade law in the field of the environment as well as human rights.[7] Considering that China has just over 100,000 lawyers, or about one for every 11,000 people compared with one per 300 in the United States, participatory legalism and endless arcane debates over whether or not customary international law should override the WTO may be a rather difficult game to play, let alone to win. (Strangely enough, however, China in 2000 decided to reduce the number of new lawyers sharply because of concern over their growing potential for disruptiveness!)[8]

So one view of the impact of Chinese accession expressed in the corridors in Geneva is that a flood of disputes could overwhelm the already over-burdened system. There is serious concern that China would be likely to regard these actions as political and, to save face, simply reject the process itself. Indeed, as many China scholars have underlined, Chinese foreign policy is deeply state-centric and protection of sovereignty is at its core. A Chinese rejection or attack on the dispute settlement mechanism would seriously undermine its credibility.

But another view shared by some, especially multinational corporations with experience in China, is that there will be very few if any disputes. Businesses will be fearful of complaining to their governments because of retaliation by Chinese officials. They would prefer informal behind-the-scene government-to-government talks so that some new deal could be worked out. This scenario would involve a two-track trading system: one set of transparent dispute settlement rules for all WTO members except China and another set of opaque bilateral arrangements for China. Other countries – India, for example – are likely to regard this as unfair, to put it mildly.

Both scenarios could threaten the long-term viability of the WTO. Both would involve an indefinite period of 'partial integration' for the Chinese – to be and not to be. If that is a suggested answer it should be directly con-fronted. Surely a longer transition period, with clearly specified monitoring

---

[6] Richard Shell, 'The trade stakeholders model and participation by nonstate parties in the World Trade Organization' (1996) 17(1) *University of Pennsylvania Journal of International Economic Law* 370.

[7] Sylvia Ostry, 'Dissent.Com: how NGOs are re-making the WTO' (2001) *Policy Options* 6–15.

[8] 'Beijing to slash number of new lawyers', *Financial Times*, 21 November 2000, p. 8.

mechanisms and benchmarks as well as provisions for co-ordinated and tar-geted legal training assistance, would have been a more effective approach? Variants of these ideas have been proposed by a number of policy wonks over the past several years, myself included,[9] but have been ignored by the ne-gotiators. In addition to this more comprehensive transition arrangement it would be essential to include specific mechanisms to secure relevant in-formation and to encourage mediation and negotiation for the settlement of seriously contentious disputes. Indeed, I would argue that the issue of the increasing litigiousness of the WTO dispute settlement mechanism is a broader issue that the Chinese accession will amplify but does not create.

This brings me to my final point: what impact will China have on the North–South gridlock during the new round of negotiations? As argued above, the North–South divide remains, despite the Doha success, and many Asian countries, not least India, are fearful of the impact of Chinese accession on their labour-intensive exports (especially textiles and clothing) and also on technology-intensive products, especially in the consumer elec-tronics sector. Hence, it is unlikely that China will replace India as a 'leader' of a southern block. Rather, I would speculate that China will be pragmatic and carefully weigh the costs and benefits for China. Given the formidable structural change that will ensue from WTO accession – especially the im-pact on the 900 million rural population and the widening rural–urban and inland–coastal income inequality – it seems highly unlikely that further lib-eralization would be welcome, whatever the long-term welfare gains, so the negotiations and industrial products may be very difficult. Yet perhaps the Chinese should take other factors into account, although they cannot be quantified even in a dynamic model. The Doha Round makes a start in some rebalancing of the asymmetry of the Uruguay Round, but it does not include some crucial issues of structural reform, such as a strengthening of the executive capability of the institution (internal transparency) or the creation of a policy forum for the discussion of questions concerning the in-tersection between domestic policy space and international rules or the role of non-state actors in the domestic and international policy-making pro-cess (external transparency). Thus far there has been no significant effort to pursue even minor incremental reform in the WTO, an organization with a

---

[9] See Sylvia Ostry, 'Coherence in global policy-making: is this possible?', *Asia and the Future of the World Economic System*, mimeo, Chatham House, London, March 1999, and Groombridge and Barfield, *Tiger by the Tail*.

virtually non-existent executive arm, an extremely weak legislative arm, and the strongest judicialized dispute system in the history of international law. But most southern countries have impeded even discussion of reform.[10] China should consider encouraging a new role for southern countries: to promote reform of the WTO. After all, this is the institution housing the rules-based multilateral system that benefits the weaker countries most of all. Perhaps *that* may be the answer?

---

[10] Sylvia Ostry, 'What are the necessary ingredients for the world trading order', the Kiel Institute of World Economics, June 2002 (publication forthcoming).

China and the 'constitutionalization' of international trade law

DEBORAH Z. CASS

Introduction

I am told that the Chinese language character for crisis is the same, or similar to, the character for opportunity. This chapter suggests that China's entry to the WTO may have similarly ambiguous consequences in relation to what has been called the 'constitutionalization' of the international trading system.[1] I focus on two aspects of the phenomenon, namely China's influence upon the trade constitutionalization process and its influence upon China.

I argue, first, that the constitutionalization of international trade law will be largely strengthened by China's accession. Secondly, from China's point of view, constitutionalization has the potential to affect China negatively, as well as creating favourable conditions for change. In short, both crisis and opportunity characterize the relationship between China and the constitutionalization of international trade law.

But first, what is constitutionalization? The term has been bandied about for a number of years, and in a variety of international contexts: Europe as a constitutional structure, the UN Charter as a blueprint for world order, and now the World Trade Organization agreements as some kind of incipient constitution for the legal regulation of international trade. This chapter adopts some of these various meanings in order to explore some implications of China's entry to the WTO.

---

[1] For a general discussion of constitutionalization of international trade, see D. Z. Cass 'The "constitutionalization" of international trade law: judicial norm generation as the engine of constitutional development in international trade law' (2001) 12(1) *European Journal of International Law* 39–75.

The chapter is divided into two parts. In the first part I examine constitutionalization from the perspective of the international trade law system generally, namely what is likely to be the effect of China's entry to the WTO upon the constitutionalization process. Here I draw upon three different interpretations of the phenomenon of constitutionalization: (1) constitutionalization as a rights-based system; (2) constitutionalization as an institutional order; and (3) constitutionalization as a metaphysical community. In short, I suggest that if constitutionalization is seen as a *rights-based* transformation, then China's entry to the WTO may have little effect on the constitutionalization process. Conversely, if constitutionalization is defined *institutionally*, the constitutionalization of trade would be strengthened by China's entry. Finally, if a *metaphysical* interpretation of constitutionalization is accepted, then China's entry might, counterintuitively perhaps, also strengthen that process by broadening the underlying architecture of the international trade community.

In the second part of the chapter I examine the flip-side of the question, by asking what implications will follow *for China* of the constitutionalization of trade. I take two commonly accepted examples of constitutionalization and briefly explore how they may affect China. The features of constitutionalization I discuss are: (1) standard of review used by the Appellate Body in assessing national decision-making; and (2) the requirement under the covered agreements for the provision of remedies. Drawing upon this discussion I argue that China, more than most states, is particularly vulnerable to the changes wrought by the constitutionalization process.

Implications of China's entry to the WTO upon the constitutionalization process

In discussing some possible implications for the constitutionalization process of China's entry to the world trading system it is first necessary to outline what the term means. The current literature contains at least three models of constitutionalization, which I have previously characterized as rights-based, institutional and metaphysical.[2]

---

[2] Ibid., n. 7.

Rights-based constitutionalization

The first model – rights-based constitutionalization – is based upon arguments made by leading GATT scholar Ernst Ulrich Petersmann. In a series of works spanning twenty years, Petersmann has suggested that international trade law *should* be a rights-based system of international law.[3]

A key feature of the rights-based view of international trade law constitutionalization is that GATT/WTO law encapsulates a series of individual economic rights (right to trade, right to intellectual property protection, right to remedies in national courts against trade discriminatory actions of another state). Moreover, and as a consequence of this view, (a) these rights should belong not just to states but to individuals who could rely on them in challenging national law and, as a corollary, (b) aspects of GATT/WTO law should have direct effect in municipal legal systems. Hence the description 'constitutional', because under a rights-based system of law governments would be restrained from introducing protectionist measures.

The radical nature of Petersmann's claims should be immediately apparent, especially to those schooled in the traditional conservatism of international law, which conceptualizes treaties as state-to-state agreements and requires those treaties to be incorporated by local statute in order for them to have effect in any municipality. This view is safeguarded by the actions of the European Union and the United States following the Uruguay Agreements, both of which enacted measures explicitly to preclude any direct reliance upon WTO laws to challenge national measures.[4] However, according to Petersmann's image of international trade constitutionalization, the freedoms encapsulated in the WTO agreements ought to be construed as rights of citizens. Moreover, occasionally he goes even further and suggests that some provisions of the WTO agreements 'imply' that they are 'directly applicable'.[5] Ultimately then, if a broad reading of Petersmann's

---

[3] See, e.g., E. U. Petersmann, 'Introduction' in E. U. Petersmann (ed.), *International Trade Law and the GATT/WTO Dispute Settlement System* (The Hague, 1997), pp. 5–122.

[4] European Council Decision of 22 December 1994 on the conclusion of an Agreement Establishing the WTO, OJ 1994 No. L 336, 23 December 1994, p. 2 and Section 102, Uruguay Round Agreement Act, Pub. L. No. 103–465, 108 Stat. 4809 (1994).

[5] Petersmann, 'Introduction', p. 72. It is important to note here that although Petersmann recognizes that the incorporation of WTO law will depend on the constitutional system of the state concerned, he nevertheless states that these implicitly directly applicable provisions 'reflect a clear determination to increase the effectiveness of WTO law by linking it to domestic dispute settlement and enforcement mechanisms': ibid.

work were to be accepted, individuals within states might rely on GATT law when arguing that their individual rights to trade, for example, have been infringed by the state's failure to fulfil its WTO obligations.

In some respects, Petersmann's claim is merely part of a broader trend at the international level to strengthen the effect of international trade law obligations in municipal legal systems. Other developments reflect that trend. First, GATT/WTO law is regularly referred to politically as a non-binding source of national obligation.[6] Secondly, even unincorporated treaties (including trade treaties) may have an effect in national law, for example by aiding in the interpretation of national law. Thirdly, although the European Court of Justice (ECJ) recently affirmed that WTO law is not generally judicially enforceable within the European Union, it also recognized that EU secondary legislation might be reviewable in the light of WTO law, at least where implementing measures explicitly intend to implement WTO law.[7] Fourthly, a modified form of the international law doctrine of state responsibility has long held sway in GATT/WTO law. According to this principle, a state that maintains discriminatory legislation (even in the absence of its concrete application) may be acting inconsistently with the agreements.[8]

In the light of these factors Petersmann's rights-based view has a plausibility that obliges one to consider its effects in the context of China and the WTO.

In my view, China's entry to the WTO does not lend support to a rights-based vision of international trade law constitutionalization. Chinese constitutional and general law practice suggests that international law must be incorporated into local law before it can be relied upon directly, and that incorporation practice is erratic.[9] China has clearly stated that it will

---

[6] The controversy in March 2002 between the United Kingdom and the United States over the imposition of steel safeguards by the United States and remarks by British officials implying that the United States had breached its international obligations *despite* the fact that the WTO agreements are not incorporated into US law, are an illustration in point.

[7] *Portugal v. Council*, ECJ Case C-149/96, [1999] ECR I-08395, 23 November 1999. See discussion in S. Griller, 'Judicial enforceability of WTO law in the European Union' (2000) 3 *Journal of International Economic Law* 441–72.

[8] See, e.g., GATT Report, *US – Taxes on Petroleum (Superfund or Oil Fee case)*, June 1987, BISD 34S/136, para. 5.2.2; WTO Panel Report *United States – sections 301–310 of the Trade Act of 1974*, WT/DS152/R, 22 December 1999.

[9] Q. Kong, 'China's WTO accession: commitments and implications' (2000) 3(4) *Journal of International Economic Law* 655–90, at 678–80.

observe its obligations in good faith and ensure its laws are in conformity with the WTO Agreement. Moreover, it is currently revising all domestic laws and regulations to this purpose.[10] Furthermore, Professor Kong has argued that although the General Principles of Civil Law provide that, in cases of conflict between international law and Chinese law, international law prevails, in practice non-self-executing treaties still require local implementation in order to have local effect.[11] Also, Chinese implementation practice is inconsistent, and is subject to State Council implementation being overridden by the National People's Congress (NPC). In short, in key respects, the situation is not so different from that which applies in many western legal states. The Chinese situation offers little support for the Petersmann argument for a constitutionalized system of international trade law.

Apart from the local effect of WTO law, the rights-based view depends on the claim that international trade law contains *a series of individual trade rights* – the right to trade, to judicial remedies for violations of such, the right to intellectual property protection. In this respect, too, Petersmann's thesis does not sit comfortably with current Chinese practice. For example, for many years China continued to state that foreign enterprises and individuals wishing to trade in China must comply with local formalities of registration.[12] What weight can be given to a right to trade (in the Petersmann sense) if it is conditioned upon a requirement of local incorporation? Similarly in relation to IP protection, administrative and judicial remedies in IP disputes remain underdeveloped. Again, the efficacy of any right to intellectual property protection may be limited by the lack of remedies under Chinese law.

In sum, China's entry to the WTO does not conform particularly well with the idea of the constitutionalization of international trade representing a system of rights protection.

Institutional constitutionalization

The second form that 'constitutionalization' is said to be taking is an institutional form. This argument is largely associated with the work of Professor

---

[10] Draft Report of the Working Party on the Accession of China to the WTO, in *Inside US Trade*, January 2001, insidetrade.com

[11] See Qingjiang Kong's chapter in this volume (chapter 9).

[12] 'Agriculture demands divide WTO members in China', *Inside US Trade*, 15 December 2000, insidetrade.com

John Jackson.[13] The key feature of this view of the trading system is, un-surprisingly, the existence of strong institutions with the capacity to take binding decisions of law, which have an effect at the inter-state level. As evidence for this form of institutional constitutionalization one need look no further than the creation of the Dispute Settlement Body with its inde-pendent adjudicators, expedited procedures and two-tier appellate review.

So what would be the effect of China's entry to the WTO upon this model? First, the inclusion of China greatly increases the number of people covered by the international trading system and strengthens the institu-tional structure of the world trading system and so lends weight to the institutional thesis. Moreover, consistent with general international legal principles, the institutional structure has been broadened in its diversity. The WTO now includes significant states from both the North and South, the first, second and third worlds. It includes developed, developing, tran-sitional, market-based and mixed economies. China's entry enhances the representative nature of its membership.

On the other hand, there are some concerns about the effects of China's membership on the dispute settlement system itself. For example, some have questioned whether China's entry might weaken the dispute set-tlement system.[14] Non-compliance with Appellate Body rulings is one scenario;[15] overload of the dispute settlement system is another,[16] as is the development of a 'two-track' system whereby companies fearful of re-taliation by China fail to bring inconsistencies to the attention of their home states.[17]

In relation to non-compliance it is simply not in China's political, eco-nomic or strategic interests to take this course of action. Refusal to comply would lead to other states' reluctance to bargain trade concessions in any following round. Much more likely is the use by China of the many pos-sibilities for appeal under the WTO Understanding on Dispute Settlement (DSU), and exploitation of any uncertainties of interpretation, such as those involved in the relationship between Articles 21.5 and 22 of the DSU. But this conduct is hardly isolated amongst members (the United States, European Union, Australia), and, in any event, conflicts of interpretation

[13] The key work here is J. H. Jackson, *The World Trade Organization: Constitution and Jurisprudence* (London, 1998).
[14] See Sylvia Ostry's chapter in this volume (chapter 2).   [15] Ibid.
[16] See John Jackson's chapter in this volume (chapter 1).
[17] See Sylvia Ostry's chapter in this volume (chapter 2).

of DSU provisions seem more likely, in the long run, to lead to greater clarification of its provisions, and hence strengthen the institutional structure overall.

Idiosyncratic interpretations of key provisions is another matter. For example, in response to concerns of some Member States that China should only not use balance-of-payments provisions in a protectionist manner, China has indicated that it will make 'full use' of the balance-of-payments provisions to protect its balance-of-payments situation.[18] In relation to subsidies, China has stated that it will 'decide whether to apply and on which conditions to apply the developing country provisions [of the SCM] in the light of its own conditions and needs'.[19]

It is still too early to tell whether these differences will lead to problems with the dispute settlement system. However, looking to other contentious issues one can see that, over the longer term, these contests over interpretation sometimes lead to an increase in the institutional strength of the organization and perhaps its legitimacy. For example the Appellate Body's jurisprudence from the *Tuna Dolphin* case to the *Shrimp Turtle* decision, on the interaction between trade and environment, indicates that it is possible for different visions of liberal trade to develop and improve a system of adjudication.[20] Interpretive disagreements between China and its contracting partners may ultimately produce similar results.

In short, if we envisage the constitutionalizing process as an institutional one, the process is enhanced, rather than diminished, by China's entry. Participation through membership is strengthened, representation is increased, legitimacy through dynamic interpretation is deepened.

Metaphysical constitutionalization

The third category of constitutionalization is one I am calling metaphysical. This definition of constitutionalization is not taken from the field of international trade, but from European Community law. Here I am drawing on the work of Joseph Weiler, who, along with others, has conceptualized

---

[18] Draft Report, cited above, n. 10.

[19] Statement by H. E. Vice-Minister Long Yongtu, head of the Chinese Delegation, at the Fourteenth Session of the Working Party on China, Geneva, 8 December 2000.

[20] *United States – Import of Certain Shrimp and Shrimp Products*, Report of the Appellate Body WT/DS58/AB/R, adopted 6 November 1998; *United States – Restrictions on Imports of Tuna* (1991) 30 *ILM* 1594.

the constitution of the European Community as inclusive of a metaphysical element. In recent years Weiler has focused on the deficiencies of the constitution of Europe from that perspective. He has argued that Europe cannot be properly described as constitutionalized until it embodies a European polity, a sense of binding community, or, as he put it, a *demos*, to authorize and legitimize its existence.[21]

There can be no doubt that if the European Community is not yet constitutionalized because it lacks a *demos*, then the international trading system is even less so (unless, of course, one views the small community of international trade policy and legal elites as constituting an authorizing community sufficient to legitimize its activities). The ongoing controversy, which peaked at Seattle, regarding the law-making activities of the WTO and related bodies, is testimony to a belief in a democratic deficit in this respect.

If Weiler is correct, what lessons might be drawn from the metaphysical approach to constitutionalization from China's entry to the WTO? Here, two views are possible. If European diversity of language, history, values and ideologies is an obstacle to constitutionalization, then the international trade system is even less likely to constitutionalize, in the Weiler sense. Moreover, China clearly stands outside any supposed liberal community of states. Its history, political, social and economic organization have clearly marked it as an outsider. On this view, China's entry can do nothing but exacerbate an already fragmented international trade community and remove any possibility of a trade constitution in this metaphysical sense.

However, if one conceives of the international community or *demos* in a different sense, emphasizing the importance of channels of the creation of a 'political public sphere',[22] then perhaps China's entry would further the avenues for East–West communication. For example, some argue that, in spite of the existence of a multitude of international actors, interests and values, there may be process-based solutions to the problem of participation and community (and hence legitimacy). In Jürgen Habermas' view, one way of creating a legitimate politics for a diverse, multipolar world is to

---

[21] Weiler has a large body of work on the topic, much of which is collected in J. H. H. Weiler, *The Constitution of Europe* (Cambridge, 1999).

[22] J. Habermas, 'Remarks on Dieter Grimm's "Does Europe need a constitution?"' (1995) 1 *European Law Journal* 303.

create public spheres for transnational communication.[23] In these public spheres it is people, not just states, who would communicate and decide issues of common inter-state interest. Applied to the concrete problems of international trade law, Miguel Maduro has argued that a proceduralist approach could lead to a different interpretation of Article 28 (ex Article 30) of the EC Treaty, which prohibits quantitative import restraints.[24] For example, he suggests that interpretation of Article 28 of the Treaty does not require a choice between an anti-protectionist approach (under which only protectionist legislation would be banned) and laissez-faire economic liberalism (according to which any government measure inhibiting economic activities of individual traders could fall). A better interpretation of Article 28 would ask whether, and to what extent, non-state interests had participated sufficiently in the national decision-making process which led to the particular discriminatory prohibition being put in place. The emphasis would be on participation and process – that is, on strengthening community – rather than on finding any 'true' or 'correct' meaning of non-discrimination. On this view, Article 28 mandates only that we live in an interdependent international community, where nation states can no longer, legitimately, decide national policy questions without being aware of their extra-territorial trade implications.

Hence, although the absence of shared values between China and other contracting partners may make it difficult to think of constitutionalization occurring at a metaphysical level, the practice may prove otherwise. If notions of community, legitimacy and democracy can be furthered *procedurally* then China's entry may present just the opportunity that this form of constitutionalization thrives upon. China's entry will lead to an opening up of the channels of communication between different interests. It will necessarily lead to China and other contracting partners confronting each others' interpretations of the covered agreements. The representation of conflicting viewpoints will be heard in formal and informal committees, in adjudication, and at General Council.[25] In other words, the public sphere of the world trading system will necessarily be widened by China's inclusion. In this sense a more metaphysical concept of what it means for the trade system to constitutionalize might be enhanced by China's entry.

[23] Ibid.
[24] M. Maduro, *We the Court: the European Court of Justice and the European Economic Constitution* (Oxford, 1998).
[25] See Jeffrey Gertler's chapter in this volume (chapter 4).

Implications of constitutionalization for China

This part of the chapter reverses the question and briefly points out some issues relevant to the other side of the equation. What are some implications of the constitutionalization of international trade law upon China as it enters the WTO, recognizing, of course, that these issues affect all Member States? However, it will be a premise of the discussion that not all states are equal in relation to the extent of that effect, and that China may be more vulnerable than other states to some of the key developments in the constitutionalization process. I make two brief points.

Standard of review

The correct standard of review a panel must apply in reviewing a national agency decision is a good case in point. Elsewhere I have argued that the Appellate Body's discussion of the correct level of national judicial deference appropriate to the standard of review a panel must use is a key indicator of the constitutionalization process.[26] The reason for this is that implicit in the discussion about review are questions about how to divide decisional power within an inter-state legal system. In other words, constitutional questions are embedded in the issue of review standard. Hence the Appellate Body's decision in the *Eu – Beef Hormones* case[27] neither to defer to state decision-making nor conduct full-scale merits review but, instead, objectively to assess the matters before it, which is one example of the construction of a constitutional-type structure for international trade law.

If constitutionalization is represented by the standard of review issue then constitutionalization will clearly affect China in profound ways. Just as the European Community discovered to their disadvantage in relation to beef hormones and Australia in relation to salmon that states may not resist Panel review with arguments of absolute sovereignty, so too will China be precluded from arguing that the WTO cannot review national agency decisions with discriminatory effects. For example, in the area of sanitary and phytosanitary measures some members of the Working Party have expressed concerns about current levels of China's trade-restrictive health measures. As a consequence of constitutionalization (read here review

---

[26] Cass, 'The "constitutionalization" of international trade law', 58.

[27] *European Communities – Measures Affecting Meat and Meat Products (Hormones)*, WT/DS26, WT/DS26/AB/R, Report of the Appellate Body, adopted 13 February 1998.

standard), decisions about levels of sanitary protection will be objectively assessed by any WTO Panel in order to determine whether they are scientifically justified. The constitutionalization process, therefore, will condition the manner in which China exercises its national health and environment policy-making functions, at least where they are trade-related.

Moreover, this aspect of the constitutionalization process may be magnified because of the nature of Chinese governmental arrangements, which are unitary in theory but highly devolved in some areas of practice. Despite this hybrid form of government, it would seem that China will be under an obligation to its international partners to take 'reasonable measures' to ensure that its sub-national entities comply with WTO obligations.[28]

Provision of remedies

The other example of the effects of constitutionalization upon China itself concerns the requirement to provide judicial and administrative remedies under various of the covered agreements. This development is a further illustration of the constitutionalization of international trade law, especially if that phenomenon is defined in an institutional form. This key innovation of the Uruguay Round deepens the structural architecture of the international trading system and facilitates the creation or modification of national institutions to enforce GATT law. In a trend somewhat reminiscent of the reference procedure in the European Community, these provisions implicate national authorities in the maintenance of GATT law, and hence enhance constitutionalization by interlinking national judicial and administrative structures with international adjudicative structures.

This example of constitutionalization has implications for China especially in relation to its internal administrative and judicial structure and the area of intellectual property enforcement. For example, China's maintenance of a filing-fee system for civil judicial actions, which is based upon the amount of damages requested and makes large-scale intellectual property infringement actions costly, will now be open to examination. Similarly, new administrative sanctions for IP infringement may be required. In short, China may be required to update and modify existing institutions and, indeed, to create new ones. Hence the constitutionalization of international trade, present in the requirement to provide remedies, has a particular resonance when applied to China's intellectual property enforcement regime.

[28] See Ravi Kewalram in this volume (chapter 22).

Conclusion

The first part of the chapter introduced three different ways of defining constitutionalization of international trade law – rights-based, institutional and metaphysical. I argued that China's entry to the WTO will affect constitutionalization differently depending upon the model one adopts. The purpose of this analysis is not to say one view of the constitutionalization process is the 'right' view, but simply to use constitutional modelling in order to tease out some of the implications of China's entry upon that process, however defined.

The examples of constitutionalization given in the second part of this chapter – standard of review and the requirement to provide remedies – briefly illustrate the thesis that the constitutionalization of international trade law will have profound consequences for China when it enters the WTO.

In conclusion, China's entry to the WTO will have significant effects upon the constitutionalization of international trade law, but the effects will vary depending on how that process is defined. If one thinks in terms of the rights-based model the practices introduced into international trade law by China's entry provide little support for the model. If an institutional approach is taken, China's entry will strengthen and expand the constitution of international trade. Adopting a metaphysical approach may at first sight lead to the conclusion that China's entry is a setback, but on reflection problems associated with legitimacy and community have the potential to be overcome. China's accession to the WTO will be deeply implicated in constitutional changes, however defined.

The second part of the chapter suggested that the constitutionalization process itself will have ramifications for China. Key aspects of the process, including introduction of an objective standard of review of national agency decisions, and introduction of a requirement for states to provide remedies, illustrate China's vulnerability to the changes wrought by constitutionalization.

In sum, both crisis and opportunity are present. We stand at the crossroads of an important moment in the constitutionalization process, in which China is a key player both in affecting and being affected by these transformations.

PART II

The accession

4

China's WTO accession – the final countdown

JEFFREY L. GERTLER

Introduction

With the gavelling of the accession package at the conclusion of the Working Party meeting on 17 September 2001, the negotiation on China's accession to the WTO was finally brought to a close. Thereafter, the WTO Ministerial Conference approved the terms of China's accession in Doha (Qatar) on 10 November 2001 and the Chinese government notified its acceptance on 11 November. In line with customary practice, and as set out in China's Protocol of Accession, China became a member of the WTO thirty days later, on 11 December 2001.

Each accession to the WTO is a unique event, but few would argue with the proposition that China's accession is in a class of its own. After all, China was one of the twenty-three original Contracting Parties to the GATT in 1948 and her application for readmission to the multilateral trading system dates back fifteen years to July 1986, easily making it the longest and most arduous accession negotiation in the history of the GATT/WTO.

After China's revolution in 1949 and the split between Mao Zedong and Chiang Kai-Shek, the government in Taiwan announced in 1950 that China would leave the GATT. Although the government in Beijing never recognized this withdrawal decision, nearly forty years later, in 1986, the People's Republic of China notified the GATT of its wish to resume its status as a GATT Contracting Party and its willingness to renegotiate the terms of its membership.

A working party to examine China's status was established in March 1987 and met for the first time in October of that year. The GATT Working Party on China's Status met on over twenty occasions, but without

The views expressed in this chapter are those of the author and are not to be attributed to the WTO, its members or the Secretariat.

conclusion. With the coming into being of the WTO in 1995, the GATT Working Party was converted into a WTO Working Party on the Accession of China. The WTO Working Party met eighteen times. Right from the beginning, the Working Party was chaired by Ambassador Pierre-Louis Girard of Switzerland.

Article XII of the Marrakesh Agreement Establishing the World Trade Organization (the 'WTO Agreement'), which governs accessions, is striking in its brevity. The operative provision reads: 'Any State or separate customs territory... may accede to this Agreement, on terms to be agreed between it and the WTO.' There are currently twenty-eight accession working parties. Sixteen new members have acceded since entry into force of the WTO Agreement. With China and Taiwan (known in the WTO as 'Chinese Taipei') joining this winter, there are now 144 members, including three separate customs territories (Chinese Taipei; Hong Kong, China; and Macau, China).

The final stages of the China accession process can be naturally classified under three headings: (1) conclusion of bilateral market-access negotiations; (2) conclusion of multilateral negotiations in the Working Party, including the draft Protocol and its Annexes, as well as the Working Party Report, these documents together setting out the terms of China's accession to the WTO; and (3) approval and acceptance of these terms of accession by WTO members and by China, respectively.

Before delving into a description of these three steps, it may be worth reviewing, briefly, the many ups and downs China experienced along its accession trail. Beginning in the late 1980s, significant progress was made just prior to the Tiananmen 'incident', although for almost two-and-a-half years following Tiananmen there was virtually no activity on the accession front. Nevertheless, during the early 1990s, China participated in the Uruguay Round negotiations but failed to conclude discussions on its status as a GATT Contracting Party in time for it to be considered as an original member of the WTO. Then in December 1995 the GATT Working Party was converted into a WTO accession Working Party, leading to considerable optimism about an accelerated process in early 1997. The near-conclusion of a bilateral deal with the United States in April 1999 was followed by US bombing of the Chinese Embassy in Belgrade in May 1999. The US–China bilaterals were eventually concluded in November 1999, and were followed shortly thereafter by a spate of other bilateral deals in the first half of 2000, including that with the European Union in May of that year. Further hiccups occurred thereafter, including the collision and downing of a US spy plane over the Taiwan Straits, the Bush administration's aggressive enthusiasm for a new form of Star Wars (the so-called Missile Defense System) and, finally, the terror attack in the United States in September 2001 and the US-led retaliatory actions since then.

Clearly, China and WTO members have been on a roller-coaster ride of major proportions over the past fifteen years.

Bilaterals

Some forty-four WTO members (counting the fifteen Member States of the European Union as one) expressed interest in concluding bilateral market-access negotiations with China. As these deals were struck and notified to the WTO, China's consolidated Schedule of Concessions and Commitments on Goods (China's 'Goods Schedule') and its consolidated Schedule of Specific Commitments on Services (China's 'Services Schedule') were prepared with assistance from the WTO Secretariat. Thereafter, they were reviewed in the Working Party and 'multilateralized' – that is, extended on a most favoured nation (MFN) basis to all WTO members, as China's Goods and Services Schedules, annexed to the Protocol of Accession. In other words, these bilaterally agreed commitments have become part of the multilateral treaty terms of China's membership in the WTO.

China was only able to make rapid progress in concluding its bilateral negotiations with most other WTO member governments once it reached bilateral agreement with the United States in November 1999 and then with the European Communities in May 2000. Thereafter, the negotiations picked up pace.

It was only in the final days of the Working Party that China was able to conclude negotiations with Mexico, the last of the forty-four WTO members seeking bilateral market-access commitments. The sticking point there was that the two countries had to agree on how to deal with hundreds of anti-dumping orders that Mexico continued to maintain against products of Chinese origin. In the end, Mexico agreed that it would terminate these allegedly WTO-inconsistent measures six years after China's accession.

In addition, El Salvador, which recognizes Taiwan and not the PRC (as is true of some other WTO members as well), did not request bilateral negotiations with China and invoked the 'non-application' provision of the WTO Agreement (Article XIII) against China.

One element contributing to pressure on China and members to conclude bilateral accords rapidly was the US administration's agreement with

China – as a *quid pro quo* for China's market-access concessions – that
the United States would provide China with permanent MFN status, thus
eliminating the annually renewed conditional MFN provided under the
Jackson–Vanik amendment to the US Trade Act. After much debate, the US
Congress finally passed unconditional MFN status (what it calls 'permanent
normal trade relations' or 'PNTR') for China in September 2000.

Multilateral steps

With the bilateral market-access negotiations nearing completion,
members and China showed renewed interest in wrapping up the many
outstanding multilateral elements of the accession package. In order to
finalize the negotiated package, and in recognition of the fact that much
of the information China had submitted to the Working Party was incom-
plete or out of date, the Working Party requested China to submit updated
information (notifications of laws, regulations and other policy measures)
on all key aspects of China's trade regime. Clearly, such information was
indispensable to the members' assessment of the consistency of China's
trade regime with WTO rules, as well as to finalizing negotiations on various key provisions of the Protocol and the Report. Identifying the trouble
spots and agreeing on the timing – including possible transition periods –
for China to bring any WTO-inconsistent policy measures into compliance
with WTO obligations, presented major challenges for all concerned.

The final meeting of the Working Party in 2001, with informal sessions
in the week of 10 September and the formal meeting on 17 September, was
devoted to completing the technical 'clean-up' and verification of the Goods
and Services Schedules, followed by an overall review of the documents to
ensure consistency among the various elements of the accession package.

China and Working Party members finally reached agreement on all outstanding issues. By the conclusion, agreement was reached on: preambular
and general provisions; commitments relating to the administration of the
trade regime, including uniform administration, special economic areas,
transparency and judicial review; commitments on non-discrimination,
special trade arrangements, state trading, non-tariff measures, tariff-rate
quota administration, import and export licensing, price controls, taxes
and charges levied on imports and exports, export subsidies and domestic
support in agriculture, sanitary and phytosanitary measures; trading rights;
and standards and technical regulations.

Agreement was also reached on a special transitional provision on price comparability in determining subsidies and dumping, lasting fifteen years; the establishment of both a transitional product-specific safeguard mechanism and a separate transitional textile safeguard; immediate implementation of the Agreement on Trade-related Aspects of Intellectual Property Rights (TRIPs); a host of technical, sectoral issues in trade in services; a transitional review mechanism to oversee compliance with the terms of the Protocol; and final provisions. An impressive list.

While China has reserved the right to exclusive state trading for products such as cereals, tobacco, fuels and minerals, and to maintain some restrictions on transportation and distribution of goods inside China, many of the restrictions that foreign companies currently face in China will be phased out over a three-year transition period. During a twelve-year period, WTO members will have access to a transitional safeguard mechanism in cases where imports of products of Chinese origin cause or threaten to cause market disruption to the member's domestic producers.

In the area of textiles, upon accession China became a party to the Agreement on Textiles and Clothing and, as for all WTO members, quotas on textiles will end on 31 December 2004. But a special safeguard mechanism will remain in place until the end of 2008, permitting WTO members to take action to curb imports in case of market disruption caused by Chinese exports of textile products.

Until very late in the game, there was lack of agreement on the availability to China of WTO provisions in favour of developing countries relating to domestic support in agriculture and industrial subsidies. The United States, in particular, objected to providing China with the full benefit of developing-country provisions in these areas. The matter was eventually resolved through China agreeing not to resort to certain of these WTO provisions and accepting a cap on domestic support in agriculture at 8.5 per cent, below that available generally to developing-country members under the WTO Agreement. It is doubtful, however, whether this cap of 8.5 per cent on domestic subsidies will have any truly detrimental impact on China's ability to help its farming sector adapt to the new and evolving conditions of competition, mainly because this 8.5 per cent figure is still well above existing budgetary outlays from the Chinese government.

Also going down to the wire, it proved exceptionally difficult to reach agreement on the regime relating to trading rights. The basic regime eventually agreed to by China calls for a fully liberalized right for foreign companies to gain trading rights in China after a three-year transition period, except in respect of state-traded products.

There was also considerable difficulty in reaching agreement on China's handling of its regime dealing with technical regulations and standards, the key issue here being how to ensure non-discrimination ('national treatment') in the application of this regime. After repeated urging, spanning several years, China finally committed to unifying its administrative structure responsible for the inspection and conformity assessment procedures (under the State General Administration of the People's Republic of China for Quality Supervision and Inspection and Quarantine (AQSIQ)) for both domestic and imported goods, thus allaying many of the concerns raised in relation to the dual and separate systems of inspection that previously existed.

As part of the concluding phase, the Working Party also reviewed and obtained amendments and clarifications to many of the transitional Annexes of the Protocol. This was done on the basis of updated and revised drafts of these Annexes provided by China. They include Annexes on: Products subject to State-trading; Products subject to Designated Trading; Non-tariff Measures subject to Phased Elimination; Products and Services subject to Price Controls; Notification and Phase-out of Subsidies; Export Taxes and Charges; Restrictions Maintained Against China; Issues to be Addressed in the Transitional Review; and the Schedule of Concessions and Commitments on Goods, as well as the Schedule of Specific Commitments on Services.

The Protocol and Working Party Report essentially contain a one-way set of commitments (from China's side only), although these documents also contain some 'soft' commitments by members – for example, regarding the non-abuse of domestic procedures in anti-dumping actions and restraint in the use of the special safeguard. Additionally, there is an unusual Annex to the Protocol, containing commitments by certain members to phase out inconsistent measures maintained against China over a transition period (of up to five years).

Approval and acceptance

Once consensus was achieved in the Working Party on the final accession package, this was forwarded to the General Council for decision. Given the timing of the Fourth Ministerial Conference in mid-November, it was decided that these documents should be forwarded to Doha for approval by ministers, rather than being decided upon at the level of the General Council in Geneva.

In accordance with established procedures, the Ministerial Conference approved the Decision on Accession and the Protocol on the terms of China's accession on 10 November, and, as mentioned earlier, the acceding government became a member of the WTO thirty days after it accepted its Protocol of Accession, which China did on 11 November, notifying the director-general that the Standing Committee of the People's Congress had ratified the terms of accession. Thus, China became the 143rd Member of the WTO on 11 December 2001.[1]

Although Article XII.2 of the WTO Agreement provides that 'the Ministerial Conference shall approve the agreement on the terms of accession by a two-thirds majority of the Members of the WTO', pursuant to Article IX.1 of the same agreement and a 1995 decision of the General Council, all accession decisions are to be approved by consensus (with possible recourse to voting only where consensus is not achievable). All sixteen WTO accession decisions to date, including that of China, have been taken by consensus.

China's accession in the context of the WTO's basic principles

It is interesting to consider, briefly, how China's accession fits within the context of the five fundamental principles of the GATT and the WTO. Simply put, these principles cover: (1) non-discrimination; (2) market opening; (3) transparency and predictability; (4) undistorted trade; and (5) preferential treatment for developing countries.

There are two types of *non-discrimination* of interest: the MFN principle; and the national treatment principle. Under the MFN principle, a member may not discriminate between its trading partners: goods and services and service providers are to be accorded MFN (i.e. equal) treatment. At the same time, a member must provide national treatment: it may not discriminate on its internal market between its own and foreign products, services and nationals.

Where do things stand in terms of China's accession *vis-à-vis* the principle of non-discrimination? China, like all other members, has committed to abide by all the WTO agreements, including those provisions requiring

---

[1] Chinese Taipei, whose terms of accession were approved by ministers on 11 November 2001, became a WTO Member on 1 January 2002.

application of MFN and national treatment. In its Accession Protocol, China has agreed to undertake additional commitments in order to ensure the smooth phasing in of these non-discrimination principles. Of particular note are commitments to eliminate dual-pricing practices and to phase out within three years most of the restrictions on importing, exporting and trading currently faced by foreign enterprises. All foreign enterprises, including those not invested or registered in China, are to be accorded treatment no less favourable than that accorded to enterprises in China.

The principle of *market opening* is promoted in the WTO through successive rounds of multilateral trade negotiations aimed at the progressive lowering of trade barriers. New members are also pressed to liberalize their trade regimes during accession negotiations. Trade ministers kicked off the latest round of multilateral negotiations at the Doha Ministerial Meeting in November 2001.

With respect to market opening, China has very significantly reduced its tariff and non-tariff barriers as part of its bid to join the WTO. The breadth and depth of the cuts are there for all to see. China's willingness progressively and substantially to open up its services sectors to foreign competition is also undeniable. As for the Doha Development Agenda, China has already demonstrated its intention to play a significant role in this new round of trade negotiations.

Transparency and predictability are key elements of the multilateral trading system. The basic transparency principle, contained in Article X of the GATT, calls on member governments promptly to publish all trade-related laws, regulations, judicial decisions and administrative rulings of general application, to administer all such measures in a uniform, impartial and reasonable manner, and to provide for independent judicial review procedures for the prompt review and correction of administrative actions. The predictability principle is ensured through a legal hierarchy giving preference to tariffs over less transparent and less secure non-tariff measures such as quotas and licences, and by encouraging members to 'bind' their market-opening commitments in goods and services. In the goods area, this binding amounts to setting ceilings on customs-tariff rates.

China has committed to abide by the WTO's transparency obligations across the board, including with respect to uniform application of its trade regime and independent judicial review, and has made additional commitments in each of these areas. While difficulties may exist with respect to variations in treatment in different parts of China's customs territory, as well as with the perceived lack of independence of the judiciary, there can be little doubt that the Chinese government is committed to carrying through the necessary reforms to implement these obligations in a uniform and impartial manner. Also, as noted, China's accession commitments will be the subject of a special transitional review mechanism for the first ten years of membership.

With China as a member, her producers and exporters will more confidently be able to make long-term business decisions on the expansion of their activities. The more open the Chinese economy becomes, the more China will benefit from the legal security of the rules-based trading system. Not just foreign investors, exporters and importers, but also all Chinese citizens, will benefit from the more open, non-discriminatory reforms China is currently undertaking.

In terms of producing a more predictable and secure trading environment, China, in the goods area, has bound all its import tariffs. China has also committed to the phased reduction and removal of tariff barriers, mostly by 2004, but in no case later than 2010. China's average bound-tariff level will decrease to 15 per cent for agricultural products, ranging from 0 to 65 per cent, with the higher rates applied to cereals. For industrial goods, the average bound-tariff level will go down to 8.9 per cent, with a range from 0 to 47 per cent, the highest rates applied to photographic film and automobiles and related products. In services, China has made a more comprehensive set of initial commitments than those offered by most developed countries during the Uruguay Round. Of particular note are China's commitments in services sectors covering telecommunications, banking and insurance.

The WTO system also promotes *undistorted trade* through the establishment of disciplines on subsidies and dumping, allowing members to respond to unfair trade through the imposition of countervailing or anti-dumping duties. In addition, the treaty allows individual members to impose temporary safeguard measures, under strict rules, when faced with a sudden surge in imports causing serious injury to a domestic industry.

As in other areas, China has undertaken to abide by all WTO disciplines relating to subsidies and countervailing measures, anti-dumping and safeguards. As noted above, it has also committed not to use export subsidies on either industrial or agricultural goods, and has accepted special provisions sought by other members in relation to determinations of dumping or subsidies, as well as a special product-specific safeguard mechanism and a separate textile safeguard. China has also indicated its intention to join the plurilateral Agreement on Government Procurement, which is aimed at ensuring fair competition rules in purchases by government procurement agencies.

The principle of *preferential treatment for developing countries* permeates the entire WTO Agreement, providing transition periods to developing countries and countries in transition to market economies, to adjust their systems to many of the new obligations resulting from the Uruguay Round. A Ministerial Decision gives additional flexibility to the least-developed countries in implementing the various Uruguay Round agreements, and calls on developed-country members to accelerate their implementation of market-access commitments on goods exported by the least-developed countries.

Although China has not been granted across-the-board preferential treatment as a developing country, it has negotiated specific transitional arrangements in certain areas of its trade regime. Examples include the phasing out of quotas and import licences, and the phased liberalization of the right for foreign entities to trade in China. In contrast, despite the availability of more preferential treatment under the WTO Agreements, China has accepted a special cap on its ability to provide domestic production subsidies in agriculture and has agreed not to use export subsidies. It has also committed to immediate implementation of the TRIPs Agreement.

Institutional implications

Turning to some of the institutional implications of China's WTO membership, no one can contest that China's participation in the WTO will affect the operations of this organization in substantial ways and over the long term. China is joining as the seventh-largest exporter and eighth-largest importer of merchandise trade, and as the twelfth-leading exporter and tenth-leading importer of commercial services. It has the largest population and largest potential market of any WTO member.

Undoubtedly, China's membership will have implications for the regular work of the WTO's many committees administering the many agreements of this institution. China will surely be active in the newly launched and future rounds of multilateral trade negotiations, in agriculture, in services but also in other areas of mutual concern. It will participate, too, in fashioning the improved institutional operations of the WTO. Clearly, also, China's membership is likely to result in expanded recourse to the dispute settlement procedures of the WTO, both by China and by other members in relation to China's implementation of its WTO commitments. The first such case was that recently brought by China, similar to that brought by many other WTO members, against the US steel safeguard measures. And we should, of course, expect to see some new faces in the Secretariat.

Concluding remarks

Since the mid-1980s, the process of reform in China has matured considerably, and China's trade performance has reflected this. China has become a very important player in international trade, on both the import and the export side. Moving from an earlier phase of import planning to one of import licensing and then, more significantly, to one of import tariffs, has brought prices and the market mechanism into play as the key determinants of China's future trade relations with the rest of the world.

Accession should allow China to lock in the accumulated benefits of the trade-reform process that the Chinese government has undertaken to date, and provide a platform from which China can sustain its reform process into the future. By placing China's reforms within the broader context of trade liberalization by all WTO members, Chinese producers and exporters can increase the returns from trade reform in China through reciprocal market access abroad, and help the Chinese government resist pressure domestically to reverse the process of reform.

For China, WTO accession will provide the 1.3 billion Chinese people with secure, predictable and non-discriminatory access to the markets of 143 trading partners. It will also give this same enormous population secure and non-discriminatory access to the goods and services of these other WTO members. But, from China's perspective, membership will also for the first time commit this new WTO player, at the international level, to implement legal and domestic policy reform, ensuring much greater transparency and security on a uniform basis. China has made incredible strides at reform over the past twenty years; however, committing itself to abide by international treaty rules and the rule of law in the conduct of trade and in domestic policy reform is likely to take this process forward at an even more impressive pace.

Accession will also mean that China can replace the many risky and uncertain bilateral relationships it has had to use until now to shape its trade with its major trading partners, by a single, multilateral trade relationship with the rest of the world.

In the final few months, there was little doubt that WTO members and China were very eager to see the negotiation brought to a rapid and successful conclusion. This desire to achieve closure on China's accession was also shared by the secretary of the Working Party.

Of course, what lies beyond China's accession is the major and, in many ways, imponderable task of implementation by China of its WTO accession commitments. As China approaches this task, the question uppermost in the minds of many Chinese and foreigners alike is whether and how China will be able to ensure uniform and impartial implementation of her trade commitments. At this stage, it is difficult to predict the speed with which WTO members and China will resort to the WTO's dispute settlement procedures. There is little doubt, however, that China and its trading partners will eventually take full advantage of WTO dispute settlement to resolve trade disputes between them. While considerable emphasis may initially be placed on the ten-year transitional review mechanism provided in China's Protocol, it must be said that this mechanism does not contain any enforcement provisions.

It is hard to overstate the difficulties many sectors of Chinese society will face in the months and years following accession. The impact on loss-making state industries, less-developed agricultural communities and myriad government-financed projects across the country will be dramatic. Moreover, so-called 'adjustment' to new, more competitive market conditions, will, for many millions of individuals and families, mean unemployment and significant 'displacement'. There can be no doubt that it will take many years for large segments of China to establish a new equilibrium, during which time many citizens may well face considerable hardship.

But one should bear in mind that this adjustment process has already begun, and not just yesterday. The Chinese people are hardly strangers to this process. Already in the early 1990s China introduced a bankruptcy law and other legislation making state industries in principle responsible for their own profits and losses. Additionally, over at least a decade now, China has radically reduced state subsidies and encouraged development of private enterprise in many sectors. Since the mid-1990s in particular, and as a member of the IMF, China has rationalized and liberalized handling of its foreign-exchange market. In addition, China has progressively, yet dramatically, reduced its import tariffs and other non-tariff restrictions on foreign participation in the Chinese market.

The difficult adjustment continues and is far from complete. At this stage, therefore, we can do little more than wish China and its people 'bon courage' as they venture down the extremely challenging and tortuous path that stretches before them.

5

China's accession to the WTO: improving market access and Australia's role and interests

GRAEME THOMSON

The negotiations surrounding China's accession to the World Trade Organization were the most important and challenging since the conclusion of the GATT Uruguay Round of multilateral trade negotiations in 1993. Australia's role, as a medium-sized power and significant player in international trade relations, provides a useful perspective through which to view the accession.

The negotiations were so challenging because China's accession required a comprehensive and largely new set of commitments by China to a rules-based system as well as large-scale trade liberalization. In addition it required reasonable assurance that China's membership of the WTO would not undermine Australia's interests in the operational effectiveness of both the rules-based system itself and the benefits that are derived by Australia from existing WTO member commitments.

Moreover, the Chinese market is relatively more important for some compared to other key WTO members engaged in the accession negotiations. For example, Australia sent a total of 4.7 per cent of total exports by value in 1999 to China compared with 0.9 per cent for the European Union, 1.9 per cent for the United States, 1.9 per cent for India, 2.2 per cent for Argentina, 2.7 per cent for Malaysia, 2.7 per cent for New Zealand and 3.5 per cent for Thailand. Only Indonesia (4.8 per cent), Japan (5.6 per cent) and the Republic of Korea (9.5 per cent) have higher proportions of their exports sent to China.

With other WTO trading partners Australia shares an interest in industrial products and service-sector liberalization in China. Key sectors

The views expressed are those of the author and do not necessarily represent the views of the government of Australia.

include banking, insurance, distribution and professional services. In addition, Australia also has the widest range of agricultural interests in the Chinese market of any WTO member. As a middle-level power, Australia also sees great value in the multilateral rules-based system and the commitments and security that China's accession to the WTO offers. Unlike larger WTO members, Australia (and most other WTO members) does not readily command the ability to negotiate bilateral deals. China is Australia's fifth-largest export market and the balance of bilateral trade is well in China's favour. In two-way trade terms, China is Australia's third-largest trading partner. Australia is also a significant investor in China.

It has been fashionable to refer to the size of the Chinese population at around 1.3 billion people as representing the size of the Chinese market. While an accurate number, this overstates the economic significance of China to the global marketplace at present. None the less, China is growing in importance and is now in the top fifteen international trading entities. But China is a difficult country to generalize about – it has many of the characteristics of a developing country yet is, by any standard, a massive industrial and agricultural producer and also possesses significant technological and intellectual property capability. There are wide divergences in economic development and performance between regions in China, and its transformation from a highly regulated, interventionist economy is continuing but still with much state control and intervention evident. Clearly China's entry into the WTO, with its more comprehensive coverage of issues and stronger rules than the GATT, was going to be a challenge and has proved to be so, as evidenced by the lengthy WTO accession negotiations.

What does WTO accession mean?

Put simply, for a non-member accession to the WTO means two things – a demonstrable commitment by the acceding entity to apply all of the WTO rules unless transitional arrangements have been granted by the WTO membership and implementing 'catch-up' trade liberalization to bring the acceding entity's protective trade regime broadly into line with comparable WTO members. Satisfying the first requirement has been a 'set-piece' negotiation, though with some novel China-specific challenges (for example, trading rights and judicial review) and a desire by the membership to see clear evidence of implementation as well as commitment in principle. The second requirement of agreeing catch-up trade liberalization has been a more 'free-wheeling' negotiation but with linkages to China's acceptance of the WTO rules to ensure market-access commitments are not nullified or impaired. Given the position of isolation from which China emerged in 1978, achievement of these two requirements has amounted to a major challenge. The extent of the achievement – and the remaining challenges facing both China and the WTO membership – can be judged in part from the following examples.

China's move to a much more transparent rules-based system for its trade and trade-related regime will require fundamental changes in both recent and traditional Chinese governance. China's governance has been mostly rule by decree – rule by law rather than rule of law – and this change will present it with major challenges, so that its acceptance of judicial review of its trade and trade-related regime is at once both a fundamental change as well as an untested step.

Similarly, it remains to be seen whether, in fact, China's agreement in the WTO to the uniform administration of all of its trade and trade-related po-lices throughout the country will sweep away overnight the many different applications of policy there, for example in special economic zones, au-tonomous regions, border trade regions, open coastal cities, and economic and technical development zones.

Without detracting from the degree of change negotiated in the accession, achieving, measuring and monitoring compliance is certain to be an issue for a WTO member the size, complexity and commercial significance of China. Compliance is sure to be an active area in the WTO and bilaterally in the years following accession. Indeed, in anticipation of issues of compliance arising, the terms of accession for China include special arrangements to raise issues relating to the implementation of its obligations. For example, for at least eight years after accession the transitional review mechanism – a US-led requirement – will provide for issues of implementation to be raised in and reported on by relevant WTO committees.

The negotiations for accession have also resulted in comprehensive, detailed commitments on trade liberalization by China covering agricul-tural, industrial products and services sectors. China will also undertake a range of commitments on investment liberalization. For goods, China will bind all of its tariffs and make reductions in tariffs on about 80 per cent of all tariff lines below 1998 applied tariff rates. China will also open tariff-rate quotas for certain agricultural products, apply low tariff rates to in-quota volumes and apply agreed growth rates to the tariff-rate quotas volumes for an agreed period after accession, usually three or five years. Such tariff-rate quotas will also apply to a small number of industrial products (such as certain fertilizers). In addition, China has been granted concessions by the WTO membership to maintain otherwise illegal import quotas, tendering or import licensing on a few industrial products. Most of these will expire by 2003, but for automobiles and a limited number of automobile parts, China can maintain such measures until 1 January 2006. All such quotas will have a 15 per cent compound annual growth rate. China has also entered a quite extensive range of commitments on trade in services of varying value amounting both to greater transparency and security of access as well as general, usually staged, improvements in market access.

Overall, the China draft Schedules of Commitments on Goods and Services amount to significant improvements in access, though they contain some disappointments in outcomes, including for Australia.

Issues in the final negotiating phase

By April 2001 the number of issues on which there was disagreement had been narrowed to around a dozen subjects and the overall negotiation was ripe for conclusion. The Working Party met twice in July and again in September, in the course of which all outstanding issues were agreed.

The key issues in this final phase were:

Quota administration. Finalization of the details of tariff-rate quota administration, especially provision for scope to allocate access on a first-come, first-served basis for wool and wool tops, and commitments by China on the publication date for the allocative systems and allocations of access under them to operate from accession.

Agricultural subsidies. China, responding to concern by WTO members about its large agricultural production and export capacity, agreed to accept a derogation from developing-country status for certain of her agricultural support measures (input subsidies and the *de minimis* commitment of the WTO Agreement on Agriculture (Articles 6.2 and 6.4b)).

Conformity-assessment procedures. Reflecting concern that it could not provide national treatment according to the Agreement on Technical Barriers to Trade, China agreed to substantially reform responsibility for conformity assessment in China (these arrangements provide a transitional phase).

Subsidies. Again reflecting WTO members' concern over China's very large industrial capacity, China agreed to derogations from developing-country entitlements under certain Subsidy Agreement provisions.

Market access. So as not to impair the value of bilateral market-access concessions, China agreed to broadened definitions of 'chain store' and 'large-scale commercial risk' as these were more liberal conditions to apply to the choice of joint venture partners in investments in certain services sectors and less onerous provisions for mandatory reinsurance requirements. Only the outcome on branching rights for insurance investments which concerned MFN treatment for new market entrants (the only issue that was not settled until the final phase of the last Working Party) was agreed with language that is quite open to differing interpretation.

Trading rights. The precise arrangements for applications for access to import quotas in circumstances where trading rights were being liberalized remain to be granted.

Safeguards. Provisions were agreed for safeguards and countervailing actions, which satisfied the differing procedures of WTO members and China's concerns.

Verification. There was also verification and acceptance of China's Schedules of Commitments on market access for goods and services.

Australia had an important interest in most of these issues and was active in the small-group negotiations to find solutions to these issues. It is noteworthy that some significant improvements were achieved in market access during this final phase (for example, for the in-quota tariff rate for sugar) and that no concessions were granted to China in the application of the WTO rules – as were often sought by China.

Role played by Australia in the accession negotiations

Negotiations for China to enter the GATT effectively began in 1988 with particular bursts of activity in 1993 and 1994 but were not completed by the time of the establishment of the WTO on 1 January 1995. China announced its intention to become a WTO member in 1995. Throughout this long period Australia played a fully engaged role in the Accession

Working Party meetings, with China and with key GATT and, since 1995, WTO members.

Apart from Australia's important interests detailed above in the negotiation, Australia brought a 'clean' hand to the discussions, not having in place WTO-inconsistent measures against China – in contrast to, for example, the United States, European Union, Mexico and some developing countries, which had in place a variety of discriminatory quotas and/or WTO-inconsistent anti-dumping measures. Australia did not seek to be a 'free rider' in the negotiations but pressed for a range of outcomes and has been successful in achieving significant outcomes across the country's own negotiating agenda.

Particular interests of Australia have included: a full commitment to the WTO rules; a balance in the agriculture outcomes, including liberalization of wool imports, which are an industrial input; commitment by China not to seek flexibility to pay export subsidies on agricultural products; an unhindered capacity to compete for improved agricultural trading opportunities and similarly improved access for resource and industrial products ranging from coaxial cables to fast ferries; no import quotas on steel; liberalization of trade in petroleum products; improved access for a wide range of services, including particular licence approvals and improved operating conditions for Australian banking, insurance and professional-service providers such as architects, engineers, educators, accountants and lawyers; and a strong commitment across all of the WTO rules to ensure that the multilateral trading system is not impaired directly or indirectly. Given China's mixed socialist/market economy development model this led to a particular interest in seeking to ensure that WTO norms such as tariff bindings would not be nullified or impaired, for example by long-term controls over trading rights.

Australia also took a special interest in systemic issues such as the liberalization of trading rights, transparency, access and convertibility of currency, technical barriers to trade and sanitary and phytosanitary issues, and tariff-rate quota and import quota administration. Other issues that impinge directly or indirectly on market-access commitments or on the applicability of the WTO rules to China included any adverse implications for the effectiveness of the WTO rules in areas such as safeguards, textiles and clothing, treatment of negative support in the determination of agricultural support commitments and TRIPs. In regard to some of the latter issues, the US/China bilaterally negotiated provisions are weaker than WTO safeguards, both the product-specific safeguard and textile and clothing safeguard. Australia alone spoke out in the Working Party against these latter two proposals because they impair the value of the WTO rules. It is not in Australia's (or China's) interest for weaker safeguard provisions. For Australia, as a major supplier to China of imports for processing and re-export (for example, wool, cotton, ferrous and non-ferrous minerals), more restrictive access to markets for textiles and clothing or manufactures will ultimately be to Australia's detriment.

Given its trading interests, Australia was particularly active on tariff-rate quota administration matters in seeking and obtaining improvement in the US/China-negotiated provisions that were included in the headnote provisions of China's Schedule of Commitments on Goods. Australia also obtained China's agreement in writing to protect the competitive position of a range of products that compete with like products for markets in China, particularly as such markets are progressively opened up to import competition. This means, for example, that products such as canola oil (in which Australia is competitive) are not disadvantaged by different and higher tariff rates than, say, soya-bean oil (which is a major US specialization). Australia has commitments of this type across a number of product sectors, such as edible oils, sugar and sweeteners and forage feeding stuffs. Australia also has a commitment from China to continue to provide duty drawback on sugar imported for processing and re-export.

Australia's bilateral market-access settlement covered around 1,500 tariff lines and the equivalent of forty-one UN Central Product Classification Categories (CPC) for trade in services.

Australia's settlement in May 1999 – coming ahead of the United States, European Union, Canada, Japan (services), Argentina, Brazil, Uruguay, Chile, India, Norway, Thailand, Malaysia and Switzerland, to name just some WTO members who followed Australia's settlement – was an important building block and clearly maintained momentum for the negotiations. This was important for the process but even more important for the Chinese negotiating team, who at that point faced a very bleak domestic outlook given the failure in Washington the month before, followed by the bombing of the Chinese Embassy in Belgrade. In this regard it is noteworthy that Australia negotiated improved outcomes on around forty tariff lines, which was better than the United States was offered by China in their ultimately unsuccessful April 1999 agreement (which was substantially accepted in October 1999). Australia played an important role in the market-access results and in advancing the acceptance of the WTO rules by China.

Conclusion

China's accession to the WTO is undoubtedly a significant event for that country, for trade and investment liberalization with and beyond China, for an increased acceptance of the rule of law there and for the multilateral trading system itself. The outcome creates both opportunities and challenges economically for China and its trading partners in the WTO, as well as managerially for the WTO.

For maximum benefits to be obtained for all interests concerned it will be necessary not only for China fully to implement its WTO commitments but also to continue to implement reforms across the whole of the Chinese economy. The importance of the latter will be critical for China's success in continuing to grow and transform its economy but will also be important in fulfilling its WTO commitments and obtaining maximum benefit from them.

The major effects of trade and investment liberalization, inside and outside China, will be gradual/incremental after the initial step of liberalization at accession. However, the greatly improved transparency, greater certainty of market access and decision-making, together with more uniform administration in China and surveillance of Chinese compliance, should contribute to a progressively better business climate in and with China, with positive results for investment and trade in many areas of the Chinese economy. A second stage of liberalization will be important to follow the conclusion of the accession transition phase. Here the launch and conclusion of a new round of multilateral trade negotiations under the WTO will be important, though it is to be hoped China will also continue with its own programme of liberalization.

A more open, transparent, predictable, equitable and efficient Chinese economy following accession will be a sizeable step forward for traders and investors. Moreover, given China's economic size, these openings and the improved competitiveness they foreshadow should be felt regionally and globally. In as much as China continues with its reform process – and in particular if it applies across all sectors – other countries will need to accelerate their own liberalization and openness if they are not to lose competitiveness and attractiveness as investment destinations and trading partners. These effects will be a particular challenge for developing countries and emerging economies and will need to be heeded by them. But there will also be challenges for developed countries.

Provided China continues with reform the WTO should be strengthened by the addition of China, which should bring many positive trade-liberalizing positions to WTO debates. If China does not maintain its reform path its influence in the WTO and the value for the Chinese market for WTO members will be marginalized.

So China's entry to the WTO is very likely to be a major milestone in the world economy. There are sure to be problems and challenges and the WTO will be changed as a multilateral institution being pushed to operate more as a true multipolar institution. Adjusting to this will be but one element of integrating China into the global market and a more rules-based system of order than presently is the case. The gains from WTO membership are relatively clear – as are the challenges and risks.

Appendix

Improved and WTO-bound market access for agricultural products

Wool. China is opening global tariff-rate quotas of 242,000 tonnes of wool and 65,000 tonnes of wool tops, at tariff levels of 1 per cent and 3 per cent respectively, with this access to grow with annual increments to 287,000 tonnes and 80,000 tonnes respectively by 2004.

Sugar. China is opening a global tariff-rate quota of 1.6 million tonnes at a tariff of 20 per cent, reducing to 15 per cent on 1 January 2004, growing with annual increments to 1.945 million tonnes by 2004, with consultative arrangements on re-exports to provide some security of access to China's domestic market.

Wheat. China is opening a global tariff-rate quota of 7.3 million tonnes, growing with annual increments to 9.6 million tonnes by 2004, at a tariff of 1 per cent.

Rice. China is opening a global tariff-rate quota of 2.66 million tonnes, growing with annual increments to 5.32 million tonnes by 2004, at a tariff of 1 per cent.

Cotton. China is opening a global tariff-rate quota of 743,000 tonnes, at a tariff level of 1 per cent, growing with annual increments to 894,000 tonnes by 2004.

Canola. China has agreed to reduce the tariff on canola seed to 9 per cent in 2000, and to provide global access for canola oil of 600,000 tonnes at a tariff level of 9 per cent, with this level of access to grow with annual increments to 1.105 million tonnes by 2005.

Barley. Will be subject only to a tariff at a tariff level of 3 per cent bound, although China had earlier been seeking agreement to a tariff quota regime which would have been much more restrictive.

Tariffs on other products. China will bind and reduce its agricultural tariffs significantly. Tariffs will be cut on accession and fully phased in by 2004. For example, tariffs will be reduced on the following products (table 5.1).

Improved and WTO-bound market access for industrial products

Tariffs. Tariffs will be bound and generally reduced on a broad basis, with many tariffs falling to 10 per cent or lower levels. Tariffs will be cut on accession and further cuts will be phased in by 2005 with some exceptions. For example, bound tariffs will be as follows (table 5.2).

Non-tariff measures. China will reduce significantly its non-tariff measures and eliminate all quotas, tendering and import licensing by no later than 2005. Quotas on Chinese imports of automobiles and parts will grow by 15 per cent annually from a level of around US$6 billion in 2000, and these quotas will be eliminated by 2005.

Information technology. China will participate in the WTO Information Technology Agreement, which will result in the elimination of tariffs on a range of computer and other high-technology products.

Improved market access in the services sector

China has agreed to make substantial market-access commitments in the services sector, including to adopt WTO rules on trade in services and to undertake significant liberalization in the key sectors of interest to Australian services exporters. Australia has been assured that China sees no substantive difficulties in granting additional licences to Australian firms in the near term in the insurance and banking sectors, and for legal and accountancy practices.

China will significantly open its market to services trade by substantially deregulating both the conditions of entry and the scope of operation for businesses in China. Key market-access commitments in sectors of particular interest to Australian exporters include the following.

Table 5.1 *Improved and WTO-bound market access for agricultural products*

Product	Reduced tariff (%)	Current tariff (%)
Chilled or frozen beef cuts	12	45
Beef carcasses/half-carcasses, chilled	20	45
Beef carcasses/half-carcasses, frozen	25	45
Frozen unboned meat of sheep	12	23
Other meat of lamb and sheep	15	23
Frozen pork	12	20
Butter	10	50
Cheese, other than blue-veined	12	50
Cheese, blue-veined	15	50
Yoghurt	10	50
Milk powder	10	25
Butter and other fats and oils derived from milk	10	50
Cabbage, cauliflowers, lettuce, celery	10	13–16
Apples	10	30
Pears, other than Ya, Hseuh, etc.	10	30
Cherries, peaches, nectarines, plums, fresh	10	30
Oranges	11	40
Mandarins	12	40
Grapes, fresh	13	40
Guavas, mangoes, mangosteens	15	25
Wheat gluten	18	30
Animal fats and oils and fractions, hydrogenated, etc.	5	40
Canola seed	9	currently TRQ
Lupins	9	15
Sugar confectionary, not containing cocoa nes	12	15
Pasta, uncooked or stuffed	15	25
Soups and broths and preparations	15	45
Wine including sparkling	14	65
Dog and cat food, for retail sale	15	30
Raw skins of sheep or lambs, wool on	7	9
Skins of sheep or lambs, without wool	7	9
Lobsters, rock lobsters and other sea crawfish	15	30–5
Prawns, shrimps frozen	5–8	30

Table 5.2 *Improved and WTO-bound market access for industrial products*

Product	Reduced tariff (%)	Current tariff (%)
Coking coal	3	3
Steaming coal	6	6
Liquefied natural gas	6	6
Mineral ores and concentrates	0	0
Alumina	8	18
Pigments and preparations of titanium dioxide	6.5	14
Various chemicals	5.5–6.5	8–16
Various pharmaceuticals	4–6	9–14
Various medicaments	4–6	9–14
Gold, semi-manufactured, non-monetary	7	9
Steel, semi-finished	2	3
Steel, flat rolled	3–8	3–10
Steel, flat rolled, stainless	10	15–20
Aluminium, unwrought, bars, rods, etc.	5–8	9–12
Motor-vehicle engines, >1,000cc.	10	25–45
Various other motor-vehicle parts	10	20–50
Motor vehicles	25	80–100
Optical fibre cables	0	12
Optical fibres	5	15
Coaxial cable	10	12
Ultrasonic diagnostic apparatus, etc.	4–7	11–15

Telecommunications: adoption of WTO regulatory principles, and commitment to phase out geographic and foreign equity restrictions. For mobile telephony, China will allow foreign operators 25 per cent equity upon accession, moving to 49 per cent three years after accession.

Insurance: commitment to phase out geographic, foreign equity and business-operating restrictions on life and non-life insurance operations, and to remove limitations on choice of operating partner. Foreign firms will be able to provide health, pension and group insurance in life, and all non-life activities except for mandatory third-party-liability auto insurance.

Banking: commitment to phase in renmimbi lending and deposit-taking by foreign firms to Chinese firms (within two years of accession) and individuals (within five years), and to phase out geographic restrictions. Also, non-financial institutions will be able to give credit facilities for the purchase of all motor vehicles.

Accountancy: commitment to reduce limitations on forms of establishment and operations, and to provide national treatment for foreigners who have passed the Chinese CPA examination.

Legal: commitment to phase out numerical and geographic restrictions. Foreign law firms will be able to provide information to their clients on the Chinese legal environment. The prior experience requirements for foreign lawyers, other than the chief representative, has been reduced to two years.

Education: commitment to bind the provision of English-language training by foreigners, and the operation of joint venture schools.

Architecture: commitment to bind foreign-majority ownership in joint venture operations, and to allow foreign architects to provide scheme design services.

PART III

China – the domestic sphere

6

The state of the Chinese economy – structural changes, impacts and implications

LIGANG SONG

Structural changes: what is at stake?

The question of how well China can cope with the impact of its entry to the World Trade Organization on its economy has drawn renewed attention since the country's formal admission to the organization on 11 December 2001. This is not only because competition from overseas has become imminent, but because the changes required under the terms for entry are huge, complex and, in many ways, challenging. A key to comprehending this issue is to have a clear understanding of the state of the Chinese economy, which in turn can only be understood in the context of structural changes that have been taking place in China since reform started in the late 1970s.

Structural adjustments have both underpinned the progress in economic development that has been made during the reform period, and revealed the difficulties in resolving the remaining structural issues. These difficulties are generally regarded as the fundamental causes of many of the existing problems in the Chinese economy, which in turn may form obstacles for China in implementing its commitments as a member of the WTO. It is, therefore, important to identify what has been achieved and what remains to be done with respect to structural changes in the economy and their policy implications.

This chapter reviews briefly the nature of, and basic approaches to, structural changes in economic transformation, outlines what has been achieved and what remains to be done in carrying out structural changes, and discusses how the structural changes affect the state of the Chinese economy. It then discusses the implications for implementing China's WTO commitments and points out some potential risks that exist in certain areas of the economy. Finally, it elaborates how China's entry to the WTO affects the long-term prospects of the Chinese economy.

Nature of, and basic approaches to, structural reform

Despite the different views with regard to the scope and speed of, as well as approaches to, reform, there has always been a general consensus about the nature of structural changes in China right from the early period of reform – that is, to transform the economic system from a centrally planned to a market system and thereby to achieve the goal of efficient allocation of resources and an improved standard of living. A prominent feature of this transformation is structural change, which is required in order to create those conditions in which incentives can be raised and both macro- and microeconomic efficiency can be improved.

Reform programmes in several areas drive the continuing structural changes in the economy, including various measures taken to establish a market system, to adjust industrial structure according to its comparative advantage, to reform ownership, open up the economy and adjust the role of government in managing economic activity.

Structural changes during the earlier period of reform included the removal of price controls on producer as well as consumer products, decentralization of the relationships between government and enterprises and between central and local government, and liberalization of the economy. More recent reform measures include privatization of state-owned enterprises (SOEs), establishment of equity markets, reform of the banking sector, and institution-building including the establishment of a regulatory and legal framework, legal enforcement of property rights and reform of government and corporate structure.

While the government continues to play an instrumental role in pushing for structural changes, changes have taken place largely as reactions to market signals by both consumers and producers including those from overseas. These market-induced structural changes have become more influential compared to government-driven outcomes as reform deepens. Government reform programmes have been adopted and implemented in a gradual fashion influenced by political, economic and social factors. They have achieved successes, as well as creating new frictions in the process of structural changes.

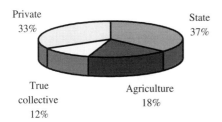

Private
33%

State
37%

True
collective
12%

Agriculture
18%

Figure 6.1 Ownership shares in China's GDP: 1988
Source: Made using figures from table 2.3 in Neil Gregory, Stoyan Tenev and
Dileep Wagle, *China's Emerging Private Enterprises: Prospects for the New Century*
(International Finance Corporation (IFC), Washington DC, 2000), p. 18.

What has been achieved?

Progress in structural reform can be described by following the fundamental
shifts taking place in the economy.

First, there has been a continual shift from a planned to a market economy. As a result, the major proportion of both producer and consumer
products are being exchanged through the market. The government now
controls the prices of only a few products. There has accordingly been a
shift from direct control by the government to indirect management of
the economy. Government planning has become indicative, serving only
as guidance to economic agencies conducting their own business activities
rather than as a compulsory instrument for direct intervention, as was the
case under the planned economy. Shifts have also occurred from indirect
to direct financing, owing to the development of equity markets.

Secondly, there has been a significant shift from the state to non-state
sector in the economy despite various constraints imposed on non-state,
especially private, enterprises (figure 6.1). Domestic private enterprises have
witnessed phenomenal increases in their shares of total GDP, industrial
outputs, employment, foreign trade and taxation revenues in comparison
with SOEs. In line with such a shift, the state has been gradually pulling
out from more competitive sectors of the economy, giving way to non-
state enterprises in these industries. For example, the state's share in total
industrial output has fallen considerably, accounting for less than one-third
of the total by the end of the 1990s. Given the differences in their respective
growth rates, the state's share in the total economy will continue to shrink
as the private sector continues to expand.

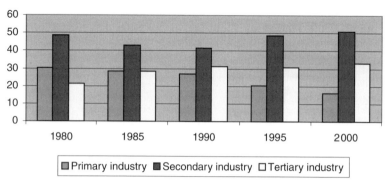

Figure 6.2 Industrial structure of the Chinese economy (%)
Source: Statistical Yearbook of China, 2001 and previous years.

Thirdly, there have been continual adjustments in the industrial structure of the economy, characterized by a gradual decline in the primary (agriculture) sector and a steady rise in the secondary (industry) and tertiary (service) sectors (figure 6.2). Within the industrial sector, the share of heavy industry is in decline while other industries, which are more in conformity with China's comparative advantages, are on the rise, transforming shortages of many manufactured products to oversupply.

Fourthly, China has been transformed from a closed to an open economy, as a result of policies of trade liberalization. Foreign trade and investments have been playing an important role in domestic consumption, production and trade. Domestic enterprises have continued to benefit from positive externalities generated from opening up the economy. Trade liberalization has proved to be an indispensable part of economic transition from a centrally planned to a market economy.

Impacts on the state of the Chinese economy

These structural changes have had a profound impact on the state of the Chinese economy. Most prominent is the emergence of the private economy – regarded as the third economic transformation following the introduction of the household responsibility system in the late 1970s and the development of township and village enterprises (TVEs) in the 1980s. This latest transformation is a natural progression from the others, but more significant in that it affects the basic fabric of Chinese society. The transformation has taken place quietly due to various constraints on its development, but has affected almost every corner of the society, and is the most public manifestation of the reality of continuing structural change in the Chinese economy. It has now been recognized in China that this transformation is necessary to maintain the dynamism and stability of the economy.[1]

The development of the private sector at this stage of economic transformation plays an important role in a number of areas. It increases employment, both by recruiting new workers into the non-farm economy and by absorbing laid-off workers from reformed SOEs. It creates competition, nurturing entrepreneurship and instigating innovation. It helps channel an increasing proportion of investment into more efficient uses and hence increases the overall efficiency of the economy. It helps to drive the regulatory and institutional framework into becoming more compatible with a market system, thereby facilitating improved performance in state-owned and collective enterprises. It also accelerates growth with less risk to macroeconomic stability than would expansion of state-owned enterprises, since private firms are subject to hard budget constraints.

However, difficulties have also emerged in the process of structural change, which have important implications for China's entry to the WTO. These centre on the following areas: agriculture, state-owned enterprises, finance (especially the banking sector), income distribution and regional disparities.

In agriculture, the biggest problem associated with the structural changes is that the fall of the sector's share in the total economy has not been accompanied by a corresponding reduction in its share of total employment. For example, agriculture contributed 15.9 per cent of China's GDP but still accounted for 50 per cent of total employment in 2000 (figures 6.2 and 6.3). Converting agricultural to non-agricultural labour holds the key to raising productivity and thus per capita income in the agricultural sector. This structural problem, along with the slowing down of rural industrial enterprises in recent years, largely explains why the increase in per capita income in rural areas has been stagnant. This problem also increases the difficulty of opening the agricultural sector to overseas competition.

The reform of SOEs has come to a stage where large enterprises need to be tackled since most of the small and medium-sized SOEs have been

---

[1] Ross Garnaut, Ligang Song, Yang Yao and Xiaolu Wang, *Private Enterprise in China* (Canberra, 2001).

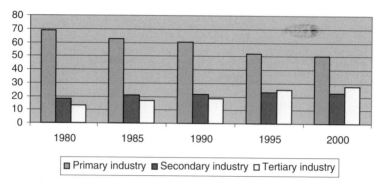

Figure 6.3 Employment structure by industry (%)
Source: Statistical Yearbook of China, 2001 and previous years.

privatized. Reform of SOEs has progressed through the responsibility, contract and shareholding system, but problems with regard to incentives,
soft budget constraints, productivity and profitability remain. Pressures for
upgrading and innovation are enormous, given the oversupply of a large
number of manufactured products. A social safety net, which alleviates the
impact of adjustment on employment, is yet to be adequately established.
Current practices with regard to market entry and exit, monopoly, competition and governance need to be changed, since many will be inconsistent
with the requirements of the WTO.

A modern, well-functioning financial system is an essential part of a
market economy, and China has come to the stage where further financial-
market reform is critical to its ability to achieve greater structural change in
the economy. The mismatch between the lending and financing needs of the
emerging private sector highlights the urgency of resolving the problems
in the financial sector (table 6.1). Further reform will undoubtedly help
channel more funds from the state to non-state sector, leading to more
efficient investment decisions and consequently raising production and
economic growth. The development of a non-state banking sector will be
a significant factor in rectifying the structural imbalance in the financial
sector and aiding the further development of the private sector.

China's commitments to open the financial sector to foreign competition under the WTO agreements will force domestic state-owned banks to
become more competitive, but will also create great challenges for managing
the complex process of financial-system liberalization – especially banking-
sector reform. Challenges include market fragmentation characterized
largely by substantial differences between official and informal lending rates

Table 6.1 *Bank lending to private enterprises, 1999 (RMB 100 million)*

Items/Date	Q1	Q2	Q3	Q4
State banks				
Total loans	69,409.2	71,589.5	73,757.3	73,695.9
Loans to private sector	222.8	256.5	282.7	301.0
(per cent)	0.32	0.36	0.38	0.41
All banks				
Total loans	87,825.5	90,620.3	93,390.4	93,734.3
Loans to private sector	483.5	518.1	556.0	579.1
(per cent)	0.55	0.57	0.60	0.62

Note: The figures are end-of-quarter balances and loans made to private enterprises include loans to sole proprietors.
Source: Calculated from tables 3.7 and 3.8 in (2001) 17 *Quarterly Statistical Bulletin* 89–90.

due to the government policy of controls on interest rates, the large number of non-performing loans held by state-owned banks, the risks to the domestic banking sector from greater financial competition, the need to meet macroeconomic policy goals and an inadequate financial infrastructure.

Market-oriented structural changes have led to increased income as well as regional disparities. Income gaps are widening not only among urban residents but also between rural and urban people. In general, people living along the coastal region are benefiting more from the structural changes than those in inland regions.

While the welfare of the urban workers has begun to depend more on the social welfare system, notwithstanding the difficulties in setting up such a system, people living in rural areas continue to be left to fend for themselves. This gives rise to disparities, which raise concerns about the social stability that may be critical for carrying through the difficult tasks of structural reform.

Implications of China's entry to the WTO

China's membership of the WTO affects the structural reform programmes and, hence, the long-term prospects of the economy in many ways. For example, it helps strengthen the domestic reforms aimed at building market-compatible institutions, particularly a modern regulatory and legal system providing full protection of private property rights. Increased competition induces further structural changes by levelling the playing fields for both domestic and overseas enterprises, widening trade and investment opportunities and by disseminating information and new technologies. Viewed from this angle, China's entry to the WTO represents a grand strategy to ease the burden of reform.

However, there are some adjustment costs and potential risks associated with China's accession to the WTO owing to the structural problems existing at this stage of reform. Of particular concern is the problem of unemployment, which has been exacerbated by the ongoing reform of SOEs and increased labour surplus in rural areas. The latter is created by the slowing down of TVEs and the shrinkage in agricultural lands in recent years. Both the industrial and agricultural sectors are already faced with the problems of over-capacity and slow growth in income. Depending upon how well these sectors adjust to the external shocks, unemployment may get worse in the short run before the long-term positive effects of China's entry to the WTO are generated.

China's WTO commitments apply to the country as a whole, not just to certain sections or regions of the society. Poorer inland provinces are not on an equal footing in competition with coastal regions. There has been an unequal distribution of benefits and costs of greater openness as far as regional economies are concerned. There will be increased pressures to balance regional and income disparities as well as pressure from sectoral interests to maintain social stability.

An important factor that affects the pace of structural changes is macroeconomic stability. While a stable macroeconomic environment is certain to be conducive to economic restructuring, macroeconomic instability (such as inflation in the past and deflation at present) is likely to cause difficulties in carrying out further structural reform. Deflationary pressure persists, forcing the government to continue to rely on fiscal measures to stimulate the economy (table 6.2).   ·

Finally, some longstanding structural weaknesses remain, notwithstanding the pressing timetable for sectoral liberalization, including weaknesses in the agricultural and financial-service sectors. In fulfilling its commitments, which in essence require more profound structural changes in the economy, the government has reduced its freedom to decide the pace and depth of reform. Both political determination and management skills will be essential. The government has to navigate between Scylla and Charybdis. Scylla is the prospect of pushing ahead with more dramatic reform so fast as

Table 6.2 *Macroeconomic indicators, 1995–2000*

	1995	1996	1997	1998	1999	2000
Real GDP (% real change)	10.5	9.6	8.8	7.8	7.1	8.0
Industrial value added (% real change)	14.0	12.5	11.1	8.9	8.5	9.9
Inflation (retail price % change)	14.8	6.1	0.8	−2.6	−3.0	0.4
Growth of M2 broad money supply (%)	29.5	25.3	19.6	14.8	14.7	112.3
Exchange rate (RMB/US$)	8.32	8.30	8.28	8.28	8.27	8.27
Fixed asset investment (% nominal change)	17.5	14.8	8.8	13.9	5.2	9.3
Retail sales (% nominal change)	26.8	20.1	10.2	6.8	6.8	9.7
Exports (% changes in US$)	23.0	1.5	21.0	0.5	6.1	27.8
Imports (% change in US$)	14.2	5.1	2.5	−1.5	18.2	35.8
Merchandise trade balance (US$ billion)	16.7	12.2	40.3	43.6	29.1	24.1
International reserves (US$ billion)	73.6	105.03	139.89	144.96	154.68	165.6

Note: Figures for 2000 are from the State Statistical Bureau's Report on National Economy and Social Development, *Economic Daily*, 1 March 2001.
Sources: State Statistical Bureau, *Chinese Statistical Yearbook 2000* (Beijing, 2000) and *China Financial Outlook 2000* (Beijing, 2000).

to go beyond socially accepted limits, thereby triggering some kind of social dislocation, which in turn would disrupt the reform process. Charybdis is the prospect of China drawing back from its WTO commitments when faced with insurmountable difficulties in tackling the hardest part of the system.

What remains to be done?

China still faces many challenges in meeting the terms of its accession to the WTO while keeping domestic reform on track. They include:

levelling the playing field for all types of enterprises;
carrying out industrial upgrading;
further reducing the state's share in credit, finance and investments;

opening up more industrial sectors to non-state enterprises;

speeding up the pace of urbanization and development of the service sector;

reforming state-owned banks through further reform of SOEs;

allowing non-state financial institutions to develop and compete;

nurturing and strengthening product, labour and equity markets;

improving the legal and regulatory system;

continuing the change in the government's function from provider to regulator;

building a modern enterprise system;

developing a modern social-security system; and

reducing income and regional disparities through the market and government policies.

Conclusions

Progress that has been made in China in establishing a market economy during the past two decades or so has paved the way for deepening the continuing structural changes in the economy. However, major risks in carrying out further reforms exist, due largely to lack of reform in certain areas. These risks are likely to be concentrated in areas such as agriculture, finance (especially the banking sector), state-owned enterprises, income distribution and regional disparities. Resolving some of these problems may require long-term solutions, but success in ameliorating potential risks in these areas is crucial if further reform and liberalization targets are to be achieved without major hindrance.

The economic outlook hinges upon progress being made in several areas. Improvement is dependent upon successful structural reform of SOEs and the banking sector, healthy development of non-state enterprises, achievement of economic growth, technological advancement and improved management. Future growth also depends upon a revitalized agricultural sector, a stable and favourable external environment, social stability through narrowing income and regional disparities and the effectiveness of government policies, particularly fiscal policies in the wake of deflation. Success in carrying out further structural changes in line with the requirements of its accession to the WTO will be a key factor in determining the long-term prospects of the Chinese economy.

7

Trade policy reform and China's WTO accession

ELENA IANCHOVICHINA AND WILL MARTIN

Introduction

Accession to the WTO was a milestone in China's development, modernization and integration into the world economy. The reform era in China, and
other East Asian transition economies, has been a period of extraordinary
growth in trade and output.[1] Part of the growth has flowed from economic
reforms that stimulated the opening up to the outside world, and part from
economic growth that opening up to the world has done much to facilitate.
Recognition of the benefits of openness for growth and poverty reduction
has been an important element in China's willingness to make the difficult
reforms involved in WTO accession.

Like economic reform in China generally, trade-policy reform has been
complex and incremental. The reforms required by WTO accession will
begin from policies that contain many features inherited from earlier eras,
such as state trading monopolies that date to the command economy, and
duty exemptions and rebates that date from the need in the early reform
era to stimulate labour-intensive exports of manufactures despite a regime
of high trade barriers.

China's accession agreement is complex. It reflects the interests and concerns of policy-makers in China and in WTO members involved in the
negotiations. While the agreement will involve widespread reductions in
protection, it cannot be represented as a move to free trade or a simple pro-
portional cut in protection, as many studies have tried to do.[2] While WTO
accession and the process of liberalization that preceded it represent one of

---

The views expressed in this chapter are personal and should not be attributed to the World Bank.

[1] W. Martin, 'Trade policy reform in the East Asian transition economies', World Bank Policy
Research Working Paper No. 2535 (Washington, D.C., 2001).

[2] See, for a survey, J. Gilbert and T. Wahl, *Applied General Equilibrium Assessments of Trade Liberalization in China*, mimeo, Washington State University, 2001.

the most profound liberalizations in recent economic history, China will still be far from fully open. In many areas, significant policy interventions remain, and their effects need to be taken into account in any evaluation of the accession package, or in consideration of future reforms. An area of particular interest will be the role of policies inherited from earlier regimes, such as state trading in agriculture, and the system of duty exemptions for exports.

This chapter forms an initial assessment of some of the likely major implications of the trade reforms involved in China's accession to the WTO, building on recent work by Zhai Fan and Li Shantong,[3] and drawing on new data becoming available as the accession process nears completion. The objectives are twofold – to assess the implications of the reforms, and to identify areas where further analysis will be helpful in guiding further reform.

Because of the importance of understanding China's current regime, the chapter begins with a discussion of policy reforms and China's current trade regime. It then examines the nature of the reforms associated with accession and outlines the modelling approach that we have used to analyse this liberalization. It takes into account the special features of the initial trade regime and the trade reforms associated with accession. Finally, some results from the analysis are discussed.

China's trade policies

The pre-reform Chinese trade regime

The pre-reform Chinese trade regime was dominated by between ten and sixteen foreign trade corporations (FTCs) with effective monopolies in the import and export of their specified ranges of products.[4] Planned import volumes were determined by the projected difference between domestic demand and supply for particular goods, with export levels being determined by the planners at levels necessary to finance the planned level of imports.

Under the pre-reform regime, price-based measures, such as tariffs, were unimportant, since the planning system was based on quantity decisions rather than behavioural responses to prices. There was little need for quotas

---

[3] Zhai Fan and Li Shantong, 'The implications of accession to WTO on China's economy', paper for presentation to Third Annual Conference on Global Economic Analysis, Monash University, Australia, 27–30 June 2000.

[4] N. Lardy, *Foreign Trade and Economic Reform in China, 1978–1990* (Cambridge, 1991).

or licences since the quantities to be imported could be controlled by planners through the monopoly trading corporations.

Reform of China's trade regime

Reform of China's trade regime had four major dimensions: increasing the number and type of enterprises eligible to trade in particular commodities beyond the FTCs; developing indirect trade policy instruments such as tariffs, licences, quotas and duty-exemption schemes that were absent or unimportant under the planning system; reducing and ultimately removing the exchange-rate distortion; and reforming prices so that they could play a role in guiding resource allocation. These reforms of the trading system were inextricably linked with reform of the enterprise sector to allow indirect regulation through market-determined prices to replace direct regulation of outputs.

The number of FTCs with trading rights was expanded, with trading rights provided to branches of the FTCs controlled by the central government and to those controlled by regions and localities until there were thousands of these firms. Since 1984, these trading enterprises have been legally independent entities[5] and state-owned trading enterprises of this type now appear to operate strongly along commercial lines.[6] Joint ventures between domestic and foreign firms, and firms located in the special economic zones, were also allowed to trade their own products early during the reform process. At a later stage, large producing firms began to gain direct foreign trade rights.

Despite the large number of trading firms, there are two groups of commodities for which the number of firms entitled to engage in trade is tightly restricted. One of these groups is subject to state trading, the other to designated trading.[7] The seventy tariff lines subject to state trading on the import side are drawn from the commodity groups set out in table 7.1, as are the 115 tariff lines covered by state trading on the export side. The 229 tariff lines subject to designated trading are primarily importables.

---

[5] Y. Kueh, 'Economic decentralization and foreign trade expansion in China', in J. Chai and C. K. Leung (eds.), *China's Economic Reforms* (Hong Kong, 1987), pp. 441–81.

[6] S. Rozelle, A. Park, Jikun Huang and Jin Hehui, *Bureaucrat to Entrepreneur: the Changing Role of the State in China's Transitional Commodity Economy*, mimeo (Stanford University, 1996).

[7] Under designated trading, trading rights are restricted to a relatively small number of firms, many of which have geographically restricted trading rights.

Table 7.1 *Products covered by state trading and designated trading.*

	Imports	Exports
State trading	Grain, vegetable oils, sugar, tobacco, crude oil, refined oil, chemical fertilizer, cotton	Tea, maize, soybeans, tungsten, coal, crude oil, refined oil, silk, unbleached silk, cotton, antimony
Designated trading	Rubber, timber, plywood, wool, acrylics, steel and products	Rubber, timber, plywood, wool, acrylics, steel and products

Source: Government of China, 1997.

The system of co-ordination and control used for major state-traded commodities, such as grains and fertilizer, follows the basic lines used under the traditional planning system. Recent empirical research concludes that, rather than helping to stabilize domestic grain prices, this inflexible system contributes substantially to volatility[8] and other problems.[9] While state trading is clearly legal under the GATT, there appears to be a strong case on economic grounds for reforming these arrangements.

An important reform was the introduction of special arrangements for processing trade, such as duty exemptions. Imports of intermediate inputs for use in the production of exports were almost completely liberalized, as were capital-goods inputs for use in joint ventures with foreign enterprises. These categories of imports came to represent a large share of total imports, with intermediate inputs into exports accounting for almost half of total imports in 1996.

The primary transitional device used to reduce, and then remove, distortions in commodity prices and exchange rates was the two- (or more) tier pricing system. Under this system, the plan price continued to operate for the quantity of the commodity that producers were contracted to supply. To stimulate output, producers were allowed to supply additional output at a secondary market price. The two-tier system for foreign exchange

---

[8] World Bank, *China: Long-term Food Security* (Washington, D.C., 1997).

[9] Colin Carter, Jing Chen and Scott Rozelle identified many of the classic features of the traditional monopoly trading system in the grain trade – an 'airlock' between buyers and suppliers; poor quality matching; unpredictable timing of deliveries. In addition, they found many of the features of poorly operating markets, particularly concerns that traders are using their superior information to take advantage of buyers in China. See C. Carter, J. Chen and S. Rozelle, 'China's state trading in grains: an institutional overview', memo, University of California at Davis, 1998.

Table 7.2 *Changes in average tariff rates in China (%)*

	All products		Primary products		Manufactures	
	Simple	Weighted	Simple	Weighted	Simple	Weighted
1992	42.9	40.6	36.2	22.3	44.9	46.5
1993	39.9	38.4	33.3	20.9	41.8	44.0
1994	36.3	35.5	32.1	19.6	37.6	40.6
1996	23.6	22.6	25.4	20.0	23.1	23.2
1997	17.6	18.2	17.9	20.0	17.5	17.8
1998	17.5	18.7	17.9	20.0	17.4	18.5

Source: World Bank, *World Development Indicators* (Washington, D.C., 1999), p. 340.

involved an overvalued official exchange rate and a higher secondary-market rate, and distorted trade by discouraging both exports and imports.[10] Over time, gaps between official and secondary-market prices were narrowed or eliminated, and the foreign exchange rate unified in 1994.

Non-tariff and tariff barriers

Over the 1990s China made substantial progress in reducing non-tariff barriers (NTBs). Nicholas Lardy (in a personal communication) estimates that the number of products subject to quotas and licences fell from 1,247 tariff lines in 1992 to 261 in 1999. The average protective impact of the complete set of NTBs in China was estimated to be 9.3 per cent.[11] The protective effect of these NTBs has clearly declined since then, because of the progressive phasing out of NTBs during the accession process.

The pace of tariff reform in China has also been rapid. While average tariffs were high in the early 1990s, they fell sharply after 1994. Significant tariff reform was implemented in October 1997, reducing average tariffs below 20 per cent. Some basic data on average tariff rates are given in table 7.2.

Progressive reductions in tariffs since 1992 have reduced average tariffs by more than half and even more in the manufacturing sector. Hence,

[10] See W. Martin, 'Modeling the post-reform Chinese economy' (1993) 15(5 & 6) *Journal of Policy Modeling* 545–79; World Bank, *China: Foreign Trade Reform* (Washington, D.C., 1994).

[11] World Bank, *China Engaged: Integration with the World Economy* (Washington, D.C., 1997).

reduction to the levels proposed in the WTO negotiations will be less abrupt than would otherwise have been the case. The reforms have also reduced the dispersion of tariff rates – with the standard deviation of tariffs falling from 32.1 per cent in 1992 to 13.1 per cent in 1998. This can be expected greatly to reduce the costs of protection.[12]

An important feature of the reforms has been the exemptions for processing trade and for foreign investment. According to China's customs authorities, 75 per cent of imports entered either duty-free or subject to reduced duties. The exempt and reduced categories, with their 1998 import shares in parentheses, were processing trade (50 per cent, exempted), initial investment of joint ventures (10 per cent, exempted), bonded warehouse imports (5 per cent, exempted) and other exempted/reduced (10 per cent).

China's reliance on exemptions for goods used to produce exports has stimulated the development of export processing industries that rely on imported intermediates. This assists China's integration into production-sharing globally. However, high protective barriers and major exemptions discriminate against industries that rely more on domestic inputs. Continued high tariffs on goods used indirectly to produce exports raises the price of locally produced goods.[13] Further, protection raises the price of non-traded goods (the real exchange rate effect) and hence discriminates against exports that embody significant amounts of domestic value added. These factors contribute to China's reliance on processing-sector exports that frequently embody little domestic value added.

Comprehensive liberalization should reduce this problem. With lower tariffs, the costs of domestic inputs to exporters will fall. This, in turn, can be expected to result in greater reliance on exports that embody a greater amount of domestic value added.

China's WTO accession package

The details of China's WTO accession package were not known when the analysis in this chapter was undertaken. However, the November 1999 agreement between China and the United States, and the May 2000

[12] Christian Bach, Will Martin and Jennifer Stevens found that reductions in the variance of tariffs associated with China implementing its (then) proposed WTO accession package accounted for a large share of the benefits. See C. Bach, W. Martin and J. Stevens, 'China and the WTO: tariff offers, exemptions and welfare implications' (1996) 132(3) *Weltwirtschaftliches Archiv* 409–31.
[13] In principle, China's tariff exemptions allow for indirect use, but these provisions do not always work effectively.

agreement with the European Union, will form its basis. The US agreement captures most of the reforms and was used in the analysis in this chapter because its details were publicly available when this analysis was undertaken.

WTO entry will require China to bring its rules into line with WTO norms, perhaps most importantly, on non-discrimination between suppliers in accordance with the most favoured nation (MFN) principle, and the abolition of most NTBs. However, WTO rules require much more, including implementation of intellectual property regimes consistent with the TRIPs Agreement, and procedures consistent with WTO rules in areas such as customs valuation, safeguards, standards and phytosanitary restrictions.

The Protocol of Accession will also require measures to increase the transparency of China's trade regime; procedures for judicial review of administrative action, phasing out of general restrictions on trading rights; the elimination of multi-tier pricing; and will require state-owned enterprises to make purchasing and sales decisions solely on commercial grounds. It is also likely to include procedures to enable China's trading partners to impose product-specific protective barriers during the transition period, when China's trade mix is likely to need to adjust sharply in response to liberalization.

After WTO accession, China will move towards a trade regime based on tariffs. Quotas, licences and designated trading are all to be phased out. State trading is allowed to remain on the commodities listed in table 7.1 (above), subject to WTO rules and tariff-rate quota (TRQ) arrangements with non-state traders. Participation in TRQ imports similar to those used in agriculture will be introduced for crude oil, processed oil and fertilizer.

In addition, protection on merchandise and services will be reduced. China has committed to bind all agricultural and industrial tariffs.[14] The weighted average tariff on manufactures is to be reduced to 6.95 per cent, a substantial reduction from the 24.3 per cent reported in table 7.4 for 1995. The weighted average tariff for agriculture was 17 per cent, and we assumed it would remain unchanged in table 7.4 (below) for all primary products. China has also committed not to use agricultural export subsidies. In bilateral negotiations with the European Union, China agreed to tariff

---

[14] US Trade Representative, Statement of Ambassador Charlene Barshefsky regarding broad market access gains resulting from China WTO negotiations (Washington, D.C., 8 April 1999).

reductions on a number of additional products, including butter, olives, textiles, leather, spirits and a range of machinery products.

The arrangements for textiles and clothing are particularly important for China. Unlike most other developing-country exporters, China was excluded from the Uruguay Round Agreement on Textiles and Clothing.[15] Under the agreement China will benefit from the integration of textile and clothing into the GATT, and hence abolition of quotas, that has occurred since 1994.[16] This paves the way for expansion of China's exports of textiles and clothing, with all existing quotas to be phased out by 2005, and any special textile safeguards introduced under the agreement phased out by 2008. This is the only important instance where China benefits in terms of improved market access; all of the other benefits arise from China's commitments to reduce its own barriers.

In agriculture, the main impact is likely to be reduction in uncertainty about agricultural trade policies. While state trading will be retained for some important commodities, the WTO's rules impose significant disciplines on the protection that state trading enterprises can provide.[17] They require importing state trading enterprises to meet market demand, and limit their ability to restrict imports to the extent that the domestic price would consistently exceed the agreed tariff binding.

The disciplines on agricultural protection may become important if comparative advantage continues to shift against agriculture in China. China might have followed the East Asian pattern of sharply rising agricultural protection,[18] but as table 7.3 shows, most of the agricultural bindings agreed by China are low by East Asian standards, and may save China from developing an inefficient agricultural sector. Chinese policy has not hitherto favoured agriculture with non-tariff barriers. The bindings will inhibit, but not prevent, a swing toward increased agricultural protection. Table 7.3 also compares the bindings in the current proposal with those that China had offered in the Uruguay Round – illustrating how far China has been willing to come.

[15] This agreement applied only to members of the GATT 1947.
[16] World Trade Organization, *The Results of the Uruguay Round of Multilateral Trade Negotiations* (Geneva, 1994).
[17] W. Davey, 'Article XVII GATT: an overview' in T. Cottier and P. Mavroidis (eds.), *State Trading in the Twenty-first Century*, Studies in International Economics, The World Trade Forum, 1, (Ann Arbor, 1998).
[18] K. Anderson and Y. Hayami, *The Political Economy of Agricultural Protection: East Asia in International Perspective* (Sydney, 1986).

Table 7.3 *Final tariff bindings on selected agricultural products (%)*

Commodity	Uruguay Round final binding	Likely final bindings
Almonds	30	10
Apples	40	10
Barley	91	9
Beef	40	12
Citrus	52	12
Grapes	40	13
Pork, frozen cuts	40	12
Poultry, frozen cuts	40	12
Soybeans	114	3
Wheat, maize, rice	114	65
Wine	135	14

Source: WTO, *Uruguay Round of Multilateral Trade Negotiations: Legal Instruments Embodying the Results of the Uruguay Round of Multilateral Trade Negotiations, Vol. 4* (Geneva, 1994); Xiwen Chen, 'The WTO and the Sino-US agricultural agreement', Symposium on WTO and the Chinese Economy sponsored by the State Information Center (Beijing, 22–3 May 1999); USTR, Statement of Ambassador Charlene Barshefsky regarding broad market access gains resulting from China WTO negotiations (Washington, D.C., 8 April 1999); C. Carter and Jikun Huang, 'China's agricultural trade: patterns and prospects', memo, University of California at Davis (1998); EU 2000, 'The Sino-EU agreement on China's accession to the WTO: results of the bilateral negotiations' (http://europa.eu.int/comm/trade/bilateral/china/wto.htm).

The agricultural trade regime includes TRQs that provide for lower tariffs on specified quantities of imports. These commitments provide for some private participation in in-quota imports. The main effect is to provide rent transfers, rather than to liberalize, but it also makes the difference between border prices and the internal prices of agricultural goods transparent.

China's commitments on services under the GATS include commitments on distribution and tourism; on telecommunications, insurance, banking, construction, professional and audiovisual services. The commitments on distribution are important for merchandise trade because of the transparency they create, and because they preclude the emergence of *de facto* import barriers through controls on distribution. The coverage of these commitments exceeds the average for high-income countries in the Uruguay Round, and far exceeds that for developing countries.[19]

Liberalization resulting from accession

To assess the implications of accession for trade barriers, a comparison is made of protection after accession with what would have prevailed in the absence of accession. Given rapid changes in China's protection rates since the early 1990s, it is not clear what the counterfactual rate of protection would be. In general, we assume that the tariffs applying in the GTAP (Global Trade Analysis Project) Version 4 database for 1995 would have continued to apply.[20] An estimate follows of the protection applying after accession as the lesser of the applied and the bound rate.

In agriculture, this chapter assumes that protection rates will not decline from initial levels. There is uncertainty about both the initial level of agricultural protection in China, and the effects of the WTO Agreement on important commodities such as wheat, corn and rice. The tariff equivalents of agricultural trade barriers in China have been variable, but appear to have been consistently negative in the 1980s.[21] In more recent years, taxation of China's agriculture has been reduced, and some estimates of protection rates have become positive in some years. However, many studies still find negative protection rates in most periods.[22] The WTO commitments seem likely to allow protection to rise to the binding rate (65 per cent) for wheat, and hence are unlikely to reduce protection of this important import, while China is typically a net exporter of rice and maize.

For industrial products, there is detailed information on 1995 tariff rates. These were aggregated up to the GTAP level of aggregation using data from the UN COMTRADE system. This chapter uses trade-weighted average tariff rates as a conservative estimate of the initially applied rate of protection. Protection created by NTBs seems to have fallen substantially from the

---

[19] E. Ianchovichina, W. Martin and C. Wood, *Effects of the Vietnam–US Bilateral Trade Agreement*, mimeo, World Bank, 2000.

[20] In doing this, we are effectively treating the tariff reductions after 1995 as being undertaken as part of China's campaign to enter the WTO.

[21] C. Findlay, W. Martin and A. Watson, *Policy Reform, Economic Growth and China's Agriculture* (Development Centre Studies, OECD, 1993).

[22] e.g. C. Carter, 'China's trade integration and impacts on factor markets', mimeo, University of California at Davis, 2001.

Table 7.4 *Weighted average tariffs in China with and without WTO accession (%)*

	Baseline	With accession
Foodgrains	0.00	0.00
Feedgrains	6.03	6.03
Oilseeds	4.16	4.16
Meat and livestock	10.14	10.14
Dairy	26.74	26.74
Other agriculture	22.09	22.09
Other food	27.68	27.68
Beverages and tobacco	123.50	20.38
Extractive industries	3.59	1.26
Textiles	57.10	9.39
Wearing apparel	75.99	14.85
Wood and paper	21.57	4.80
Petrochemicals	20.17	6.94
Metals	17.52	6.22
Automobiles	129.07	13.76
Electronics	21.69	3.44
Other manufactures	23.53	6.74
Total – Agriculture	17.09	16.88
Total – Manufactures	24.27	6.95
Total	21.41	7.85

9 per cent estimated by the World Bank.[23] In the absence of better information, we preferred to adopt a known lower-bound estimate of protection, rather than add a speculative estimate of the rates of protection contributed by NTBs.

Estimates of the rates of assistance to various sectors pre- and post-accession

Table 7.4 shows China's average tariff rates in the baseline (column 2) and in the case of WTO accession (column 3).[24] Although the tariff bindings are

[23] World Bank, *China Engaged.*
[24] The tariff rates are the statutory tariff rates, and not the *de facto* rates after adjusting for duty exemptions. The *de facto* rates will be smaller.

estimated to be above the previous rates of protection, as Joe Francois and Will Martin have emphasized,[25] once the stochastic nature of protection is taken into account, even bindings above applied rates may reduce both the mean and the variance of protection, and hence its cost.

The table highlights the substantial nature of the offer for industrial products. On average, tariffs on imported manufactures drop from 24.3 per cent to about 7 per cent. Protection of textiles and apparel, automobiles, electronics and petrochemicals falls dramatically. The decline in protection to electronics is related to China's agreement to implement the Information Technology Agreement as part of its accession package. The reduction in protection to the automobile sector is larger than it appears, since quota protection is to be phased out. Overall, China's offer lowers the weighted average tariff protection on imports to the country from 21.4 per cent to 7.9 per cent.

Assessing China's accession to the WTO

China's economy is likely to continue growing fast, causing substantial changes in the composition of output. Liberalization associated with WTO accession is also likely to have implications for the structure of output, the orientation of production between domestic and international markets, and the benefits from liberalization.[26] To evaluate the impact of accession in this dynamic context, this chapter assesses the likely future growth in China's economy using an extended version of the GTAP model, which models duty exemptions.[27]

This chapter looks at two scenarios – a baseline scenario in which China does not enter the WTO, and a companion scenario under which China enters the WTO. All experiments broadly replicate World Bank projections for overall output growth in each region, and use projections of factor input growth and a residually determined level of total factor productivity growth to ensure broad consistency between the two. To avoid the increase in

[25] J. Francois and W. Martin, 'Multilateral trade rules and the expected cost of protection', Discussion Paper No. 1214 (Centre for Economic Policy Research, London, 1995).

[26] C. Bach, B. Dimaranan, T. Hertel and W. Martin, 'Market growth, structural change, and the gains from the Uruguay Round' (2000) 8(2) *Review of International Economics* 295–310.

[27] E. Ianchovichina and W. Martin, *Comparative Study of Trade Liberalization Regimes: The Case of China's Accession to the WTO*, mimeo, World Bank, 2001.

agricultural prices that would otherwise occur,[28] we specify a higher rate of productivity growth in agriculture.[29] The protection rates used throughout were based on tariffs in (or near) the model's base year of 1995.

Because the available projections suggest that the growth of factor endowments in high-growth regions such as East Asia will be highly unbalanced, the structure of output can be expected to change sharply as a result of Rybczynski effects. These pressures for change are in addition to those resulting from differences in the income responsiveness of different consumer goods. The simulations have been performed over the period from the model's benchmark year of 1995 to 2005.

Details are given in table 7.5 for 1995/2005.[30] These projections were generated by combining historical and forecast data from World Bank sources. The skilled-labour projections, based on forecasts of the growth in the stock of tertiary-educated labour in each developing country[31] and projected growth rates of skilled labour in developed countries from the World Bank, provide an indication of changes in the stock of those qualified as professional and technical workers. Projections of the stock of physical capital were calculated using a Harberger-type perpetual inventory method – that is, by adding investment net of depreciation to update the capital stock in each year. Data for initial physical-capital stock for 1995 as

---

[28] Capital:labour and capital:output ratios appear to have been rising worldwide (see V. Nehru and A. Dhareshwar, 'A new database on physical capital stock: sources, methodology and results' (1993) 8(1) *Revista de Análisis Económico* 37–59) and, under these circumstances, Rybczynski effects tend to pull resources out of the relatively labour-intensive agricultural sectors: see M. Gehlhar, T. Hertel and W. Martin, 'Economic growth and the changing structure of trade and production in the Pacific Rim' (1994) 76 *American Journal of Agricultural Economics* 1101–10.

[29] See for evidence W. Martin and D. Mitra, 'Productivity growth and convergence in agriculture versus manufacturing' (2001) 49(2) *Economic Development and Cultural Change* 403–22. The productivity growth rates in this study differ not only by region but also by sector. Based on work by Bernard and Jones for OECD agriculture 1970–87, we assume that annual productivity growth in agriculture is 40 per cent faster than that of manufacturing, in services it is half of the rate in manufacturing, in mining productivity growth is zero. See A. Bernard and C. Jones, 'Productivity growth across industries and countries: time series theory and evidence' (1996) 78(1) *Review of Economics and Statistics* 135–46.

[30] For further discussion, see W. Martin, B. Dimaranan, T. Hertel and E. Ianchovichina, 'Trade policy, structural change and China's trade growth', Working Paper No. 64, Stanford Institute for Economic Policy Research (Stanford, 2000), and K. Anderson, J. Francois, T. Hertel, B. Hoekman and W. Martin, 'Potential gains from trade reform in the new millennium', paper presented at Third Annual Conference on Global Economic Analysis, Monash University, 27–30 June 2000.

[31] V. Ahuja and D. Filmer, 'Educational attainment in developing countries: new estimates and projections disaggregated by gender', Policy Research Working Paper 1489 (World Bank, Washington D.C., 1995).

Table 7.5 *Percentage growth rates over the period 1995–2005 (annual rates in parentheses)*

Regions	Population	Unskilled labour	Skilled labour	Capital	Manufacturing TFP*
North America	11 (1.05)	14 (1.29)	39 (3.33)	63 (4.98)	low
Western Europe	1 (0.10)	0 (0.03)	29 (2.60)	30 (2.70)	medium
Australia/ New Zealand	10 (0.97)	11 (1.09)	66 (5.20)	38 (3.29)	low
Japan	2 (0.20)	−3 (−0.29)	32 (2.83)	29 (2.59)	low
China	9 (0.83)	12 (1.17)	43 (3.66)	174 (10.62)	medium
Taiwan	8 (0.73)	13 (1.21)	51 (4.18)	102 (7.28)	high
Other NICs	9 (0.84)	8 (0.73)	66 (5.18)	71 (5.54)	low
Indonesia	14 (1.31)	21 (1.96)	79 (6.00)	21 (1.96)	low
Other Southeast Asia	19 (1.73)	26 (2.36)	79 (6.00)	38 (3.30)	low
India	17 (1.59)	23 (2.11)	73 (5.65)	85 (6.36)	medium
Other South Asia	23 (2.10)	33 (2.92)	77 (5.87)	56 (4.52)	medium
Brazil	13 (1.26)	22 (2.04)	70 (5.46)	25 (2.22)	low
Other Latin America	18 (1.63)	23 (2.11)	89 (6.55)	25 (2.22)	low
Turkey	15 (1.44)	22 (2.02)	104 (7.41)	66 (5.19)	low
Other Middle East and North Africa	27 (2.43)	37 (3.17)	109 (7.64)	15 (1.37)	low
Economies in transition	3 (0.27)	6 (0.60)	69 (5.37)	30 (2.70)	low
South African Customs Union	23 (2.06)	29 (2.59)	64 (5.06)	15 (1.43)	low
Other Sub-Saharan Africa	33 (2.87)	37 (3.19)	88 (6.50)	19 (1.78)	medium
Rest of World	18 (1.65)	21 (1.90)	83 (6.22)	88 (6.51)	low

*The low, medium, and high growth assumptions for total factor productivity (TFP) in manufacturing correspond to annual growth rates of 0.1%, 1.0% and 2.0%, respectively.

well as annual forecasts of gross domestic investment were obtained from the World Bank.

The workforce in China is projected to grow faster than the population over the period, although not greatly because much of the demographic dividend[32] resulting from the decline in the birth rate has now passed. Most important for the growth and structure of the economy are the high

---

[32] D. Bloom and J. G. Williamson, 'Demographic transitions and economic miracles in emerging Asia' (1998) 12(3) *World Bank Economic Review* 419–56.

projected growth rates for skilled labour and for physical capital. This aug-
mentation of physical and human capital can be expected to have profound
implications for growth and structural change.

Under the baseline scenario, tariff rates on industrial products remain
constant, and Multi-Fibre Arrangement (MFA) quotas are projected to
grow at the rates determined in each country's agreements. Tariff rates
on agricultural products are also held constant, in line with the move to
tariffication in the Uruguay Round. Since MFA quota growth rates for
WTO members are subject to quota growth-rate acceleration,[33] but those
for non-members such as China are not, MFA quota growth rates become
an increasing burden for China without WTO accession.

The estimated impact of China's liberalization due to accession and its
growth till 2005 are shown in tables 7.6 to 7.9. These suggest some interesting
conclusions. The first is the rapid growth in China's shares of world output
and exports even in the absence of WTO accession.[34] Without accession,
China's share of world output is projected to increase between 1995 and
2005 from 3.4 to 5.3 per cent, and its share of exports from 3.7 to 4.8 per cent.
The accession offer has almost no impact on the share of output. However,
it has a very significant impact on China's share of world trade.[35] With
the implementation of the accession offer, China's share of world export
markets rises to 6.8 per cent, and of world import markets to 6.6 per cent.

At the sectoral level, the most important impact of accession is on China's
output of apparel. Production of apparel rises by 264 per cent over the ten-
year period, compared to 57 per cent in the baseline (columns 2 and 3,
table 7.7), and results in an increase in China's share of world output of
apparel from 8.84 per cent in the baseline to 20.10 per cent in the case
of accession (columns 3 and 4, table 7.6). This is because of the lifting
of the burdens imposed by the MFA on China's exports, and because
reduced protection of domestic inputs lowers the cost structure of the
industry.

---

[33] WTO, *The Results of the Uruguay Round of Multilateral Trade Negotiations* (Geneva, 1994).

[34] China's demand for foodgrains and other agricultural products grows rapidly without WTO
accession, which is reflected in growing shares of both output and imports in the world market.
This result is consistent with a strong income growth averaging 7.4 per cent per year for ten
years, and high income elasticities with respect to agricultural commodities and food embedded
in the GTAP data (www.agecon.purdue.edu/gtap).

[35] The result that extra trade leads to no extra growth can be explained with the fact that we have
not included an endogenous growth linkage between openness and growth.

Table 7.6 *Output, exports and imports as a share of the world economy*

	Output 1995–2005			Exports 1995–2005			Imports 1995–2005		
		Without accession	With accession		Without accession	With accession		Without accession	With accession
Foodgrains	14.29	19.59	19.39	0.30	0.06	0.06	6.45	16.35	16.02
Feedgrains	8.33	10.55	10.43	0.72	0.12	0.12	3.20	9.18	9.13
Oilseeds	5.13	6.22	6.34	4.05	0.76	0.70	1.15	3.94	4.04
Meat and livestock	6.70	11.62	12.12	3.51	0.51	0.46	2.02	8.88	9.63
Dairy	0.75	1.34	1.42	0.08	0.03	0.02	0.17	0.61	0.62
Other agriculture	10.58	15.65	15.42	2.32	0.36	0.35	2.74	9.62	9.80
Other food	2.27	3.15	3.15	2.61	1.21	1.27	3.10	6.39	6.15
Beverages/tobacco	4.89	7.02	4.37	2.42	1.03	0.99	0.89	1.29	16.24
Extractive industries	8.07	12.29	11.88	1.69	0.12	0.14	1.55	9.09	8.50
Textiles	10.79	13.88	14.16	8.43	8.84	10.60	13.35	17.96	25.47
Wearing apparel	7.02	8.84	20.10	19.58	18.54	47.14	1.04	1.09	3.69
Wood and paper	2.41	3.67	3.35	2.19	2.59	3.00	2.57	3.86	4.64
Petrochemicals	5.00	7.57	7.06	2.56	3.06	3.42	4.02	5.76	6.33
Metals	5.45	8.99	8.40	3.38	5.47	6.48	4.23	5.77	6.62
Automobiles	1.91	3.76	1.10	0.13	0.69	2.16	1.95	1.81	4.83
Electronics	2.63	4.53	4.81	4.97	7.79	9.79	3.57	5.25	5.72
Other manufactures	6.40	10.41	9.81	5.49	8.05	9.86	4.23	5.89	7.45
Utilities	2.69	3.90	3.79	5.82	6.70	7.51	1.20	1.73	1.46
Trade/transport	2.55	3.73	3.69	1.70	2.79	3.07	2.03	2.41	2.19
Construction	3.29	6.22	6.07	0.00	0.00	0.00	1.82	2.81	2.69
Business/finance	0.89	1.34	1.31	1.92	2.50	2.68	1.49	1.95	1.82
Government services	1.58	2.37	2.34	1.01	0.62	0.65	0.72	1.31	1.22
Total	3.38	5.26	5.13	3.71	4.78	6.76	3.36	5.34	6.61

Table 7.7 *China's output and wages (percentage change 1995 to 2005)*

	Output	
	Without accession	With accession
Foodgrains	46.3	44.5
Feedgrains	28.9	26.9
Oilseeds	32.4	32.3
Meat and livestock	75.0	81.3
Dairy	74.9	84.4
Other agriculture	53.2	50.0
Other food	50.5	51.8
Beverages/tobacco	80.7	13.8
Extractive industries	61.9	60.2
Textiles	71.6	88.0
Wearing apparel	57.0	263.5
Wood and paper	103.6	93.9
Petrochemicals	105.8	98.6
Metals	135.7	126.2
Automobiles	189.6	−3.8
Electronics	142.5	169.1
Other manufactures	131.7	125.5
Utilities	103.2	101.2
Trade/transport	110.9	114.4
Construction	147.9	149.0
Business/finance	104.6	105.1
Government services	85.0	85.9
Wages of skilled labour	39.2	42.2
Wages of unskilled labour	83.0	87.1

China's apparel exports increase by 375 per cent over the decade, compared to 45 per cent in the case of no accession, for the same reason (columns 4 and 5, table 7.8). As a result, China's share of world export markets for apparel increases to over 47 per cent. The expansion of the apparel sector stimulates demand for imported textiles, which increase by 272 per cent by 2005.

The automobile sector, and some high-tech sectors, experience increases in exports under the accession scenario, as their costs fall following liberalization. Despite this increase in exports, the output of the automobiles sector contracts in the case of accession, as its protection falls from

Table 7.8 China's trade by commodity and composition of value added (% changes between 1995 and 2005)

	Imports (cif weights)		Exports (fob weights)		Composition of value added	
	Without accession	With accession	Without accession	With accession	Without accession	With accession
Foodgrains	240.4	233.9	−76.9	−77.9	−26.1	−29.5
Feedgrains	263.5	260.5	−81.7	−82.8	−34.9	−38.1
Oilseeds	321.2	331.7	−82.0	−83.6	−33.1	−35.4
Meat and livestock	451.7	507.3	−85.5	−86.8	−11.6	−11.5
Dairy	318.1	324.2	−70.0	−71.9	−11.6	−10.0
Other agriculture	352.1	363.6	−84.8	−85.4	−22.6	−26.8
Other food	154.1	144.7	−48.8	−46.2	−24.0	−25.9
Beverages/tobacco	148.4	6718.5	−25.4	−14.9	−8.7	−44.5
Extractive industries	719.9	681.6	−92.6	−90.9	−18.2	−21.8
Textiles	86.8	271.9	44.5	106.8	−13.3	−8.3
Wearing apparel	57.9	818.1	45.3	374.8	−20.6	77.4
Wood and paper	105.0	184.3	63.0	96.8	2.9	−5.4
Petrochemicals	96.3	140.7	64.8	90.6	4.0	−3.1
Metals	88.0	138.9	134.2	190.1	19.1	10.4
Automobiles	24.7	550.7	647.8	2522.6	46.3	−53.0
Electronics	101.4	146.6	125.9	194.9	22.5	31.3
Other manufactures	95.2	186.6	113.5	175.6	17.1	10.1
Utilities	95.0	64.5	57.2	79.7	2.7	−1.8
Trade/transport	63.4	46.7	113.0	133.5	6.6	4.6
Construction	101.2	92.7	5.6	20.2	25.3	21.5
Business/finance	75.2	63.3	82.4	98.5	3.4	0.1
Government services	156.8	140.4	−20.5	−15.9	−6.5	−9.3

Table 7.9 *Welfare change due to China's accession to the WTO*

Countries/ Regions	Income in 1995 (million US$)	Income change in baseline w/o WTO, 1995–2005 (million US$)	Income change due to WTO (million US$)	Income change due to WTO as a share in base 2005 income (%)
China	713,567	576,698	28,622	2.2
Developed countries	22,141,335	5,240,158	19,708	0.1
North America	7,976,177	2,561,244	9,456	0.1
Western Europe	8,649,828	1,828,018	7,115	0.1
Japan	5,095,149	724,361	2,921	0.1
Australia and New Zealand	420,182	126,535	216	0.0
Developing countries	5,464,721	1,935,271	7,752	0.1
East Asia	1,447,568	581,945	12,462	0.6
Taiwan	280,853	176,771	5,191	1.1
Other NIEs	624,308	237,664	7,819	0.9
Indonesia	199,799	49,903	−171	−0.1
Other Southeast Asia	342,609	117,607	−377	−0.1
South Asia	440,769	248,625	−3,963	−0.6
India	331,447	188,060	−3,190	−0.6
Other South Asia	109,322	60,565	−773	−0.5
Latin America	1,360,294	405,957	57	0.0
Brazil	700,697	190,848	−31	0.0
Other Latin America	659,597	215,109	88	0.0
Middle East and North Africa	848,233	277,828	−360	0.0
Sub-Saharan Africa	319,542	110,366	77	0.0
Eastern Europe and FSU	792,466	178,760	−245	0.0
Rest of the World	255,850	131,790	−276	−0.1
Total	28,319,624	7,752,127	56,082	0.2

129 per cent in the baseline to only 13.8 per cent under accession (table 7.4, above).[36] The output growth of the high-tech sector ('electronics')

[36] This model underestimates the increased efficiency of China's automobile sector, since it assumes constant returns to scale. With high protection and the presence of economies of scale, the automobile industry in China is currently grossly inefficient, as manifested by an excessive entry of firms and models, and sub-optimal scale. China has been trying to deal with this issue for twenty years or more by controlling entry through restrictions on the import of assembly lines and related equipment. But, as in other countries, these controls have been ineffective. Reducing protection, however, will force increased economies of scale, and hence efficiency. This in turn implies that China might become a much bigger exporter than these results suggest.

is export driven, the export share growing from 7.8 per cent to almost 10 per cent. The export shares of all manufacturing sectors grow under WTO accession due to a rapid increase in intra-industry trade. Table 7.6 shows an increase both in the export and import shares of all manufactured goods.

Wages of unskilled workers are expected to grow at twice the rate of those of skilled workers during 1995–2005, given the projections of 12 per cent growth in unskilled labour compared to 43 per cent growth in skilled labour over the same period.[37] In aggregate, membership in the WTO is expected to have a positive effect on wages, due to expansion under accession of China's labour-intensive apparel sector. This increase in demand for labour translates into a slight increase in wages due to accession (table 7.7). This slight strengthening of the labour market could have favourable impacts on inequality and poverty, a result consistent with that of Zhi Wang and Zhai Fan.[38]

China becomes a much bigger market for its trading partners following accession to the WTO. Although protection of agriculture is assumed to remain largely unchanged, China increases its agricultural imports of oilseeds, meat and various food products due to the strong shift in comparative advantage away from agriculture (implied by the baseline-growth scenario in the last two columns of table 7.8). This is a typical outcome of successful economic development, and a sign of improved food security for the population in that they can more readily acquire food from domestic or foreign sources. It is associated with growth in agricultural production in addition to positive growth in agricultural imports and a decline in agricultural exports (table 7.7).

Table 7.9 shows regional income and welfare changes due to China's accession both in value and as a percentage of income in 2005. It suggests that China will be the biggest beneficiary of accession to the WTO, followed by the industrialized economies and newly industrialized countries in East Asia. While the developing countries as a whole and the world as a whole also benefit, most developing countries competing with China in third markets will lose from China's accession to the WTO. Countries in South Asia are expected to be hurt the most, followed by Indonesia and some

---

[37] Ahuja and Filmer, 'Educational attainment in developing countries'.
[38] Zhi Wang and Zhai Fan, 'Tariff reduction, tax replacement, and implications for income distribution in China' (1998) 26 *Journal of Comparative Economics* 358–87.

other Southeast Asian countries, mainly because of the removal of MFA restrictions on China's apparel exports. Losses to countries elsewhere are negligible.

Conclusions

Trade reforms associated with China's accession to the WTO are part of a long-term movement to greater openness and integration into the world economy. Their full effects can only be understood if they are considered in the context of China's existing trade policies, and particularly the important duty exemptions provided for processing trade.

China has committed to make substantial reductions in the tariffs applied on manufactures. In agriculture, it is much more difficult to ascertain the extent of liberalization because of our limited knowledge about current protection rates, and the complex nature of protection under the TRQ system for some commodities. In contrast with other studies, such as that of Zhai Fan and Li Shantong,[39] we conclude that little short-run liberalization of agriculture will be required, but that much more work is needed before much confidence could be placed in this conclusion. In the longer run, however, it is likely that accession will help China retain an efficient agricultural sector. Another important aspect of liberalization will be the phasing out of the MFA quotas that have hampered China's textile and clothing sector.

The analysis in this chapter is conducted in the context of rapid growth and structural change in the Chinese economy. The findings in this chapter suggest that accession has a strong impact on China's trade growth but, because the chapter has not included an endogenous growth linkage between openness and growth, a smaller impact on its shares of output. With accession, China's share of world exports rises from 3.7 per cent in 1995 to over 6.8 per cent. While accession has an impact on China's export shares, its effect is smaller than found in other studies that do not incorporate the effects of duty-exemption schemes in the base.[40] The duty exemptions represent partial liberalization, and this needs to be taken into account.

---

[39] Zhai Fan and Li Shantong, 'The implications of accession to WTO on China's economy'.

[40] e.g. T. Walmsley and T. Hertel, 'China's accession to the WTO: timing is everything', (2001) 24 (8) *World Economy* 1019–49.

At the sectoral level, the most important impact of accession is on the apparel market, where China increases its share of world export markets to 47 per cent. While enormous, this is smaller than estimates obtained without taking the implications of tariff exemptions into account.

In our analysis, accession has favourable impacts on demand for skilled and unskilled labour. This follows from the expansion of labour-intensive sectors such as clothing and modest expansions in some labour-intensive agricultural sectors such as meat production. Due to further lowering of trade distortions under the final offer, China's gains from joining the WTO will be magnified as a result of the improved efficiency of the Chinese economy and increased investment flow into the region. This analysis, however, ignores important dynamic considerations that might augment the estimated gains for China.

The benefits of China's accession to the WTO will mainly accrue to China but also to some developing and developed countries. Indonesia and South Asia may lose out due to increased competition from China outweighing their gains from increased direct trade.

These results highlight areas where more research is needed if appropriate policies are to be adopted: agricultural trade, where lack of knowledge about the base level of agricultural protection creates uncertainty about whether accession will have a substantial liberalizing effect; the abolition of the textile quotas, whose impacts are likely to be enormous, but for which this analysis has relied on dated estimates of protection; and the automobile sector, which will undergo wrenching changes during transition to a more efficient and export-oriented sector and whose features are not well captured by our model. The contingent protection measures included in the agreement will require careful analysis and policy responses if they are not greatly to hinder China's integration into the world economy.

8

China's WTO entry in labour surplus and Marxist terms

RAJ BHALA

Indeterminacy: spotting the issue

This chapter contributes to the subject of China's WTO accession from a more theoretical perspective than that which underlies questions of the economic impact of entry on various sectors, the substantive legal regime that will be in force, or the consonance of China's trade laws and practices with that regime. At the same time, neither can nor should the discussion here avoid an occasional foray into empirical matters.

This chapter considers the US and EU bilateral deals with China from two different schools of thought in development economics, one capitalist and one Marxist. Each school permits a different inference to be drawn about the terms of these deals. These inferences are not inconsistent, but neither is cheerful.

The capitalist framework is the Fei–Ranis labour surplus model. In this framework, the story of economic growth is a story of transition from a largely agricultural economy to a largely industrial economy. International trade plays the role of handmaiden, not protagonist, in this story. To facilitate the agriculture-to-industry transition, a developing country can be helped by market access for industrial products in which it seeks to gain an international comparative-exporting advantage. That country can also be helped by imports of goods and services it needs in the

I would like to thank Deborah Cass and Brett Gerard Williams of the Australian National University for their help on this project. I shall be discussing the labour surplus model, and its variants such as the neo-classical two-sector model, in greater detail in *Trade and Development* (Carolina Academic Press, 2003). See also M. Gillis, D. H. Perkins, M. Roemer and D. R. Snodgrass, *Economics of Development* (4th edn, Oxford 1996), pp. 51–7.

industrial export sectors (for example, raw materials, intermediate goods, capital equipment and technical assistance) and to alleviate strains in the agricultural sector during the industrialization process (such as certain foodstuffs).

What can one draw from applying this model to the US and EU bilateral deals? These deals appear not entirely consistent with the role (albeit limited) granted to trade in the Fei–Ranis model; that is, their terms do not go far enough to facilitate the economic transition China must continue to make from agricultural to industrial society. The terms ensure a great deal can be imported. But, on the export side, few promises are made by China's trading partners beyond most favoured nation (MFN) treatment, a benefit China has, or could have, through a web of bilateral trade deals and regional trade agreements.

In the Marxist–Leninist paradigm the story is more radical, and so too is the inference drawn. Economic growth is possible only through exploitation – at the enterprise level, of a worker by a capitalist, and at the national level, of one country by another. From this second theoretical perspective, the US and EU bilateral deals are lopsided – former President Clinton said so himself of the US deal. With precious few limitations (for example on the telecommunications, insurance and cultural sectors), these deals could be said to permit China to be carved up by foreign economic interests to a degree not seen since the Opium War era.

Depending on the theoretical framework through which the US and EU bilateral agreements are viewed, one can come to different conclusions about the meaning for China's economy of its terms of entry to the WTO.

Two contextual points

Why choose the Fei–Ranis and Marxist–Leninist Models? Is the Fei–Ranis model rather old-fashioned? Did Marx and Lenin have a model of modern economic growth (as distinct from the historical progression of capitalism)? The direct answer is that China made the choice of models. Until the mid-1970s, China followed the latter model. Since then, it has pursued the former model.[1] Yes, it is true that no model captures reality perfectly. Hence, it is always reasonable to inquire whether applying a model is worth the trouble.

---

[1] See Gillis et al., *Economics of Development*, p. 59.

My sense is that the two models do a good job of capturing what Chinese planners had in mind for their country.

The labour surplus model is the standard paradigm of modern cap-italist economic growth. The Marxist–Leninist Model appears to form the basis for positions taken by the anti-globalization movement. I argue elsewhere that Marxist–Leninist concepts lay at the foundation of the claim that the WTO is 'anti-Third World'.[2] These concepts echo in the minds of some Chinese leaders. Consider a *Financial Times* report of 20 November 2000. Li Yining, a well-known economist and deputy direc-tor of the Finance and Economy Committee of China's National People's Congress (NPC) spoke of the shocks that will strike China's economy after WTO accession, and of the emergence of a 'new left' in Chinese politics that 'strongly believe that the disadvantages [of WTO accession] outweigh the advantages'.

The Fei–Ranis model and the bilateral deals

The three-panel Fei–Ranis labour surplus model

The Fei–Ranis labour surplus model is expressed through three graphs: the agricultural production function, the agricultural labour market (the marginal productivity curve), and the industrial labour market (the labour supply and demand curves). The Fei–Ranis model is the placement of these three graphs – one on top of the other – on the same page (see figure 8.1).

Note that the agricultural production function is flipped over, upside down. That way, all three graphs can be read in the same manner – an outward horizontal movement represents a shift in workers from the agri-cultural to the industrial sector. Thus, in the top left of the agricultural production function in figure 8.1, all workers are employed in farming. The marginal productivity of each worker is nil or negative. The assump-tion is relaxed as the graph proceeds to the right – that is, as the labour surplus is withdrawn and as non-surplus farm workers shift to industry. In the bottom right-hand corner, all workers have shifted out of farming and into industry. In that situation, the marginal productivity of one worker in the agricultural sector would (in theory) tend toward a large number – she

118   RAJ BHALA

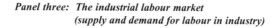

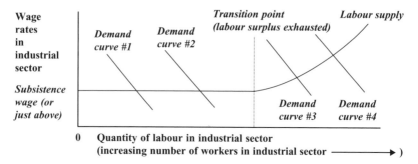

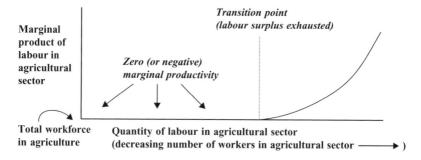

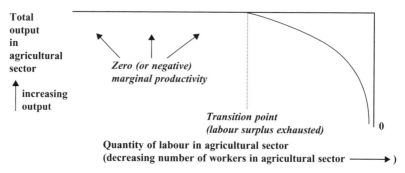

Figure 8.1 The Fei–Ranis labour surplus model

is the only producer in that sector, hence her marginal contribution is the same as total agricultural output.

Flipping the agricultural production function also means the vertical (y-) axis must be read with care. In a standard depiction, a movement upward (from zero to the top of the axis) signifies an increase in farm production. When the graph is inverted in the way shown in figure 8.1, moving from the bottom to the top of the page still represents an increase in total agricultural output. Conversely, by moving along the curve from the top to the bottom, total agricultural output declines. As explained below, this decline results from industrialization after the transition point – that is, the successive withdrawal of workers from the agricultural sector who are productive (as measured by a positive marginal productivity) – and signifies a change in the terms of trade (the relative price) of industry to agriculture.

Taken together, all three panels in figure 8.1 portray the industrialization process made possible by a pool of surplus labour. The agricultural production function in Panel One shows a decrease in agricultural output as this labour surplus is withdrawn from rural areas and put to work in urban factories. This decrease is evident by recalling that the function is presented in an inverted way, so a movement from left to right means the supply of labour to agriculture is decreasing, and a movement from top to bottom means agricultural output is decreasing.

However, farm output decreases only after the transition point, when the labour surplus is exhausted. By definition, the labour surplus that is withdrawn has a zero or negative marginal product – hence the label 'labour surplus': withdrawing them from farm work does not harm total agricultural output. On the contrary, getting these workers off the farm helps the remaining farmers work more efficiently than when the land was over-worked, over-crowded, and subject to diminishing, zero and negative returns. Yet once all surplus workers have moved out, and workers with positive marginal productivity are siphoned off, total farm output begins to suffer because workers now shifting to industry had contributed positively to agricultural output.

Panel Two shows the familiar marginal productivity of labour curve. At the bottom left, all workers are engaged in farming. Once again, a rightward movement signifies a transfer of the labour surplus from agriculture to industry. Marginal productivity is flat (zero), or even negative, for as long as surplus labour remains on the farms. When industrialists have exhausted the pool of surplus farm labour, the economy reaches the transition point.

After this critical point, marginal productivity in the agricultural sector begins to rise, because the remaining farmers can do their jobs unfettered by workers who are under- and un-employed, and make better use of the other factor inputs (land, technology and so on).

Marginal productivity in the agricultural sector is the basis for the labour supply curve to the industrial sector (because workers are willing and able to sell their labour for the value of their marginal product – that is, for their marginal revenue product). The labour supply and labour demand curves are portrayed in the upper-most panel of figure 8.1 (Panel Three). As long as the labour supply curve is perfectly elastic, workers can be enticed away by the captains of industry for subsistence wages (or just above that level). When all labour surplus is gone, farm workers need a higher wage if they are to leave the idyllic countryside for an urban factory job. Hence, the industrial wage rate must rise if the demand on the part of capitalists for labour continues to increase.

Corresponding to this increase in wage rates in the industrial sector is a decline in total agricultural output. Once past the transition point, any workers who shift from farms to factories are, by definition, productive (that is, they have a positive marginal productivity). Thus agricultural output falls. As in any market, if output declines, then (*ceteris paribus*) prices rise. Hence, the terms of trade of industry relative to agriculture (that is, the price of industrial versus farm goods) deteriorate. Urban factory workers must pay more for their food, so need higher wages.

Here is why the transition point is so critical. Industrialization before the point continues apace on the benefit of the labour surplus transferred from agriculture. After the point, steady agricultural output can no longer be taken for granted. Continued industrialization imposes demands on agriculture that have to be addressed if economic growth is to continue without straining that sector beyond limits.

The bilateral deals from a labour surplus perspective

The role of trade

Can industrialization, made possible through the labour surplus, be enhanced (that is, accelerated) by international trade? The answer is 'of course'.[3]

---

[3] See, e.g., Dan Ben-David and L. Alan Winters, *Trade, Income Disparity and Poverty* (WTO Special Studies No. 5 1999) (available on the WTO website www.wto.org).

If the captains of industry have overseas markets to which they can export the output from their factories, then no doubt they will have all the more incentive to expand production. To do so, they will hire the labour surplus from the agricultural sector more quickly, and thus the transition from agriculture to industry will be hastened. However, this trade-enhancing effect of industrialization is not a predominant feature of labour surplus models, such as the Fei–Ranis model. These models leave open the question of where industrial output is sold – that is, they tend not to specify whether the consumers are at home or abroad.

Another potential role for trade is in mitigating the demands placed by industrialization on the agricultural sector after the transition point is reached. How can the fall in domestic agricultural output after this point be addressed?

One answer is to provide the remaining farmers with better technology, such as high-yield and disease-resistant seeds. A second answer is better physical capital, in the form of mechanized tools (such as tractors). A third is to train the remaining farmers – to raise their level of human capital. A fourth answer is to expand the land that is available for cultivation, so that the remaining farmers can realize economies of scale. That expansion may occur through land reclamation (from the seas) or steppe farming (in mountainous areas).

There exists another answer: trade. The developing country that has passed the transition point can export its excess industrial output resulting from continued expansion of the industrial sector. In exchange, it can import agricultural commodities. Indeed, that bargain may enhance the process of industrial-product specialization, thus hastening the agriculture-to-industry transformation.

China adopted this policy in the late 1970s.[4] Faced with a labour-surplus economy, planners sought to accelerate the agriculture-to-industry transformation, being careful not to repeat the disaster of the Great Leap Forward of the late 1950s and early 1960s, during which an extraordinary number of people died from starvation during an industrialization effort that all but neglected domestic food production. Thus, China increased food imports to cover the needs of its expanding urban factory labour force. But increasing food imports may cause political difficulties.

---

[4] See Gillis et al., *Economics of Development*, p. 59.

Agricultural imports

The concessions offered by China to the United States and European Union are substantial, but, viewing modern economic growth in China through the lens of a labour surplus model, are these concessions likely to accelerate industrialization?

It is difficult to offer an affirmative answer. These concessions are market-access commitments for foreign exporters and investors. They represent market opportunities for them in China, not the other way around. In the Fei–Ranis model, what China needs is market access for its industrial products, coupled with additional agricultural imports to avoid excessive demands on Chinese farmers during the industrialization process. In that paradigm, the American, European and Chinese negotiators got it half right – they liberalized China's agricultural-import regime, or at least capped agricultural protections, but did little to open up foreign markets for Chinese capitalists.

The 'other half': market access for Chinese industrial products

What about the 'other half': overseas market access for Chinese goods? Through WTO entry, these goods will get the benefit of permanent, unconditional MFN treatment from all WTO members. However, it appears Chinese trade negotiators have already obtained such treatment from many countries through bilateral trade deals. Even in the all-important American market, China got MFN treatment, though it had to be renewed annually. To the extent that Chinese trade negotiators had not yet got around to obtaining MFN treatment from certain countries, they could have continued to do so – in the absence of WTO membership – on a bilateral basis.

So, one way to put the question from the vantage of the Fei–Ranis model is whether the bilateral deals create market-access opportunities for Chinese industrial products, beyond MFN treatment, and thereby accelerate further the industrialization process? The answer is 'no'.

There is no broad-scale provision of preferential treatment for Chinese industrial products. For example, there is no commitment on the part of the United States or European Union to offer duty-free treatment to these products. There is no preferential treatment for specific industrial sectors. For instance, neither the United States nor the European Union offered special help to China's petrochemical, textile or steel sectors. On the contrary, as discussed in the context of applying the Marxist–Leninist model, the deals are oriented to assure expanded access for foreign exporters and investors to the Chinese markets.

Worse, some of the terms and conditions of the US–China deal allow for a denial of even MFN treatment. Examples are the special safeguard mechanism against textiles that will remain in place after the Uruguay Round Agreement on Textiles and Clothing (the ATC Agreement) expires, the non-market economy (NME) dumping margin rules that facilitate an affirmative dumping margin calculation through clever choice of a proxy for normal value (NV), and the Product-Specific Safeguard. Another example is the ability to apply countervailing duties against exports of former state-owned enterprises on the basis of subsidies the exporter received while still in state hands. The United States and other WTO members can use these devices to slap import restrictions on Chinese products, assuming the legal prerequisites are satisfied, hence denying them MFN treatment.

Such restrictions would retard China's efforts to exhaust its surplus labour and move rapidly past the transition point. I am told by specialists on China's economy that a large amount of China's industrial output during the past several years has ended up as accumulated inventories, not as actual sales. The terms of the bilateral deals will do little, if anything, to clear these inventories through export.

Thus, applying the Fei–Ranis model, there is a case to be made for special and differential treatment for exports of low-value-added industrial products in which China is seeking (or can aspire to) a comparative advantage. In addition to textiles, steel and simple petrochemical products, examples would be shoes and basic consumer electronic items. Had China received, say, duty-free treatment on these sorts of items, then large numbers of surplus farm labourers could be moved into factories making these items for export. The result could well be an acceleration of the agriculture-to-industry transformation that Professors John Fei and Gus Ranis say is the touchstone of modern economic growth.[5] Had China received less aggressive treatment on trade remedies, then the prospect of retarding the transition would have been diminished.

All this is not to imply that China's transition will stop upon entry into the WTO; far from it. The question is how quickly it will occur, and the severity of the adjustment costs the Chinese people will endure. In a trade sense, the question is whether the terms of the bilateral deals allow imports

---

[5] *Development of the Labour Surplus Economy.*

and exports to play the supporting role left to them by the Fei–Ranis model as successfully as possible. The slower the pace of transformation, and the more painful it becomes to absorb the costs, the more difficult it may prove to continue the course of economic reforms – and political liberalization then may be yet further off.

The Marxist model and the bilateral deals

Be prepared

Understanding what a Marxist approach to the US–China and EU–China bilateral concession agreements might be presupposes knowledge about the Marxist–Leninist model of economic growth and, in particular, about the role trade plays therein. That model underlies many of the charges levelled at the multilateral trading system and the WTO by advocates of third-world causes.[6]

It is easy to think of China as an emerging dragon after touring Shanghai's Pudong industrial zone or the Shenzhen Stock Exchange. But tour towns and villages elsewhere and a different picture emerges. There is a great deal of uncertainty about everyday matters, from pensions and bank accounts to finding a flat and having a child. There is deep concern about the rule of law, cynicism about corruption and fear about what globalization might mean for China. Some Chinese textile and steel workers dread foreign competition, revealing the same insecurities harboured by their American competitors.

There is no 'one China'. There are many Chinas, and in some of these Chinas the concerns about international trade articulated in the Marxist–Leninist model still resonate, though typically without the 'Marxist–Leninist' rubric. China was 'lost' once in the twentieth century because of a failure to appreciate why Marxism–Leninism was attractive to average and lower-class Chinese.[7] It would be a tragic irony to 'lose' it again owing to a similar sort of stupidity. If Premier Zhu's bet on China's future does not pay off, then many of his critics in China (and perhaps elsewhere, such as Russia) will take aim at global capitalism.

One therefore needs to be aware of how the terms and conditions of the US–China and EU–China bilateral deals could (and I emphasize the word

---

[6] See Bhala, 'Marxist origins'
[7] Not everyone failed to see the attraction. See Edgar Snow, *Red Star Over China* (Geneva, 1936).

'could') be viewed through a Marxist–Leninist prism (whether or not it is called that).

The question on which to focus is whether wealthy countries block economic growth in the third world by limiting access to their markets for third-world exports? That is, do the wealthy countries talk like free traders, but at the negotiating table behave like mercantilists, with the goal of maximizing market access for their own multinational corporations (MNCs)? This question was put by Karl Marx, and taken up by Lenin, hence the appellation 'Marxist–Leninist model'.

In this model, the answers are a resolute 'yes'. The basic storyline in Marx's classic critique of capitalism is clear enough:[8] competition among capitalists will doom their economic system. The chain of causation was historically determined. Marx urged that in the competitive process, capitalists will exploit not only workers in their own countries, but also workers in poor countries, and, indeed, the poor countries themselves.

A different concept of 'surplus', coupled with an insatiable appetite for new markets

Marx's critique of capitalism posits two critical factors of production: labour and capital. 'Labour', of course, refers principally to workers on a factory assembly line. 'Capital' means physical capital, such as machine tools on an assembly line. The model does not ascribe much importance to other factors, such as land or human capital. In the model, 'capitalists' are the class of businessmen who own capital, and who employ labour to work with capital in the production of goods. The goal of capitalists – as free-market economists champion in their classical and neo-classical models – is to maximize profits. In the Marxist terminology, it is a relentless drive for 'surplus',[9] meaning profits.

Capitalists face a number of costs and the only one over which they have much control is the price of labour. Marx predicted that capitalists would drive down wages in order to maximize 'surplus'. Likewise, capitalists do

---

[8] Parts I and II of *The Marx–Engels Reader* contains Marx's essential writings on this critique. The famous expression of this Marxian theory of history is, of course, *The Communist Manifesto*, reprinted in *The Reader* (New York, 1978), pp. 469–500. See also Karl Marx, *The Grundrisse*, Section H ('The end of capitalism'), reprinted in *The Reader*, pp. 291–2 (discussing the contradictions of capitalism that lead to its self-destruction).

[9] See, e.g., Marx, *The Grundrisse*, Section C ('The dynamics of capitalism'), reprinted in *The Reader*, pp. 247–50.

not have much control over sales revenues. In the long run, they cannot generate higher returns to capital by raising prices. In their competition with one another, capitalists over-produce, hoping to sell more if they cannot charge more. Capitalists tend to saturate, then super-saturate, the markets in which they sell their goods. The inevitable result is a decline in prices for those goods.[10] The solution is to find new markets and hence to expand overseas. Capitalists thus become imperialists and may join forces with their governments to compel other markets to open up to them.

The bilateral deals from a Marxist–Leninist perspective

Three trade–imperialism linkages

In the eighteenth, nineteenth and early twentieth centuries, the search for new markets led to overt colonialism. The expression 'trade followed the flag' meant that a colonial power could open up new trading markets by sending in its navy first.[11] In the late twentieth and early twenty-first centuries, it is not uncommon to hear it said that MNCs from developed countries are the new agents of colonialism, and international trade law is written to serve MNC interests.[12] Critics charge that the bargaining power to open up new markets is asymmetric; that is, even with larger and more powerful developing countries, such as China, India, Brazil and Mexico, it is said that MNCs (or their government representatives, such as the United States trade representative (USTR)) are able, at least in some sectors, to dictate market-access terms.[13]

In the Marxist–Leninist paradigm, there is concern that trade facilitates the exploitation of labour surplus in poor countries. First, the logic is that

---

[10] See Karl Marx, *Theories of Surplus Value*, chapter XVII, reprinted in *The Reader*, pp. 443–65.

[11] In fact, Lawrence James' examination of colonial history suggests that the opposite actually occurred in many instances – the flag followed trade in order to secure and reinforce trade routes that merchants had pioneered. See Lawrence James, *Raj – The Making and Unmaking of British India* (New York, 1997). It is sometimes forgotten that even Marx spoke of the possibility of a few salutary effects, however unintended they were, of British colonialism in India, namely the destruction of the age-old and oppressive village system that was the foundation of Oriental despotism. See Karl Marx, *The British Rule in India* (10 June 1853), reprinted in *The Reader*, pp. 657–8.

[12] See, e.g., books cited in Raj Bhala, *International Trade Law* (New York, 2001), p. xliii.

[13] Every year, this point is made with passion in my International Trade Law and Advanced International Trade Law courses by students from developing countries. Many of these students come to the George Washington University Law School after serving in senior negotiating posts with ministries of their respective governments. Could all of their anecdotes be woven from their imaginations?

as capitalists open up new markets overseas, they also locate production facilities overseas, particularly in colonies or former colonies (in modern parlance, foreign direct investment (FDI)). After all, why not make goods in the third world, where labour costs are lower than in the home countries of the MNCs, thereby minimizing returns to labour and maximizing profits? In so doing, capitalists extract surplus from third-world labourers – a colonial, or neo-colonial, surplus.

Secondly, to Marx, this extractive process is exploitative. Developing countries need the surplus to reinvest in their own economies (in new production facilities, for example). Precisely because they are poor, they lack a large endowment of resources on which to base industrialization. Draining what surplus they do have from their workers makes their growth process all the more difficult. Unfortunately for the poor countries, the principal source of investment comes from abroad – FDI. This investment generates accumulated surpluses that MNCs repatriate to the bank accounts of the capitalists that run them from plush offices in developed countries.[14] Seen through this lens, WTO rules – such as the Uruguay Round Agreement on Trade-related Investment Measures (TRIMs) – actually advance this exploitative process.

Third is the argument that during the present period of neo-colonialism, as in the colonial era of the past, capitalists advocate free-trade policies *vis-à-vis* developing countries. They push for open markets overseas as an outlet, or vent, for excess production. Simultaneously, they lobby their governments for protection from foreign imports, so as to avoid exacerbating competitive pressures in domestic markets. Here is a double standard that amounts not to pure free trade, but instead mercantilism in new garments.

Worse yet, there is nothing in the logic of capitalism to put an end to the hypocrisy. Marx and his adherents observed that the declining rates of return to capital in developed-country markets, coupled with the prospect of cheap labour overseas, mandate a push to pry open third-world markets. Yet independent of this mandate is another: natural resources. Some third-world countries have minerals and other raw materials necessary to fuel the

---

[14] From time to time, workers in the home countries of the MNCs tire of their exploitation, and threaten industrial action. Then, the capitalists can take some of the labour surplus extracted from developing countries, and use it to increase the wages of the restless workers. Of course, the increase would be the minimum amount necessary to stave off the threatened action. See Gillis et al., *Economics of Development*, pp. 30–1.

engines of capitalist production. Accordingly, so goes the critique, capitalists push to secure these sources of supply for their factories. For the third-world country, the result is over-investment in its natural-resource sector.[15] Dictating free-trade policies to developing countries, while limiting the access of developing countries to developed-country markets, hampers the integration of developing countries in the multilateral trading system, and causes over-investment in the natural resource sector. They cannot grow to become robust players, because the playing field was not level. They cannot protect their infant industries. Their agricultural and industrial sectors remain exposed to stiff foreign competition in their own domestic markets, and they have few overseas opportunities themselves. Indeed, small producers and local industries – from handicrafts to textiles – are destroyed.

Thus, wrote the renowned Brazilian development economist, Celso Furtado, serious income inequality within a third-world country can, and does, lead to an alignment of interests between local elites and foreign capitalists.[16] Why would these elites advocate a more level playing field for multilateral trade, if that would entail (1) limiting luxury-good imports (in order to preserve precious foreign-exchange reserves for imports essential to the poor, or to emerging industries), (2) a reorientation of domestic production away from luxury goods consumed by local elites and toward basic goods in which there was a broader societal interest, and (3) maybe even formal income redistribution? These questions are pondered by those in China dubious of Premier Zhu's economic reforms.

Conversely, why would foreign capitalists seek radical change, when (1) they profit from exporting luxury items to the power elite in developing countries, and (2) their own home markets are spilling over with excess production? On the contrary, the local power elite and foreign capitalists have every incentive to keep the trade regime just the way it is. Again, this resonates in the mind of some of Premier Zhu's critics who think in Marxist–Leninist terms.

The relentless drive for market access

Whether any of the links between trade and imperialism will be observed in practice as China integrates more fully into the multilateral trading system

---

[15] See ibid., p. 33.
[16] See Celso Furtado, 'The "Brazilian model" of development', in Charles K. Wilber (ed.), *The Political Economy of Development and Underdevelopment* (New York, 1979), pp. 324–33.

remains to be seen. Exploitation of labour surplus, repatriation of FDI profits abroad, increased market access in China coupled with decreased access for Chinese products may occur. I am not in a position to forecast, but the links are both plausible and possible from a Marxist–Leninist approach. All three links share a common denominator: market-access demands of capitalists from industrialized countries. What is remarkable is how easy it is to find that same denominator in the terms and conditions of the US–China and EU–China bilateral deals.

Seen through a Marxist–Leninist perspective, accession to the WTO of third-world countries is all about market access. Market access for whom? Not so much for China and other developing countries, Marx and Lenin would reply, as for the hegemonic trade powers that are already in the club. Even the American president could not help but gloat that the 15 November 1999 bilateral concession agreement between the United States and China was the most lopsided trade deal in history.[17] American MNCs won nearly everything; domestic American producers gave little.

The reduction in tariff barriers on industrial products will benefit Chinese consumers of those goods. So, too, will the lessening of non-tariff barriers, from trading and distribution rights to equity restrictions in various service sectors. Chinese consumers will be able to buy imported goods directly, rather than through a domestic 'middleman', and Chinese depositors will be able to choose healthy foreign banks for their accounts. All that is what the standard classical and neo-classical models of trade and comparative advantage, inspired by Adam Smith and David Ricardo, would tout.[18]

But neither Marx nor Lenin evaluates freer trade using marginal cost-benefit analysis and the calculation of economic effects on different sectors of a society (consumers, producers and the government). Thus, neither would highlight how Chinese consumers stand to gain, nor offer a conclusion of net welfare gain.

Through the Marxist–Leninist lens, virtually all the provisions of the US–China and EU–China bilateral deals are about the commercial exploitation by American, European and other developed-country capitalists of China. They need markets because their own are stocked full with their

---

[17] See Raj Bhala, 'Enter the dragon, an essay on China's WTO accession saga' (2000) 15 *American University International Law Review* 1469 at 1530.

[18] For discussion of these models, see Bhala, *International Trade Law*, chs. 1–2.

products and surplus is declining. With its ostensible large and increasing middle class of consumers, and its enormous pool of cheap labour, China is too attractive a source of surplus to neglect.

It is important to avoid drawing conclusions from the application of this model that are too strong. As the US–China and EU–China bilateral deals indicate, China was successful in resisting unbridled foreign-market access in telecommunications, internet services, insurance, securities regulation, fund management, cultural industries and legal services. Even as to the declines in tariff and non-tariff barriers in commodity markets, China negotiated transition periods for the phasing out of such barriers. In other words, China protected some (particularly services) markets, and negotiated for some breathing space in other (particularly goods) markets. Small comfort, perhaps, to critics inclined to wear Marxist–Leninist lenses.

Why did China do it?

The inference drawn about the US–China and EU–China bilateral concession agreements in the Marxist–Leninist paradigm is gloomier than that drawn in the Fei–Ranis labour surplus paradigm. However, neither conclusion is a happy one for China. Applying one model tells us that China's efforts at accelerating its transition from agriculture to industry, and thus achieving sustained economic growth, are not assisted by the terms of the deals. These terms fall short in terms of guaranteeing overseas market access for industrial products in which China has, or could seek, a comparative advantage. Applying the other model informs us that the terms of the deals are bordering on the evil. WTO entry, it says, spells a slicing up of the Chinese dragon by foreign capitalists. They are plagued by saturation in their home markets, and driven to search for profits in new markets and thereby extract surplus value from Chinese workers.

If there is any truth to either of these inferences, then a significant question follows: why did China seek WTO accession? China's leaders, for the most part, are aware of the labour surplus and Marxian models. They can draw inferences from the application of these models to facts at hand.

It is also quite unsatisfactory to say that the Chinese leaders sought 'face' for their country. Yes, prestige on the international arena is important to them, but they do not seem to act recklessly to gain it. China has been known to behave intemperately on the three 'T' issues – Taiwan, Tibet and

Tiananmen – and to be obstinate on 'internal' matters such as freedom of worship and Falun Gong. To be sure, from intemperance and obstinacy it is possible to infer an indifference that borders on recklessness, but it is plausible to infer cold, cost-benefit calculation. In other words, Chinese leaders would appear to have higher priorities than gaining face in the eyes of the West through WTO accession.

The answer might be at a much more human level. The leaders were simply at their wits' end. What other models are there aside from (1) the Marxist–Leninist one, to which they do not want to turn again, and (2) the capitalist Fei–Ranis style one, to which they have committed themselves for nearly a quarter century? The Brahmins in Beijing had no other choice but to repeat the same mantra on the lips of the leaders of virtually all other developing countries: we cannot be left out of the world trading system and the globalization process.

Whatever unhappy inferences might be drawn about the accession terms from the theoretical frameworks discussed above, China's leaders had no other systemic frameworks for modern economic growth to apply. So these leaders placed a bet. They turned away from the old model they had tried. They moved deeper into a capitalist framework that, at worst, permitted an inference that there was another Long March ahead.

For present purposes, I suggest that the terms and conditions of the US–China and EU–China bilateral concession agreements are not as generous in assisting the industrialization process as they might be. Both the Fei–Ranis and neo-classical models characterize modern economic growth as, at bottom, a matter of industrialization. Both models ascribe to trade – at best – a supporting, not a central, role. My point (that the terms of the bilateral deals do not allow trade to play as much of a supporting role as perhaps they could in accelerating industrialization) is equally valid whichever model is used.

9

Enforcement of WTO agreements in China: illusion or reality?

QINGJIANG KONG

Introduction

China's accession to the WTO has engaged considerable attention in trade and legal circles. Speculation has arisen concerning the potential benefits of membership to China and to her trading partners, and whether admitting China to the WTO will weaken the framework of what is, by many accounts, a most successful international organization. This chapter examines the theory and practice of implementing international treaties in China with a view to shedding light on the prospect of enforcing WTO agreements in China.

Since China adopted the open door policy in the late 1970s,[1] it has participated in high-level trade negotiation and entered numerous trade and economic agreements, both at the bilateral and multilateral level. China's size and economic leverage in combination with MFN provisions of bilateral agreements have secured it the same trade treatment *vis-à-vis* the WTO as other Member States. At the multilateral level, despite its lack of membership of the WTO China has acceded to or participated in the making of multilateral trade treaties, the most significant of which was the Multi-Fibre Arrangement. As an observer, China was a participant in the Uruguay Round and initialled the final results of the negotiation.

Despite these trade advantages China has long desired entry into the WTO, and in July 1986 officially applied to the General Agreement on Tariffs

I am grateful to Sandra Bunn-Altham, David Wall and Wenhua Shan for comments. I am particularly indebted to Deborah Cass, Brett Gerard Williams and Carlos Espósito for their kind advice and most insightful comments. Of course, I am responsible for any errors.
[1] The year 1978 saw two major trade treaties concluded – between China and the United States and between China and the European Economic Community.

and Trade (GATT), the WTO's predecessor, to resume its status as an original Contracting Party. After a series of bilateral and multilateral negotiations, China's specific obligations upon entering the WTO have been incorporated into a Protocol of Accession and accompanying schedules,[2] which were multilateralized (or extended to all WTO members) upon its accession. With their breadth and scope, and a strong enforcement mechanism, the WTO agreements will become the backbone of the trade treaties that bind China.

The essential characteristic of the post-1994 WTO agreements is that they are binding upon all Member States: the agreements comprise a single undertaking instead of the previous GATT pick-and-choose approach; compliance is strengthened by the establishment of a unified dispute settlement mechanism with power to authorize retaliation for non-compliance; and the ability of parties against whom a complaint is made to block adoption of a dispute settlement report finding them in breach of the agreements has been, effectively, abolished.

From the perspective of WTO members, enforcement of the WTO-administered agreements consists of two aspects: internal implementation by the members and external oversight by the WTO. In relation to internal implementation the Agreement Establishing the World Trade Organization provides that 'Each Member shall ensure the conformity of its laws, regulations and administrative procedures with its obligations as provided in the annexed Agreements.'[3] The WTO oversees internal implementation with a system of binding dispute settlement and a regular policy-review mechanism.[4] As a WTO member, China is responsible for any failures of its sub-national entities to comply with WTO law;[5] and its internal law cannot provide any excuse for failure to adhere to its international obligations because, according to Article 26 of the Vienna Convention on

---

[2] For a description of the accession process see Jeffrey Gertler, chapter 4, above.

[3] Article XVI.4 of the Marrakesh Agreement Establishing the World Trade Organization.

[4] The Trade Policy Review Mechanism (TPRM) was confirmed as an integral part of the WTO in Annex 3 of the Agreement Establishing the World Trade Organization. Its purpose is to 'contribute to improved adherence by all Members to rules, disciplines and commitments made under the Multilateral Trade Agreements and, where applicable, the Plurilateral Trade Agreements, and hence to the smoother functioning of the multilateral trading system, by achieving greater transparency in, and understanding of, the trade policies and practices of Members'.

[5] Article XXIV:12 of the GATT: each WTO member 'shall take such reasonable measures as may be available to it to ensure such observance by regional and local governments and authorities within its territory'. See also Ravi Kewalram, chapter 22, below.

the Law of Treaties, to which China is a party,[6] a WTO member cannot invoke its domestic law as justification for failure to carry out its international obligations.

The implementation of international treaties in Chinese domestic law

The hierarchy of sources of law in China

The status and applicability of the WTO agreements will depend, in the first place, upon the manner in which international treaties are implemented within Chinese municipal law. This depends, in turn, upon an appreciation of the hierarchy of sources of Chinese municipal law and the position and status of treaties within the hierarchy. In the Chinese legal system, the sources of law comprise: basic laws of the NPC;[7] laws of the NPC Standing Committee;[8] administrative regulations;[9] local regulations by Provincial People's Congresses;[10] local rules by people's congresses at

---

[6] China ratified the Vienna Convention on 3 September 1997, with, among other things, a reservation to Article 66 concerning submitting disputes to the International Court of Justice for judicial settlement and other procedures for arbitration and conciliation.

[7] According to the Constitution of the People's Republic of China, the National People's Congress (NPC) is the highest authority of the state. The Constitution provides that the NPC has the power to enact and amend 'basic laws [jiben fa]'. In principle, 'basic laws' refer to such laws as the General Principles of Civil Law, the Civil Procedural Law, the Criminal Law, the Criminal Procedural Law, the Administrative Procedural Law, and the Law for Self-government in the Minority Autonomous Regions, amongst others.

[8] The NPC Standing Committee is the permanent organ of the NPC. It exercises the legislative power when the NPC adjourns. The NPC Standing Committee has the power to enact and amend 'laws other than basic laws' and to supplement and amend to some extent laws made by the NPC.

[9] Under the Chinese Constitution, the State Council is the highest administrative organ of the state. It has the power to enact 'administrative regulations [xingzheng fagui]' 'in accordance with the Constitution and laws'. Like the basic laws and laws, the 'administrative regulations' are binding nationwide. Given that in China most of the normative rules take the form of administrative regulations, the role of these administrative regulations should not be underestimated.

[10] The people's congresses at provincial level and their standing committees have the power to draw up 'local regulations [difangxing fagui]', 'provided that they do not contravene the Constitution, laws and administrative regulations'; but the regulations are required to be reported to the NPC Standing Committee for the record. People's congresses in minority autonomous regions have the power to enact autonomous regulations and special regulations. It is noted that in 1992, 1994 and 1996, the NPC Standing Committee authorized the people's congresses and the people's governments of four special economic zones (Shenzhen, Zhuhai, Shantou and Xiamen) to enact 'local regulations'. Local regulations are binding only in the provinces and the SEZs concerned.

sub-provincial levels and local governments;[11] and administrative rules passed by ministries.[12]

Courts across the country must observe basic laws, laws and administrative regulations, and those within a province or special economic zone (SEZ) must observe local regulations. According to relevant judicial interpretations of the Supreme People's Court, courts may invoke 'rules [*guizhang*] and other normative guidelines [*qita guifanxing wenjian*]',[13] the latter referring to administrative rules made by ministries, local people's congresses and provincial governments.

According to the Legislation Law (2000),[14] all these laws, regulations and rules are fixed in a hierarchy: apart from the Constitution, the basic laws passed by the NPC are at the top of the hierarchy. Next are the laws by the NPC Standing Committee. Then follows 'administrative regulations' by the State Council. Next are local regulations by the people's congresses of the provinces and administrative rules by ministries.[15] These are followed by local rules by local people's congresses and people's governments.

The hierarchy means that a subordinate normative rule is null and void if it contravenes a higher one. For example, the local regulations by a provincial-level people's congress are binding in the provinces concerned only if they do not contravene the laws and regulations by the NPC and the State Council. The hierarchy also dictates that the organ adopting a higher

---

[11] The Constitution provides no reference to the power of local people's congresses at sub-provincial levels and local governments to enact regulative rules. The 1986 Organic Law of the Local People's Congresses and Local People's Governments, however, provides that the local people's congresses and local people's governments of cities where the provincial governments are situated, and of 'large-sized cities', have the power to work out local rules (*guizhang*). These local rules are binding only in the localities concerned.

[12] The Constitution provides, subject to their respective authority, that ministries and ministerial-level commissions may enact 'administrative rules [*xingzheng guizhang*]' 'in accordance with the laws and administrative regulations of the State Council'. Administrative rules are binding nationwide on the matters concerned, and may serve as reference for application when courts at different levels adjudicate relevant cases. Given the predominant role of the ministries in the economic life of China, administrative rules of ministries occupy a significant position.

[13] Section 62 of the Interpretations on Certain Questions regarding the Administrative Procedural Law (Supreme People's Court, 2000).

[14] Chapter 5 of the Legislation Law.

[15] According to Article 86(2) of the Legislation Law, in case of conflict between a ministerial rule and a local regulation by a provincial People's Congress, it is up to the State Council and even the NPC Standing Committee to determine which to apply: if the State Council finds the local regulation should be applied, that regulation applies; if the State Council finds the ministerial rule should be applied, the matter shall be referred to the NPC Standing Committee for final decision.

normative rule has the power to determine whether such a conflict occurs between that rule and a subordinate one and hence declare the subordinate rule null and void.[16] Examples are that the NPC has the power to modify or repeal inappropriate resolutions made by the NPC Standing Committee; the NPC Standing Committee possesses the authority to annul administrative regulations by the State Council and revoke local regulations by local organs of state power; the State Council has the power to annul the rules by ministries and local governments; etc.

On the other hand, a competent court possesses no authority to correct an inconsistency between two normative rules at different levels by repealing the lower rules. Moreover, according to the Legislation Law, the court is not among the competent authorities that have the power to take the initiative to make, amend or annul a statute, and therefore is presumably not in a position to refer the statutory provision to the competent authority for amendment.

In this regard, the status of a directive of the Supreme People's Court must be borne in mind. Courts may interpret laws and regulations only when adjudicating cases. Nevertheless, the Supreme People's Court has the authority to give courts at different levels directives, in the form of judicial interpretations, concerning the application of laws, regulations and rules in relevant cases.[17] As a matter of fact, its directives are binding on the courts across the country.

Chinese law and practice on the ratification of treaties

According to the Chinese Constitution, the State Council is responsible for 'conducting foreign affairs and concluding treaties [*tiaoyue*] and agreements [*xieding*] with foreign states'.[18] The power to ratify and abrogate 'treaties and important agreements' rests with the NPC Standing Committee.[19] This follows from the Law of Procedures for Concluding

---

[16] Article 88 of the Legislation Law.

[17] The Interpretations on Certain Questions regarding the Administrative Procedural Law (Supreme People's Court, 2000) is an example.

[18] Article 89(9) of the Constitution. It is noteworthy that the Constitution differentiates between treaties and agreements. However, for the sake of convenience, the term 'treaty' or 'agreement' in this article is actually referred to as any international legal instrument unless otherwise indicated in the context.

[19] Article 67(14) of the Constitution provides that the NPC Standing Committee has the power to 'decide on the ratification or abrogation of treaties and important agreements concluded with foreign states'.

Treaties (1990), which requires such ratification for 'treaties and important agreements' as well as a variety of other instruments including treaties and agreements that differ from the laws of the People's Republic of China.[20]

A combined reading of the constitutional provision with the above-mentioned law suggests that international agreements that are not 'important' are not subject to approval by the NPC Standing Committee. The Law of Procedures for Concluding Treaties confirms that all the other legal instruments shall be checked and approved by the State Council.[21] Nevertheless, for treaties and important agreements, constitutionally it appears to be a possibility that the NPC Standing Committee might refuse to ratify such a treaty referred to it for ratification. In practice, the *de facto* supremacy of the Communist Party Central Committee, and particularly its Politburo, over all the state organs ensures the conclusion and ratification of treaties in conformity with the party line. As a matter of practice, there has been no case yet in which the NPC Standing Committee refused to ratify an international treaty submitted to it by the State Council for ratification.

In the process of negotiation of the Protocol of Accession, China made clear that the WTO agreements and the Protocol of Accession specifying the terms and conditions for China's accession to the WTO fall within the category of 'important international agreements' subject to ratification by the NPC Standing Committee.[22] The perceivable substantial difference between the WTO agreements and relevant Chinese laws had led to speculation about whether the NPC Standing Committee should ratify the Protocol of Accession negotiated by the State Council.[23] In the event, no formal debate took place in the NPC or its Standing Committee; the NPC Standing

[20] Article 7 of the Law of Procedures for Concluding Treaties provides that the following 'treaties and agreements' need to be ratified by the NPC Standing Committee: (a) political treaties such as friendship and co-operation treaties and peace treaties; (b) treaties and agreements relating to territory and boundary-delimiting; (c) treaties and agreements on judicial assistance and extradition; (d) treaties and agreements that differ from the laws of the People's Republic of China; (e) treaties and agreements whose ratification is agreed on by Contracting Parties; (f) other treaties and agreements that require ratifying.

[21] See Article 8 of the Law of Procedures for Concluding Treaties.

[22] Article 7 of the Law of Procedures for Concluding Treaties.

[23] According to Article 46 of the Vienna Convention, 'A state may not invoke the fact that its consent to be bound by a treaty has been expressed in violation of its internal law regarding competence to conclude treaties invalidating its consent unless that violation was manifest and concerned a rule of its internal law of fundamental importance.' As a Contracting Party, China is bound by the provision.

Committee completed its ratification formality even before the completion of the draft Protocol on 17 September 2001.[24]

The status of treaties as a source of law in the hierarchy of Chinese domestic law

The legal status of international treaties is examined in the context of their relationship to domestic law. Essentially, this question is determined by a particular domestic system's constitutional structure, unless otherwise provided in the treaties concerned.

An international treaty concluded and ratified in due course has the force of law within a Contracting State, but it does not necessarily form an integral part of the legal order of the state until it has complied with the constitutional requirements of that state. In some states, treaties are not automatically part of the domestic law. In a dualist system of law, treaty obligations become part of domestic law only when some domestic legal instrument makes the treaty into a part of domestic law. Treaty obligations are thus *transformed* or *translated* into domestic law before they take effect domestically. In a monist system, by contrast, treaties are automatically part of domestic law without any special act of domestic law, with the result that courts may rely on the treaty directly as a source of domestic law. In these latter situations treaties are often referred to as having been automatically *incorporated* into domestic law.

It should be noted that even in a state that takes a monist approach, a treaty is not necessarily directly applicable, since there is a distinction between 'self-executing' and 'non-self-executing' treaties (in some countries, the terminology used is 'directly applicable' and 'non-directly applicable' treaties). According to conventional usage, a 'self-executing' international treaty can be applied directly without further legislative or other measures to implement it, and a non-self-executing agreement cannot be directly applied, but must be implemented by legislative or other measures.

---

[24] Early on 25 August 2000, fifteen months before China's signing of the Protocol of Accession, the NPC Standing Committee adopted the Decision on China's Accession to the WTO. The decision declared that the NPC Standing Committee was satisfied with the WTO negotiation up to that point and it 'agrees that the State Council, in accordance with the aforementioned principles, conclude the WTO accession negotiations and designate its representative to sign the Protocol on China's Accession to the World Trade Organization, thus completing the procedures on China's WTO accession subject to the ratification of the President of the country'.

Although one may argue that an international treaty may be directly applicable if its provisions are unconditional and sufficiently precise,[25] whether a treaty is self-executing or not is always a question of domestic law of the particular state, unless otherwise provided in the treaty. The practice of domestic law in dealing with this issue varies from nation to nation.

In the Chinese context, one has difficulty defining whether the state belongs to the monist or dualist system. On the one hand, there exist no statutory provisions that characterize treaties as part of the domestic legal system; on the other, from time to time, international treaties are directly applicable in practice. The Constitution remains silent as to the legal status of an international treaty in Chinese domestic law, although numerous laws provide that the international agreement shall prevail in case of conflict between Chinese law and an international treaty. For example, the General Principles of Civil Law provide, '[i]f any international treaty concluded or acceded to by the People's Republic of China contains provisions differing from those in the civil laws of the People's Republic of China, the provisions of the international treaty shall apply, unless the provisions are ones on which the People's Republic of China has announced reservations.'[26] In view of this, it can be held that in case of disagreement between an international treaty provision that allows no reservation and the relevant Chinese statutory provision, the international treaty provision shall prevail over the relevant statutory provision and apply.

In the meantime, however, the provisions of the General Principles of Civil Law appear to limit the effect of international treaties in the domestic legal order. They suggest that an international treaty is applied only when the relevant law is inconsistent with the treaty. If a Chinese domestic law is consistent with the treaty then local courts would apply Chinese law. In other words, framers of these laws aimed to promote the position that

---

[25] The Court of First Instance of the European Communities holds the same view. See Case T–115/94 *Opel Austria GmbH* v. *Council of the European Union* [1994] ECR II. For, specifically, the direct applicability of WTO agreements, see Carlos D. Espósito, 'International trade and national legal orders: the problem of direct applicability of WTO law', in Paolo Mengazzi (ed.), *International Trade Law on the 50th Anniversary of the Multilateral Trade System* (Milan, 1999), pp. 429–69.

[26] Article 142 of the General Principles of Civil Law (1986). Also, see Article 238 of the Civil Procedure Law, which reads 'Where the provisions of international treaties which China has concluded or to which China is a party are different from those of this law, the former shall apply, except those clauses to which China has made reservation.'

domestic law continues to play the main role where the issue concerned is covered by both an international treaty and a domestic law.

Direct application or implementation of treaties through domestic measures

Ultimately, the question of the status of particular treaties in the Chinese legal system depends upon whether the treaties are directly applied or implemented through domestic measures. The Chinese Constitution and laws again remain silent on whether a treaty shall be applied directly by automatic incorporation or through legislative or administrative transformation into domestic law. Therefore, Chinese practice is the only source for determining the appropriate constitutional position.

Unfortunately, practice in this regard is not consistent. When China joined the international copyright conventions in accordance with its commitments under the Memorandum of Understanding between China and the United States on the Protection of Intellectual Property in 1992, the State Council promulgated regulations to implement the agreement.[27] When China joined the Patent Co-operation Treaty in 1993, it took a similar measure to implement the agreement.[28] Moreover, sometimes the NPC Standing Committee adopts a law (statute) to implement the provisions of a treaty. The typical example is that in 1986 the NPC Standing Committee adopted a special law – Regulations on Diplomatic Privileges and Immunity – for the purpose of implementing the Vienna Convention on Diplomatic Relations.[29] It seems from the empirical evidence that the organ with legislative power over the issue in question prefers to implement international treaty obligations through transformation into domestic law.

In contrast, the judicial practice shows a preference for direct application or automatic incorporation of international treaties. In some circumstances, the Supreme People's Court instructs the courts across the country to apply directly the provisions of international treaties. For example, on 10 April 1987, in the Notice on the Implementation of the Convention on the Recognition and Enforcement of Foreign Arbitral Awards to which China has Acceded, the Supreme People's Court required the courts that receive an application or a request for judicial assistance to handle the

---

[27] Provisions on the Implementation of the International Copyright Treaties (1992).
[28] The Provisions on the Implementation of the Patent Co-operation Treaty in China (1993).
[29] China acceded to the Vienna Convention on Diplomatic Relations (1961) in 1975.

matter conscientiously, strictly in conformity with the provisions of the treaties concluded or acceded to by China.[30] Even in the absence of a directive by the Supreme People's Court, courts from time to time apply directly international treaties or permit direct invocation of international treaties by parties to litigations.[31] Two cases involving application of the Hague Rules (that is, the International Convention for the Unification of Certain Rules of Law Relating to Bills of Lading) illustrate court practice in this regard. One is *China National Supply Corp. of Xiamen Special Economic Zone of Fujian Province* v. *Europe Overseas Steamship Lines NV Belgium*, the other *Japan Sea Fire Insurance Co. Ltd* v. *Tianjin Branch of China General Foreign Trade Transportation Co.* In the former case, the plaintiff did not invoke the Hague Rules but the court applied them: in the latter, the plaintiff invoked the rules and the court upheld them.[32] In this regard, it should be noted that the Supreme People's Court's directives that favour direct application of an international treaty can only play a part where the NPC Standing Committee or the State Council has not acted to enact an implementing law or regulations for the treaty.

Implementing WTO agreements through domestic measures

Now that the general position of treaties within the Chinese domestic legal system has been outlined, the specific question of the implementation of the WTO agreements can be addressed. In the Protocol of Accession, China made clear that it would implement the WTO agreements 'through revising its existing domestic laws and enacting new ones fully in compliance with the WTO Agreement(s)'. Therefore, the Chinese government will need to transform or translate the obligations under WTO agreements into legislative instruments in the domestic sphere. This will involve the examination and review of all existing laws, regulations and rules. In

---

[30] Similarly, when the United Nations Convention on Contracts for the International Sale of Goods was ratified and became effective in 1988, the Supreme People's Court in an internal directive ordered the courts at different levels to apply the convention directly in relevant cases. See Supreme People's Court, Memorandum of the National Working Meeting on Adjudication of Economic Cases involving Foreign, Hong Kong or Macau Elements in Coastal Regions (12 June 1989), Part III, Chapter 5 (entitled 'Questions on application of laws').

[31] In theory, direct application of international treaties by the court is different from private invocation.

[32] The two cases can be found in Priscilla Leeung Mei-fun (ed.), *China Law Report 1991*, vol. 3 (Singapore, Malaysia and Hong Kong, 1995), pp. 740–4 and pp. 745–8.

principle, those that are found to be inconsistent with WTO agreements will have to be amended or repealed; where no provisions can be found corresponding to relevant WTO agreements, new laws or regulations will be enacted pursuant to the WTO agreements.

Amending or repealing inconsistent domestic law

Amending laws and regulations in line with WTO agreements has been a major issue regarding China's accession to the WTO. WTO agreements cover a great number of issues that, traditionally, are within exclusive domestic administrative jurisdiction; the scale of amendment required is unprecedented in the Chinese history of legislation and administration.[33]

It is noteworthy that the laws and regulations that need to be amended or repealed include not only those that are directly inconsistent with WTO agreements, but also those that require the Chinese government to act in a way that is inconsistent with WTO agreements. The former is obvious. For example, provisions of the Patent Law and Trademark Law supporting final decisions by administrative organs shall be repealed to comply with the TRIPs Agreement requiring judicial review. An example of the latter is that implementation of the domestic laws on special economic zones would result in conflict with the disciplines of uniform administration embodied in the Agreement Establishing the World Trade Organization.

As a matter of practice, up to 31 December 2001, the NPC and its Standing Committee was found to have revised primarily six laws that contain provisions inconsistent with the WTO agreements, namely the Chinese–Foreign Equity Joint Venture Law, the Chinese–Foreign Contractual Joint Venture Law, the Wholly Foreign-invested Enterprise Law, the Patent Law, the Trademark Law and the Copyright Law. The State Council examined 756 pieces of administrative regulation that had been adopted before the end of 2000, repealed seventy-one regulations and declared eighty void in October 2001. In addition, various regulations including the Regulations on Travel Agencies and the Regulations on Foreign-invested Financial Institutions were amended. The ministries also acted to this end. For example, the State Development Planning Commission (SDPC) had, among a total of 341 regulations and instruments released before the end of 2000, repealed

---

[33] According to Shi Guangsheng, minister of foreign trade and economic co-operation, the State Council alone had up to August 2001 revised or repealed 2,300 regulations and legal instruments.

124 price regulations and will further revamp another 51 price regulations in order to fit its price laws into the framework of the WTO.

An issue directly relevant here is the appropriate authority to mend the inconsistency between Chinese law and WTO agreements. Since legislative power is shared by numerous organs at the central and local level, it is important to identify which entity has the authority to amend or repeal WTO inconsistent provisions. Of course, with respect to the amending or repeal of laws, the NPC and its Standing Committee in particular will have to act. According to the Legislation Law, the NPC and its Standing Committee possess the exclusive legislative power regarding the state's fundamental economic system and the basic systems of finance, taxation, customs, monetary affairs and foreign trade.[34] Indeed, some relevant laws appear to require that courts in China are under an obligation to apply WTO agreements *vis-à-vis* relevant domestic law. However, in accordance with the Constitution, except for the NPC Standing Committee,[35] no organ and no body can declare a law is null and void. In fact, even a court that has identified a discrepancy between a WTO agreement and a relevant law is not in a position to annul the conflicting law. In case of inconsistent administrative regulations and rules, the court is not empowered to take measures to repeal the inconsistent provisions either.

Nevertheless, it would have been preferable if one authoritative organ had been solely responsible for amending or repealing inconsistent provisions in other sources of law. Unfortunately, in practice, amendment and repeal of inconsistent law has so far not been carried out in a unified manner. For example, although the State Council is in a position to mend any inconsistencies between WTO agreements and all sources of law except the basic laws made by the NPC and the NPC Standing Committee, all that the Council has done is to revise its own administrative regulations, leaving the rest of the task of revision up to the respective bodies responsible for enacting the laws in the first place: the ministries and local people's congress and local people's governments.[36]

---

[34] Article 8 of the Legislation Law.   [35] Article 67(7) of the Constitution.

[36] Article 89(4) of the Constitution provides that people's governments at all levels are under the leadership of the State Council, which has the power to determine the power of the administrative organs at the central and provincial levels. Hence, the State Council should be able to define the amending or repeal of rules by ministries and by local people's governments, as well as amendment and repeal of administrative regulations by the State Council itself. Moreover, given that the local people's congress rules shall not contravene administrative regulations, the State Council should also be able to exercise control over the amending or repeal of the rules by local people's congresses.

It should also be pointed out that the process of identifying which law is inconsistent inevitably involves some discretion and potentially permits a government department, agency or official to act in a way that violates the WTO agreements. Furthermore, in view of the massive changes required[37] there still exist quite a few gaps or inconsistent laws and regulations after the accession. In this context, where new provisions have not yet been enacted, or inconsistencies not mended, Article 142 of the General Principles of Civil Law shall be applied to ensure the prevalence of relevant WTO agreements over inconsistent domestic laws, regulations and rules.[38] In the Protocol of Accession, China confirmed that revision would occur 'in a timely manner so that China's commitments would be fully implemented within the relevant time frames'; 'If administrative regulations, departmental [ministerial] rules or other measures were not in place within such time frames, authorities would still honour China's obligations' under the WTO agreements and Protocol.

Introducing new rules: transforming WTO agreements into domestic law

While WTO agreements dictate obligations which have not been supported by existing domestic law, China needs to adopt new domestic laws, regulations or measures in accordance with its obligations under the WTO agreements. Prominent examples are adopting regulations permitting foreign investment in sectors where foreign participation had been prohibited, uniform application of laws and regulations and measures, and the establishment of mechanisms of judicial review.

---

[37] No measures will be taken to conform with the international treaty before the inconsistency between the statutes and the international treaty comes to the attention of the authority possessing the power to amend the inconsistent provisions. Even if the authority has noticed the inconsistency, it is still unclear how long it needs in order to take actions to remedy it. It is a worrisome fact that no Chinese law, including the Legislation Law, deals with this situation.

[38] Reservations are generally not permitted under the WTO agreements. The Agreement Establishing the World Trade Organization and the Agreement on Trade-related Aspects of Intellectual Property Rights (the TRIPs Agreement) provide two examples. See respectively Article XVI.5 of the Agreement Establishing the World Trade Organization and Article 72 of the TRIPs Agreement. There are some provisions in some Multilateral Trade Agreements that allow developing-countries to make reservations. However, from the negotiation process, it seems that China is not permitted by the Protocol for Accession to make reservations to those developing-country provisions.

Adopting regulations permitting foreign investment

In the Protocol, China committed to opening to foreign investment various industries that had prohibited or restricted foreign participation. In an effort to honour these commitments, the State Council adopted various measures allowing foreign participation in the medical care, rail freight services, printing, telecommunications services, maritime transportation, insurances, cinema and banking industries.[39]

Uniform sub-national administration of laws

According to the GATT 1994, each WTO member 'shall take such reasonable measures as may be available to it to ensure such observance by regional and local governments and authorities within its territory'.[40] The understanding on the interpretation of this provision[41] further strengthens the requirement for uniform administration by introducing the WTO dispute settlement mechanism and even sanctions where the central government of a WTO member fails to mend a breach by a regional or local government.[42]

Although China is a unitary state, the regions are different in terms of economic prosperity, degree of openness, tradition and governance structure and so on. Law enforcement varies from region to region, not only because of differing local regulations and rules, but because of its discretionary application from region to region. This may present some difficulty for the uniform administration of WTO agreements. For example, the Law for Self-government in the Minority Autonomous Regions devolves power to the minority autonomous regions to amend laws to local requirements; hence, the relevant law or regulations implementing a WTO agreement may be modified in its application in the regions.

Unifying laws and regulations and rules and ensuring their uniform implementation is an important task facing China. However, the *de facto*

---

[39] They are the Provisional Measures for Administration of Chinese–Foreign Equity and Contractual Joint Venture Medical Institutions, Provisional Measures for Examination and Approval and Administration of Foreign Investment in Rail Freight Transport Services, Administrative Regulations on the Printing Industry, Regulations on Foreign Investment in Telecommunications Enterprises, Regulations on International Maritime Transportation, Regulations on Foreign-invested Insurance Companies, Regulations on Cinemas, and Regulations on Foreign-invested Financial Institutions, which entered into force on 1 July 2000, 29 August 2000, 2 August 2001, 1 January 2002, 1 January 2002, 1 February 2002, 1 February 2002 and 1 February 2002, respectively.

[40] GATT 1994, Art. XXIV:12.

[41] For a summary of WTO interpretation and its relevance to China, see Ravi Kewalram, Chapter 22, below.

[42] See the Understanding on the Interpretation of Article XXIV of the GATT 1994, section 14.

supremacy of Communist Party Central Committee and its Politburo in the political structure, and the leading role of the State Council in the administrative structure, of the state should facilitate uniform administration of WTO agreements in the entire territory of China.

The promulgation of the Legislation Law in 2000 has provided a possibility for clarifying the limits of legislative power, thus contributing to the uniform application of law. The latest adoption of Regulations on the Procedures for Enacting Administrative Regulations and Regulations on the Procedures for Enacting Ministerial Rules on 26 November 2001, and Regulations for Filing Regulations for Record on 21 December 2001, which became effective on 1 January 2002, will further facilitate the uniform application of law by providing for procedures for the State Council to adopt administrative regulations and for ministries to adopt and file for record ministerial rules.

Nevertheless, more clarification is needed, for example by way of promulgating a law amending the Law for Self-government in the Minority Autonomous Regions and regulations concerning the grant of special treatments to SEZs, so that the latter do not extend to the WTO agreements.

Introduction of judicial review in areas covered by WTO agreements

To some extent, WTO agreements reflect the requirements of a market economy and can function well in the prevailing legal system of the established market economies. An important aspect is that the implementation of law heavily relies on an independent, fair and effective administrative legal system and a judicial review system. In view of this, the WTO agreements set out corresponding requirements. For example, the General Agreement on Trade in Services provides that 'Each Member shall maintain or institute as soon as practicable judicial, arbitral or administrative tribunals or procedures which provide, at the request of an affected supplier, for the prompt review of, and where justified, appropriate remedies for, administrative decisions affecting trade in services.'[43] The TRIPs Agreement also requires that members accord to parties an opportunity for review by a judicial authority of final administrative decisions.[44] In contrast, the Chinese Administrative Procedural Law provides that no organ or no individual can challenge before the court any administrative rules, orders and acts

---

[43] GATS, Art. VI:2(a).   [44] TRIPs Agreement, Art. 41.4.

of binding nature.[45] It further strengthens the regime by providing that courts shall not accept any suits against 'specific administrative acts that shall, as provided by law, be finally decided by an administrative organ'.[46] These provisions thus directly contravene the WTO agreements, and, as a consequence, will require amendment.

However, from the Chinese perspective, these matters are traditionally within exclusive domestic jurisdiction. Such issues are politically sensitive since any alteration to the status quo might undermine the foundation of the regime based on party and administrative control. From the perspective of the West, however, China could accommodate the demands of WTO members only when such institutions are established in China.

Of course, a pragmatic Chinese leadership has already initiated reform in limited areas which, one assumes, will gradually expand into more sensitive areas. For example, the Chinese government has introduced judicial review as required by the TRIPs Agreement through incorporating the TRIPs provisions into the intellectual property rights (IPRs) laws. It has also introduced judicial review in the Patent Law and the Trademark Law, which previously denied such review.[47]

Prospects for further implementation of WTO agreements in China

General factors affecting implementation and compliance

So what, then, are the prospects for full implementation of the WTO agreements in China? As discussed above, transformation is preferable to direct incorporation, and for this purpose it may be desirable for China to translate the WTO agreements and its commitments in the Protocol of Accession into domestic law by adopting a special law, especially since the WTO agreements require members to take measures to ensure the implementation of the agreements.[48] For the Chinese government, the translation of WTO

---

[45] Article 12(2) of the Administrative Procedural Law provides that courts shall even not accept suits concerning regulations, decrees and orders by the administrative organs.

[46] Article 12(4) of the Administrative Procedural Law.

[47] See Articles 41 and 46 of the Patent Law, and Articles 32, 33, 43 and 49 of the Trademark Law.

[48] The Understanding on the Interpretation of Article XXIV of the GATT 1994 reiterates the obligation of Article XXIV: that each member 'shall take such reasonable measures as may be available to it to ensure' observance of the provisions of WTO agreements by regional and local governments and authorities within its territories. Article XVI.4 of the Agreement Establishing the WTO is a similar provision.

agreements into domestic laws and policies is the easy part, but the non-market factors and domestic legal restraints pose the greatest challenge to the implementation of the agreements.

Numerous factors will further affect China's implementation and compliance with the WTO agreements, some positive and some negative. China's two-decades-old commitment to market reform and economic liberalization, despite resistance from the ageing industrial sector and the heavily protected agricultural sector, bode well for implementation and compliance. Recent practice in relation to international treaties has also been fairly positive. For example, further to ratification of various IPRs treaties,[49] China has spared no effort to update its IPRs system. Immediately after the China–US Agreement in 1995, the Intellectual Property Working Meeting under the State Council was set up in 1996 to overhaul China's IPRs legislation to bring it fully in line with the TRIPs Agreement. This action was taken before the conclusion of historical agreement between China and the United States on China's accession to the WTO in 1999. China committed, in the Sino-US agreement, to bring the IPRs regime into full compliance with the TRIPs Agreement and reiterated this later in the Protocol of Accession. China has conducted an intensive work programme to examine and revise the IPRs laws, administrative regulations and ministerial rules relating to the implementation of the WTO Agreement and China's accession commitments. Strictly in line with its commitments, China revised the Patent Law, the Trademark Law and the Copyright Law before China's accession to the WTO.

Despite this positive assessment, some negative factors militate against smooth WTO implementation and compliance. China possesses a distinctive legal culture that historically rejected the rule of law in favour of the rule of man (ren zhi), and although, since 1979, the latter has been substituted with legality (fa zhi), it is legal instrumentalism that now predominates. The use of liberal language, rhetoric and the ritual of law to pursue distinctly illiberal political and social objectives is often present; it is the rule through law rather than the rule of law.

Political considerations may also retard implementation and compliance. Included here are concerns about interest-group pressure, rising nationalism, the role of Taiwan and a traditional desire to place political

---

[49] Memorandums of Understanding Between China and the United States on the Protection of Intellectual Property Rights in 1992 and 1995.

considerations above economic ones (*zhengzhi guashuai*). Trade implementation and compliance are therefore likely to be hindered, perhaps more than in most countries, by domestic pressure, from, for example, state bank or factory managers fearing competition, job loss and bankruptcy.

A further set of factors that may retard implementation and compliance with the WTO agreements is the existence of institutional defects in the Chinese legal system. The transparency requirement of Article XI of the GATT is recognition that lack of a clear and consistent framework of laws and regulations is an effective barrier to the participation of foreign firms in the domestic market and, conversely, that transparency greatly enhances business conditions, promotes commerce and reduces opportunities for corruption. Hence a major institutional defect likely to affect WTO compliance is the existence of a wide variety of entities that can make statutory law in China, leading to a proliferation of legal forms and inconsistency between them. Moreover, China's bureaucracy is known for its reluctance to implement law, selective application[50] and failure to enforce law.

A second institutional defect concerns the Chinese judicial system. It is difficult to see how a country with a judicial system that is slow, corrupt or not independent of domestic political influence could offer reliable and impartial enforcement of its laws. The highly personalized nature of business in China often makes arbitration or other legal remedies impractical. Scepticism about the independence and professionalism of the Chinese judiciary and the enforceability of judgements and awards remains high in the international community. Thirdly, institutionally, China's decentralization of power to local authorities[51] has led to uneven implementation of laws, especially where local interests are restricted by the central rule,[52] and a central government impotent to affect any control in this regard.

---

[50] In countries with an established tradition of the rule of law, conflicting statutory provisions may be reconciled, for example with an adjustment of the meaning of competing provisions so as to allow the purpose of those provisions not to be frustrated and to maintain the unity of the statutory scheme. However, that might prove to be a difficult or even impossible task in China due to an unskilled judiciary and/or interested legislators.

[51] For an analysis of the decentralizing process in China, see Li Donglü, 'The trend of economic decentralizing and its impact on foreign policies' (in Chinese) (1996) 6 *Strategy and Management* 44–9.

[52] According to a survey by the State Commission for Economic Restructuring (SCER), which was directed toward local officials throughout the country, two-thirds of the official responders stated that 'for the sake of local interests, even if there exist constraints by the [central] policy, we will pursue the local interests irregardless [*sic*.] of [the constraints]'. See SCER, 'A comprehensive investigation report of local officials in China' (in Chinese) (1996) 2 *Management World* 197.

Finally, China's approach to international law will influence its WTO commitments. Traditionally, China held a negative view of international law as representative of western interests, but in the post-Maoist era there are numerous signs of a softening of this approach. For example, although China still holds to a view of its own absolute sovereignty it displays increasing acceptance of the universal applicability of rules of general international law and some national laws refer specifically to international customs and practices (*guoji guanli*).[53] Moreover, the Sino-US Agreement, Sino-EU Agreement and finally the Protocol of Accession show an increasing willingness to submit itself to international dispute settlement. Recent Chinese practice has been to recognize rights of private parties to enforce private rights at international law.[54] Ultimately, China's desire to participate in international rule-making may encourage a shift in its attitude to international law.

In relation to the traditional Chinese approach to international law, China needs first to unify its practice in applying treaties by domestic judicial and administrative organs. It may even consider revising domestic statutory provisions to the effect that the legal force of international treaties and their direct application are clearly stated.

China's approach to the WTO dispute settlement mechanism

As Professor John Jackson has pointed out, 'A very important consideration affecting a nation's willingness to accept the WTO dispute procedures

[53] For instance, Article 142(3) of the General Principles of Civil Law provides 'International practice may be applied to matters for which neither the law of the People's Republic of China nor any international treaty concluded or acceded to by the People's Republic of China has any provisions.' However, in view of China's longstanding viewpoint, it is arguable that the reference to 'international practice' is not equivalent to customary rules of international law. As a matter of fact, the empirical evidence of judiciary practice shows that the Chinese courts apply, for example, rules such as the International Chamber of Commerce (ICC)'s standard commercial terms, e.g. Incoterms, as international practice in adjudicating cases involving foreign traders.

[54] The 1985 accession to the United Nations Convention on the Recognition and Enforcement of Foreign Arbitral Awards (New York, 1958), which directly confers rights to a private party of a Contracting State to enforce an arbitral award in another Contracting State, signified the starting point; the 1992 accession to the Convention on the Settlement of Investment Disputes between States and Nations of Other States (the ICSID Convention), under which a Contracting State will be under an obligation to submit a particular dispute to conciliation or arbitration by ICSID if it gives consent in its agreement with the nationals of other Contracting States, left room for private enforcement; the 1999 conclusion of the Sino-US Market Access Agreement was the decisive step towards foreign private enforcement of China's commitments under international agreements.

is that nation's view of the role that the treaty and its institutions should play in its international economic diplomacy.'[55] Historically, China has never been shy to express its preference for amicable means of dispute settlement in diplomacy.[56] That attitude might discourage China from using, or even accepting, the adjudicating method used by WTO panels for dispute settlement, which is arguably the strength of the WTO dispute settlement mechanism.[57]

With its accession to the WTO, however, China is now bound by the WTO agreements, including the Understanding on Dispute Settlement (DSU). Unlike other international organs for dispute settlement, the Dispute Settlement Body (DSB) has compulsory jurisdiction. China cannot challenge the jurisdiction of the DSB that receives the application against China from another member. Since its inauguration, the DSB has successfully adjudicated trade disputes between members. In cases where a complainant can show that China has violated WTO rules, the WTO dispute settlement system mechanism will be in a position to recommend that China change its behaviour and comply; moreover, if compliance is not forthcoming, the DSU ensures an automatic right to retaliation by the injured WTO member.[58]

However, the WTO dispute settlement mechanism can only play a role in areas covered by WTO agreements. Where a practice receives only limited or no coverage by the agreements, or regulation in China is not conducive to liberalized trade, and the issue culminates in a dispute between a WTO member and China, the DSB might be frustrated in dealing with it.

---

[55] John H. Jackson, *The World Trade Organization: Constitution and Jurisprudence* (London, 1998), pp. 76–8.

[56] Probably, the traditional preference for consultation and other amicable means for dispute settlement will find support in a new context. A major power, with attractive market potential, is presumably to own more bargaining power in diplomacy-negotiation-oriented processes of dispute settlement. A recent example is the dispute over garlic exports with Korea. The Korean government decided to impose a 300 per cent punitive anti-dumping duty on garlic imported from China. China, which had retained a huge deficit in relation to its trade with Korea, was angered by the failure of Korea to 'give due and sympathetic consideration' to China's longstanding position of settling disputes through bilateral consultation, and responded by stopping imports from Korea of IT products including mobile telephones, for which China is a real and prospective major market. In the subsequent consultation, China won this give-and-take game, in that both withdrew their trade measures.

[57] The DSU indeed leaves room for members concerned to engage in consultation to settle their disputes. It, however, only requires parties mutually to 'give sympathetic consideration to and afford adequate opportunity for consultation'. See DSU, Art. 4.2.

[58] DSU, Art. 22.

Examples where problems of dispute settlement may occur between China and other members include SOEs, competition, anti-corruption, the environment and social regulation.

Nevertheless, subjecting itself to the dispute settlement mechanism – no matter how unwilling China might be – would lead to the desirable result that China would develop an interest in defending its rights through a generally viable and fair quasi-judicial body.

Private enforcement

While most treaties are designed to create rights and obligations between the Contracting Parties, some international treaties, including the WTO agreements, leave room for private parties to enforce their rights under the agreements. The TRIPs Agreement is an example. It requires members to provide private entities with legal remedies under domestic law, thus making available enforcement to private parties. In this regard, it should be borne in mind that the private enforcement of WTO agreements against a WTO member is different from private participation in a WTO member's enforcement of WTO agreements against another member in the context of WTO dispute settlement mechanism.[59] Moreover, private enforcement of WTO agreements encompasses two situations: enforcement by a private party against its own state and enforcement by a private party against another WTO member either in the jurisdiction of the country to which the private party belongs or in an international forum. However, the answer in both circumstances falls completely within the municipal jurisdiction of the WTO member concerned.

As explained above, Chinese practice regarding the New York Convention, the Convention on the Settlement of Investment Disputes between States and Nations of Other States (the ICSID Convention) and the Protocol show changing attitudes towards recognizing foreign private parties' right to enforce in China their rights under international treaties. While under the

---

[59] See also the WTO decisions on the private counsel representation of Saint Lucia to the *EU Bananas* case and the *Indonesia Autos* case. See WT/DS27/AB/R, 9 September 1997, and WT/DS54/R, 2 July 1998, respectively. For private participation in the enforcement of WTO agreements, see, for instance, Michael Laidhold, 'Private party access to the WTO: do recent developments in international trade dispute resolution really give private organization a voice in the WTO?' (1999) 12(2) *The Transnational Lawyer* 427–50; and Marco C. Bronckers, 'Private participation in the enforcement of WTO law: the new EC Trade Barriers Regulation' (1996) 3(2) *Common Market Law Review* 299–318.

ICSID Convention, China's submission to international arbitration is still conditioned on its consent where a dispute arises, China expressly agrees to foreign private enforcement under the Protocol wherever a dispute arises and the foreign private party desires to do so. Accordingly, the provision in the Protocol leaves room to presume that China recognizes a foreign private party's right to enforce a WTO agreement.

It is important to note that the Protocol of Accession strengthens that position, since it provides that a foreign 'minority shareholder' shall enforce his rights in the investment 'under China's laws, regulations and measures'.[60] It should also be noted that this provision leaves an important question unanswered: whether the foreign private party can enforce his right only in China. Since the right of the 'minority shareholder' is presumably based on China's commitments (namely international treaties), the 'Chinese laws, regulations and measures' should not refer to the substantive Chinese law rules that might contradict its commitments, but to the procedural rules,[61] which provide that aggrieved companies and individuals may resort to administrative reconsideration and/or litigation.

A further difficulty concerns the ability of private parties to bring administrative and judicial review actions against government for failure to comply with the WTO agreements. Can a private party bring an administrative proceeding against the Chinese government for damages incurred as a result of the non-compliance with WTO agreements by the government? The Administrative Procedural Law provides that individuals, Chinese or foreign,[62] may bring administrative proceedings against the government agency whose 'specific administrative act' causes damages to the individual. However, the same law commands courts to reject suits against

---

[60] See section 320 of the Report of the Working Party on the Accession of China, which is an integral part of the Protocol.

[61] Currently, procedural law rules are dispersed in varieties of laws, regulations and measures, including those specifically dealing with administrative consideration and administrative litigation, such as the Regulations for Administrative Considerations (the State Council, 1991), the Administrative Procedural Law (NPC, enacted 1989, revised 1990), and other laws and regulations such as the Copyright Law (Art. 50).

[62] Foreign citizens share the same right as Chinese on the basis of reciprocity. Article 67 of the Administrative Procedural Law provides that 'A citizen, a legal person or any other organization who suffers from damages because of infringement upon his or its lawful rights and interests by a specific administrative act of an administrative organ or the personnel of an administrative organ, shall have the right to claim compensation.' Article 71 provides that 'Foreign nationals, stateless persons and foreign organizations that are engaged in administrative suits in the People's Republic of China shall have the same litigation rights and obligations as citizens and organizations of the People's Republic of China.'

administrative orders that have a general binding nature.[63] In this connection, a private party may bring an administrative action against the government for damages incurred if the non-compliance constitutes a 'specific
administrative act'. Where the Chinese government infringes the interests
of private parties in implementing laws and regulations that contravene the
WTO agreements, the private parties do not have access to judicial remedy.

The Chinese procedural law rules contain no reference as to whether the
foreign private party can enforce his right against the Chinese government
outside China. Given that the Chinese government holds that it and its
property enjoy immunity in its international law practice,[64] the Chinese
intention in the above-mentioned provision may be understood to exclude
foreign enforcement unless international treaties to which China is a party
(such as the ICSID Convention) allow such enforcement.

A further question regarding private enforcement of WTO agreements is
related to the WTO dispute settlement mechanism. As explained before,[65]
WTO Panel and Appellate Body reports are presumably binding upon
China. This raises the issue of whether a foreign private party, attempting to defend its interests *vis-à-vis* Chinese trade measures in a Chinese
court, can rely on a WTO Panel finding of inconsistency between a Chinese
measure and WTO law. Given the recent judicial practice in admitting enforcement requests brought by interested individuals,[66] Chinese courts are
unlikely to discourage the foreign private party from doing so, merely by
denying that the foreign private party has standing.

Concluding remarks

Fundamental questions remain about China's ability to implement and
enforce WTO agreements. Internally, real tensions exist between the application of laws and procedures on the one hand, and constitutional and
political/ideological considerations on the other. Moreover, the huge gap

---

[63] A private party cannot challenge the non-conforming laws and regulations per se. See Article
12(2) of the Administrative Procedural Law.
[64] For instance, in the case of *Jackson v. The People's Republic of China*, China declared that it
should be free from foreign jurisdiction based on the 'internationally recognized principle of
sovereign immunity'. See *Chinese Yearbook of International Law* (in Chinese) (Beijing, 1993),
pp. 31, 47–52.
[65] Above, pp. 134–5, 142–4.
[66] For instance, see Article 90(2) of the Interpretations on Certain Questions regarding the
Administrative Procedural Law (Supreme People's Court, 2000).

between Chinese culture – legal, political and economic – and that of the West suggests difficulties for the enforcement of WTO agreements in China. Unless China is fully prepared to accept the culture of WTO agreements, trade disputes and political tensions are likely to accompany the West's efforts to enforce WTO agreements in China. On the other hand, it might be useful to remember that patience will probably pay off in dealing with a country like China.

Fortunately, China has no reason to disregard its commitments. Since 1995, WTO members are becoming ever more engaged with the detailed process of the WTO, especially its dispute settlement procedures. A pragmatic China knows that if it wants to protects its interests as a club member, it will have to treat its obligations under WTO agreements sincerely, and reform its domestic legal structure.

10

China: trade, law and human rights

ALICE E. S. TAY AND HAMISH REDD

'If the realities of life were to coincide perfectly with theory, social science would be superfluous.'

'Out of the crooked timber of humanity nothing straight was ever made.'[1]

On 15 November 1999 the United States and China sealed their bilateral WTO deal, in the most significant development between those two countries since diplomatic relations were established nearly three decades ago. On 19 May 2000, China and the European Union finally concluded an agreement, and Australia and China signed their agreement three days later.

This chapter examines economic globalization and the new global agenda, noting what role the WTO sees itself playing within this, and how its perceptions differ from perceptions external to the WTO. The second section of the chapter looks at the human rights situation in China and the linking of trade negotiations to human rights dialogue. Structural problems in the Chinese legal system are highlighted with regard to the struggle for the rule of law and the enforcement of civil judgements. Recent legislative responses to growing domestic and international concerns in the light of China's accession to the WTO and intensifying human rights dialogues are canvassed.

The opinions expressed in this chapter are those of the authors, not the Australian Human Rights and Equal Opportunity Commission.
[1] Immanuel Kant, 'Idee zu einer allgemeinen Geschichte in weltbürgerlicher Absicht', in *Kant's gesammelte Schriften* (Berlin, 1784), vol. XVIII, p. 23, as cited in Isaiah Berlin, *The Crooked Timber of Humanity: Chapters in the History of Ideas* (London, 1990), p. V.

Globalization, the WTO and human rights

Perceptions of globalization inside and outside the WTO

In an illuminating linguistic shift, Mike Moore, the former director-general of the WTO, twice during 2001 referred pejoratively to 'globalization'. In Adelaide in February 2001 he referred to it as 'that terrible word',[2] while three days later it was 'that ugly word'.[3] This is symptomatic of the frustration building within the WTO, as it is blamed for everything from civil unrest to fragile markets collapsing. Regardless of their validity, in part the criticisms are misdirected at the WTO: the organization's ominous title and the meetings around the globe invite high-profile focal points for anger not easily targeted at the effects of globalization in its infinite manifestations. The people's outrage is based on fear and anxiety in the search by the protestors, as *Le Monde* saw it, 'for a new world order, one of an open world but of a world which isn't, under any circumstances, reduced to mere merchandise'.[4] Recognizing this, Moore now prefers to talk of 'opening up' rather than 'globalization', because the latter term has lost political credibility.

In 1995, the then director general of the WTO, Renato Ruggiero, defined globalization to mean 'a multiplicity of interlocking economic relationships among national economies' and 'a natural outgrowth of technological advances in communications and transport'.[5] By 1997, Ruggiero was speaking in much broader terms:

> Our ability to move towards the construction of a truly global system for an increasingly globalized economy stands as a powerful and encouraging symbol for those *seeking solutions to the many other issues which now spill across borders, jurisdictions and cultures.* Whether we are talking about the environment, development, labour, human rights or other ethical values – in

---

[2] 'The case for the "open society" and the role the WTO Plays', speech delivered by Mike Moore to the Australia–Israel Chamber of Commerce, Adelaide, 2 February 2001 http://www.wto.org/english/news_e/ spmm_e/spmm51_e.htm

[3] 'The WTO: challenges ahead', speech delivered by Mike Moore to the National Press Club, Canberra, 5 February 2001 http://www.wto.org/english/news_e/spmm_e/spmm52_e.htm.

[4] Editorial, *Le Monde*, 30 November 1999.

[5] *The Global Challenge: Opportunities and Choices in the Multilateral Trading System*, the Fourteenth Paul-Henri Spaak Lecture delivered at Harvard, 16 October 1995, http://www.wto.org/english/news_e/sprr_e/harvar_e.htm.

all these areas there are positive signs that the policy debate is moving beyond the sterile divisions and polarities of the past.[6]

In one of his last speeches as director general, Ruggiero paved a particularly tricky path for his successor to tread: 'From human rights, to climate change, to capital flows – our globalizing world demands global solutions. And these solutions must increasingly be based on shared agreements and rules.'[7] Further, 'We can no longer treat human rights, the environment, development, trade, health, or finance as separate sectoral issues, to be addressed through separate policies and institutions.'[8] These bold statements are a coded invitation for the WTO to play its part 'in shared agreements and rules' in the new global agenda. An agenda that places states and non-state actors in a closer matrix with international problems is consistent with the trend away from statism, towards some form of liberal agenda[9] or social clause. The scope of the new agenda is unclear: although confrontation of terrorism and the prevention of the threat of nuclear, chemical and biological weapons are clearly within it,[10] it is questionable whether the plight of a billion or so people living in poverty is.[11] Human rights, however slowly, appear to be moving somewhere towards the centre of this agenda.

These themes will now inform a fuller analysis of China's accession to the WTO, and its relationship to human rights. Will this event prove not only the economic, but also the political cataclysm that Lee Kuan Yew has boldly predicted?[12]

---

[6] *A Shared Responsibility: Global Policy Coherence for our Global Age*, speech by Renato Ruggiero to the Conference on 'Globalization as a challenge for German business; export opportunities for small and medium-sized companies in the environmental field', 9 December 1997, http://www.wto.org/english/news_e/sprr_e/bonn_e.htm (emphasis added).

[7] *Beyond the Multilateral Trading System*, address to the 20th Seminar on International Security, Politics and Economics at the Institut pour les Hautes Etudes Internationales, 12 April 1999, http://www.wto.org/english/news_e/sprr_e/ih_e.htm.

[8] Ibid.

[9] Karen Knop, 'Re/Statements: feminism and state sovereignty in international law' (1993) 3 *Transnational and Contemporary Problems* 293.

[10] See A. M. Slaughter, 'The real New World Order' (1997) 76 *Foreign Affairs* 183.

[11] P. Alston, 'The myopia of the handmaidens: international lawyers and globalisation' (1997) *European Journal of International Law* 435.

[12] Lee Kuan Yew was reported as describing the accession as 'the single biggest economic and political decision China has made since 1949': quoted in Moore, 'The WTO: challenges ahead'.

Human rights in China: challenges and opportunities in the new millennium

Human rights in trade negotiations in China

The United States has been particularly loud on human rights in its trade negotiations with China. Until recently, China was subjected to a yearly scrutiny by Congress of its human rights record, before inevitably being granted most favoured nation status once more.

Looking at Singapore – where a free market is allowed wherever the state cannot be bothered to regulate – it is fair to comment that such a model does not *of itself* guarantee political freedom, or guarantee against authoritarianism. If Beijing's relations with the commercial and political communities of the Hong Kong Special Administrative Region are an indication, a wealthy but politically controlled environment might occur on the mainland as well.[13]

The US position linking human rights with trade is less about globalization and the international rule of law, and more about domestic lobbying and pressure. After all, the United States maintains tariffs on lamb imports that directly and adversely affect Australia, one of its closest allies. This is despite continuing rhetoric about trade liberalization and posturing as the guardian of the new economic order – it has happened not because the US government necessarily wants to maintain these tariffs, but because domestic pressures ensure the United States must protect its industries, and thereby its votes. By visibly linking human rights to trade negotiations when in all likelihood it would rather leave the two apart, the US government appeals to the American political imperialist sensibility, placating powerful blocks of domestic votes, particularly in its southern states.

While the pressure from the United States has indeed been immense, other countries have been quietly pursuing a track-two diplomatic approach more amenable to Chinese sensibilities. Great Britain, France, Australia, Canada, Norway, Sweden, Brazil and Japan, as well as the European Union, all conduct human rights dialogues with the Chinese government. The United States claims these dialogues have not produced improvements in the Chinese government's human rights practices, yet despite such protests in November 2000 the United States and China agreed in principle to resume

---

[13] We acknowledge that Hong Kong's economy is based on increased productivity whereas Singapore's is based on capital inflows. The point is that neither of these 'models' provide intrinsic political freedoms: these are matters that must be consciously massaged into society.

the bilateral dialogue that was suspended by China in 1999.[14] This is another example of the State Department and Congress awkwardly straddling a schizophrenic foreign policy with China. The confrontation of wills of two nations, one uncontestably huge and the other indisputably wealthy, can only be conducted on a complex, unequal and unresolvable basis.[15]

Apart from this confrontation, activities such as the Australian–Chinese dialogue and co-operative programme on human rights play their part in very gradually changing the legal culture in China, as well as addressing more tangible structural issues. In this sense, the WTO and human rights dialogues share common objectives: both desire transparency, predictability and conformity with accepted international norms. As shall be demonstrated, both face similar structural hurdles on different legislative platforms.

Catching fish in clean water

In February 2001 Beijing was fluttering its eyelashes at International Olympic Committee officials as seventeen delegates from around the globe descended for an official scrutinizing visit. Rubbish had been cleared, trees planted, hawkers and beggars removed from the streets, and grass sprayed a pleasant green. Despite these best efforts at looking clean, revitalized and neo-millennial, a thick fog shrouded Beijing,[16] symbolizing a continuing opacity that clouds so many activities in that city. In fact Pricewaterhouse-Coopers recently proclaimed China the most opaque country in the world to do business in, with the equivalent of a 46 per cent tax being levied on investments through corruption, arbitrariness and other structural quirks.[17] Both Indonesia and Russia outscored China in terms of corruption in government bureaucracy, but China had the highest level of opacity in its legal and regulatory structures. Commentators have been quick to point out that such apocalyptic figures are unlikely to deter the ever-growing number of

[14] Bureau of Democracy, Human Rights and Labor, US Department of State, *Country Report on Human Rights Practices – 2000: China*, February 2001 http://www.state.gov./g/drl/rls/hrrpt/2000/eap/index.cfm?docid = 684.

[15] For instance, contrast the Chinese reactions regarding the US plane shot down near Hainan Island in April 2001 and the allegations of bugging throughout Jiang Zemin's new American-manufactured Boeing plane. This helps demonstrate the complexity and lack of predictability between China and the United States: it is a dynamic relationship.

[16] Reuters, 'Thick fog shrouds Beijing amid Olympic inspection', 22 February 2001, http://dailynews.muzi.com.

[17] PricewaterhouseCoopers, *The Opacity Index*, January 2001, http://www.opacityindex.com.

foreign companies eager to set up operations in China now that it has entered the WTO.[18] In 2000, for instance, three firms – oil giants PetroChina, China Petroleum and Chemical Corp (Sinopec) and China's second-largest mobile-telephone company China Unicom – raised US$12 billion through overseas listings. More mega-listings are expected in 2001.[19] Further, Premier Zhu Rongji has been dangling the prospect of a free-trade zone with China's southern neighbours. Speaking at an investment forum in Hong Kong in November 2000. Zhu's colleague, the vice-minister of foreign trade, Long Yongtu, has also been hinting at reform: 'We have to create a new culture that even in clean waters, there will be fish.'[20] Yet despite all these flashes of apparently increased transparency in China, the reality is quite different. This is an enduring theme in the analysis of the Chinese legal system and one that will be touched on again below.

Enforcing civil judgements

If China's accession to the WTO can overcome some of these factors, it may help create a cultural shift in Chinese legal logic, which in turn will affect the treatment of human rights, particularly under the Criminal Law.

The decision to reconstruct the Chinese legal system was made at the same time as the decision to undertake a process of economic reform and modernization. Indeed, the 'modernization' of the legal system, urged by Deng Xiaoping as vital to the achievement of the Four Modernizations (of agriculture, industry, national defence and science and technology), soon came to be known as the Fifth Modernization. As the legislative engines were slowly cranked up again after a long period of disuse, their first major outputs were to 'perfect' the economic legal system. Inevitably, the Chinese government failed adequately to recognize that the move from a hierarchically administered economy to a market economy means more than reams of legislation: a completely new method of rule-making and enforcing is required.

Donald Clarke listed a range of factors, internal and external, that interact to create a real problem for the resolution of Chinese civil economic

---

[18] Michael Dwyer, 'China tops the world as the worst place to do business', *Australian Financial Review*, 14 February 2001, p. 11.

[19] 'Bank of China to raise $3bn in share sale', *BBC News*, 8 July 2002, http://news.bbc.co.uk/1/hi/business/2115792.stm. Paul Eckert (Reuters) 'For China, globalisation brings power, scrutiny', 20 December 2000.

[20] 'China vows new era of transparency with WTO entry', Lateline news, 19 December 2000, http://dailynews.muzi.com.

disputes,[21] not all of which need to be canvassed here. The enforcement of judgements referred to here are not Chinese–foreign disputes, but Chinese–Chinese civil economic disputes, which of course directly affect an assessment of revenue potential by foreign entities considering investing in China. The essence of the problem is local protectionism (*difang baohuzhuyi*). Local governments rely on local enterprises for revenue and employment. Such governments, therefore, have no interest in funds being sucked from such enterprises by inconvenient judgements often made by a court in a neighbouring jurisdiction. In addition, a local political leader, who will exert his influence to protect the enterprise, may well run a local enterprise.[22] Most financial/administrative aspects of local courts (budgets, housing facilities) are controlled by local party and government organs, and with no tenure to protect them, judges are particularly susceptible to party influence. As local governments will protect local enterprises, and local courts are beholden to local governments, this equation ensures local courts are reluctant to rule against their 'own' local enterprises, or reluctant to enforce adverse judgements of a court in another jurisdiction. Consistent with this institutional pressure, 'The practice of execution shows that if court work is supported and assisted by local Party and government departments, execution work goes smoothly.'[23]

The absence of an adequate separation of powers has also affected the relationship between the people, other units and organs of justice: judges are appointed by and accountable to local governments. Banks have been known to ignore judicial orders with impunity, preventing the seizure or otherwise of defendants' funds. Clarke attributes this to the fact that the court is 'essentially just another bureaucracy, with no more power to tell banks what to do than the Post Office'.[24] Unlike common law courts, the Chinese judiciary has no general power of contempt to wield when it is ignored.

It is hoped that China's accession to the WTO, along with increasing foreign investment, will strengthen the rule of law in China as the number of economic disputes rise. In the twenty-year period since the reform of

---

[21] Donald C. Clarke, 'Power and politics in the Chinese court system: the enforcement of civil judgments' (1996) 10 *Columbia Journal of Asian Law* 1, esp. 35–61.

[22] Ibid., 42.

[23] Chen Youxi and Xue Chunbao, 'The Three Major Reasons why Courts Have Difficulty in Execution', (in Chinese), *Zhejian Fazhi Bao*, 16 August 1990, 3, cited in Clarke, 'Power and politics', 51.

[24] Clarke, 'Power and politics', 56.

the legal system began, a number of important steps towards stability and transparency have been made,[25] some of which will be scrutinised in the second section of this chapter. Certainly pressure will be placed on the government to accelerate legal reform to keep pace with economic reform, for substance over form. Greater transparency in economic matters could support and increase demands and expectations from within China for more openness in other areas.

Rule of law

Of the four goals currently on the reform agenda of the secretary-general of the United Nations, the international rule of law is placed as the second priority, behind international peace and security.[26] Of course, the two concepts are artificially separated, as they are mutually dependent on each other. In China, as in many other developing countries, it has been a long struggle towards a rule of law, and it is worth taking a brief excursion to discover why.

Historically, Confucianism conspired with geo-social and geo-political factors to ferment a strong and resilient tradition of extra-judicial administration of justice.[27] Confucian ethics and political theory perceive state-imposed law (*fa*) as a human construct that is subservient to higher principles of propriety (*li*), an external force made necessary by human inadequacies. Confucianism thus relegates law to a secondary role in social control. In the Confucian conception of state and society, law was a terroristic and punitive tool wielded by the state as a last resort against those who failed to respond to the moral exhortation of Confucian values and virtues. In time, these coercive rules came to incorporate, or have embedded within them, that broader philosophical and moral scheme concerning personal and social conduct. Punishments were increased or relaxed,

---

[25] Company Law 1993 (*Zhonghua Renmin Gongheguo Gongsi Fa*); Contract Law 1999 (*Zhonghua Renmin Gongheguo Hetong Fa*); Administrative Punishments Law 1996 (*Zhonghua Renmin Gongheguo Xingzheng Chufa Fa*); Administrative Litigation Law 1989 (*Zhonghua Renmin Gongheguo Xingzheng Susong Fa*); Civil Procedure Law 1991 (*Zhonghua Renmin Gongheguo Minshi Susong Fa*); Administrative Review Law 1999 (*Zhonghua Renmin Gongheguo Xingzheng Fuyi Fa*).

[26] Palitha Kohona, chief of UN Treaty Section, Office of Legal Affairs, 'The advancement of the international rule of law – the role of the United Nations', speech delivered in Sydney, 20 February 2001.

[27] Alice E. S. Tay, 'From Confucianism to the socialist market economy: the rule of man vs the rule of law', in Alice E. S. Tay and Günther Doeker-Mach (eds.) *Asia-Pacific Handbook, Volume I: People's Republic of China* (Baden-Baden, 1998), pp. 81–142, at p. 84.

applied in accordance with status in society. The ideology of coercive but universalist law, written and knowable, severe, strictly equally applicable to all, was known as the School of Legalism (*Fajia Zhuyi*), that gained prominence during the Qin Dynasty (221–207 BC): Legalism arose in opposition to society governed on a moral precept, and in an attempt to unify rival kingdoms into one nation.[28] A corollary of this was the need for a bureaucratic fabric that provided order where the tendrils of Confucianism did not reach. Confucian virtues were achievable by and accessible to the educated; to the 'little people' who could not be reached by education and moral cultivation, the full force of the law would apply. Unlike the Confucianists, Legalists believed in the original malignity of human kind, and their emphasis, therefore, was not on moral persuasion to find virtue, but laws and punishments to prevent a state of chaos. Such legal positivism, however, was not to introduce any rule of law and conception of individual rights, but something rather different: rule by law. Law was an effective tool for controlling growing populations under Legalist jurisdiction. Although the Legalist School officially vanished with the end of the Qin Dynasty, today's leaders recall this totalitarian technique well enough, revive and indeed revitalize it, for it is now also useful for them to control and unify their nation once more.

The remnants of continuing suspicion and reserve towards law can in part be traced to these dynastic times. The absence of protection, and the relentless brutality that the law represented, prevented individuation of guilt or liability, or a respect for the law being infused into Chinese legal logic. There was no separation of administration from law or criminal subject-matter from civil, or any codes of procedure to administer justice.[29] It was a system that declared not justice but punishment. It should be no surprise that the people turned their backs on these methods and evolved a method of dispute resolution described in current western legal parlance as 'alternative'. Briefly, during the period of Nationalist rule after 1911, codes were enacted, based largely on European models, in which an apparent attempt at the rule of law was made. Not unlike the Legalists, however, law was a tool for strengthening and unifying the nation, not the creating of juridical right- and duty-bearing individuals and units. Like the Qin

---

[28] For a more thorough history of legalism, see D. Bodde and C. Morris, 'Basic concepts of Chinese law', in D. Bodde and C. Morris (eds.), *Law in Imperial China: exemplified in 190 Ch'ing Dynasty Cases* (Harvard, 1967), pp. 1–39.

[29] Tay, 'From Confucianism to the socialist market economy', p. 89.

Dynasty nearly 2,000 years earlier, Chiang Kai-shek and his legal reforms were to disappear. In the wake of Chiang, who fled with his Six Codes to Taiwan, the Communist Party rose to power and promptly abolished all existing laws.[30]

Abolishing the Six Codes meant that only a very rudimentary, experimental legal system was in place when the Chinese Communist Party (CCP) claimed power, so the Central Committee ordered that where the 'new laws of the people' did not exist, judicial work should be carried out in accordance with the concept of 'revolutionary justice' and the programmes and policies of the party.[31] This decree formalized the legal authority of party policy directives that underpins the contemporary Chinese legal system: law is the mature form of policy, the programme of the party uttered in the words of power. The work of Stalinist jurist Andrei Vishinsky further entrenched this proposition into the Chinese socialist-legal model.[32] Vishinsky declared that in the socialist state, the Communist Party, as the guiding force of the people, the representative of the ruling proletariat, should enjoy absolute control over the creation of positive law by the organs of the state.[33] The party would define the form and content of these laws to suit its evolving programme of social and economic development. Thus, even in more contemporary times, it has been a struggle for law to gain an independent existence. International trade pressures may help this process, and also drag human rights observance with it. The increasing exposure to and growing awareness within China of foreign legal systems and international law, its signing and sometimes ratification of UN treaties and covenants, together with the real pressures of globalization, have already prompted China to respond and quicken the reform of its legal system.

---

[30] 'Directive Concerning the Abolition of the Nationalist Six Codes and the Establishment of Principles of Law in the Liberated Areas', issued by the Central Committee of the Chinese Communist Party, February 1949, in *The Complete Laws of the PRC* (in Chinese) (Jilin Renmin, 1989).

[31] See Perry Keller, 'Sources of order in Chinese law' (1995) 42 *The American Journal of Comparative Law* 711, at 719.

[32] Vishinsky's central theory rejected any autonomy of law from politics and therefore called for an abandonment of rationality as an essential characteristic of law. See further Robert Sharlet and Piers Beirne, 'In search of Vishinsky: the paradox of law and terror', in Piers Beirne (ed.), *Revolution in law* (1991), pp. 136–56; see also Arkady Vaksberg, *Stalin's Prosecutor: The Life of Andrei Vishinsky* (translated by Jan Butler) (New York, 1999).

[33] See Yu Xingzhong, 'Legal pragmatism in the People's Republic of China' (1980) 3 *Journal of Chinese Law* 28, at 36.

Chinese legislative responses

Human rights breaches are often most dramatically located in the system of criminal justice. On 14 March 1997, the Fifth Session of the Eighth National People's Congress substantially approved a new criminal law, and a new criminal procedural law, after a long process of discussion on the inadequacies of the previous 1979 laws. Western scholars have been quick to analyse the Chinese criminal-justice system and expose its shortcomings – the criminal-justice system is more visible and less complex than other areas of law, thereby providing greater accessibility to the interested observer.

Criminal Law 1997

It is unclear whether the overriding purpose of the new Criminal Law of 1997 is to create greater order in a society increasingly plagued by waves of criminality, to suppress political dissent, to tidy up a criminal code that had been amended and enormously added to almost the day after promulgation, or to meet some of the criticisms levelled at the 1979 Law. The reference to Marxism–Leninism and Mao Zedong thought as the guiding ideology of criminal law has been removed from Article 1. Article 2, however, reminds us that 'The tasks of the PRC Criminal Law are to use punishment against all criminal acts to defend national security, the political power of the people's democratic dictatorship, and the socialist system.'[34] The Criminal Law, therefore, is necessary timber in socialist construction. The CCP, as the vanguard of the people's democratic dictatorship, is protected implicitly in this article, despite Article 4 that states 'Every one is equal before the law in committing crime. No one is permitted to have privileges to transgress the law.' Significantly, the new provisions removed the old Article 90 that stated 'all acts endangering the PRC committed with the goal of overthrowing the political power of the dictatorship of the proletariat and the socialist system are crimes of counter-revolution'. Under Part I of the 1997 Criminal Law (the general provisions), Article 13 now expresses a similar prohibition, but in different language:

> All acts that endanger the sovereignty, territorial integrity, and security of the state; split the state; subvert the political power of the people's democratic

[34] Criminal Law of the People's Republic of China, adopted by the Second Session of the Fifth National People's Congress on 1 July 1979 and amended by the Fifth Session of the Eighth National People's Congress on 14 March 1997. A translation of this is available at http://www.qis.net/chinalaw/lawtran1.htm.

dictatorship and overthrow the socialist system; undermine social and economic order; violate property owned by the state or property collectively owned by the labouring masses; violate citizens' privately owned property; infringe upon citizens' rights of the person, democratic rights, and other rights; and other acts that endanger society, are crimes if according to law they should be criminally punished. However, if the circumstances are clearly minor and the harm is not great, they are not to be deemed crimes.

It is not accidental that in this general list of crimes, issues of sovereignty, territorial integrity and political power are placed before economic order, state- and collectively owned property, privately owned property, and finally rights of the person, democratic rights and other rights. The specific provisions relating to crimes of endangering national security are listed in Articles 102–13 in Part II of Chapter I of the Law. Some offences can carry the death penalty when the circumstances 'are particularly vile'.[35] Local-level governments interpret these sections in accordance with centralized policy directives.

Chapter III (Articles 140–231) of the Criminal Law is headed 'Crimes of undermining the order of socialist market economy'. It covers crimes such as corporate fraud, infringement of intellectual property rights and disrupting the market order; many are new crimes, reflecting the profound social and economic changes that China has experienced. Several provisions can attract the death penalty.

In the Chinese socialist-legal history, there are 'loosening and tightening' (*fengsou*) of policy and 'political crackdowns' (*yanda*, literally 'hard strike'), which will influence the enforcement and content of these provisions. Such 'extra-legal' considerations surround the statute and cast a shadow over what are otherwise reasonably promising reforms in the Criminal Procedure Law of 1997.

Criminal Procedure Law 1997

In 1996 the NPC adopted a 110-article decision revising the 1979 Criminal Procedure Law[36] (CPL) that came into effect on 1 January 1997. Of the 164 articles in the original law, seventy were eliminated, two altered and

---

[35] Article 113 reads 'When one commits the aforementioned crimes in this chapter that endanger national security – except those stipulated in the second clause of Article 103, and Articles 105, 107 and 109 – and has incurred particularly serious harms to the country and the people, and the circumstances are particularly vile, he may be sentenced to death.'

[36] Decision of the National People's Congress on the Revision of the 'Criminal Procedure Law of the PRC', adopted 17 March 1996.

sixty-three new articles included. A greater awareness of international practice was an important stimulant to revise the CPL, as was a greater international awareness, and criticism of China's criminal law had an effect.[37]
Though the 1954 State Constitution and Organic Law of the Courts of the
same year had declared that 'the people's courts shall conduct adjudication
independently and are subject only to the law' (Article 78, and Article 4
of the Organic Law), the 1982 Constitution provides that 'the people's
courts shall, in accordance with the law, exercise judicial power independently and are not subject to interference by administrative organs, public
organizations or individuals'.[38] The 1997 Law declared courts to be the only
competent organs to judge and convict.[39]

Other provisions made fundamental changes and improvements to the
Chinese criminal-justice process: judges must now determine on presentation of the indictment whether the indictment was sufficient, in which case
the trial commences; if not, it is rejected, with the judge having no power to
send it back for further investigation or direct its further investigation. The
new Law requires the prosecution and defence to present evidence to the
court, question and debate on the evidence and examine witnesses, with
judges taking an essentially passive 'umpire' role, concerning themselves
mainly with the maintenance of court order and orderly debate, thus creating a better environment for a meaningful defence. After deliberation of
the guilt of the defendant, the collegial panel (judge and assessors) must
render judgement and may request the president of the court to transfer the
case to the judicial committee for discussion and decision only in difficult,
major or complex cases – whereas in the past such cases were automatically
discussed and decided by the judicial committee prior to the trial. Unfortunately, without an overhaul of the institutional structure of the Chinese
justice system, such provisions will remain as largely unenforceable as their
constitutional counterparts have long been.[40]

In its analysis of the revisions, the US-based Lawyers Committee for
Human Rights deciphered four areas particularly relevant to human rights:
pre-arrest detention, the right to counsel, prosecutorial determination of
guilt and the trial process.[41] For brevity's sake, only the first two of these shall

---

[37] Lawyers Committee for Human Rights, *Opening to Reform?* (New York, 1996), p. 10.
[38] Criminal Procedure Law 1997, Art. 5. The ambiguity of this provision has been quickly noticed
and noted in both Chinese and western legal analyses.
[39] Ibid., Art. 12.   [40] Constitution of the PRC 1982, Art. 126.
[41] Lawyers Committee for Human Rights, *Opening to Reform?* p. 20.

be discussed here. Pre-arrest detention had traditionally been a problem in China on the basis of people being detained for 'shelter and investigation' (*shourong shencha*), an administrative not criminal provision, because the arrest standard in the 1979 CPL was seen as too high. The revised CPL sought to address this by lowering the arrest standard[42] and also expanding the categories of people towards whom the 'shelter and investigation' provisions had originally been directed, so such pre-arrest detentions would be governed by the criminal law, not administrative regulations (and thereby governed by the courts, not the police). In theory, it was a good move as it removed a 'legal' method for police to avoid prescribed time limits and procedural requirements contained in the CPL. Yet the revisions also slipped through an increase in the time of pre-arrest detention for this class of suspects from seven to thirty days, and granted an extra four days for the procuracy to decide whether to authorize the arrest.[43] Further, the original CPL allowed for a maximum three months' detention of those suspected of committing crimes punishable by ten years or longer, while the revised version permits ten months.[44]

Another response by China to growing international concern, and also awareness amongst its expanding legal profession, of deficiencies in its criminal procedure, was to reform provisions regarding a right to counsel. Again, the commitment to meet international human rights standards is questionable. The new CPL provides suspects with a right to counsel from the moment case materials are transferred from investigating authorities to the procuracy to assess whether to proceed with prosecution, and also stipulates that suspects must be informed of that right within three days of the transfer.[45] There is no right of counsel, however, during the investigative phase when, of course, all manner of illegally obtained evidence may be introduced, and the suspect may be vulnerable to torture or other coercion. It is a deliberate tactic by the drafters, as Article 96 explains that suspects may have counsel during this stage, but there is no obligation to inform suspects of this 'right'. Acquiring competent counsel at such an early stage of pretrial detention and investigation is certainly not part of the Chinese legal culture, and in the absence of positive measures to give substance to this right, it may remain illusory. In addition, China is struggling to generate a higher number of lawyers (and higher-quality lawyers) essential to the enforcement of such rights.

---

[42] Art. 60.   [43] Art. 69.   [44] Art. 127.   [45] Art. 33.

Other legislation

China has also responded to the recognized need for a 'rule of law' environment with some other major pieces of legislation in its continuing 'modernization' of the legal system. The Administrative Litigation Law 1989 (ALL)[46] was introduced in response to a problem Deng Xiaoping (and many others) had observed: 'For a long time we have lacked strict administrative regulations... [and] clear stipulations regarding the competence of each organ and even each person; whatever the matter, more often than not there have been no regulations to follow.'[47] In other words, legislation was required to restrain official abuse of power and corruption. The ALL provides a process of judicial review of 'concrete' administrative acts, but not 'abstract' and discretionary ones, the latter being one of the primary sources of administrative abuses and corruption.[48] This is particularly of concern in the criminal law, where although there has been an attempt to relocate notorious abuses into the criminal law, and therefore out of the administrative law (note the 'shelter and investigation' case discussed above), several problems remain in administrative (non-reviewable) discretion.[49] The ALL is accompanied by four other legislative outputs, that together form a suite of administrative review for the first time in China.[50] Although the absence of an independent and competent judiciary, as already noted, largely leaves the abuse of administrative power unbridled, the importance of this suite of legislation should not be underestimated. The process of reforming the legal system in China is only two decades old, and swims upstream against a current of hostility towards the law, and emphasis of individual subordination to greater authorities. Such legislative outputs are significant steps in a cultural shift that will lead to more substantive rights and remedies, along with continuing structural reform.

---

[46] *Zhonghua Renmin Gongheguo Susong Fa*, promulgated 4 April 1989.

[47] Deng Xiaoping, *Dang he Guojia Lingdao Zhidu de Gaige* [trans: *Reform of Party and Government Leadership*] quoted in Susan Finder, 'Like throwing an egg against a stone? Administrative litigation in the People's Republic of China' (1989) 3 *Journal of Chinese Law* 1, at 5.

[48] See Alice E. S. Tay and Günther Doeker-Mach, 'Twenty years of law-making', in Alice E. S. Tay and Günther Doeker-Mach (eds.), *Asia Pacific Handbook – PRC Legislation* (forthcoming).

[49] The reach of the Security Administration Punishment Regulations 1987, for example, is extremely broad.

[50] Administrative Review Regulations 1990, State Compensation Act 1994, Administrative Penalties Law 1996, Administrative Review Act 1999.

Rhetoric versus reality

It would be premature, however, to conclude that the changes to the criminal and administrative law have led to alleviation of human rights abuses. Endemic inefficiency and corruption in the judiciary, and a questionable commitment to rectify these, continue to cause grave concern. The Justice Ministry set a target of 150,000 lawyers, 30,000 notaries and 40,000 grass-roots legal services centres by 2000, yet according to the All-China Lawyers Association, the country fell short of that goal.[51] Further, for the entire legal history of the People's Republic of China until the last few years, neither prosecutors nor judges were required to have law degrees or legal experience; most of them were retired army officers and former public security personnel. Over the last few years, a genuine effort has been made to encourage law graduates to enter the judiciary (including a call by members of the Shanghai People's Congress) and to increase judicial salaries to make a judicial career an attractive alternative opening to law practice in lucrative commercial areas.

Senior officials acknowledge that torture and coerced confessions are chronic problems.[52] Electric shocks administered with cattle prods, prolonged periods of solitary confinement, beatings and shackles remain favoured methods of torture by the security organs. The latest available official statistics indicate that 230,000 persons remain in re-education through labour camps (an administrative punishment out of the CPL's scope). While defendants can challenge their sentences under the ALL, inadequate legal counsel and short appeal times defeat the promise of the law in preventing or reversing arbitrary decisions.

Anecdotal evidence gathered by the US government indicates that the implementation of the CPL 'remains uneven and far from complete, especially in politically sensitive cases'.[53] This is indicative of two paths that change must follow: it must cascade down the various levels of government and state and it must also spread outwards from Beijing into the provinces and penetrate traditional extra-legal handling of justice in rural areas. In April 2000, the Beijing newspaper *Legal Daily* published an article on torture that concluded that the practice was due to police officials not having adequate legal or human rights training and holding antiquated ideas about a presumption of guilt.[54]

---

[51] Cited in US State Department, *Country Report on Human Rights Practices – 2000: China.*
[52] Ibid., 4.   [53] Ibid., 11.   [54] Cited in ibid., 12.

Conclusion

The 'Fifth Modernization' is a continuing process for China. The last two decades have witnessed an extraordinary amount of legal reform judging by almost any standard. Human rights, like international trade, is a new concept not easily absorbed into China's legal culture, and incompatible with its legal and constitutional structures. It has been seen that human rights and international trade face similar challenges in China as they seek to effect their separate but related causes. Granting NGOs and UN agencies WTO observer status will recognize that the international trade system has a relationship and role to play with other entities in pursuing higher living standards for all humanity.

China's accession to the WTO will provide significant impetus for further domestic reform of its legal system. Strengthening its judiciary and dismantling at least those features and aspects of the politico-legal apparatus at all levels that stand in direct opposition to legality will remain priorities for China as it responds to increased foreign investment and scrutiny. Reflecting on the changes China has experienced during the twentieth century, the legal reforms already in place together with those on the horizon, may be fairly described as a 'legal revolution'. Senior Minister Lee Kuan Yew may be overstating the accession when he proclaimed it 'the single biggest economic and political decision China has made since 1949'.[55]

The accession is a natural medium-term consequence of the reforms enacted shortly after the death of Chairman Mao, as part of the 'economic revolution'. Should the WTO embrace the new global agenda and work in partnership with civil society and UN agencies, Lee Kuan Yew may well prove the soothsayer. The danger is that progress in international trade through the WTO will remain divorced from greater social concerns. If this proves true, China may well follow in the footsteps of the country Mr Lee has created. The 'socialist' part of Deng Xiaoping's 'socialist market economy' (for which read state-controlled and licensed market economy) will define the market economy, just as Mr Lee's 'Asian values' have provided Singaporean characteristics to the Singapore miracle.

[55] As quoted in Moore, 'The WTO: challenges ahead'.

PART IV

Trade in goods

11

China's interest in the World Trade Organization's deregulation of international textiles trade

IAN DICKSON

In testimony before the House Ways and Means Committee in February 2000, former US Trade Representative Charlene Barshefsky characterized the WTO deal struck between China and the United States as a 'one-way' flow of concessions from China to the United States. Although this argument suited efforts to persuade Congress to grant permanent normal trading relations (PNTR) to China, it is not strictly true. The United States – and the European Union, Canada and Norway – have in fact committed to important changes in their treatment of goods imported from China. In particular, they will eventually be required to eliminate quotas on imports of Chinese textiles and clothing. This concession is not trivial, with important political economy issues at stake in both the United States and the European Union.

The concession is also of considerable importance to China. Textiles and clothing make up approximately one-quarter of China's total exports by value, and around one-quarter of China's textiles and clothing exports go to the United States and European Union. This chapter examines China's interest in the deregulation of textiles trade as required by WTO provisions. It focuses on changes in the United States and European Union. As the regulatory barriers in these markets decrease, the benefits to China of its WTO membership will increase.

A note on the benefits for importers

China and other textiles-exporting nations are not the only beneficiaries of textiles trade deregulation. For example, a recent study shows that textile

The views expressed here are the author's own, and not those of the Department of Foreign Affairs and Trade, Canberra, Australia, nor of the Australia Department of Treasury.

Table 11.1 *Effects of US quotas on imports from China, 1994–1999*

	Change in import volumes		
	All products	Sweaters, wool	Shirts, men's
1995/1994	−7.0%	−1.5%	−7.3%
1996/1995	−4.7%	−12.0%	−2.1%
1997/1996	11.2%	17.2%	5.6%
1998/1997	−0.3%	−0.2%	2.1%
1999/1998	2.3%	0.2%	−2.8%
1999/1994	0.5%	1.6%	−4.9%
Average quota fill rate	93.8%	97.4%	97.6%
Average annual quantities	1,726.3 mil m^2	3.7 mil m^2	45.7 mil m^2

Source: Author's calculations based on Expired Performance Reports (China) from US Commerce Department.

import quotas cost EU consumers and industry a total of US$28.4 billion per year and that the average annual loss for a family of four in the European Union is US$306.[1]

Another study, commissioned by the Australian Wool Council, shows that the complete elimination of US quotas in 1999 would allow US consumers to expand 'their consumption of textiles and clothing by switching to cheaper imports and still have US$20 billion left over to spend on other goods and services'.[2] The same study also shows that the deregulation of textiles and clothing trade will also have significant benefits for Australian wool and cotton growers. The cost in 1999 to Australian wool and cotton producers of US quotas on imports of textiles and apparel from countries including China amounted to nearly US$21 million.[3] This figure does not include the cost to Australia of EU quotas.

---

[1] J. François, H. Glismann and D. Spinanger, '*The Cost of EU Trade Protection in Textiles and Clothing*' (Working Paper 997, Kiel Institute of World Economics, 2000), p. 5. These opportunity costs are those associated with quotas on imports from all nations, not only China. In the study, the opportunity costs were presented in terms of 1997 ECU (European Currency Units), but have here been converted to US dollars.

[2] CIE (Centre for International Economics), *Barriers to Wool Fibre Products Trade: Costs to US Consumers and Australian Woolgrowers*, commissioned by the Wool Council of Australia (Canberra, 1999), p. x.

[3] Ibid., p. 19, table 3.3. The study reported this result in Australian dollar terms (A$32.3 million).

Table 11.2 *Effects of EU quotas on imports from China, 1994–1999*

	Change in import volumes		
	All products	Sweaters, all	Shirts, men's
1995/1994	38.1%	114.9%	55.4%
1996/1995	−3.9%	−14.8%	11.8%
1997/1996	15.5%	5.6%	−3.3%
1998/1997	2.0%	7.9%	1.8%
1999/1998	11.7%	0.6%	−12.4%
1999/1994	74.6%	110.1%	49.6%
Average quota fill rate	76.7%	99.8%	99.1%
Average annual quantites	316.3 th tonnes	22.8 mil m²	25.8 mil m²

Note: Square metres equivalent measure not available for 'all products'.
Source: Author's calculations based on Système Intégré de Gestion de Licenses (http://sigl.cec.eu.int).

Current US and EU restrictions on China's exports

China faces strong restrictions on its exports of textiles and clothing products to the four trading partners that maintain import quotas, namely the United States, European Union, Canada and Norway. Tables 11.1 and 11.2 provide evidence on quotas facing Chinese exporters in the United States and European Union respectively. Some background information on the US quota system is helpful for understanding table 11.1. The United States divides clothing and textile products into 147 categories for quota administration purposes. Each category contains, on average, 22 separate tariff lines. The United States groups its imports from all countries in the same way, but not all trading partners face the same quotas. For example, China faces specific limits in 81 of the 147 categories, while the number for India is 30.

   In addition to quotas on specific categories, the United States also groups individual categories into 'global' limits. In China's case, all of the 147 categories, bar one, are grouped into four overarching global quotas. Group II covers cotton, wool and man-made fibre (MMF) clothing. Group III covers non-apparel items. Group IV includes apparel items made from silk or other vegetable fibres, but not cotton. Group I is less well defined but covered 79 per cent of China's quota volumes in 2000.

The 'all products' column of table 11.1 sums these four global quotas, and shows that between 1994 and 1999, China's exports under US quotas grew by just 0.5 per cent (equivalent to a compound growth rate of 0.1 per cent per year). This growth rate is strikingly low considering the growth in the US GDP and consumption expenditure over the same period. Overall, Chinese merchandise exports to the United States grew by 96 per cent between 1994 and 1999, according to Chinese customs data.

The high average 93.8 per cent quota fill rate over the six years 1994 to 1999 suggests that China could have expanded its exports only slightly within the existing quota constraints. If China had filled its 1999 quotas completely, its textile and clothing exports to the United States would have grown by just 7 per cent between 1994 and 1999, or 1.4 per cent per year. China would, however, have faced difficulties achieving this slightly improved outcome. During several of the last few years it has exhausted quotas in commercially important categories, so that room to expand exports exists only in other product categories where customer demand is weak or non-existent. For example, in 1994, 1996, 1997 and 1999 China completely filled its global Group II quota for cotton, wool and MMF apparel products, and in the other years, 1995 and 1998, the Group II quota was 99.2 per cent and 99.3 per cent filled respectively. Where surplus quota existed for a specific product, it would have been unusable if the overarching global quotas had already been exhausted by China.

The quota fill rates in table 11.1 are based on the most liberal interpretation of quota volumes available to Chinese exporters. That is, these rates take into account through-the-year 'flexibility' adjustments to the initial quotas granted by US authorities. In accordance with principles carried over from the Multi-Fibre Arrangement, quota-maintaining nations adjust quota levels slightly at the request of exporting nations using swing, carry-over and carry-forward provisions. These measures allow for some limited variation in quotas by shifting quota between products or between years.

The European Union divides textiles and clothing products into 143 categories for the purposes of managing import quotas. Each category covers on average 10 tariff lines. China faces quotas on 61 of these product categories, compared to 17 for India.

Comparison of tables 11.1 and 11.2 shows that the rate of growth of imports under quota between 1994 and 1999 has on average been higher in the European Union than in the United States. The 76.7 per cent figure for aggregate utilization of EU quotas in table 11.2 should be treated with care, however, as it includes both commercially important categories for which quotas are tight and less restrictive categories. Indeed, China's quota utilization rate exceeded 95 per cent for twenty-seven of the total sixty-one categories affected by EU quotas and was 100 per cent in nine of those categories. Table 11.2 shows that China used 99.8 per cent and 99.1 per cent of its quotas for sweaters and men's shirts respectively. These levels take into account EU flexibility adjustments.

Quotas in the European Union and United States are defined in terms of volumes not values, so that real flows, not flows that are susceptible to exchange-rate changes, are regulated. The United States tends to express quotas in terms of dozens or square metre equivalents, while the European Union uses pieces, pairs or kilograms. Without common units of measurement, comparisons of US and EU levels are difficult. (The only feasible comparison of quantities in tables 11.1 and 11.2 is the measure of men's shirts in millions of square metres.)

Overall, the evidence shows that, in the US case, not only do quota fill rates approach 100 per cent, but the actual rate of growth of imports under the quotas is much slower than would be expected given other economic conditions. While the growth of imports under EU quotas has been faster, the high rate of utilization of EU quotas suggests that EU quotas also stifle China's exports.

Quota administration

Significantly, quota-maintaining nations do not assume the responsibility of allocating quota among importing enterprises. Exporting countries control quota allocation, with quota allocated to exporting rather than importing firms.[4]

In China's case, exports of textile and clothing to the United States are governed by a 1997 memorandum of understanding (MOU) that replaced a similar MOU for the 1994 to 1997 period. The 1997 MOU was due to expire after December 2000, but was extended into 2001 as a stop-gap until

---

[4] K. M. Krishna and L. Tan, *Rags and Riches: Implementing Apparel Quotas under the Multi-Fibre Arrangement* (Ann Arbor, 1998), survey of quota-allocation arrangements used in Hong Kong, Korea, Indonesia, India, Pakistan and Bangladesh.

China joined the WTO. The MOU established growth rates for quotas on China's exports to the United States, as well as flexibility provisions and penalties for rule of origin violations and illegal transhipments.

Implementation of the agreement on the US side is conducted by CITA, the Committee for Implementation of Textile Agreements. CITA is an inter-agency body steered by the US Commerce Department with representatives from the Department of Labor and the Treasury and the US Trade Representative.

CITA sets quota levels each year and directs US Customs to enforce them. CITA is also responsible for monitoring compliance and subtracting 'charges' or 'triple-charges' from quotas where US authorities suspect that transhipment violations have occurred. For example, in May 1998, the United States imposed triple charges, which contributed to the decline in China's exports of quota-restricted clothing and textiles during that year – see table 11.1. Again in December 2000, the United States announced punitive charges which were estimated to reduce Chinese exports by US$9 million per year.[5] This figure compares with US penalties that reputedly cost China US$120 million in lost sales between 1994 and 1996, and with EU penalties that cost China US$50 million in 1995.[6]

US monitoring of clothing and textile imports from China is assisted by the Electronic Visa Information System (known as 'ELVIS'). Under ELVIS, Chinese authorities issue visas to domestic enterprises exporting to the United States. The visa is stamped to the commercial invoice or export licence accompanying the shipment to the United States, and includes visa information, which is also transmitted separately to US authorities by e-mail. Before releasing goods that have arrived at US ports, US customs authorities cross-check the visa information in accompanying documentation against the visa information in the e-mail message from Chinese authorities. ELVIS was introduced at US behest to prevent visa fraud and illegal routing of exports to the United States, but has helped importers and exporters by speeding up customs clearance.

The US role in the implementation of textile quotas is simple and essentially limited to counting imports as they are cleared through customs, and charging those imports to the annual quota. When the quota is filled, no more imports are permitted. The United States leaves it to China (or to other countries affected by quotas) to determine how best and how

---

[5] *South China Morning Post*, 14 December 2000.   [6] *Textile Asia*, December 1999, p. 58.

quickly to exhaust their quotas throughout the year. The United States takes no role in deciding to whom visas and quotas are issued – that also is left to China.[7] It is up to US importers to find Chinese suppliers capable of obtaining the necessary visas and export licences from Chinese authorities.[8]

Quota rents

By staying out of the business of quota allocation, the United States forfeits most of the rents associated with quotas.[9] Yongzheng Yang, Will Martin and Koji Yanagishima comment that nations restricting imports from developing countries 'felt it necessary to purchase compliance' by handing over control of quota allocation and the quota rents that go along with this control.[10] The United States also avoids messy issues of political-economy and corruption that can accompany quota allocation exercises.

In China, 60 per cent of export quotas for twenty-one commercially significant product categories have been auctioned since 1999. The remaining 40 per cent of quotas for these product categories, and 100 per cent of quotas for all other categories, are allocated on the basis of past performance. Neither auctions nor administrative allocation has led to entirely satisfactory outcomes.

Administrative allocation inevitably short-changes some deserving firms. Investigation of competing claims is unavoidable but generates bureaucracy. Each year China's State Textile Industry Bureau analyses the records of thousands of textile enterprises to appraise claims for export quota. The system can never be entirely transparent, free from subjectivity or immune from the possibility of corruption.

---

[7] US customs authorities do, however, publish lists of producers suspected of transhipment violations in order to discourage US importers from doing business with them.

[8] The Chinese term for textile export-quota licences is *beidong chukou pei-e zheng*. The word *beidong*, which means 'passive' or 'to act under order', makes clear that China does not choose to impose quotas of its own volition.

[9] Importing countries will recover some of the rents as a result of the buying power of the large retailers that do much of the importing: see K. Krishna, R. Erzan and L. Tan, 'Rent sharing in the Multi-Fibre Arrangement: theory and evidence from US apparel imports from Hong Kong' (1994) 2(1) *Review of International Economics* 62–73.

[10] Y. Yang, W. Martin and K. Yanagishima, 'Evaluating the benefits of abolishing the MFA in the Uruguay Round package', in T. W. Hertel (ed.), *Global Trade Analysis: Modelling and Applications* (Cambridge, 1997), pp. 253–79, at p. 255.

The auction system should, in theory, lead to more transparent and efficient outcomes but, in practice, in the few years it has operated, it has led to a rapid escalation in costs passed on by exporters to their overseas customers. According to one report about the situation in Guangdong, the cost of clothing exports under quota rose by 60–70 per cent in 1999.[11] European importers, led by the Brussels-based Foreign Trade Association, have complained about China's quota-auction system.[12]

Escalating costs partly reflect the fact that the auction process has helped China to realize potential rents. Previously, China may have been extracting less rent than it could have, because quota was allocated administratively for free or low charges and because markets for resale of quota were imperfect or illegal. The rise in costs may also reflect the fact that US and EU quotas on imports from China have been growing more slowly than latent consumer demand, increasing the protective effect of quotas over time.

Fundamentally, US and EU importers who complain about quota-induced import costs have their own governments to blame, rather than China. None the less, difficulties associated with the timing and organization of China's auctions may have exacerbated the cost increases associated with the quotas. If only limited opportunities exist to acquire or redistribute quota, auction participants may react precipitately. Many Chinese exporters have first obtained orders from US and EU importers and then scrambled to secure the necessary quota at auctions.

To maximize utilization of quotas, and to curb hoarding of quotas and other activities aimed at manipulating quota prices, China's Ministry of Foreign Trade and Economic Co-operation (MOFTEC) recently introduced new rules on the use of quotas. MOFTEC will debar firms from participating in auctions if they do not return unused quota to authorities by certain deadlines.[13] But in so doing, China may be helping its customers, by keeping a lid on rent escalations that consumers in importing countries will ultimately pay for.

The prospective abolition of quotas on China's exports to the United States and the European Union raises the issue of what will happen to the rents that China currently enjoys. Quota liberalization is not without

---

[11] *Textile Asia*, March 2000, p. 58.   [12] *Textile Asia*, July 2000, p. 4.

[13] *Textile Asia*, August 2000, p. 85. Year 2000 rules required that auctioned quota unused by 31 August had to be surrendered to the government, whereupon deposits paid on the unused portion would be refunded. Enterprises failing to surrender unused quota exceeding 5 per cent of the original allocation would be forbidden from participating in quota auctions for the next two years. If the wastage exceeded 30 per cent, the ban would last for three years.

cost to China itself. However, Yang, Martin and Yanagishima conclude that the benefits of international textiles-trade deregulation for restricted and efficient textiles exporters such as China outweigh the accompanying loss of quota rents.[14] Moreover, while China controls quota allocation, it does not control quota volumes, which are set by the quota-maintaining nations; nor is it the only exporter to those nations. Unlike a monopolist, therefore, China is not able to dictate price or supply levels to maximize rents. The rents that it receives are almost certainly sub-optimal from its point of view.

The Agreement on Textiles and Clothing

Having joined the WTO, China will benefit from the provisions of the WTO's Agreement on Textiles and Clothing (ATC).[15] The ATC came into force on 1 January 1995, when it replaced the Multi-Fibre Arrangement (MFA), which governed international textiles trade between 1974 and 1994. The ATC also has a limited lifespan, being a transitional arrangement for phasing out the discriminatory barriers permitted under the MFA. By the time the ATC expires on 1 January 2005 there should no longer be any need for an agreement devoted solely to textile products, with trade in textiles governed entirely by the General Agreement on Tariffs and Trade (GATT).

Only WTO members are bound by the obligations of the ATC, and only WTO members may enjoy its benefits. In contrast, the MFA included members such as China that were not also GATT/WTO members. China's textile exports were governed by bilateral agreements during the period between the expiry of the MFA and China's WTO accession.

The MFA basically served the interests of textile industries in developed nations, but even then those nations sometimes considered it necessary to abridge the limited principles the MFA contained for the benefit of exporting countries. The MFA legitimized the discriminatory use of quotas and other barriers in textiles trade, but supposedly in a way that restrained their use and allowed for continued expansion of international textiles trade. Several safeguard and quota measures were included, but none were to grow at an annual rate of less than 6 per cent. Growth in China's export quotas has been lower than 6 per cent, as tables 11.1 though 11.9 show.

China's right to the benefits of the ATC is established in provisions of the Working Party Report on China's WTO accession, as incorporated into

---

[14] Yang et al., 'Evaluating the benefits', pp. 268, 275.
[15] These benefits are compromised to some extent by the discriminatory safeguards which are included in the terms of China's accession, as discussed later.

the Protocol of Accession.[16] The text of these provisions is almost identical to wording in the 1999 bilateral US–China agreement on China's WTO membership.

The ATC requires that WTO members notify and bind any restrictions on textile imports that they had in place on the 'day before the date of entry into force of the WTO Agreement' (Article 2.1). This requirement applies both to restrictions maintained under the former MFA and to non-MFA restrictions. For purposes of applying this obligation to quotas on China's imports, the Working Party Report deems Article 2.1 to refer to 'the day prior to the date of China's accession'. Thus in China's case the restrictions that the United States, European Union and other members are obliged to notify are those that were in effect against China when China joined the WTO. As with all such previous notifications, the notifications must include both the restraint level and the growth rates. Restrictions not notified must be terminated.[17]

Quota integration

The most important function of the ATC is to integrate 790 Harmonized System (HS) tariff items into GATT provisions.[18] This transition takes place in four steps, occurring prior to 1995, 1998, 2002 and 2005 respectively. At each stage, countries that notified a right to continue using restrictions inconsistent with GATT provisions must abandon this right with respect to a certain percentage of the 790 tariff lines. The percentages are based on the volume of imports each member had in 1990. On 1 January 1995 members were required to integrate into GATT rules tariff lines that accounted for 16 per cent of their 1990 imports. A further 17 per cent and 18 per cent were to be integrated by January 1998 and January 2002 respectively. The balance, 49 per cent, is integrated by 1 January 2005, the date that the ATC terminates.[19]

---

[16] WT/L/432, which incorporates obligations set out in certain paragraphs of the Working Party Report, WT/ACC/CHN/49.

[17] ATC, Art. 2.4.

[18] Although the ATC specifies 790 tariff categories for integration into the GATT, the number of affected tariff lines in the United States and European Union exceeds 790. This is because the United States further subdivides the 790 categories into 3,654 tariff lines for its administrative purposes, while the European Union subdivides the categories into approximately 1,410 lines.

[19] WTO members maintaining the right to use ATC's transitional safeguard mechanism must also participate in the integration process. Initially, fifty-five members retained the right to use the safeguard, including the four – the United States, European Union, Canada and Norway – which use import quotas. By the end of 1997, the number had decreased to forty-three.

Table 11.3 *Number of tariff lines under quota: all textiles and clothing*

Market		Exporting country			
		China		India	
		Number	%	Number	%
US	Lines under quota in 2000	2,067	100	777	100
	Lines under quota in 2001	2,015	97.5	777	100
	Lines under quota 2002–5	1,788	86.5	774	99.6
	Lines under quota after 2005	0	0	0	0
EU	Lines under quota in 2000	730	100	369	100
	Lines under quota in 2001	677	92.7	369	100
	Lines under quota 2002–5	535	73.3	344	93.2
	Lines under quota after 2005	0	0	0	0

Sources: Author's compilation using data from http://otexa.ita.doc.gov/ fedreg/gatt94.htm, http://otexa.ita.doc.gov/fedreg/finalfr.htm, http://europa.eu. int/comm/trade/goods/textile/legitext2.htm, and OJ 1996 No. L314, 4 December 1996, p. 1 and OJ 2000 No. L286, 11 November 2000, p. 1.

Therefore, by the date of China's accession in December 2001 quota-maintaining nations must have integrated tariff lines accounting for 33 per cent of their 1990 textiles and clothing imports. On accession, China benefited from the immediate removal of quotas on this 33 per cent of tariff lines. Moreover, in January 2002, quotas were abolished on a further 18 per cent of tariff lines.

However, the design of the integration process, based as it is on 1990 import volumes and not values or actual quotas, gives quota-maintaining nations considerable flexibility. Many of the tariff lines for which the ATC requires integration do not actually have quotas, and, particularly during the initial stages, quota-maintaining nations can easily avoid integrating any tariff lines which involve quotas. For instance, in the first stage of integration, the United States did not abolish any quotas at all.

Table 11.3 reports the number of tariff lines under quota for China's exports to the United States and European Union. For comparison purposes, India's exports to those markets are also examined.[20] The figures in

[20] EU data for 1999 show that India was the largest supplier of textiles to Europe, exporting US$1.675 billion. China was a close second, with US$1.457 billion in exports. But China was by far the largest supplier of apparel to Europe, with US$6.315 billion in exports. India was in fourth place with US$1.664 billion in exports (*Textile Asia*, June 2000, p. 13).

table 11.3 differ for India and China. This result follows from the fact that
the European Union and United States do not apply the same restrictions
to each exporting country.

Table 11.3 confirms that the United States and European Union have
postponed liberalization of the majority of quotas until 1 January 2005,
the last date possible under the terms of the ATC. For instance, in respect
of China's exports to the United States, elimination of 86.5 per cent of
quotas by tariff line will wait until 1 January 2005, with only 13.5 per cent
liberalized before then. The United States does not restrict as many tariff
lines for imports from India, but less than 0.4 per cent of the restrictions
that India currently faces will be liberalized before 2005.

The same situation applies with respect to liberalization of quotas on
exports to the European Union. For quotas on exports from China, 535 or
73 per cent of the total 730 quota-restricted tariff lines will be integrated
into the GATT on 1 January 2005. Only 195 tariff lines with quotas will be
liberalized before then. India faces fewer restrictions, but will face most of
these restrictions until 2005. In India's case, 93 per cent of quotas will be
liberalized on 1 January 2005. Only 7 per cent of currently restricted tariff
lines will be liberalized before then.

The ATC requires that quota-maintaining nations integrate some tariff
lines from each of four product groups – yarns, fabrics, made-ups and
apparel – at each stage of the integration process. Table 11.4 shows how
US and EU integration programmes will affect quotas on apparel exports,
the most important product category for China. In addition, table 11.5
provides a breakdown for quotas on exports to the United States of clothing
and textile products made from wool. These tables show that exports of
clothing and woollen products are highly restricted.

Quota acceleration

In addition to requiring the abolition of quotas through the process of integrating tariff lines, the ATC also requires that quota-maintaining nations
increase the size of quotas that have not yet been abolished. As with the
provisions on quota integration, the method for increasing quotas gives
considerable leeway to quota-maintaining nations and is not as generous
to exporting countries as might be expected.

The ATC applies a 'growth-on-growth' formula for which the baseline
is the growth rate notified under Article 2.1. The formula stipulates three

Table 11.4 *Number of tariff lines under quota: apparel*

Market		China		India	
		Number	%	Number	%
US	Lines under quota in 2000	1,227	100	470	100
	Lines under quota in 2001	1,175	95.8	470	100
	Lines under quota 2002–5	1,018	83.0	470	100
	Lines under quota after 2005	0	0	0	0
EU	Lines under quota in 2000	294	100	109	100
	Lines under quota in 2001	264	89.8	109	100
	Lines under quota 2002–5	200	68.0	84	77.1
	Lines under quota after 2005	0	0	0	0

Sources: Author's compilation using data from http://otexa.ita.doc.gov/ fedreg/gatt94.htm, http://otexa.ita.doc.gov/fedreg/finalfr.htm, http://europa.eu. int/comm/trade/goods/textile/legitext2.htm and OJ 1996 No. L314, 4 December 1996, p. 1 and OJ 2000 No. L286, 11 November 2000, p. 1.

Table 11.5 *Number of tariff lines under quota: wool products (US market only)*

Market		China		India	
		Number	%	Number	%
US	Lines under quota in 2000	338	100	0	0
	Lines under quota in 2001	338	100	0	0
	Lines under quota 2002–5	338	100	0	0
	Lines under quota after 2005	0	0	0	0

Sources: Author's compilation using data from http://otexa.ita.doc.gov/fedreg/ gatt94.htm and http://otexa.ita.doc.gov/fedreg/finalfr.htm.

successive increases to the rate at which quotas grow. As outlined in ATC Article 2.13, 16 per cent increase in the growth rate of quotas occurs with the commencement of the first stage on 1 January 1995. In the second and third stages, quotas remaining in effect as at 1 January 1998 and 1 January

Table 11.6 *Effects of ATC acceleration on quota volumes and growth rates*

	Base rate of growth of quota		
	1%	6%	12%
Annual compound rate of growth 1995–2004, assuming ATC acceleration	1.5%	8.9%	17.7%
Increase in quota, 2004/1994, assuming ATC acceleration	16%	134%	411%
Increase in quota, 2004/1994, if no ATC acceleration	10%	79%	211%

Source: Author's calculations.

2002 have their annual growth rates increased by 25 per cent and 27 per cent respectively.

This 'growth-on-growth' formula benefits textile-exporting nations if the annual rates of growth which were notified and bound at the ATC's inception were already high. However, in reality the most commercially important categories of textiles and clothing had and have low rates of growth, sometimes below the old MFA's stipulated minimum 6 per cent growth rate. Quotas on many of China's exports to the United States and European Union have been growing at 1–2 per cent per annum.

Table 11.6 shows the effect of the ATC quota-acceleration process on quotas growing at 1, 6 and 12 per cent per annum respectively on the eve of the ATC's introduction. For quotas growing at an annual rate of 1 per cent, the acceleration programme has the effect of lifting that growth rate to just 1.5 per cent per annum over the life of the ATC. The quota itself will be 16 per cent bigger in 2004 than it was in 1994, but it would have been 10 per cent larger anyway without ATC's acceleration programme. However, table 11.6 also shows that the benefits of the acceleration programme improve as the base rates of quota growth increase.

Tables 11.7 to 11.9 examine the effects of the acceleration programme in the particular cases of China and India. Table 11.7 provides overall results, while tables 11.8 and 11.9 provide breakdowns based on apparel and woollen products. The quota growth rates in these tables reflect EU and US interpretations of their obligations to China. The most generous

Table 11.7 *Effects of ATC quota-acceleration programme: all clothing and textile products*

Market		China, as a WTO member		China, if no WTO membership		India	
		Number of tariffs under quota	Average annual growth rate of quotas (%)	Number of tariffs under quota	Average annual growth rate of quotas (%)	Number of tariffs under quota	Average annual growth rate of quotas (%)
US	2001 to 2002	2,015	1.7	2,067	1.7	777	8.6
	2002 to 2005	1,788	2.1	2,067	1.7	774	10.9
	After 2005	0	—	2,067	1.7	0	—
EU	2001 to 2002	677	2.1	730	1.9	369	5.0
	2002 to 2005	535	2.3	730	1.9	344	6.1
	After 2005	0	—	730	1.9	0	—

Sources: Author's calculations based on same sources as for tables 11.3 to 11.5, plus 'Summary of Current Agreements' at http://otexa.ita.doc.gov/sofa200.htm to .../sofa899.htm and Système Intégré de Gestion de Licenses (http://sigl.cec.eu.int/).

Table 11.8 *Effects of ATC quota-acceleration programme: apparel*

		Exporting country					
		China, as a WTO member		China, if no WTO membership		India	
Market		Number of tariffs under quota	Average annual growth rate of quotas (%)	Number of tariffs under quota	Average annual growth rate of quotas (%)	Number of tariffs under quota	Average annual growth rate of quotas (%)
US	2001 to 2002	1,175	1.4	1,227	1.4	470	8.6
	2002 to 2005	1,018	2.0	1,227	1.4	470	10.9
	After 2005	0	—	1,227	1.4	0	—
EU	2001 to 2002	264	2.8	294	2.5	109	7.1
	2002 to 2005	200	3.4	294	2.5	84	8.7
	After 2005	0	—	294	2.5	0	—

Sources: http://otexa.ita.gov/sofa200.htm to .../sofa899.htm and Système Intégré de Gestion de Licenses (http://sigl.cec.eu.int/).

Table 11.9 *Effects of ATC quota-acceleration programme: wool products (US market only)*

		Exporting country					
		China, as a WTO member		China, if no WTO membership		India	
Market		Number of tariffs under quota	Average annual growth rate of quotas (%)	Number of tariffs under quota	Average annual growth rate of quotas (%)	Number of tariffs under quota	Average annual growth rate of quotas (%)
Wool Products	2001 to 2002	338	0.7	338	0.6	0	—
	2002 to 2005	338	0.8	338	0.6	0	—
	After 2005	0	—	338	0.6	0	—

Sources: Author's calculations based on same sources as for tables 11.3 to 11.5, plus 'Summary of Current Agreements' at http://otexa.ita.doc.gov/sofa200.htm to .../sofa899.htm and Système Intégré de Gestion de Licenses (http://sigl.cec.eu.int/).

interpretation of the relevant text of China's Working Party Report would have resulted in the benefits of the first two stages of quota acceleration being passed on to China when it became a member on 11 December 2001. Accordingly, quota growth rates for China's products would have been immediately increased by a compound rate of 45 per cent on that date. However, the European Union and United States have not interpreted the Working Party text in this way and have refused to pass to China the benefits of the first stage of quota acceleration.[21] In addition, the United States has decided to grant to China only part of the benefits of the second stage.[22]

As a consequence, the effects on China's quota growth rates have been negligible, as the figures for overall textile and clothing products in table 11.7 show. In the short period between China's accession and the commencement of the third stage of quota acceleration on 1 January 2002, China's quota growth rates for exports to the European Union increased from 1.9 to 2.1 per cent, while there was virtually no impact on quota growth rates for exports to the United States. In comparison, India's quotas in the European Union and United States expanded by 5 per cent and 8.6 per cent respectively between 2001 and 2002.

With the third and final stage of quota acceleration on 1 January 2002, India enjoyed a further boost to its quota growth rates, while the effects for China continued to be more modest. According to the calculations in table 11.7, growth of India's quotas in the United States and European Union rose to 10.9 per cent and 6.1 per cent respectively, compared with growth rates of 2.1 per cent and 2.3 per cent for China.[23] The results highlight the

---

[21] The relevant text of China's Working Party Report says: 'To these base levels, the increase in growth rates provided for in Articles 2.13 and 2.14 of the ATC should be applied, *as appropriate*, from the date of China's accession' (my emphasis). The United States and European Union have emphasized the words 'as appropriate' in their responses.

[22] The US has pro-rated benefits under the second stage of quota acceleration to reflect the fact that China was a full member of the WTO for only twenty-one days of 2001. As a result, the second stage increase to China's quota growth rates in the United States was merely 1.4 per cent instead of the full 25 per cent. The European Union, by contrast, passed on the full 25 per cent increase.

[23] For some categories the rate of expansion of quotas will actually slow with the onset of the third stage in the acceleration process. For example, the available data show that the rate of growth of quotas for China's exports to the United States of silk products declined from 2 to 0.9 per cent. This result arises because quotas affecting some ninety-nine tariff lines have been abolished at the same time as the growth rates were increased. The quotas that were abolished were growing relatively quickly, while the remaining quotas were and are growing very slowly.

uneven – and in China's case, very small – effects of the ATC's quota acceleration programme.

EU and US strategies for quota liberalization

Information in the previous sections – plus other studies[24] – makes clear that both the European Union and the United States are waiting until 2005 before phasing out most of their import quotas. In doing so, neither the United States nor the European Union are breaking any rules that can be strictly interpreted. However, the ATC's preamble notes that quota integration should be progressive in nature, and Article 1.5 states that WTO members should allow for 'continuous autonomous industrial adjustment and increased competition in their markets'. By waiting until the end of the ATC before liberalizing most quotas, the United States and European Union are maintaining protection for their domestic industries as long as they possibly can, and arguably are slowing the process of autonomous industrial adjustment.

The lack of progressiveness in the quota phase-out programmes of both the United States and European Union might suggest that political leaders in those countries have no strategy for coping with the political reaction from domestic textile producers who suddenly find their quota protection terminated in 2005. Indeed, a cynical view of the ten-year duration of the ATC is expressed neatly by Laura Baughman et al.

> It is easy to see how such a long transition period found favour with importing countries. In effect the terms of office of most political leaders of importing countries is less than ten years (in the case of the US it is at most eight years). Thus for incumbents the decision to propose and/or support a ten-year transition period is an easy one: they will receive national and especially international accolades for enlightened statesmanship but know that most of the politically unpopular and economically disruptive costs of liberalisation will be postponed until after they leave office. Additionally, an incumbent has less incentive to pay attention to crafting an import liberalisation program.[25]

---

[24] e.g. L. Baughman, R. Mirus, M. E. Morkre and D. Spinanger, 'Of tyre cords, ties and tents: window dressing in the ATC?' (1997) 20(4) *World Economy* 407–34; D. Spinanger, 'Textiles beyond the MFA quota phase-out' (1999) 22(4) *World Economy* 455–76; CIE, *Barriers to Wool Fibre Products Trade*; François et al., *The Cost of EU Trade Protection*.

[25] Baughman et al., 'Of tyre cords, ties and tents', pp. 410–11.

Clothing and textile manufacturers in both the European Union and the United States are, however, well aware of the looming abolition of quotas required by the ATC.[26] The strategy of US and EU producers is to shift labour-intensive aspects of their operations abroad – usually to neighbouring countries with low wage levels – while retaining the more capital-intensive yarn- and fabric-making operations at home. Their governments are attempting to buy time for them. EU and US authorities are also providing incentives to domestic producers to shift parts of their operations to neighbouring countries.

In the US case, domestic producers are shifting sewing and assembly operations to Mexico, and also to Caribbean Basin countries. This activity has been assisted by the North American Free Trade Agreement (NAFTA), which allows duty- and quota-free treatment for clothing and textile imports from Mexico subject to strict rule of origin requirements. US apparel imports from Mexico increased by 611 per cent between 1 January 1994 – when NAFTA went into effect – and the end of 1998. Notably, the content of US yarns and fabric in clothing imported from Mexico and other parts of the western hemisphere is higher than for imports from Asia.

In addition to NAFTA, President Clinton signed into law Caribbean Basin Initiative (CBI) trade enhancement legislation in May 2000. This legislation allows for quota- and duty-free treatment of imports from Caribbean countries of clothing made from US fabrics and yarn. Similar though less attractive treatment was allowed for clothing made from Caribbean fabrics but stitched using US yarn. Up to twenty-four Caribbean Basin countries are eligible for the benefits of the legislation, depending on whether their customs procedures have been brought into line with US requirements.

European clothing and textile producers are also increasingly moving abroad labour-intensive sewing and assembly operations. European producers are choosing central and eastern European countries (CEECs), North Africa and Turkey as their preferred partners. In January 1998, the European Union eliminated all duties and quantitative restrictions on exports of clothing and textiles from CEECs. The European Union also provides incentives for outward processing using materials manufactured in the European Union.

[26] e.g. see letter to the USTR from the American Apparel Manufacturers Association (AAMA) of 7 February 2000, posted at www.americanapparel.org/News_FTR_Feb7.html. Also see AAMA statement, 'For the Record', on internet at www.amicanapparel. org/News_FTR_LM.html.

Labour costs in the countries benefiting from the trade diversionary effects of US and EU quotas and outward-processing arrangements are generally higher than labour costs in China, India, Pakistan and other major developing-country textile producers. Nevertheless, at least part of the sewing and assembly operations shifted from the European Union and the United States to these preferred locations will survive the ATC-mandated removal of quota restraints on imports from relatively efficient producers such as China. One of the advantages that these locations possess is proximity to markets, a factor which can be important for retailers in an environment of rapidly changing fashions and trends and just-in-time inventory management. In addition, the special textiles and product safeguards that will apply to China for some years after it joins the WTO will continue to foster some uncertainty among traders about the advisability of sourcing products from China.

Tariff reciprocity and the European Union's focus on Article 7

Another thread to the strategy of quota nations for coping with the phasing out of textile quotas is to emphasize that the exporting nations should also lower their own barriers to textile imports, especially tariff barriers. Textiles and clothing tariffs are generally higher in developing countries than in the European Union or United States.[27] The European Union, in particular, has made this demand. To advance its argument, the EU cites the ATC's Article 7, which requires in broad terms that WTO members improve market access for trade in textiles and clothing products.

The European Union has explicitly linked the pace of its own quota-integration programme under the ATC to improvements in access to the markets of the clothing-exporting nations.[28] Indeed, the European Union adopted a new strategy for opening bilateral negotiations with third countries on 9 November 2000. It announced this strategy at the same time as it published a list of products for the ATC's third stage of quota integration to commence on 1 January 2002. As part of the strategy, the European Union is prepared to offer faster quota phase-out than outlined in its third-stage

---

[27] Though Baughman et al., 'Of tyre cords, ties and tents' note at 409 that EU and US tariffs on textile products are higher than tariffs on other manufactures.

[28] See, for example, EU Commission statements posted at http://europa.eu.int/comm/ trade/pdf/ tlm.pdf and http://europa.eu.int/comm/trade/goods/textile/whatson02b.htm.

list to countries that are prepared to reduce their own barriers on imports from the European Union.

The European Union has backed up its arguments with studies examining tariff barriers to its exports of clothing and textiles,[29] but the argument that other WTO members are not meeting obligations under Article 7 has limited applicability in the case of China, at least for now. China will, as part of its accession commitments, lower the simple average tariff for 1,054 tariff lines in HS Chapters 50 and 63 (which encompass products in the ATC) from around 27 per cent to just under 12 per cent, a reduction of over 50 per cent in China's clothing and textile tariffs.

Motivations for joining the WTO

The statistics discussed above suggest one reason why, in late 1998, China decided to reinvigorate its efforts to join the WTO. Between 1995 and 1998, work on China's WTO application essentially stalled, as China was unwilling to make concessions attractive enough to its negotiating partners in the WTO.[30] But by late 1998 China's leaders were renewing their interest in the Organization. This renewed interest stemmed from a range of political, economic and strategic considerations, one of which may have been the threatened loss of competitiveness of China's clothing and textile exporters if China did not join the WTO soon. Under that situation, competitors with WTO membership would benefit from quota integration and acceleration while China would not. For example, if China had not joined the WTO by 2002, it would have faced US quotas on 2,067 tariff lines with quota growth averaging 1.7 per cent per year, compared with India, which would face US quotas on 774 tariff lines with quota growth at 10.9 per cent per year (table 11.7, above).

Chinese policy-makers may also have been conscious of the increasing competitiveness of Mexico, Caribbean nations, North Africa and the CEECs in US and EU markets. In addition, the European Union has promised

---

[29] See e.g. F. Dehousse, K. Ghemar and T. Iotsova, *Market Access Analysis to Identify Barriers in China and Russia Affecting the EU Textiles Industry: Final Report*, Centre d'Etudes Economiques et Institutionnelles (Brussels, 2000); background notes posted at http://europa.eu.int/comm/trade/goods/textile/legis.htm, and comparative tariff analysis posted at http://europa.eu.int/comm/trade/goods/textile/texttarif.htm.

[30] At the same time, China unilaterally cut tariffs, from a simple average of 35.6 per cent in July 1995, to 16.5 per cent in January 1999. None the less, many important non-tariff barriers remained in place.

to provide duty- and quota-free access to its market to forty-eight least-developed countries. These countries include Bangladesh, which is a large exporter of textiles and clothing and which already benefits from duty-free access to EU markets under the generalized system of preferences.

While important, the significance of this motivation for China to join the WTO should not be over-emphasized. Textiles make up around 25 per cent of China's exports, and quota-maintaining nations take approximately 25 per cent of China's textile exports. In other words, textile-quota liberalization would affect exports currently amounting to 6.25 per cent of China's total merchandise exports. As other markets where quotas are not used are also important outlets for China, China's State Textile Industry Bureau (STIB) does not expect large overnight increases in textile exports as a result of China's accession.[31] None the less, the potential exists for the proportion of China's exports occupied by textile exports to the United States and European Union to increase as the restrictions are removed.

Four safeguards

In addition to quotas, prior to joining the WTO China's textiles exports were subject to safeguards (or 'consultation provisions') in bilateral agreements with the United States and European Union. Since joining the WTO, these bilateral safeguards were replaced by no less than four separate measures. The first is Article XIX of the GATT (titled 'Emergency action on imports of particular products'). Importantly, however, the conditions for using Article XIX are relatively strict, and Article XIX cannot be used to discriminate against particular countries. Use of Article XIX is also governed by the detailed WTO Agreement on Safeguards.

Secondly, Article 6 of the ATC provides for a transitional safeguard for clothing and textile products not yet integrated into GATT rules. As at the end of 1997, forty-three WTO members retained the right to use this safeguard, including the four quota-maintaining members. The transitional safeguard can be applied for a duration of three years or until the affected product lines are integrated into the GATT, whichever comes first, and it will not be available after 2005. If the duration of the safeguard exceeds one year, then the restraint level must rise by at least 6 per cent in each subsequent year. In contrast to Article XIX of the GATT, the transitional

---

[31] Author's discussions with STIB, April 2000.

safeguard may be applied in a discriminatory manner against imports from particular countries.

Thirdly, China alone among WTO members will be subject to a textiles-specific safeguard for products covered by the ATC.[32] China agreed this safeguard would be available to WTO members until 31 December 2008, or up to four years after the ATC terminates and quotas on its products are completely phased out. A ninety-day consultation period applies to this safeguard, during which China is expected to hold its exports of affected textile products to a level no greater than 7.5 per cent above the amount entered during the first twelve months of the fourteen months preceding the month in which the request for consultations with China was made.[33] If no satisfactory agreement is reached after ninety days, the WTO member requesting consultations with China can continue the safeguard until the end of the calendar year, or up to one full year if the consultations were called during the last three months of the calendar year.

WTO members will be able to use this safeguard measure prior to 2005, potentially impairing the increased market access that China will enjoy as a result of the immediate liberalization of US and EU tariff lines already integrated into the GATT at the time of its accession. The absence of quota protection on these tariff lines may encourage the United States and European Union to use the China-specific textiles safeguard instead.

Fourthly, in addition to facing its own specific textiles safeguard, China's exports will also be subject to a product-specific safeguard, which will be available to members for up to twelve years after China's accession. The requirements for using this China-specific product safeguard are more rigorous than the textiles-specific safeguard that China faces, but not more rigorous than requirements for Article XIX of the GATT. However, no restriction exists on the type of penalties that may be imposed under the product safeguard, although the safeguard is supposed to remedy and not overcompensate for market disruption. Restrictions should not be imposed for longer than is necessary to prevent or remedy the market disruption.

---

[32] See Working Party Report, para. 242, which by virtue of para. 342 of the WP Report and Article 2 of the Protocol is incorporated into the Protocol.

[33] In the case of wool products, China is expected to limit annual growth to 6 per cent. The lower growth rate for wool products reflects the fact that wool and wool products have traditionally been relatively sensitive and highly protected in the US market. See also tables 11.5 and 11.9, above.

China has the right to suspend the application of equivalent concessions to the country using the product-specific safeguard after two years if the safeguard was instituted in response to an increase in the market share of China's exports, or after three years if the safeguard was used in response to an absolute increase in China's exports to the country concerned.

Will the China-specific safeguards be used?

The back-loading evident in the phase-out programmes of quota-maintaining nations, the abruptness with which the majority of quotas will be terminated as a result of that back-loading, and the attempts by the United States and European Union to give their domestic producers as much time and leeway as possible to restructure, all suggest that the EU and US will be inclined to use available measures to assist their domestic producers. After all, China is the world's single largest clothing-exporting nation and is one of the main competitive threats to producers in the United States and European Union.

An important feature of the textile and product safeguards included in China's WTO accession agreements is that these safeguards will be easier to invoke than either the ATC transitional safeguard or Article XIX of the GATT. This feature also increases the chances that the European Union and United States will use the China-specific safeguards, as does the history of application of the ATC transitional safeguard. In the ATC's first year, the transitional safeguard was invoked on twenty-four occasions, all by the United States. In the second year, 1996, the United States invoked it once, and in 1997 twice.

What effect will the safeguards have?

Though the history and political economy of quota liberalization in the importing countries suggests that the China-specific safeguards will often be used, their coverage and restrictiveness is not as great as the textile quotas that will be eliminated by 2005. It would be impractical – and would provoke serious friction and debate in WTO councils – for the United States or other members to place a safeguard on each and every category of products that was formerly subject to quotas.

In any case, the 7.5 per cent growth rate required under the China-specific textiles safeguard (or 6 per cent in the case of wool products) compares favourably with existing growth rates for quotas on China's products. Quotas on China's textile exports to the United States and European Union have been growing at a rate of 1.7 per cent and 1.9 per cent per year respectively (table 11.7, above). Quotas on wool product exports to the United States have been growing at 0.6 per cent (table 11.9, above), just one-tenth of the minimum allowable rate under the China-specific textiles safeguard. Thus, although that safeguard is unwelcome for China, it will not impede an increase in the general rate of export growth compared with the situation under the existing quotas.

A safe conclusion would appear to be that in the period after quotas have been abolished (by 2005) but before the textiles and product safeguards end (in December 2008 and December 2013 respectively), China's textile exports will have scope for growth rates which are moderately higher than at present. Growth rates will be held back to some extent by the ad hoc application of safeguards, and the threat of safeguard actions may discourage US and EU retailers from sourcing their products from China. None the less, China's competitive position, in terms of regulatory barriers in key export markets, will improve after quotas are abolished by 2005.

Conclusions

China is facing an increasingly competitive situation in world textile markets. It is the largest clothing- and textile-exporting nation now, but other suppliers are increasing their market share in the United States and European Union, in part as a result of the uneven application of trade liberalization measures. Preferential trading arrangements and geographical proximity are increasing the competitiveness of nations adjacent to the European Union and the United States, but WTO member nations such as India and Pakistan are also enjoying decreases in barriers as a result of the application of the ATC. Given these trends, China needs WTO membership to maintain its market share with respect to trading partners that currently maintain quotas, as quotas on imports from China would not have been proscribed if it had remained outside the Organization.

The trend of rising competition will also erode the value of quota rents currently received by China. In the improbable event that the value of those rents exceeded the benefits that China would obtain from the dismantling of barriers on its exports, any such cost-benefit outcome is unlikely to hold true beyond the next few years.

Thus, China had a real economic imperative to join the WTO. Its reasons for joining were not limited to the diplomatic and symbolic gains associated with its desire to become a full and equal partner in a major international organization, as is sometimes suggested. Staying outside would have had significant adverse implications for China's clothing and textiles producers.

The immediate benefits of the ATC for China are, in and of themselves, not great. The vast majority of China's quota-restricted clothing and textile exports to the European Union and United States will remain under quota until 2005. Even after quotas are eliminated, China will still be subject to discriminatory safeguards and, not outlined here, anti-dumping methodologies. But China's leaders are likely to have taken a long-term view. The discriminatory barriers featured in the terms of China's WTO accession will not last forever (twelve to fifteen years) and have sunset clauses.

In summary, China needed to join the WTO just to stay competitive and cannot look forward to major overnight gains from membership. The clothing and textile industry will certainly not be the fastest-growing sector of China's economy during these first years of its participation, at least until 2005. WTO membership will, however, pave the way for substantially improved export opportunities for China's textile industry in the longer term.

12

China and the Agreement on Technical Barriers to Trade

ICHIRO ARAKI

Introduction

The Agreement on Technical Barriers to Trade (TBT Agreement) sets out rules to be observed by WTO members in their administration of technical regulations and standards, as well as conformity assessment procedures. Under the TBT Agreement, technical regulation is defined as a 'document which lays down product characteristics or their related processes and production methods, including the applicable administrative provisions, with which compliance is mandatory'. The Agreement further notes that technical regulations 'may also include or deal exclusively with terminology, symbols, packaging, marking or labelling requirements as they apply to a product, process or production method'.[1]

The TBT Agreement defines a product or process standard as a 'document approved by a recognized body that provides, for common and repeated use, rules, guidelines or characteristics for products or related processes and production methods, with which compliance is not mandatory'. As in the case of technical regulations, the Agreement further notes that standards 'may also include or deal exclusively with terminology, symbols, packaging, marking or labelling requirements as they apply to a product, process or production method'.[2] Conformity assessment procedures are defined as 'any procedure used, directly or indirectly, to determine that relevant requirements in technical regulations or standards are fulfilled'. The Agreement further notes that 'conformity assessment procedures include, *inter alia*, procedures for sampling, testing and inspection; evaluation, verification

---

[1] TBT Agreement, Annex 1, para. 1.   [2] Ibid., para. 2.

and assurance of conformity; registration, accreditation and approval as well as their combinations'.[3]

Trade negotiators have long been aware that national and local rules governing technical regulations, standards and conformity assessment procedures can be used, intentionally or unintentionally, as trade barriers against foreign products. This is the reason why the old Agreement on Technical Barriers to Trade (Standards Code) was negotiated in the Tokyo Round.

At the conclusion of the Tokyo Round, the director-general of the General Agreement on Tariffs and Trade (GATT) observed as follows, explaining the rationale behind the newly negotiated Standards Code:

> Technical regulations are essential in modern society. They are adopted to protect human and animal life and health; to ensure that products offered to the consumer meet the necessary levels of quality, purity, technical efficiency and adequacy to perform the function for which they are intended; to protect the environment; and for reasons connected with safety; national security; and the prevention of deceptive practices.
>
> However, international trade can be complicated and inhibited by disparities between regulations, adopted at local, State, national or regional levels; by insufficient information on the often complex and detailed requirements; by the introduction of regulations without allowing time for producers, especially foreign ones, to adjust their production; by frequent changes to regulations which create uncertainty; by the drawing up of regulations in terms of design rather than performance in order to suit the production methods of domestic suppliers, thus causing difficulties to suppliers using different techniques; by exacting testing requirements; by the denial of access to certification systems; and finally by the manipulation of regulations, testing or certification to discriminate against imports. The problem has been to strike a balance between the essential needs referred to in the preceding paragraph and the demand of exporters that their goods should not unreasonably or unfairly be excluded from the market.[4]

This explanation is still valid today. These considerations were also the driving force behind the new Agreement on Technical Barriers to Trade, negotiated in the Uruguay Round.

The new TBT Agreement builds upon the old Standards Code, making it a more effective tool for preventing technical regulations, standards

---

[3] Ibid., para. 3.

[4] GATT Secretariat, *The Tokyo Round of Multilateral Trade Negotiations*, report by the director-general of GATT (Geneva, 1979), p. 62.

and conformity assessment procedures from being used as a means of arbitrary or unjustifiable discrimination between countries where the same conditions prevail or as a disguised restriction on international trade.

The most significant feature of the new TBT Agreement is that the new dispute settlement mechanism under the Dispute Settlement Understanding, with its enhanced automaticity and stronger enforcement, is applicable to it.[5] One might question then why there have been so few disputes involving technical barriers to trade adjudicated under the DSU. This presents a stark contrast with the Agreement on the Application of Sanitary and Phytosanitary Measures (SPS Agreement). The SPS Agreement, which was newly negotiated in the Uruguay Round as a companion to the TBT Agreement, has been invoked in a number of controversial disputes, including the famous *Beef Hormones* case.[6]

This is not to say that there has been no complaint where the TBT Agreement was formally invoked. Starting with the *Gasoline* case,[7] the very first case to reach the Appellate stage, a number of complaining parties alleged violations of the TBT Agreement as part of their claims. However, to date, there has been no case where a dispute settlement panel found violation of the TBT Agreement. In many cases, parties reached a mutually agreed solution before the panel was established or even when it was established, before it made a definitive ruling on TBT issues. In other cases, panels declined to rule on TBT issues for the sake of judicial economy.[8]

Recently, Canada alleged violation of the TBT Agreement in its complaint against the European Communities on asbestos. Again, the panel avoided a ruling on the TBT Agreement, arguing that a general ban on asbestos was not a 'technical regulation' within the meaning of the TBT Agreement.[9] Although this part of the panel's finding was reversed by the Appellate Body, which found that the measure, viewed as an integrated whole, constituted a 'technical regulation' under the TBT Agreement, the Appellate Body

---

[5] TBT Agreement, Art. 14.

[6] WTO Panel and Appellate Body Reports, *EC Measures Concerning Meat and Meat Products (Hormones)*, WT/DS26/R/USA, WT/DS48/R/CAN, WT/DS26/AB/R, WT/DS48/AB/R, adopted 13 February 1998.

[7] WTO Panel and Appellate Body Reports, *United States – Standards for Reformulated and Conventional Gasoline*, WT/DS2/R, WT/DS2/AB/R, adopted 20 May 1996.

[8] See, for instance, the Panel Report in the *Gasoline* case, at para. 6.43: 'In view of its findings under the General Agreement, the Panel concluded that it was not necessary to decide on issues raised under the TBT Agreement.'

[9] WTO Panel Report, *European Communities – Measures Affecting Asbestos and Asbestos-containing Products*, WT/DS135/R, adopted 5 April 2001, para. 8.72.

declined from examining Canada's specific claims regarding the violation of the TBT Agreement due to the lack of an adequate factual basis.[10]

However, the fact that there have been no violation findings on the TBT Agreement does not diminish its utility. As Craig Thorn and Marinn Carlson argue, 'the most important provisions of the TBT Agreement are those relating to procedural requirements, and the Agreement's principal (not insignificant) contribution to the international trading system has been to promote transparency and information exchange'.[11]

TBT issues in China

In view of China's long history of state control over economic activities, it is not surprising that many foreign traders doing business in China have complained about the lack of transparency in, and the discriminatory nature of, China's technical regulations, standards and conformity assessment systems. For instance, the United States trade representative pointed out a number of TBT issues as trade barriers of China in the 2000 National Trade Estimates (NTE) Report:

> It is often difficult to ascertain what inspection requirements apply to a particular import, as China's framework of import standards is not fully developed. Moreover, the United States and other countries have complained that safety and inspection procedures applied to foreign products are more rigorous than those applied to domestic products. Foreign suppliers have also had difficulty in learning exactly how and who conducts inspections.

Inspection standards

Chinese law provides that all goods subject to inspection by law or according to the terms of a contract must be inspected prior to importation.

China maintains statutory inspection requirements known as 'conformity assessment procedures' on about 800 imported goods, and an even greater number of exported products. Chinese buyers or their purchase agents must register for inspection of imported goods at the port of entry. The scope of inspection includes quality, technical specifications, quantity, weight, packaging, and safety requirements.

---

[10] WTO Appellate Body Report, *European Communities – Measures Affecting Asbestos and Asbestos-containing Products*, WT/DS135/AB/R, adopted 5 April 2001, para. 83.

[11] Craig Thorn and Marinn Carlson, 'The Agreement on the Application of Sanitary and Phytosanitary Measures and the Agreement on Technical Barriers to Trade' (2002) 31(3) *Law and Policy in International Business* 841–54, at 842.

Quality licenses

For manufactured goods, China requires that a quality license be issued before the goods can be imported into China. Obtaining quality licenses is a time-consuming process. While requirements vary according to the product, U.S. exporters have complained that they are burdensome and contrary to principles of national treatment.

Safety licenses

China also imposes safety licensing requirements on certain products under the terms of the 'Import and Export Commodity Inspection Law' of 1989. National health and quarantine regulations in addition require that all imported (but not domestic) food items be marked with a laser sticker as evidence of the product's safety. Importers are charged between 5 and 7 cents per sticker. Major problems with China's safety licensing system include the lack of transparency, lack of national treatment, difficulty in determining relevant standards. Examples include:

Electronic products. On January 1, 1999 China imposed mandatory safety inspections for imports of electronic products, including personal computers, monitors, printers, switches, television sets, and stereo equipment. As of January 1, 2000, these same products require an import commodity safety license.

Cosmetic regulations. In mid 1999, the Ministry of Health imposed strict testing standards on imports of cosmetic products containing sunscreens, skin lighteners or hair restorers. Industry sources say the testing requirements create an effective import barrier, as they require individual testing requirements for each individual product containing one of the regulated substances, making them expensive to carry out.[12]

Many trading partners of China also shared these concerns. For instance, a report published by Japan's trade ministry has made the following observation:

In China, different authorities or institutions are in charge of product inspections depending on whether the product is domestic or imported. The standards by which products are inspected often lack transparency. When pressed to create a uniform system, China claims that this dual certification regime is non-discriminatory because common standards are used. Applying common

---

[12] Office of the United States Trade Representative, *2000 National Trade Estimate Report on Foreign Trade Barriers* (available from the USTR website at http://www.ustr.gov/html/ 2000_contents/html).

standards alone, however, is not enough. There must also be common procedures for certification and a single authority inspecting both imports and domestic goods. Otherwise, it will be difficult to allay suspicion that imported products are more rigorously inspected and thus discriminated against. We hope that China will undertake active efforts in this regard, especially given the peculiarity of the dual certification system by international standards. Certification standards and procedures, including the detailed implementations, should be published, and should take international standards into account in accordance with the TBT Agreement.

The Sino-Japanese bilateral negotiations [of September 1997] resulted in a commitment from China to improve specific features of its standards and certification regime upon accession. The industries involved, however, report that there have been no significant improvements, even in the simplification of procedures requiring redundant markings (Great Wall Mark, CCIB Mark) for consumer electronics. Japan urges China to adhere faithfully to its commitments in the Sino-Japanese Agreement. These issues will need to be taken up during the negotiations on the protocol issues.[13]

Indeed, these issues were considered by the Working Party on the Accession of China. In particular, the discussions on TBT issues were given a high priority after the work on the Accession Protocol and the Working Party Report was reactivated in March 2000.

The starting point of their discussion was the text of the draft Protocol, which had remained unchanged since May 1997. The draft Protocol provided as follows:

Standards and technical regulations

1. The list of *[import]* products subject to statutory inspection in China, together with the applicable technical regulations and standards, the objective which they fulfil and their necessity to fulfil those objectives, are specified in Annex 7 of this Protocol.
2. China's standards, technical regulations and conformity assessment procedures shall be based *[, to the maximum extent possible,]* on relevant international standards, where they exist, except where use of different standards, technical regulations and conformity assessment procedures are justified to the TBT Committee pursuant to Article 2.4 of the TBT Agreement as

---

[13] Industrial Structure Council, *Report on the WTO Consistency of Trade Policies by Major Trading Partners* (Tokyo, 2000), pp. 296–7 (available from the website of the Ministry of Economy, Trade and Industry at http://www.meti.go.jp/english/report/index.html). See also Working Party Report, WT/MIN(01)/3, para. 196.

necessary to fulfil: the legitimate objective of national security; prevention of deceptive practices; or protection of human health or safety, animal or plant life or health, or the environment. Any such standards, technical regulations and conformity assessment procedures shall be administered so as not to create unnecessary barriers to trade. Government inspection agencies shall not apply to imported products compulsory standards which relate solely to fulfilling unspecified criteria of quality, quantity, or weight, nor apply statutory inspection to products by reason of the volume of such imports.

3. China shall publish in the official journal complete commodity inspection criteria, whether formal or informal.

4. *Government-mandated inspection agencies shall not inspect imported products for compliance with the terms of commercial contracts.*

5. China may inspect imported products and/or require conformity assessment only upon justification that third-party testing or certification is not able to fulfil the legitimate objectives listed in the TBT Agreement. *[Pending the conclusion of a Mutual Recognition Agreement with the WTO Member concerned, China shall comply with Article 6 of the TBT Agreement.]*

6. China shall not maintain requirements which have the effect of acting as barriers to the operation of foreign and joint-venture commodity inspection agencies.

7. In implementing the TBT Agreement, China shall submit its Statement on Implementation and Administration of the Agreement (Article 15.2 of the TBT Agreement) in line with the relevant Decisions adopted by the Committee on Technical Barriers to Trade of the Tokyo Round Agreement on Technical Barriers to Trade (TBT/16/Rev.7).

8. Further to China's application of the provisions of the GATT 1994 and the TBT Agreement 1994, China shall *[, by [x date],]* eliminate the two-tiered system used for imports and domestic products, and otherwise consolidate the standards, technical regulations and conformity assessment procedures (e.g. testing, inspection, certification, quality system registration, laboratory accreditation) to ensure that the same measures applied to domestic production are applied to imports and in the same way.[14]

---

[14] *Inside U.S. Trade*, 14 March 1997. The text is also available to the subscribers of World Trade Online ('Around the World, China'), http://insidetrade.com. The text was distributed to members of the Working Party on the understanding that 'those positions on which there is substantial agreement are reproduced in bold type. Those which have not yet been fully discussed or on which there is not yet agreement appear in italics and/or in brackets.' There were no bold-type parts in section 15 of the draft Protocol, indicating that there was not yet substantial agreement on the whole issue. Those parts which were particularly controversial were indicated with italics and/or brackets in accordance with the understanding above.

While these provisions served as certain indicators of various difficulties encountered by non-Chinese economic operators, many delegates felt that the language used in this part of the draft Protocol was imprecise and lacked coherence. This chapter now briefly describes the ensuing Working Party process regarding TBT issues, highlighting the changes that were made to the 1997 draft Protocol.

Statutory inspection

Paragraph 1 of the draft Protocol related to the practice of the State Administration for Entry–Exit Inspection and Quarantine of China (CIQ-SA), where many imported and exported products are subjected to inspection at the port of entry or exit, as described in the USTR Report above. While this was an important issue, many delegates felt that placing this at the top of the section on TBT in the Protocol was not appropriate. In particular, if the Working Party were to endorse the content of Annex 7, it was feared that it might send a wrong signal to the Chinese side by creating the appearance that Annex 7 had a special legal status. 'Statutory inspection' is a terminology unique to China, and the listing does not have any legal significance apart from providing information for transparency purposes. Furthermore, the listing did not represent the entire gamut of technical regulations in China.

For these reasons, the Working Party decided to move the content of this paragraph to a section on TBT in the Working Party Report. Accordingly, Annex 7 was removed from the Protocol, and transcribed into separate notification lists expressly said by the Working Party Report not to prejudice the legal status of the measures.[15]

Harmonization with international standards

Paragraph 2 of the draft Protocol was essentially a restatement of the provisions of Article 2.4 of the TBT Agreement.[16] However, China and the

---

[15] See Working Party Report, para. 190, referring to WT/ACC/CHN/31 and WT/ACC/CHN/32. Following this deletion, Annex 8 (Reservations by WTO Members) in the draft Protocol was renumbered as Annex 7.

[16] Article 2.4 provides as follows: 'Where technical regulations are required and relevant international standards exist or their completion is imminent, Members shall use them, or the relevant parts of them, as a basis for their technical regulations except when such international standards

members of the Working Party were not able to reach consensus on the bracketed language. China insisted on the inclusion of the phrase 'to the maximum extent possible', and many Working Party members were opposed to the inclusion of this phrase.

This issue was part of the more general discussion regarding China's status as a developing country. China argued that since as a developing country it was entitled to the 'special and differential treatment' provisions of the TBT Agreement (Articles 12.4 and 12.8 in particular), it was unreasonable for the Working Party members to expect immediate and full harmonization with relevant international standards by China. China also pointed out that even those developed countries that were asking for deletion of this phrase themselves maintained some technical regulations that were not based on international standards. At the same time, China stressed that it intended to comply fully with the requirement of the TBT Agreement upon accession.

In response to this argument, some members of the Working Party sought explicit commitment by China not to invoke Articles 12.4 and 12.8. As was expected, China refused to accommodate this request, claiming that the issue of developing-country status was a matter of principle. However, as a practical matter, China said that it had no intention of seeking exceptions from the obligations under the TBT Agreement. China also stressed that, since 1980, the country had taken the active adoption of international standards as a basic policy for accelerating industrial modernization and promoting economic growth. According to China, due to its efforts in the past twenty years, the rate of adoption of international standards had been raised from 23 per cent to 40 per cent.

In view of these exchanges, it became futile for the Working Party to pursue a mutually acceptable language on the basis of paragraph 2 of the draft Protocol. Members of the Working Party worked to draft appropriate Working Party Report language, which would accommodate the two sides' positions. The final Protocol says only that China will comply with the TBT Agreement but is silent upon the right to have recourse to Article 12. The Working Party Report contains a commitment to increase the use of international standards by 10 per cent in five years.[17]

---

or relevant parts would be an ineffective or inappropriate means for fulfilment of the legitimate objectives pursued, for instance because of fundamental climatic or geographical factors or fundamental technological problems.'

[17] Working Party Report, para. 184.

Transparency

Paragraph 3 of the draft Protocol is essentially a transparency provision. Although the issue of transparency is dealt with elsewhere in the Protocol in a more general manner, it was considered necessary to reiterate the importance of transparency in TBT issues, in view of the current lack thereof in China. With modifications to make it more consistent with the TBT Agreement, this became section 13.1 of the final Protocol.

Commercial contracts

During the protocol negotiations in 1997, paragraph 4 was bracketed, reflecting the disagreement about whether China should be able to continue its practice of inspecting imported products to verify compliance with the terms of commercial contracts. China argued that government-mandated inspection agencies (CIQ-SA in particular) should be allowed to carry out such inspections when the parties to the contracts so request.

The agreed compromise in the final Protocol includes commitments by China that conformity assessment bodies will determine the conformity of imported goods with commercial terms of contracts only if authorized by the parties to such contract and that such inspections will not affect customs clearance or the granting of import licences for such goods.

Conformity assessment

China and the members of the Working Party agreed that paragraph 5 of the draft Protocol should be made more generic. The final Protocol includes a statement that China will apply conformity assessment procedures to imported goods to determine compliance with technical regulations and standards that are consistent with the provisions of the Protocol and the WTO Agreement.[18]

Regarding mutual recognition, the content of the bracketed sentence in paragraph 5 was deleted. It was clearly unnecessary. The Working Party Report was amended to include a note of the obligation applying under Article 6.1.

---

[18] Protocol, section 13.3.

Foreign commodity inspection agencies

Paragraph 6 of the draft Protocol dealt with the issue of foreign commodity inspection agencies. It was deleted from the Protocol but became the basis for paragraph 195 of the Working Party Report.

TBT Committee

The obligations relating to China's obligation *vis-à-vis* the TBT Committee of the WTO, contained in paragraph 7 of the draft Protocol, were made more comprehensive and included in paragraph 177 of the Working Party Report rather than in the Protocol.

Two-tier system

This was the most controversial issue in the whole TBT negotiations. As discussed in the Japanese report cited above, imported products were subject to inspection and certification by CIQ-SA, while domestic products were subject to a separate standards and certification regime under the auspices of the China State Bureau of Technical Supervision (CSBTS).

Although paragraph 8 of the draft Protocol referred to China's commitment to 'eliminate the two-tiered system used for imports and domestic products, and otherwise consolidate the standards, technical regulations and conformity assessment procedures', it was never clear what was meant by this paragraph. Did it mean that China had to unify the two regimes operated by CIQ-SA and CSBTS into a unitary system of technical regulations, standards and conformity assessment procedures? Or was it sufficient for China to accord national treatment to imported products while maintaining the coexistence of CIQ-SA and CSBTS?

Many members of the Working Party took the former view, while China adhered to the latter view, claiming that how to allocate responsibilities among different administrative agencies was a sovereign decision of China and that asking for more than national treatment would be a 'WTO-plus' requirement.

The negotiations thus seemed to have reached a stalemate at one point. However, after months of negotiations, a compromise was formulated in the spring of 2001 with the following elements:

- Upon accession, China will ensure that the same standards, technical regulations and conformity assessment procedures are applied to both imported and domestic products.
- Upon accession, China will ensure that all certification bodies and agencies are authorized to undertake certification of both imported and domestic products.
- All inspection bodies and agencies will be authorized to undertake inspection for both imported and domestic goods (after a certain transition period).
- The choice of body or agency will be at the discretion of the applicant.
- With respect to the treatment of imported and domestic products, all bodies and agencies will issue the same mark and charge the same fee. They will also provide the same processing periods and complaint procedures for imported and domestic products. Imported products will not be subject to more than one conformity assessment.
- [After a certain transition period,] China will assign the respective responsibilities of its authorizing bodies solely on the basis of the type of product without any consideration of the origin of such product, *and will authorize only one body to oversee all conformity assessment bodies and procedures falling within a particular assigned scope of responsibility.*[19]

Following a further agreement that the first of the transition periods referred to above would be twelve months and the second would be eighteen months, this compromise became section 13.4 of the final Protocol (with the exception of the italicized part, which was perhaps considered unnecessary because of the merger of CIQ-SA and CSBTS into the State General Administration for Quality Supervision and Inspection and Quarantine (AQSIQ)).[20]

Thus, the whole negotiations on TBT issues reached a close.

Conclusion

On one view, it is not necessary to dwell too much upon what was being debated during the negotiations. It may even be harmful to record too

[19] Elements of a 'non-paper' distributed among interested delegations within the Working Party at the final phase of the negotiations. The original document is on file with the author.
[20] Working Party Report, para. 188.

much of a subjective negotiating history in view of the principles of treaty interpretation enshrined in Article 31 of the Vienna Convention, which is so often cited by the Appellate Body. After all, China acceded to the WTO Agreement on terms that were agreed between China and the WTO.[21] Those terms are set out in the Protocol and the Working Party Report. If a dispute arises regarding the interpretation of those terms, one should rely on the ordinary meaning of the terms in light of the context, as well as the object and purpose of the Accession Protocol. What was at the back of the negotiators' mind is not relevant.

However, as a personal note, it was interesting to observe case law being developed by the Appellate Body, while the same type of issue was being debated at the Working Party – on the issue of the two-tier system. Many members of the Working Party cited the precedent of the *Section 337* case[22] in support of their position that the very existence of the two-tier system (CIQ-SA for imports and CSBTS for domestic products) was in violation of the national-treatment requirement under Article III of the GATT because it was origin-based distinction and was per se illegal.

The panel in the *Korea – Beef* case held a similar view. The Panel Report stated that 'any regulatory distinction that is based exclusively on criteria relating to the nationality or the origin of the product is incompatible with Article III and this conclusion can be reached even in the absence of any imports (as hypothetical imports can be used to reach this conclusion) confirming that there is no need to demonstrate the actual and specific trade effects of a measure for it to be found in violation of Article III'.[23] The Appellate Body reversed this part of the panel's finding. According to the Appellate Body, a formal difference in treatment between imported and like domestic product was neither necessary nor sufficient to show a violation of Article III:4. Whether or not imported products are treated less 'favourably' than like domestic products should be assessed instead by examining whether a measure modifies the condition of competition in the relevant market to the detriment of imported products.[24]

---

[21] Marrakesh Agreement Establishing the World Trade Organization, Art. XII.1.

[22] *United States – Section 337 of the Tariff Act of 1937*, GATT Panel Report, adopted 7 November 1989, BISD 36S/345.

[23] WTO Panel Report, *Korea – Measures Affecting Imports of Fresh, Chilled and Frozen Beef*, WT/DS161/R, WT/DS169/R, adopted 10 January 2001, para. 627.

[24] WTO Appellate Body Report, *Korea – Measures Affecting Imports of Fresh, Chilled and Frozen Beef*, WT/DS161/AB/R, WT/DS169/AB/R, adopted 10 January 2001, paras. 137–8.

Had China maintained the two-tier system, a WTO dispute regarding the operation of the system would have made an excellent opportunity for clarifying what the Appellate Body really meant in its *Korea – Beef* Report. However, the issue is now moot because CIQ-SA and CSBTS were merged into AQSIQ, and the legislation implementing China's obligation under the TBT Agreement was promulgated in December 2001.[25] Nevertheless, the above-mentioned episode in the negotiation demonstrates that China's accession process was closely following the cutting edge of the developing jurisprudence in the WTO.

[25] See Working Party Report, para. 188.

PART V

Trade in services and competition policy

13

WTO membership and professional services regulation in China

CHRISTOPHER ARUP

In this chapter, China's commitments to liberalization of trade in professional services are assessed against the norms and disciplines of the General Agreement on Trade in Services (GATS) and the regulatory measures that other WTO Member States have maintained. The focus is on the outcome for legal services, making some mention too of accountancy services.[1]

The significance of any liberalization by China depends on the legal resources it will free and, possibly, favour. Consequently, this chapter provides all-too-brief comment on how WTO membership might affect competition between different types of law and styles of 'lawyering'. China's accession to the WTO may constitute a significant moment in the globalization of law.

The strength of the legal profession in China

Through all the shifts in China's turbulent history, whether the context has been one, say, of Confucianism or communism, law and lawyers have been regarded with some scepticism.[2] During the Cultural Revolution, the government promulgated an edict concerning the abolition of 'underground lawyers and litigation tricksters'.

The Chinese government now seems prepared to encourage the development of a legal profession. While their ratio to the population is still

---

[1] I rely on earlier papers for a comprehensive analysis of China's commitments thus far on trade in services and professional services in particular; see B. Williams and D. Cass, *Legal Implications for Regulation of Trade in Services of China's Accession to the WTO* (Working Paper No. 2 of the China and the WTO Project, School of Law, Australian National University, Canberra, 2000).

[2] For background, see J. Chen, *Chinese Law* (The Hague, 1999); regarding lawyers, W. Alford, 'Tasselled loafers for barefoot lawyers: transformation and tension in the world of Chinese legal workers' (1995) 141 *The China Quarterly* 22.

low, the number of lawyers has been rising rapidly, from some 11,000 in 1979 to 110,000 in 1998. More legal practices are operating independently of state funding as co-operatives or partnerships.[3] Greater devotion to the notion of rule according to law, if not to the rule of law itself, means there are more situations when legal services are productive. Demand for lawyers has increased with procedural reforms that give lawyers greater opportunities to participate in legal proceedings. The liberalization of the economy gives private parties greater autonomy from the state in ordering their legal relations.

However, several local factors mean that those professionals whose expertise lies with the mastery of rules and assertion of rights are likely to remain marginal for some time.[4] These factors include China's distinctive brand of relational or *guanxi* capitalism, its executive and administrative style of government decision-making, and its preference for deference and consensus. China's law is both complex and unstable. It is complicated by the indeterminacy of local legislative instruments, the discretion afforded executive and administrative officials at the multiple levels of government, the lack of legal education and respect for legal skills among the judiciary, and even the obstacles to having judgements enforced.[5]

While these conditions are being ameliorated, not least through the build-up at the national level of a much stronger legislative corpus and judicial branch, the gap between the law in theory and the law in action remains significant. The uncertain position for lawyers is not just the product of past neglect. In the current climate, it reflects a tension: between the desire to reap the benefits of economic liberalization and the urge to maintain political stability and control.[6]

Lawyers may still prove useful if they can deploy skills that are not rule-oriented, such as those of networking, brokering, lobbying and the avoidance of disputes. A foreign lawyer confirms this when he says that the

---

[3] See Li Yuwen, 'Lawyers in China: a flourishing profession?', *China Online*, 11 May 2000, at www.chinaonline.com.

[4] For my characterization of law in China, I rely on Chen, *Chinese Law*; also S. Lubman, *Bird in a Cage: Legal Reform in China After Mao* (Stanford, 1999). See further P. Potter, *The Chinese Legal System: Globalization and Local Legal Culture* (New York, 2001).

[5] For example, R. Peerenboom, 'Law enforcement and the legal profession in China', paper at Conference on Implementation of Law in the People's Republic of China, Leiden University, The Netherlands, 8–10 November 2000; also see J. Cooper, 'Lawyers in China and the rule of law' (1999) 6 *International Journal of the Sociology of Law* 71.

[6] J. Gray, *False Dawn: The Delusions of Global Capitalism* (London, 1999), ch. 7.

practice of law is quite different in China from at home in Australia: a 'flexible approach' is taken to law.[7] Another states emphatically that there is no black-letter law in China. Of course, empiricists have long been saying that rules are only part of the 'law in action' in western societies.[8]

Paradoxically, as it seeks to develop a separate legal profession,[9] China is building professional restrictions around the freedom to supply law-related services. Elsewhere, the traditional mode of regulation, stressing strict entry requirements, rationing of places, reserved areas of practice, codes of conduct, and obligations to the legal system and public institutions, has been a defining characteristic of a legal profession. Now this character is being challenged by new demands, both for multidisciplinary and multinational business services and for lawyers to play a constructive role in ameliorating social problems.[10]

One would expect that the highest volume of demand will be domestically oriented towards expertises such as criminal law, family law, employment law and small-business law. Smaller numbers of lawyers will be needed for work in internationally oriented areas of commercial law. But here the sophisticated and specialist nature of the practice stretches the quality of the education and training of Chinese lawyers. Many lawyers currently do not have a university education, let alone a law degree, and much of that education has been oriented to political and legal doctrine.[11] New lawyers now have to pass the national bar examination, but the emphasis is said to be on rote learning rather than critical thinking and problem solving. The pass rate for the examination has been running at a conservative 10 per cent.

China has some fine law schools and the State Educational Commission and Ministry of Justice plan to reform legal education.[12] While legal education has been more politically sensitive than, for example, nursing or

---

[7] Such insights are from a two-part story: 'Fast boat to China – legal opportunities in the new PRC', *Lawyers Weekly* (Australia), 17 November 2000, p. 10, and 24 November 2000, p. 10.

[8] C. Jones, 'Capitalism, globalization and the rule of law: an alternative trajectory of legal change' (1994) 3 *Social and Legal Studies* 195.

[9] Culminating in the Law of the PRC on Lawyers and Legal Representation (1996), see (1996) 10(6) *China Law and Practice* 28.

[10] See H. Kritzer, 'The professions are dead: long live the professions: legal practice in a post-professional world' (1999) 33 *Law and Society Review* 713.

[11] See Lubman, *Bird in a Cage*; Li, 'Lawyers in China'; also Peerenboom, 'Law enforcement'.

[12] IDP Australia, *Internationalisation of Australia's Legal Education Opportunities in the New Millennium*, report for consortium of Australian law schools, August 1998 (author's copy).

business education, there are signs of increasing willingness to partner foreign universities in international postgraduate courses.[13] Eventually, independent bar associations will make a contribution too, for example through
continuing legal-education programmes. Membership of the WTO will
itself provoke more local interest in international and comparative law.

Old-fashioned regulation, such as restrictions on form, size and location
of practices, may continue to put local lawyers at a disadvantage, unless
foreign lawyers are subject to the same or stricter limitations.[14] So, too,
extra-legal factors – such as the lack of strong, competitive internal markets
for professional services and demanding local clients – have told so far
against the development of international legal capacity.

The attractions of foreign professional services

Once China decided to participate in the international economy again, it
was bound to attract the attentions of foreign lawyers. Foreign firms seeking
joint ventures in China brought lawyers with them. Subsequently, Chinese
exporters sought advice from foreign lawyers when encountering obstacles
overseas.

The liberalization of capital markets around the world and the accompanying global flows of funds have affected the demand for international
legal and accounting services markedly. Within China, economic liberalization and privatization in sectors such as manufacturing, banking and
finance have increased the market for inwards foreign investment (from the
Chinese diaspora as well as the developed nations), while Chinese investors
search for opportunities overseas.

While business continues to depend on local approvals and clearances,
lawyers with local legal knowledge have an advantage. Physical proximity, time and connections may all be necessary for the acquisition of that
knowledge. In China, connections are especially important in achieving
favourable decisions.[15] For foreigners, effective access will thus depend on

---

[13] None the less, China has not made commitments to liberalize trade in education services under
the GATS.

[14] Few Chinese firms are more than thirty lawyers strong and they are just beginning the process of
merger and inter-regional alliance, see Li, 'Lawyers in China'. The Chinese government has given
an ambivalent reception to Chinese lawyers educated and experienced abroad: see Hongming
Xiao, 'The internationalisation of China's legal services market' (2000) 1(6) *Perspectives* 3.

[15] All commentators stress this point; see e.g. Lubman, *Bird in a Cage.*

preparedness to live and operate under local conditions as well as with the assistance of local practitioners. However, with globalization promoting greater cross-border interaction and giving business more choice about location, such national differences can actually suit professionals who make comparisons between jurisdictions, putting together the most favourable package for the client, even routing components of a business package through different national regimes.

Such ability to exploit differences is said to advantage the big Anglo-American law firms, who were the first on to the international stage, developing deal-making and dispute-resolution skills.[16] They have the economies of scale and scope to offer one-stop services. These firms already have a presence in China.[17] But the same opportunities now challenge traditional professional boundaries and attract even larger and more internationally organized accounting firms, which are, where regulation permits, building legal departments and merging with law firms.

Competitive advantages accrue also to foreign firms when legal models characteristic of one national regime or another are injected into the processes of global law-making. With so many countries in economic transition, there is a 'market' for legal models, met, for instance, through the provision of aid and consultancy services. One would expect the economies looking outward to be attracted to the models operating in their biggest markets. However, historical associations also play a part – in China's case until recently with Germany and the Soviet Union.[18] Concerns about political sovereignty and cultural integrity can be influential, too – for example in resistance to American models and interest in best practice from less imposing but like-minded common law jurisdictions, such as Australia and New Zealand.

Such explanations continue to stress the role of local factors in the reception and transplantation of models. In legal fields, exporting nations and multinational business may seek preferment by having their versions adopted in international law-making processes of various kinds.[19] Choice of law clauses in international financial transactions, for example, are said

---

[16] Y. Dezalay and B. Garth, *Dealing in Virtue: International Commercial Arbitration and the Construction of a Transnational Order* (Chicago, 1996).

[17] For a list of firms, see *Lawyers Weekly*, 'Fast boat'.

[18] Regarding legal transplantation in China, see Chen, *Chinese Law*.

[19] See J. Braithwaite and P. Drahos, *Global Business Regulation* (Cambridge, 2000).

generally to favour New York or English law.[20] The WTO might itself become a forum for the dissemination of legal models, if it were to move from a predominantly deregulatory preoccupation on to a reregulatory agenda. The TRIPs Agreement already provides a very strong indication of the WTO's prescriptive or reregulatory potential; the GATS, as this chapter shows, less so.

The regulation of professional services by WTO members

In each national case, the advantages different suppliers enjoy, on technical, economic or cultural grounds, interact with the conditions of competition created by the domestic and international regulation of professional services. Any survey of national measures will reveal how intricate domestic regulation has been – all over the world.[21] Governments typically grant foreign professionals limited rights of access and practice in order to avail local industries of access to wider legal expertise, especially those aiming to participate in the international economy, and to reassure foreign investors who may have reservations about the expertise or allegiance of local professionals. At the same time, governments try to control the impact on the local legal profession and, indeed, the local legal system. Rarely do jurisdictions wholly sacrifice the privileges of local lawyers for the sake of overall international gains. But few now exclude foreigners altogether.

Regulation generally restricts the provision of some services to those who are qualified members of the local legal profession. The scope of these reservations varies. Where it has been modest, as in Japan, there have been greater opportunities for unqualified foreign lawyers, or professionals of other kinds, to compete, unless another type of regulation acts as a barrier. These restrictions have generally not been constructed as a defence against foreigners but reflect the strength of legal professionalization locally.

Where restrictions apply, the key to access is the conditions of entry into the profession. Overt forms of discrimination such as nationality requirements are disappearing, and local education and training requirements are

---

[20] C. Silver, 'Globalization and the U.S. market in legal services – shifting identities' (2000) 31 *Law and Policy in International Business* 1095.

[21] C. Arup, *The New World Trade Organization Agreements: Globalizing Law through Services and Intellectual Property* (Cambridge, 2000), ch. 5.

appearing as the main obstacles to entry.[22] In some jurisdictions there is pressure to minimize these entry requirements or to afford some recognition to education and experience in other countries.[23] These requirements do not simply protect incumbent professionals; local knowledge may be seen to enhance the quality of service to consumers and the level of respect for local legal and political institutions.

Access is also restricted, on a non-discriminatory basis, by quotas applied to the numbers licensed for practice – for instance, limits on places in law degrees or pass rates for bar examinations. Again, the reasons may not simply be industrial; some jurisdictions, certainly in Asian countries, have concerns about the impact of lawyers generally on local styles of decision-making and dispute resolution.[24] These kinds of restrictions are often not preoccupied with foreign influences but reveal a wider distrust of lawyers.

It is common now for foreign lawyers to be allowed to offer services in carefully circumscribed areas outside the profession, for example as legal consultants. They may be limited to giving advice on their home-country law or public international law, though the precise delineation varies from country to country. Even so, the host government may remain wary about the impact of these foreigners on the local legal profession and the legal system overall, so a licensing scheme may be employed to control numbers and to apply conditions to the manner in which services may be supplied.

Choice of business structure may be limited more than for local practitioners. Commercial or natural presence may be required (though policing the provision of legal services across borders, especially on-line, is bound to be problematic).[25] The form of establishment may be restricted, for example to the representative office or the single branch of the home firm.

The nature of the professional relationship with local lawyers is often regulated. In contrast to other professional sectors, in which joint ventures and local participation are required, the employment of locals and partnerships

---

[22] OECD, *International Trade in Professional Services: Assessing Barriers and Encouraging Reform* (Paris, 1997).

[23] e.g. in the European Union, see Arup, *The New WTO Agreements*, ch. 5.   [24] Ibid.

[25] This policy was evident in the limitations Member States entered into schedules at the end of the Uruguay Round: see WTO, Council on Trade in Services, *Legal Services: Background Note by the Secretariat*, S/C/W/43, 6 July 1998, at the WTO website www.wto.org. Schedules are set out in WTO, *Legal Instruments Embodying the Results of the Uruguay Round of Multilateral Trade Negotiations* (Geneva, 1994), vols. XXVIII–XXX.

with or acquisition of local practices may be banned. The regulators may fear that, until they have had the chance to develop the capacity to compete, local lawyers risk domination by foreign practitioners, the best talent being bought up, the most lucrative work siphoned off, and unsympathetic styles of 'lawyering' encouraged.

Foreign lawyers must find ways to work within such restrictions, which are both anti-competitive and impose extra costs and uncertainties. In China, before the licensing system for foreign lawyers was instituted, such lawyers operated, very much under sufferance, as in-house counsel within foreign industrial corporations or consultancy firms.[26]

Previous Chinese regulation

Enactment of the Tentative Regulations on Foreign Law Firms Establishing Offices in China in 1992 had the virtue of giving formal recognition to the place for foreign lawyers and standardized a set of restrictions.[27] Under the Regulations, foreigners can obtain licences to establish representative offices. These offices are to be representative of firms back home; lawyers cannot come and offer legal services as 'natural persons'.

Each firm is confined to one office in China and the number of offices over all, as well as the geographical locations for offices, are rationed. The authorized locations have, apart from Beijing, largely been cities in the economically more liberalized coastal regions – a total of ten in 1999. By 1999, licences had been granted to 103 firms, mainly firms originating in the United States, United Kingdom and Germany, together with Hong Kong firms which are themselves a mixture of Chinese and foreign-linked firms. Effort is being made to spread the licences around firms from different countries.

Staffing is regulated, too. The main representative must be a partner with at least three years' practice experience in his or her home country. Representatives must reside in China for at least 180 days each year.

The clearest restriction is on the scope of permitted activities. Licensed offices are confined to the provision of advice on the law of their home countries (where they are members of the profession), together with

---

[26] Xiao, 'Internationalisation'.
[27] PRC, Ministry of Justice, State Administration for Industry and Commerce, Foreign Law Firms Establishing Offices in China Tentative Regulations (1992).

international treaties and practices. This scope is not only restrictive but uncertain, presenting a risk that foreign firms might fall foul of the licensing authority, the Ministry of Justice.[28]

The Regulations prohibit giving advice on Chinese law and possibly some kinds of international law, such as private international law, as well as third-country law. Still, according to at least one report, foreign firms do give advice on Chinese law from time to time:[29] because of the natural interaction in some situations, it would be difficult not to.

Foreign firms are banned from representing clients in Chinese courts. Within the permitted legal areas, they may, however, represent clients in arbitrations on Chinese soil, a significant concession given the emphasis in China on alternatives to litigation. They may also represent clients in either arbitration or court cases outside China.

The Regulations prohibit partnerships with local professionals; nor can Chinese lawyers be employed by foreign firms unless they give up their own practice licences. In fact, locally qualified and experienced lawyers are employed in foreign-owned offices, and profit-sharing may occur informally. Matters may also be referred to Chinese law firms case by case and informal inter-firm alliances have developed. Foreign firms need indigenous lawyers, not only for their local legal knowledge and language skills, but also for their links into the all-important networks of business people, national, regional and municipal government officials, and members of the judiciary.

These direct bars are important because the lack of full professionalization of lawyers in China could otherwise enable readier access than in some other countries for foreign firms. Local firms may assume various business structures, including limited liability, and, on an informal basis at least, can form joint ventures with other types of business. In practice, the lawyers' hold over the areas of legal work recognized by the Law on Lawyers and Legal Representation is not tight.[30]

A contrast can be made with accountancy, where there has been an explicit policy of partnering Chinese firms with the Big Five international accountancy firms. Local firms may become 'member offices' of the international firms in China. The government has been clear about the need

---

[28] Peerenboom, 'Law enforcement'.   [29] *Lawyers Weekly*, 'Fast boat'.

[30] Li, 'Lawyers in China'; Alford, 'Tasselled loafers'. This is not to say a foreign business could simply take over a Chinese legal firm; there are laws of a general nature limiting foreign ownership and control of companies, partnerships and joint ventures in China; see Williams and Cass, *Legal Implications*.

to provide Chinese business and industry on the one hand with expert accounting, taxation and management consultancy services, and foreign investors and international capital markets on the other hand with reliable financial information, both directly and through the skills development of local certified public accountants (CPAs).

Yet, even here, there has been ambivalence. While the international firms have been able to establish their own representative offices, these offices have not been allowed to employ Chinese CPAs. The firms have been limited to a minority investment stake in the local member firms. Until recently, the government was reluctant to let international firms audit Chinese enterprises.[31] It has been slow to adopt international accounting standards.[32]

GATS norms

Membership of the WTO means that a country signs up for a package of agreements, including the agreement most relevant to this chapter, the GATS. Indeed, membership necessitates making a schedule of commitments under the GATS in the first instance and through this agreement engaging in successive rounds of negotiations to achieve higher levels of liberalization, the first of which has commenced (slowly) in 2000.[33]

There are interesting slippages between the obligations assumed by the original members and those seeking approval for accession subsequently. Inevitably the course of negotiations differs when the focus is on one country seeking to join. In the case of the GATS, the in-built approach to the negotiation and listing of commitments means the outcomes are always going to be the product of unilateral offers and bilateral bargaining as much as multilateral prescriptions.

The GATS is impressively broad. Though the concept of 'services' was never defined, in operational terms it has covered professional services,

---

[31] Note the change made in 2000: Notice on Management of Temporary Licences for Overseas Accounting Firms to Audit Financial Institutions Seeking Public Listing (jointly issued by China Securities Regulatory Commission and the Ministry of Finance).

[32] M. Burke, 'China's stock markets and the World Trade Organization' (1999) 30 *Law and Policy in International Business* 361. Lack of accounting standards has also been a feature of the non-performing loan problem: see Jianbo Lou, 'China's bank non-performing loan problem: seriousness and causes' (2000) 34 *The International Lawyer* 1185.

[33] For the texts of the WTO agreements, see WTO, *The Results of the Uruguay Round: The Legal Texts* (Geneva, 1994).

including legal and accountancy services. Four broad modes of service supply are covered: cross-border supply, consumption abroad, supply through natural presence, and supply through commercial presence – each relevant to professional services.

Despite its 'bottom-up approach', the GATS contains several substantive obligations for members. They are general in the sense that, once covered by the Agreement, governments must make all their measures affecting trade in services conform to these standards.

The primary obligation is that of most favoured nation treatment. It applies to legal services. The cautious openings to foreign lawyers afforded by jurisdictions in the developed countries were commonly conditioned on material reciprocity.[34] Under the GATS, countries including the United States, Japan, the European Union and Australia gave up insistence on this condition. China's Tentative Regulations have included a reciprocity requirement.

Insistence on reciprocity can well be a hard-headed decision, using access as leverage to extract concessions for home-grown legal-services exporters. But reservations can also represent political and cultural considerations. Countries may be more willing to give access to lawyers from what they regard as sympathetic cultures – in national, legal or other terms. They may be other common law lawyers, French-speaking lawyers or, in the case of China, lawyers from Hong Kong, Taiwan and Macao. The GATS makes provision for members to list exemptions from the MFN obligation (Article II:2).

The heart of the GATS is its approach to commitments on national treatment and market access. GATT jurisprudence offers interpretation of these key norms but its application to the new field of services will require further consideration. In relation to professional services, the GATS definition of national treatment exposes to scrutiny measures that are not simply formally or, on their face, discriminatory (Article XVII:2). As regulation moves away from overt discrimination, such as nationality requirements, it will invite questions such as whether local residency or qualification requirements are more onerous for foreigners to meet than locals – and in effect discriminate against them.

In giving content to the norm of market access, the GATS 'proscribes' three types of discriminatory measures (Article XVI:2). Each of these

---

[34] Arup, *The New WTO Agreements*, ch. 5.

measures is to be found in professional services regulation in various jurisdictions. The measures proscribed by Article XVI:2 are as follows:

- Regulations prohibiting foreign investment in professional firms or specifying that any foreign investment remains a minority interest.
- Restrictions on choice of business structure (the specific type of legal entity or joint venture through which services may be supplied), which act as a barrier for foreigners too. Multinational practices may be obstructed because the permitted structures in each jurisdiction do not mesh. A more general inhibition is the result of the common policy that legal firms can only be owned and controlled by those admitted to the local profession. One commentator has argued that 'the very strict rules intended to maintain the necessary independence of lawyers and ensure the practice of law remains a liberal profession . . . have also prevented the establishment of large multi-speciality firms, especially in the field of corporate law, despite a clearly growing demand from businesses'.[35] However, allowance for multidisciplinary partnerships and equity participation in incorporated firms would obviate the need for foreign professionals to qualify as lawyers if they wished to associate with locals.
- Limitations on the number of service suppliers, whether numerical quotas, monopolies, exclusive service suppliers or an economic needs test. Here, controls, for example stringent tests for entry into professional courses or passage through a professional examination, would lead to an analysis of issues which were contested in the photographic film and paper dispute, such as the outer limits to the definition of 'measures affecting trade'.[36] Unless they operate as explicit quotas, such restrictions might anyway be regarded as qualitative rather than quantitative limitations.

In the case of the GATS, these issues can be kept at bay because each member has the option, subject to the pressures of negotiations, of withholding the sector or subsector from the scrutiny of the norms or listing limitations in its schedule of commitments. In the Uruguay Round, all sorts of countries took advantage of these options in relation to legal services.[37]

Even this 'list-it-or-lose-it' position seems to have been modified. The working principle is that members do not have to list those limitations on

[35] S. Nelson, 'Legal services', in OECD, *International Trade in Professional Services*, p. 47.
[36] WTO Panel Report, *Japan – Measures Affecting Consumer Photographic Film and Paper, Complaint by the United States*, WT/DS44/R, adopted 22 April 1998.
[37] WTO, *Background Note*.

market access that fall outside the proscriptions in Article XVI:2 – those, roughly speaking, that are qualitative rather than quantitative limitations.[38] Furthermore, members have been allowed to say in their schedules that limitations on a particular mode of supply will be 'unbound', meaning they have not even committed themselves to a standstill position.

China's commitments

China's commitments are contained in its Schedule of Specific Commitments on Services. These commitments should represent, on the basis of MFN, the most liberal commitments made in the various bilateral agreements.[39] Overall, the commitments are more liberal than China's current regulation and its limitations, at least on paper, are little different from those maintained by other Member States.

For legal services, the subsector inscribed in the Schedule, and hence the scope of activities exposed, is described as 'legal services (CPC 861, excluding Chinese law practice)'.[40] The United States was seeking China's agreement to permit foreigners to take the Chinese lawyers' qualification, so they could be licensed to practise local law. However, it appears that sensitivities remain, in part possibly about political matters being raised in the local courts.[41] The List of Article II MFN Exemptions does not indicate that any exception has been made for lawyers of other Chinese nationalities.[42]

Reflecting the format adopted for scheduling commitments at the conclusion of the Uruguay Round, the Schedule has separate columns for limitations on market access and national treatment, together with a column for additional commitments (which has not been used). The 'limitations' are then broken down into the four modes of supply.

---

[38] WTO, *Legal Instruments*, vol. XXVIII, Introduction, p. iii.

[39] In particular, the agreements with the United States, see The US–China Business Council staff, 'The US–China Bilateral Agreement and the United States' (2000) 27(1) *The China Business Review* 20, and with the European Union, see J. Lapres, 'The EU–China WTO deal compared' (2000) 27(4) *The China Business Review* 8.

[40] See WTO, *Report of the Working Party on the Accession of China*, Addendum, Schedule of Specific Commitments on Services/List of Article II MFN Exemptions, WT/ACC/CHN/49Add.2, 1 November 2001, available at the WTO website.

[41] Xiao, 'Internationalisation'.

[42] *Report of the Working Party on the Accession of China*, Schedule of Specific Commitments on Services/List of Article II MFN Exemptions.

For cross-border supply and consumption abroad, the entries say 'no limitations'. Not all countries making commitments on legal services in the Uruguay Round were prepared to free these modes.

For the supply mode of natural presence within the territory, the limitations are 'unbound', enabling China to step them up at some point in the future if it saw fit. Even in this restricted sphere of consultancies, economic and political sensitivities may remain. Like most countries, China has general controls on entry and temporary stay for the purpose of work. The exception is its horizontal commitments, across all sectors included in the Schedule, whereby several restricted categories are afforded entry rights. These categories include managers, executives and specialist senior employees of a corporation that has established a representative office, branch or subsidiary, if they are temporarily moving as intra-corporate transferees.

The mode of supply given most detailed attention in China's Schedule is commercial presence. Foreign firms are limited to providing legal services in the form of representative offices. At the same time, the Schedule counters a horizontal limitation by making it clear that the offices can engage in profit-making activities.[43] Foreign firms are still confined to one representative office each, in one of nineteen enumerated cities. However, China undertakes to eliminate these geographic and quantitative limitations within one year of its accession – that is, by the end of 2002.

The staffing of the offices remains regulated. The representatives of the firm shall be members of the bar or a law society in one of the WTO Member States. The chief representative must be a partner or equivalent of a law firm in such a country. These commitments represent a liberalization in the sense that lawyers no longer need to be qualified in their original home country, making it easier for multinationals to post staff who have practised elsewhere.[44] Still, lawyers must have practised at least two consecutive years outside China, and a 180-day residency requirement applies to each representative, reducing flexibility in staffing.

Uncertainty will be created by the cryptic nature of the expression used in the Schedule. It seems, by inference, that the offices may now employ Chinese, nationally registered, lawyers, though not outside China. They may entrust the Chinese legal affairs of their foreign clients to Chinese legal firms, including instructing Chinese lawyers directly to appear in court.

---

[43] Ibid. On the possible scope of these horizontal commitments, see Williams and Cass, *Legal Implications*.

[44] Xiao, 'Internationalisation'.

They may enter into contracts to maintain long-term entrustment relations with Chinese law firms for these legal affairs, though they may not take majority control of firms practising Chinese law. Such half-way-house arrangements are reminiscent of the relationships allowed by Japan in 1994.[45]

So, too, the business scope of the offices is unclear. Representing a commitment made in the EU–China bilateral agreement, they are permitted to 'provide information on the impact of the Chinese legal environment'. They may handle, when entrusted by clients or Chinese legal firms, legal affairs of the country/region where the lawyers of the foreign law firm are permitted to engage in lawyers' professional work. But missing from the Schedule, in a seemingly exhaustive list, is mention of professional work in relation to third-country law, or international conventions and practices.

Effective from 1 January 2002, China's commitments were given national legislative form in the Administration of Representative Offices of Foreign Law Firms in China Regulations. The Regulations faithfully implement the commitments but, in simply reproducing the wording of the Schedule to the Protocol, they do not clear up any of the uncertainties regarding the extent of the liberalization.[46]

GATS disciplines

The main impact of WTO membership is economic rather than political or legal. None the less, it is possible a more open economy will lead, indirectly, to demands for changes in domestic law; for instance, foreign lawyers may bring certain expectations of law with them. If one concentrates on the direct impact of the WTO, it is possible to see some tentative moves in the direction of legal guarantees for economic activity.

Strongest is the TRIPs Agreement, which requires member governments to guarantee foreign nationals intellectual property rights, including

---

[45] Arup, *The New WTO Agreements*, p. 163.

[46] The text of the Regulations can be found in 2000 16(2) *China Law and Practice* 43. For a commentary in the same issue of *China Law and Practice*, see H. Wong and O. Cox, 'Foreign firms set to expand in China', at 54. Also see A. Subrahmanyan, 'Hong Kong and Macao law firms in China: still "foreign" to the MOJ', (2002) 16(4) *China Law and Practice* 32. For further specification, see now the Regulations Implementing the Administration of Representative Officer of Foreign Law Firms in China, (2002) 16 (7) *China Law and Practice* 37, particularly in regard to 'Chinese legal affairs'.

providing administrative and judicial means domestically against infringement. Even the TRIPs Agreement concedes some choice of legal form to members. They are free to determine the appropriate method of implementing the provisions of the Agreement within their own legal system and practice (Article 1.1). But the decision in the US–India dispute over patent protection indicates that the method should none the less lend legal certainty and predictability to the implementation.[47] In China's case, the Protocol on Accession contains clarifications and commitments concerning the legal texts and procedures that will ensure compliance with the TRIPs Agreement.[48]

The GATS has much less of a reregulatory momentum than the TRIPs Agreement. However, it, too, will have an influence on domestic law. Where countries make commitments to liberalization in their schedules, they offer a standard by which they can be held to account, through the WTO process of dispute settlement, for non-compliance. Furthermore, in those sectors which they do inscribe, limitations that have not been listed may be tested for consistency with the norms of national treatment and market access. Often, though, there is room for argument, because the precision needed to treat the commitments and norms as hard and fast rules may be found wanting.

One should also note that the process for obtaining compliance is by government-to-government dispute settlement. Those service suppliers who seek to benefit by liberalization cannot directly hold governments to account in international or domestic courts. It is a matter for each member's constitutional law whether the local courts will give force to undertakings that the member government has failed to implement by legislation.

On a government-to-government level, the WTO dispute settlement process is developing a legal flavour with its procedural rights, sanctions for non-compliance, and the charge to the Panels and Appellate Body to preserve the rights and obligations of members under the covered agreements (Article 3.2 of the WTO Agreement). None the less, the emphasis remains on settlement between the parties and diplomatic and political, as well as legal, considerations come into play. Despite the high take-up rate for the

---

[47] WTO Appellate Body Report, *India – Patent Protection for Pharmaceutical and Agricultural Chemical Products*, WT/DS50/AB/R, adopted 16 January 1998.

[48] WTO, Protocol of the Accession of the People's Republic of China, WT/L/432, 1 December 2001, Part VI.

dispute settlement process generally, very little has gone through to the Panels under the cover of the GATS.[49]

The GATS is mindful that the domestic regulation of services supply is likely to continue. Hence, it applies disciplines to these measures in order to minimize their impact on trade; some such disciplines concern the legal form that regulation may take. Measures affecting trade in services must meet the general obligation of transparency in Article III. Members must publish or make readily available all relevant measures of general application which pertain to or affect the operation of the Agreement. For China, transparency represents a substantial new discipline.[50] The Working Party Report and the Protocol contain a considerable elaboration of China's obligation in respect of transparency.[51] In relation to services regulation, licensing procedures and conditions attract particular attention.

Article VI of the GATS requires members to ensure that measures of general application affecting trade in services are administered in a reasonable, objective and impartial manner. It requires each member to maintain or institute judicial, arbitral or administrative tribunals or procedures that provide for prompt review of and, where justified, appropriate remedies for administrative decisions affecting trade in services. The Working Party Report and the Protocol contain provisions on uniform administration and judicial review that appear to strengthen this obligation.[52] While Article VI:2(b) of the GATS states that its provision does not require procedures or tribunals inconsistent with the constitutional structure or nature of a member's legal system, this obligation should still prove significant. The exercise of discretion in so many government approvals and clearances means that reform of China's administrative law is a focal point of foreign representations.[53] Yet reform remains a sensitive matter, for it reaches into the heart of the Chinese state.

---

[49] The *Bananas* case includes a ruling on the nature of MFN treatment under the GATS; see WTO Appellate Body Report, *European Communities – Regime for Importation, Sale and Distribution of Bananas*, WT/DS27/AB/R, adopted 25 September 1997, at *DSR* 1997: II. The 'behind the border' nature of services regulation will mean that, if they do attract adjudication, disputes under the terms of the GATS will be significant jurisprudentially, for example complaints by the United States against Japan (WT/DS45) (distribution services) and against Mexico (WT/DS204/1) (telecommunications services).

[50] See S. Ostry, 'China and the WTO: the transparency issue' (1998) 3 *UCLA Journal of International Law and Foreign Affairs* 1.

[51] Protocol of Accession, Part I, Art. 2(c); also Part V.

[52] Ibid., Part I, Art. 2(A) and (D).

[53] See Lubman, *Bird in a Cage*; also J. Chen, 'The development and conception of administrative law in China' (1998) 16(2) *Law In Context* 72.

If one looks generally at the jurisprudence of the GATT and WTO, especially the principle of the least trade-restrictive measure, one can see a tendency to narrow national choice of regulatory instrument. In the case of professional services, the WTO is also being more proactive. Article VI:4 of the GATS charges the Council of Trade in Services to develop disciplines for measures relating to qualifications and licensing requirements. The disciplines should ensure that such measures are based on objective and transparent criteria, be no more burdensome than necessary to ensure the quality of a service, and (in the case of licensing procedures) not be in themselves a restriction on the supply of the service.

At Marrakesh, the Decision on Professional Services set up a Working Party that produced Guidelines for the Recognition of Qualifications in the Accountancy Sector.[54] The GATS allows for members to make mutual-recognition agreements and arrangements, while at the same time encouraging them to extend their benefits to other countries (see Article VII). However, in the absence of a complete convergence of law across the world, mutual recognition has to find a balance between recognition of foreign qualifications and respect for local learning. In matters of professional conduct as well as qualification, serious differences have been experienced, even between western countries. Recently the bar associations of the United States, Europe and Japan have been broaching the task of harmonization through participation in forums on transnational practice.[55]

The Guidelines were followed in December 1998 by Disciplines on Domestic Regulation in the Accounting Sector.[56] These Disciplines aim to channel members towards those measures which are no more trade restrictive than necessary to fulfil their regulatory objectives. Interestingly, the WTO gives legitimacy to certain regulatory objectives: the Disciplines recognize, *inter alia*, the protection of consumers, the quality of the service, professional competence and the integrity of the profession. Transparency is a priority; otherwise the Disciplines urge members to consider measures less restrictive than a residency requirement and to take account of

---

[54] See WTO Press Release PRESS/73, 29 May 1997, where the Guidelines were appended.

[55] Law Council of Australia and International Legal Services Advisory Council, *Transnational Practice for the Legal Profession*, Report of the Law Council of Australia Delegation to Paris and Geneva, 8–13 November 1998, available from the Council.

[56] WTO, Council on Trade in Services, *Disciplines on Domestic Regulation in the Accountancy Sector*, see WTO Focus no. 36, December 1998, or go to WTO website.

qualifications acquired in the home territory that are equivalent in education, experience and/or training levels. Work has begun slowly on disciplines for other sectors.

Summary

This chapter considered the impact of WTO membership on legal services in China, drawing some contrast with accountancy services. The immediate point of interest has been the degree of liberalization of China's current restrictions; the broader interest is the impact on competition between different types of law and styles of lawyering for ascendancy, both within China and in its relations with the world.

The commitments are a cautious advance on current restrictions. On a somewhat uncertain basis, they will expand the opportunities for the large international firms to provide services; but they will not open the legal 'market' to them generally. At the same time, membership begins to expose China to the norms and disciplines of the GATS, along with those of the other WTO agreements. Membership will thus have an impact on China's legal system, both directly and indirectly. It is not possible to explore these second-order consequences here.[57] None the less, it is safe to say that it will be a gradual and negotiated process of change. The WTO's role will be to mediate, rather than order, the competition between local and foreign versions of what legal services and law should be in China.

---

[57] An attempt is made in C. Arup, 'Lawyers for China' (2001) 4 *Journal of World Intellectual Property* 741.

14

The impact of China's WTO accession upon regulation of the distribution and logistics industries in China

DENE YEAMAN

Introduction

From the perspective of a foreign company, the legal and logistical problems associated with distribution of products in the People's Republic of China is arguably the most difficult aspect of doing business in China. Since it embarked on its course of economic reforms and the opening of its economy to foreign investment in the late 1970s, the Chinese government has consistently pursued a policy preference for attracting foreign capital, manufacturing technology and management expertise while restricting the ability of foreign companies to import, distribute and sell their products. Despite this, foreign companies have been excited by the possibilities that have been offered by the gradual breakdown of China's command economy and socialist distribution network. However, the combination of diverse markets, poor infrastructure, local protectionism and corruption, together with the restrictions imposed by state laws and policies on the ability of a foreign company to sell and deliver its products to customers has often proved an overwhelming challenge for foreign investors and has retarded the development of an efficient and modern distribution system in China.

In the early to mid-1990s, foreign distribution and logistics companies began to establish themselves in China with a view to bringing western-style supply-chain management systems to what was, and continues to be perceived as, a market of immense opportunity. The unbridled enthusiasm of such companies in the early 1990s gave way, initially, to pessimism and then to a more balanced approach to meeting the challenges of the China market, as foreign investors adjusted their expectations and strategies in the light of the many legal and practical difficulties they confronted. However, notwithstanding incremental relaxation of the Chinese regulatory environment for foreign participation in distribution services in the late 1990s, the vast majority of foreign logistics-service providers remain unable to offer the full range of logistics services that they are able to provide in most developed jurisdictions. They have often had to adopt convoluted legal and operational structures in order to obtain approval for even very limited business scopes. It is against this background that foreign companies generally, and foreign distributors and logistics providers in particular, have great hopes that China's accession to the World Trade Organization will result in fresh opportunities for foreign participation in distribution services.

The Protocol on the Accession of the People's Republic of China to the WTO was approved at the Fourth Ministerial Conference of the WTO in Doha, Qatar on 10 November 2001. Having been pre-approved by the National People's Congress, the Protocol was accepted by the government of the PRC on 11 November 2001 and entered into force on 11 December 2001.

The various market-access commitments that China has agreed to are set forth in the Schedule of Specific Commitments (the Services Schedule), annexed to the Protocol and which form part of the General Agreement on Trade in Services. The Services Schedule sets forth, *inter alia*, the service sectors to which China will apply its GATS market-access and national-treatment obligations as well as the exceptions from these obligations which it intends to maintain. If China fully implements the basic WTO principles under the GATS, in particular the principles of non-discrimination (or most favoured nation treatment)[1] as well as national treatment in those sectors for which it has agreed to grant market access,[2] China's accession will herald genuine new opportunities for foreign service suppliers and, over time, radically change the way foreign companies do business in China. Such MFN and national treatment principles essentially require China to accord equal treatment to all WTO-member service suppliers on terms no less favourable than it accords to its own domestic service suppliers in areas where market access has been granted. Of course, whether this happens remains to be seen. Even with genuine will on the part of the Chinese government, local protectionism is so entrenched in many provinces and regions far removed from Beijing that implementation of these principles will be a significant challenge.

[1] GATS, Art. II.   [2] Ibid., Art. XVII:1.

China must publish its laws, regulations and administrative measures that relate to general implementation of its GATS commitments.[3] Moreover, many existing PRC laws and regulations will need to be extensively overhauled to conform with China's WTO commitments. While this process is already under way, it will undoubtedly continue for some time. In certain areas, the lack of an administrative framework for China's agreed commitments in the immediate aftermath of accession has led to confusion and uncertainty.

In order to assess the likely impact of WTO changes, this chapter first considers China's pre-accession and existing regulatory framework together with the principal pre-accession restrictions impacting on the distribution and logistics sectors respectively, and then examines how WTO changes are likely to affect foreign investment in the relevant distribution and logistics subsectors.

Outline of general legal and regulatory issues impacting on the provision of distribution and logistics services

Sales of self-made products

Under the current PRC policy framework, foreign-invested enterprises (FIEs) such as equity or co-operative joint ventures (JVs) and wholly foreign-owned enterprises (WFOEs) that have been approved to engage in manufacturing activities can generally only import products for their own use and sell only what they manufacture themselves.[4] This restriction has frustrated foreign investors with manufacturing operations in China, especially investors that have several FIEs, each producing different products. Many foreign companies wish to offer a family of products or range of complementary or interdependent products, but it is currently impossible to offer the full range of locally manufactured products together with imported products to Chinese customers through the same corporate sales entity. Foreign goods for resale to third parties in China must be imported

---

[3] 'Each member shall promptly and at least annually inform the Council of Trade in Services of the introduction of any new, or any changes to existing, laws, regulations or administrative guidelines which significantly affect trade in services covered by its specific commitments under this Agreement': ibid., Art. III:3.

[4] See further discussion at p. 253, below. The general prohibition on sales of non-self-manufactured products is derived from the restrictions on domestic commerce under earlier versions of the PRC Catalogue for Guiding Foreign Investment in Industry and effected in practice through business scope limitations.

by enterprises called foreign trade corporations (FTCs), authorized by the PRC government to engage in 'foreign trade'.

Business-scope limitations

Another significant factor impacting on the ability of foreign investors generally to conduct business in China is that, under current Chinese law, FIEs are only authorized to engage in a relatively narrow and specifically defined scope of business. In addition to being limited to carrying out directly business within their authorized scope, FIEs may only sub-contract third parties to carry out business that is within the authorizing FIE's approved scope of business. If an FIE engages in activities beyond its approved scope of business, it could be penalized by the relevant governmental agencies and, in a worst-case scenario, could be subject to revocation of its business licence. Similarly, if an FIE sub-contracts activities that are not specifically listed in its business scope, the contract may be declared invalid.

Article XV1:2(e) of the GATS prohibits restrictions as to the type of legal entity through which a foreign service supplier may supply a service in sectors where China has made a market-access commitment (unless an exception is specified in China's Services Schedule). However, China may still impose various business-scope restrictions such that only certain entities in a particular class of entity will be able to conduct particular services. For example, a JV that is authorized to engage in wholesaling may provide wholesaling services, but a JV authorized only to engage in manufacturing may not. Such business-scope limitations are not fully addressed in the Protocol or Services Schedule and will continue to restrict the activities of FIEs after accession.

Restrictions on establishment of FIE branches

Assuming that an FIE is able to obtain a business licence to engage in certain permitted distribution activities such as wholesaling or to provide certain logistics services such as freight-forwarding, the ability to establish an effective branch network is an essential key in developing a China-wide distribution network. In this regard, all FIEs are given a licence that enables them to operate in a particular city or other relevant local jurisdiction, such as a development zone. In practice, they are able to establish an on-the-ground presence in other localities only through opening a branch or a liaison office (upon approval of the relevant authorities in the FIE's home jurisdiction and in the area where it proposes to set up the branch). However, service-oriented FIEs are often not permitted or are otherwise discouraged from establishing branches outside their home jurisdiction as a result of statutory, policy or other restrictions directed towards protection of local interests. For example, leaving aside geographical restrictions, a freight-forwarding JV cannot establish branches until the expiry of a twelve-month waiting period, payment in full of capital contributions, and the addition of at least US$120,000 per branch to the registered capital of the JV. The establishment of a liaison office only permits a limited range of activities not including the provision of services, execution of contracts, and other direct business activities and is therefore not generally a viable or attractive alternative for service-oriented FIE's.[5]

Distribution services

Distribution services are broadly regulated under the Catalogue for Guiding Foreign Investment in Industry (the 'Foreign Investment Catalogue') as well as the Regulations for Guiding Foreign Investment (the 'Foreign Investment Regulations') both of which were revised with effect from 1 April 2002 to conform with China's WTO commitments.[6] Previously, distribution services fell under 'domestic commerce' (referring to the ability to buy, sell and trade products and services in China) and had been regulated under restricted category B of the December 1997 version of the Foreign Investment Catalogue. 'Domestic commerce' has now been replaced by a range of more specific distribution activities, each under separate headings. For example, 'wholesale and retail trade industries' and 'transportation and storage' are now partly regulated under a new, consolidated restricted category (which replaces the old restricted categories A and B) and partly under the encouraged category. These changes are clearly marked in the Foreign

---

[5] See Article 18 of the Detailed Implementing Rules of the PRC for the Administration and Registration of Enterprise Legal Persons, promulgated by the State Administration of Industry and Commerce on 3 November 1988.

[6] The new Foreign Investment Catalogue was issued by the State Development and Planning Commission, the State Economic and Trade Commission and the Ministry of Foreign Trade and Economic Co-operation, approved by the State Council on 4 March 2002 and promulgated on 11 March 2002. It replaces the previous version issued by the same authorities on 31 December 1997. Similarly, the new Foreign Investment Regulations were promulgated by the State Council on 11 February 2002 and replace the Provisional Regulations for Guiding Foreign Investment promulgated by the State Planning Commission, the State Economic and Trade Commission and the Ministry of Foreign Trade and Economic Co-operation on 20 June 1995.

Investment Catalogue as having been implemented to conform with China's accession commitments.

Investment projects falling in the restricted category may now be approved by provincial-level authorities if the value of investment is within such authority's authorised approval limit. This is a development of great practical significance. Previously, the establishment of any entity proposing to conduct 'domestic commerce' activities required PRC central government approval. In practice, such approvals were generally not granted.

Article 12 of the Foreign Investment Regulations makes clear that where procedures for examination and approval of foreign investment projects are specified in relevant laws and regulations, such procedures will prevail over the Foreign Investment Catalogue. As a result, notwithstanding that aspects of distribution activities may nominally be classified as 'encouraged', they may still be restricted by the terms of specific legislation.

Principal investment vehicles for foreign investment in distribution services under current laws and regulations

Wholesaling

Since the introduction of the Trial Measures on Foreign Investment Commercial Enterprises (the 'Trial Measures') on 25 June 1999, foreign investors have been able to establish wholesale and retail commercial enterprises (*shangye qiye*) in the form of JVs. These are referred to in the Trial Measures as joint venture commercial enterprises or 'JVCEs'. The promulgation of the Trial Measures ended a longstanding ban on foreign investment in the wholesale sector and set forth more comprehensive measures for foreign participation in retail sales. However, both the retail and wholesale industry is still restricted to those foreign investors which meet the high threshold conditions specified under the Trial Measures.

The possibility of establishing a wholesale JVCE has been particularly attractive to foreign investors wishing to engage in effective distribution of both locally manufactured products and foreign-imported goods. However, the threshold requirements applicable to foreign investors wishing to establish a wholesaling JVCE are extremely high, ruling out all but the largest of multinational investors. For example, Article 5 of the Trial Measures stipulates that the foreign party to a wholesaling JVCE must have assets exceeding US$300 million and have average annual sales exceeding US$2.5 billion in the three years prior to filing an application for establishment of a JVCE. Chinese partners must also satisfy stringent, but lower, threshold requirements. For example, a Chinese party to a wholesaling JVCE must have assets of at least RMB 50 million (approximately US$5.96 million) or at least RMB 30 million (approximately US$3.62 million) if based in central or western areas of China.

Notwithstanding the implementation of the Trial Measures and the concomitant relaxation of policy restrictions on foreign investment in the wholesaling sector in China, it remains difficult as a matter of practice to establish a wholesaling JVCE, even where the parties satisfy the difficult criteria set forth in the Trial Measures. As of mid-2002, there had been very few wholesaling JVCEs successfully approved in accordance with the Trial Measures.

In addition to high financial threshold requirements under the Trial Measures, wholesaling JVCEs may only be established in capital cities of provinces and autonomous regions, municipalities under the direct administration of the central government, special economic zones and all cities listed separately under state plans (the 'trial cities'). However, Ministry of Foreign Trade and Economic Co-operation (MOFTEC) and State Economic and Trade Commission (SETC) officials have indicated informally that as of mid 2002, notwithstanding the provisions in the Trial Measures, a wholesaling JVCE will only be permitted to be established in Beijing, Shanghai, Tianjin or Chongqing and not in other trial cities. Moreover, under current central government policies, only *one* wholesaling JVCE will be permitted to be headquartered in each of Beijing, Shanghai, Tianjin and Chongqing, again a more restrictive quota than that specified in the Trial Measures. Foreign wholesalers therefore may be shut out of some of these cities once a quota is filled in a particular city.

There are a host of other restrictions set out in the Trial Measures.[7] Collectively, these ensure that for all but the largest foreign investors, establishment of a wholesaling JVCE as a distribution vehicle to provide a range of goods and related services is not a viable option.

Retailing

As previously mentioned, the Trial Measures allow for the establishment of JVCEs that can engage in the provision of both retail and wholesale services. Under Article 6(4) of the Trial Measures, retailing JVCEs can also engage in limited wholesaling activities as a 'secondary business'. The threshold

---

[7] For example, minimum capitalization requirements (Art. 6); maximum term of operation (Art. 6); royalties payable to the foreign party (Art. 7); scope of business (Art. 12); and import restrictions (Art. 16).

requirements applicable to a foreign investor in a retailing JVCE are some-what lower than those required to establish a wholesaling JVCE, although are still highly restrictive.[8]

In most other respects, the requirements applicable to retail JVCEs are the same or similar to those for wholesale JVCEs. However, a significant difference is that if the JVCE operates three stores or less, the foreign party will be permitted to hold up to a 65 per cent equity stake, upon approval. Even where more than three stores are operated, it may be possible for a retail JVCE to hold a majority interest if certain domestic sourcing and export commitments are met and State Council approval can be secured.

Holding companies

Since their introduction in the mid-1990s, following promulgation of the Interim Regulations Concerning Investment in and Establishment of Investment Companies by Foreign Business Entities (the 'Holding Company Regulations'),[9] a foreign-invested holding company in the PRC has been permitted to undertake sales agency services for or provide assistance to its directly owned subsidiary companies in China in connection with the sales and marketing of products produced by its subsidiary FIEs. MOFTEC interpreted the Holding Company Regulations to permit holding companies to be paid a commission on sales but did not permit holding companies to take title to the goods sold. However, in August 1999, MOFTEC issued a notice that substantially changed its earlier position, thereby permitting holding companies to engage in a limited form of distribution.[10] Although they could not distribute products produced by their ultimate parent investor, offshore affiliates or companies other than their subsidiary ventures in China, holding companies could in effect engage in *some* of the wholesale and retail distribution rights promised under China's Services Schedule as from August 1999 and have continued to do so following accession.

However, it should be emphasized that the threshold requirements for authorization to establish and maintain a holding company remain very high.

---

[8] For example, under Article 5(2) of the Trial Measures, the average annual sales of the foreign party to a retailing JVCE in the three years prior to the application must exceed US$2 billion and assets shall exceed US$200 million in the year prior to the application, as opposed to US$2.5 billion and US$300 million respectively for a wholesaling JVCE. Capitalization requirements are also lower – see Article 6(3).

[9] Holding Company Regulations, promulgated by the MOFTEC, with effect from 4 April 1995.

[10] Supplementary Regulations of the Ministry of Foreign Trade and Economic Co-operation Concerning the Interim Regulations Concerning Investment in and Establishment of Investment Companies by Foreign Business Entities, promulgated 24 August 1999.

Foreign companies are required to have already invested US$10 million in China and to pledge a further US$30 million to future ventures or products.[11] Holding companies must also maintain investments in at least ten separate FIEs in order to qualify as a holding company under the Holding Company Regulations.[12]

Bonded zone trading companies

Bonded zone trading companies (BZCs) have in recent years become one of the most popular vehicles for international trade and, though legally questionable, also for conducting domestic distribution activities. Bonded zones, sometimes also referred to as 'free trade zones', are not regarded as part of China for customs purposes. Goods entering and exiting a bonded zone from and to destinations outside China are exempted from customs duties and value added tax. It is only when goods, products or raw materials enter into China proper, from the bonded zone, that customs duties and VAT are imposed. Regulations applicable in the bonded zones permit FIEs to engage in a wider scope of business than is permitted in China proper and, within the zone, lift the normal restrictions imposed on foreign investment in trading, distribution and service activities.[13] BZCs have been attractive to foreign investors because FIEs have been able to engage in otherwise impermissible distribution activities by interposing a BZC in the sales chain.

Overview of China's principal accession commitments for regulation of distribution services

The Services Schedule provides for a phased-in opening to foreign investment in four specific subsectors under the heading of 'distribution services', namely commission agents' services, wholesaling, retailing and franchising.

Commission agents' services and wholesale services

Commission agents' services and wholesale trade services are dealt with in the same way. The key operative provisions provide that within one year

---

[11] Holding Company Regulations, Art. 2.   [12] Ibid.

[13] The State Council and General Administration of Customs have approved thirteen bonded zones as at mid-2002. The Regulations on Shanghai Waigaoqiao Bonded Zone, promulgated by the Shanghai Municipal People's Congress, with effect from 1 January 1997, are a good example of typical bonded zone regulations.

after accession foreign service suppliers will be permitted to establish joint ventures to engage in commission agents' business and wholesale business of all imported and domestically produced products (except certain sensitive products including, amongst others, books, newspapers, magazines and pharmaceutical products, which foreign-invested wholesalers will only be permitted to handle from the beginning of the fourth year after accession, and chemical fertilizers, processed oil, and crude oil, which may be handled from the beginning of the sixth year after accession). Salt and tobacco are completely excluded from the Services Schedule.

'Sales agency business' is specifically regulated under the restricted category of the Foreign Investment Catalogue providing expressly for foreign participation in agency businesses including 'cargo transport, freight and advertising, etc'.[14] However, at present, there is no specific implementing framework for the establishment of FIE commission or sales agencies. Thus, while the theoretical possibility of establishing such an FIE exists, in practice there is no clear approval or registration process for doing so.

The Services Schedule provides that within one year after accession foreign investors will be permitted to engage in wholesaling by way of joint venture. The Trial Measures already allow for the establishment of wholesaling JVCEs, as discussed above. JVCEs established prior to accession were 'grandfathered' (protected from change or alteration) upon accession. However, whether the Trial Measures will be amended to reflect China's WTO commitments, or replaced with entirely new WTO-consistent legislation, remains to be seen. At the time of writing, new or amended legislation is expected in due course. While the Services Schedule clearly deals with the phasing-out of equity and geographical restrictions (discussed further below), it is by no means clear that the onerous capitalization and other requirements[15] for foreign investors, Chinese partners and for wholesaling JVs themselves will be eliminated or even reduced. National treatment principles may only partially solve these issues.

For the first year following accession, China was not obliged to allow foreign-majority ownership in wholesaling or commission agent ventures. From the beginning of the third year after accession, foreign-majority ownership (but not 100 per cent foreign ownership) will be permitted without geographic or quantitative restrictions. Only from the fourth year after accession will restrictions on ownership and form of establishment be

---

[14] Foreign Investment Catalogue, restricted category B, item 14(7).
[15] See pp. 245–6, above.

removed, implying that foreign investors will be permitted to establish wholesaling WFOEs at that time.

Retailing

Restrictions in the retailing sector are to be liberalized leading to the elimination of almost all geographic, quantitative, equity or form of establishment restrictions by the beginning of the fourth year after accession. At such time it should theoretically be possible for a foreign investor to establish a retail sales venture anywhere in China, in the form of a WFOE.[16]

Upon accession, foreign retail-service suppliers will be permitted to establish retail joint ventures in five special economic zones (Shenzhen, Zhuhai, Shantou, Xiamen and Hainan) and in specified cities (Beijing, Shanghai, Tianjin Guangzhou, Dalian, Qingdao, Zhengzhou and Wuhan). At such time, in Beijing and Shanghai, a total of no more than four retailing joint ventures will be permitted. In each of the other cities except Zhengzhou and Wuhan, the number of retailing JVs will be limited to two. In Beijing, two of the four JVs will also be permitted to establish additional branches in Beijing.

Starting no later than the beginning of the third year after accession, foreign-majority control will be permitted in retailing JVs and all provincial capitals; Chongqing and Ningbo will also be open to retailing JVs.

Upon accession, foreign service suppliers will be permitted to engage in the retailing of nearly all products except for: (a) the retailing of books, newspapers and magazines, which will be permitted no later than one year after accession; (b) the retailing of pharmaceutical products, pesticides and processed petroleum oil, which will be permitted no later than three years after accession; and (c) the retailing of chemical fertilizer, which will be permitted no later than five years after accession. Upon accession, foreign service suppliers will be allowed to provide the full range of related subordinate services including after-sales services for the products they distribute.

The provisions of the Services Schedule do not substantially improve the position for foreign participation in retailing at least until such time as all geographic, quantitative, equity and form of establishment restrictions are removed at the beginning of the fourth year after accession. As

---

[16] Note, though, the exception in China's GATS Schedule for non-branded chainstores with more than thirty outlets and selling certain listed products.

with wholesaling, it is unclear whether the relevant provisions of the Trial Measures will be scrapped or amended so as to reflect China's commitments.

Finally, it remains unclear what treatment will be given to foreign retailers, which have established an extensive retail presence in China on the basis of locally approved JVs and/or other franchise arrangements that do not conform with the provisions of the Trial Measures.[17] On the one hand, corporate structures and other arrangements that were illegal prior to accession have not formally been 'grandfathered' after accession. On the other hand, there are a number of retailers, notably Carrefour, that have continued to operate throughout China with huge investments, without MOFTEC and SETC approval at the central level, in contravention of the Trial Measures.[18] Ultimately, China will either have to enforce its stated regulatory restrictions on an MFN basis or find itself continually involved in WTO dispute settlement procedures.[19]

Franchising and other commitments

In the absence of a specific framework for franchising, foreign investors have had to rely on trademark, trade name and other licensing agreements with FIEs or domestic PRC companies to create an effective franchise arrangement. Many of these arrangements have been questionable, viewed collectively, in that they have often been adopted so as to circumvent approval requirements at the central government level in restricted industries, although each element of an arrangement (such as an arrangement

---

[17] A series of central government notices (see, for example, the Notice on Immediate Cessation of Unauthorised Approval and Covert Establishment of Foreign-Invested Commercial Enterprises, of 13 November 2000, and the Notice on Strengthening Rectification of Non-Trial Foreign Invested Commercial Enterprises, of 6 August 2001) have directed that illegally approved retailers conform their operations with the provisions of the Trial Measures. Very few foreign retailers have done so or been penalized for failure to do so.

[18] See 'Vive la différence', *Business China*, Economist Intelligence Unit, 12 February 2001; 'Beijing jumps on Carrefour for flouting retailing rules', *Financial Times*, 8 February 2001. Carrefour's operations in China have also received a great deal of attention in the Chinese press (during February 2001). However, while Carrefour and other foreign retailers have been subject to government rectification requirements, some uncertainty remains, as some notices have not been publicly issued. For example, a circular issued as document *Guo Jing Mao Wai Jing* [2001] No. 354 by SETC, MOFTEC and SAIC relating to Carrefour's operations remains 'neibu' – a restricted internal document.

[19] The WTO trade disputes mechanisms, which China is obligated to abide by on accession, flow primarily from the Uruguay Round Understanding on Rules and Procedures Governing the Settlement of Disputes. WTO disputes may be commenced by WTO Member States. There is no private right of action.

to provide management consulting services in conjunction with a trademark licence and trade name licence) considered alone, may not breach any
laws and otherwise be unexceptional. Foreign investors will therefore welcome the elimination of all restrictions on franchising as from the fourth
year after accession, thereby removing legal doubts in connection with
the arrangements which many foreign service suppliers currently adopt.
However, there will be no major changes to the status quo until the fourth
year following accession and until a clear regulatory framework has been
developed.

Wholesale or retail services, away from a fixed location, are also dealt
with in China's accession commitments. At the beginning of the fourth
year following accession, foreign companies will be able to establish WFOEs
to engage in direct marketing/sales activities. Foreign companies such as
Amway and Avon were hugely successful in utilizing door-to-door sales in
China, until PRC authorities banned such sales methods in April 1998 on
the basis of public-interest concerns, namely that such practices coerced or
deceived consumers and that the bulk of direct marketers used 'disreputable
business practices'.[20]

Likely impact of China's accession commitments on corporate entities for foreign investment

The Services Schedule and other bilateral market-access agreements do
not deal fully with government approval requirements. Thus, even for the
specific entities discussed in the Services Schedule, central government approval may still be required even after all geographic, equity, quantitative
and form of establishment restrictions are removed. It remains too early
to tell what impact this will have on the implementation of China's agreed
commitments.[21] It is, however, significant to note that paragraph 84(a) of
the Report of the Working Party on China's Accession provides, *inter alia*,

---

[20] See Notice Concerning the Prohibition of Direct Marketing Business Activities, issued by the
PRC State Council in April 1998, issued as document *GuoFa* [1998] No. 10, and the Notice
Concerning Change of Sales Method of Foreign Invested Direct Marketing Enterprises, jointly
issued by MOFTEC, the State Administration of Industry and Commerce and the State Bureau
for Internal Trade on 18 June 1998.

[21] GATS, Art. VI provides, *inter alia*, that Member States must deal with applications for approval
to provide a service where a specific commitment has been made and inform the applicant
within a reasonable period of time. This provides a minimum safeguard against abuse, but there
is nevertheless much room for abuse of the approval process.

that China promises to eliminate its system of examination and approval of trading rights within three years after accession, thereby presumably allowing all FIEs to import and export all goods except those listed in Annex 2A to the Protocol. Nevertheless it is equally important to understand that such rights do not allow importers to *distribute* goods within China.

Manufacturing FIEs

While the restriction on sales of non-self-made products continues to be actively applied to FIEs,[22] there is no legislative or other legal rule to this effect. The restriction is effected through limitation of the business scope of a manufacturing FIE contained in the business licence issued to it by the local Administration of Industry and Commerce. Business-scope restrictions are likely to remain for several years after accession. China's specific services commitments do not require China to remove this system. The Services Schedule in effect merely states what is already the case: namely that, upon accession, FIEs are permitted to distribute their products manufactured in China. However, expectations were raised by the US government's summaries of its November 1999 bilateral market-access agreement with the PRC (the 'US–China Agreement'), which indicated that foreign companies would be able to distribute *imported* products as well as those made in China. The Services Schedule, however, only establishes that FIEs specifically established for wholesale, wholesale agency or retail distribution will be able to distribute imported products.

Despite the rapid pace of state-sector and industry reforms in China, it is possible that in the foreseeable future manufacturing FIEs will continue to be regulated in the same way as they are at present, subject to tight restriction on distribution rights. There are no specific phase-in distribution rights for manufacturing FIEs. Even once all restrictions on distribution functions referred to in the Services Schedule have been removed, it is possible that manufacturing FIEs will continue to have somewhat limited distribution functions as a result of business-scope limitations. However, the interaction between the GATT and the GATS is important here. China will have to be careful that treatment of distribution of imports does not accord imports less favourable treatment than like domestic goods in violation of Article III of the GATT. Discriminatory restrictions on who can distribute imported

---

[22] See pp. 242–3, above.

products may infringe the GATT even if they do not infringe specific GATS commitments.

Holding companies

Following the discussion above in respect of manufacturing FIEs, the Services Schedule does not oblige the PRC to extend wholesale and retail rights to existing FIEs (including holding companies) other than dedicated wholesale and retail FIEs. Pre-accession holding companies ought, however, to have had their distribution rights grandfathered upon accession.

Bonded zone trading companies

Once FIEs generally are granted trading rights, and once geographic and other restrictions are eliminated, it seems reasonable to assume that BZCs will no longer be attractive as a vehicle for circumventing restrictions on domestic distribution.

Logistics services

The United Nation's Development Programme uses the term 'logistics' to refer to 'that part of the supply chain process that plans, implements, and controls the efficient, effective flow and storage of goods, services and related information from the point of origin to the point of consumption in order to meet customers' requirements'.[23] This is a useful definition in that it covers the wide range of services auxiliary to the distribution of goods necessary for their efficient delivery from place of production to markets. However, in China such definition is also somewhat deceptive, as the 'logistics industry' is in fact a number of different industries, regulated separately both at the state and provincial levels.

On 1 March 2001 several Chinese government authorities, namely the SETC, the Ministry of Railways (MOR), the Ministry of Communication (MOC), the Ministry of Information Industry (MII), MOFTEC and the Civil Aviation Administration of China (CAAC), jointly issued the Several

---

[23] 'Background on China's logistics industry', report issued by UN Development Programme on opening of the International Conference on Modern Logistics and E-Commerce, Beijing, 29 October 2000. Available at www.unchina.org/undp/news/html/bk001029.htm.

Opinions on Accelerating the Development of Modern Logistics in China (the 'Logistics Opinion'). The Logistics Opinion is the first PRC governmental document that recognizes and defines the concept of 'logistics'. Paragraph 2 of the Logistics Opinion defines logistics as 'a complete process where raw materials or finished products flow from the starting point to the destination point together with the effective flow of related information'. The Logistics Opinion also considers transportation enterprises, warehousing/delivery enterprises, freight-forwarding enterprises and coordinated transportation enterprises as 'logistics enterprises'.

Regulatory treatment of foreign participation in logistics

As of August 2002, the regulatory regime governing logistics is in a state of flux. Building on the policy developed in the Logistics Opinion, MOFTEC issued the 'Notice on Issues Relating to the Launch of Pilot Projects for the Establishment of Foreign-Invested Logistics Enterprises' (the 'Logistics Notice'). The Logistics Notice, which became effective on 20 July 2002, represents the first integrated approach to the regulation of the various services discussed above that together comprise 'logistics services'. It is therefore a very significant development. The Logistics Notice permits a foreign-invested logistics enterprise, established in accordance with the provisions thereof, to provide a relatively wider scope of services than is available to logistics service-providers established under other existing regulations. Under the Logistics Notice foreign-invested logistics enterprises may, upon approval, operate some or all of the following services:

logistics services for international distribution: import/export business and related services, including the business of importing or exporting goods, import/export agency services for export processing enterprises and provision of international freight-forwarding services for goods to be imported or exported by sea, air or land;
third-party logistics services: general cargo transport by road, storage, loading, unloading, processing, packaging, distribution, related information-processing services and/or consulting services, domestic freight-forwarding services and operation of logistics services through computer networks.

Until issuance of the Logistics Notice, there has been no over-reaching legislation governing the establishment and operation of FIEs that wished

to provide comprehensive logistics services, from the provision and operation of physical infrastructure to the supply of sophisticated services for
supply-chain and inventory management. Prior to issuance of the Logistics
Notice, FIEs whose scope of business allowed them to engage in 'logistic
services' (including related consulting and management services) had been
established as warehousing and consulting entities, trucking companies or
as freight-forwarding enterprises. These are the principal corporate entities
through which 'logistics services' have been conducted with foreign-equity
participation in China, although the Logistics Notice now opens fresh pos-
sibilities. Under current regulatory restrictions, only warehousing can be
conducted utilizing a WFOE and only then in a few locations, as discussed
further below.[24] Freight forwarding and trucking must be carried out, for
the time being, on a joint venture basis.

As of August 2002, no foreign invested logistics enterprises have been
established (or approved) under the Logistics Notice, so it is too early to tell
what practical impact the Logistics Notice will have on the development of
the PRC logistics industry. However, in theory, the Logistics Notice ought
to give greater flexibility to foreign logistics service providers that wish to
provide a range of integrated services in the 'Pilot Areas' described below.
This is because any enterprise approved under the Logistics Notice will not
have to characterize itself purely as a freight-forwarding company, trucking
company or storage company etc., as is the case under other existing regulations (as discussed further below). Notwithstanding this business scope
flexibility, the Logistics Notice only expressly permits the establishment
of foreign-invested logistics enterprises on a joint venture basis and only
in pilot areas designated by MOFTEC. At present these areas are Beijing,
Tianjin, Shanghai, Chongqing, Zhejiang, Jiangsu, Guangdong and the
Shenzhen special economic zone (the 'Pilot Areas'). Outside these Pilot
Areas the pre-Logistics Notice regime will continue to apply and, confus-
ingly, even within the Pilot Areas, pre-Logistics Notice legislation, such as
the IFF Regulations and Road Transport Regulations (discussed below),
will continue to apply. The Logistics Notice also makes clear that where
departments other than MOFTEC have jurisdiction to approve, say, road
transport services or computer-based logistics services, a JV that wishes to
provide such services will still be required to obtain the relevant department's approval under existing laws and regulations.

[24] See pp. 260–1.

The prospect, under the Logistics Notice, of a one-stop-shop MOFTEC approval to obtain a wide-ranging business scope permitting fully integrated logistics services may therefore, at least in the short to medium term, prove illusory. Moreover, the Logistics Notice contains relatively high threshold capital requirements as a pre-condition for establishment of a JV logistics enterprise, which will restrict market access to all but large foreign investors.

In a perhaps unintended way, the Logistics Notice reaffirms continuing ad hoc regulation of separate logistics services by a number of different government agencies. While MOFTEC clearly prefers an integrated approach, it may be expected that other departments will continue to protect their own turf. Clearly, State Council or higher level legislation will be required in the future to ensure such an integrated approach prevails. Until such time, other legislation regulating various logistics services will remain important and is examined further below.

Freight forwarding

The week following China's accession to the WTO saw MOFTEC issue the Administrative Regulations on Foreign Investment in the International Freight Forwarding Industry (the 'IFF Regulations'), which took effect on 1 January 2002. The IFF Regulations replace the Regulations on the Examination and Approval of International Freight Forwarding Enterprises with Foreign Investment (the 'IFFEFI Regulations') of 9 September 1996.

The IFF Regulations are clearly based on China's agreed commitments on freight-forwarding services and introduce some significant new developments. In some cases the IFF Regulations provide for more liberal market-access conditions than commitments agreed in China's Services Schedule. However, the IFF Regulations do not cover domestic courier services and do not appear specifically to regulate domestic freight forwarding, both of which are permissible, upon accession, under the terms of the Services Schedule. Accordingly, a number of issues remain to be clarified and some freight forwarders may yet find that they are unable to obtain in practice a suitable business scope or otherwise face practical restri[...] cific approval can be obtained under the provisions of th[...] to provide such domestic courier or domestic freight-fo[...]

Article 9 of the IFF Regulations has enlarged the[...] that an international freight-forwarding enterprise with[...]

(an IFFEFI) may be permitted to engage in. Significantly, freight-forwarding of personal articles, distribution, transhipment and short-distance freight services as well as international multimodal transport and container transport have been added as possible new business items under Article 9.

Under current policy, no 100 per cent foreign-owned subsidiaries are permitted. In fact, for the time being, the foreign party to an IFFEFI is limited to holding no more than 50 per cent of the IFFEFI's equity.[25] However, Article 4 of the IFF Regulations contemplates an unspecified timetable for foreign-majority equity ownership and eventually for the introduction of WFOEs. A foreign party that invests in the establishment of an IFFEFI is prohibited from investing in the establishment of a second IFFEFI until the first IFFEFI has been in operation for two years, a substantial reduction from the five years required under the IFFEFI Regulations.[26] In addition to these restrictions, an IFFEFI will only be approved to establish branches at the central level after having completed one full year of operation.[27] If the branch is to be established in a different location from the headquarters, there are often further difficulties associated with obtaining local approval in the area where it is proposed to register the branch. Finally, additional minimum capital requirements are imposed: US$120,000 must be added to the original registered capital of the IFFEFI in respect of each new branch to be established.

It is therefore difficult for foreign logistics providers to deliver comprehensive and integrated logistics services using an IFFEFI structure, partly because of equity limitations, partly because of the practical difficulty in obtaining a sufficiently broad business scope and partly because of the restrictions on establishing a second and further IFFEFIs as well as branches thereof, through which additional logistics services could theoretically be provided.[28] Issuance of the Logistics Notice may solve some of these problems, but not all, and will only be effective in Pilot Areas.

As with other restricted industries, such as wholesaling and retailing, there are high threshold conditions that both the Chinese and foreign parties must meet in order to set up an IFFEFI, though the threshold requirements

---

[25] IFF Regulations, Art. 4.
[26] Ibid., Art. 7; IFFEFI Regulations, Art. 7.   [27] IFF Regulations, Art. 12.
[28] MOFTEC officials have indicated to me, informally, that a second IFFEFI may in practice be allowed if established by a separate subsidiary of the foreign investor and if such affiliate provides different (if similar) services.

for Chinese partners have been relaxed under the IFF Regulations and certain import/export volume requirements have been removed.

MOFTEC has considerable discretion in approving applications for the establishment of an IFFEFI. Article 6 of the IFF Regulations is a case in point. While somewhat narrower than the same provisions in the IFFEFI Regulations, it provides that wharves, harbours, airports and 'enterprises which have the capacity to bring unfair competition to the freight agency industry' may not act as investors in IFFEFIs. Typically, there are no legislative or judicial fetters that operate in any way to limit MOFTEC's power to interpret such provisions.

Trucking/ground transportation

The Administrative Regulations on Foreign Investment in the Road Transport Industry ('Road Transport Regulations') became effective on 20 November 2001. They have been clearly based on China's WTO commitments and replace 1993 legislation, which was broadly framed and highly discretionary.[29]

The Road Transport Regulations allow for foreign investment in trucking JVs with (in theory) up to a 99 per cent maximum equity limit as from 20 November 2001. The new legislation clearly contemplates the possibility of trucking WFOEs in due course, though trucking WFOEs are not generally permitted at the present time.[30]

The Road Transport Regulations appear to simplify the process of examination and approval for trucking JVs and give greater structure and certainty to the substantive and procedural requirements that were in place prior to accession. They appear to be even more liberal than the WTO commitments China agreed to in the Services Schedule, in that freight trucking businesses may be established as foreign-majority owned JVs, rather than with foreign equity capped at 49 per cent until the beginning of the second year after accession.

---

[29] See the Tentative Regulations of the PRC Ministry of Communications Governing Foreign Investment Projects to be Established in the Road Transportation Industry, promulgated by the Ministry of Communications, December 1993.

[30] The Interim Procedures of Examination and Approval of Wholly Foreign-owned Shipping Companies, promulgated by MOFTEC, 28 January 2000, allow for a WFOE structure. I am aware of several such shipping companies that, prior to accession, were also approved to operate trucking businesses on a wholly owned basis through the shipping WFOE. Presumably such operations have been grandfathered under the terms of China's accession.

Under the pre-accession regulatory framework it was not easy to obtain MOC approval for the establishment of a trucking JV. In cases where approval was obtained, the trucking JV was often frustrated by the difficulty of establishing branches across China. Protection of domestic trucking companies plays a significant role in the general reluctance of local authorities to consent to the establishment of a branch in its own local area. However, without such a branch network, it is impossible, as a practical matter, for a foreign-invested trucking JV to offer comprehensive domestic trucking services in China. It will be interesting to see to what extent implementation of the new Road Transport Regulations are also hampered by these concerns.

Warehousing

Since the 1 April 2002 revision of the Foreign Investment Catalogue, 'storage' appears in both the encouraged and restricted categories, although there is no specific mention of 'warehousing services'. Moreover, there is no specific statutory framework governing the establishment and operation of warehousing FIEs.[31] In the absence of specific rules applicable to warehousing FIEs, requisite approvals are difficult to obtain. In the past, where FIEs have been able to obtain approval to provide warehousing services, they have been generally only authorized to handle customs declarations for their own goods and not for the goods of their customers. In any event, warehousing FIEs cannot obtain a scope of business that includes any of the principal freight-forwarding business items, transport, delivery or wholesaling. Subject to these restrictions, in certain special zones, warehousing WFOEs are permitted on the basis of local approvals. The Pudong New Area and the Guangzhou Economic and Technological Development Area (GEDA) are two such zones, as are the Waigaoqiao and other bonded zones. Manufacturing FIEs have also sometimes been able to include warehousing within their scope of business, but only in connection with the warehousing and storage of their own goods.

Some smaller foreign logistics providers that cannot meet the threshold requirements to establish an IFFEFI or that do not have sufficient political capital to obtain approval for establishment of a trucking JV, have

---

[31] Under the encouraged category of the Foreign Investment Catalogue, 'storage' appears to be limited to storage in connection with listed transportation services (section VI, item 13). As regards warehousing services provided on an agency basis, I believe the correct view, supported by my discussion with MOFTEC officials, is that such services would be regulated under section VI, item 6 of the restricted category rather than under section V of the restricted category.

sometimes developed highly convoluted structures, often utilizing ware-housing WFOEs and, perhaps, a consulting FIE to provide management services. Such arrangements are often used in conjunction with a web of agency agreements, and trademark and trade name licences with PRC domestic service companies, in order for a foreign logistics company to provide comprehensive logistics services in its own name while attempting to remain within the scope of prevailing laws and regulations. However, such arrangements are cumbersome, inflexible and almost universally unsatisfactory. No improvement is likely in the short term. Even with the 1 April 2002 changes to the Foreign Investment Catalogue, an entity established purely to undertake third-party warehousing services is unlikely to prove an attractive or viable option for foreign logistics providers until such time as specific rules governing approval and establishment of such entities have been put in place.

Impact of China's accession commitments on foreign service providers in the logistics sector

As with distribution services, transport and logistics services are subject to phased-in liberalizations. The categories set forth in the Services Schedule do not correspond precisely with existing regulatory categories discussed above. However, most of the services relevant to foreign logistics providers are dealt with to some extent in the Services Schedule.

Freight forwarding

Under the Services Schedule, equity restrictions are relaxed one year after accession, and most other restrictions are eliminated within five years after accession. There is no discussion in the Services Schedule of what subsectors are covered by the term 'freight-forwarding agency services'. One presumes that, at a minimum, it covers the subsectors that constitute freight forwarding under Article 9 of the IFF Regulations, although questions arising as to the scope of domestic freight-forwarding activities are not dealt with specifically by the new IFF Regulations. The market-access provisions in the Services Schedule are in fact remarkably similar to the regulatory framework set out in the new IFF Regulations.

The liberalizations in the Services Schedule will be welcomed by foreign investors. However, substantive concerns remain. Not insignificant minimum capitalization requirements continue beyond the date for elimination of all foreign-equity restrictions. Of particular concern to foreign investors is the limitation of a twenty-year term of operation of a freight-forwarding FIE. While FIEs in non-sensitive, unrestricted industries can probably extend their term of operation without undue difficulty, China is not obliged to renew or extend the term of a foreign-owned freight-forwarding agency under the terms of the Services Schedule. This could be used in all sorts of coercive ways by the PRC government, as a carrot or a stick, and could still impact on market access years after the expiry of China's agreed accession timetable.

Freight transportation by road and rail

Under the Services Schedule, foreign service suppliers are able to take a minority interest of up to 49 per cent in a JV upon accession. In practice, freight trucking service suppliers are able to take a majority equity share (less than 100 per cent) now and will be free of all restrictions by the beginning of the fourth year after accession. In rail-transportation services, foreign service suppliers will be able to hold a majority equity share within three years and be free of all the restrictions by the beginning of the seventh year, at which time a WFOE should theoretically be possible.

While it is now theoretically possible for FIEs to be structured with up to 99 per cent foreign ownership in the road-freight sector, it may still prove very difficult in practice for foreign entities to obtain approval for such high equity ownership. Foreign logistics firms will be focusing on the beginning of the fourth year after accession, when the trucking sector ought to be open to genuine foreign competition, as WFOEs become possibilities. Other multinationals will position themselves to invest in the operation of rail operations, a sector which is to all practical effects off-limits to foreign participation at present. It should be noted that in both of these transport sectors, PRC government approval requirements have not been eliminated.

Storage and warehousing services

The Services Schedule provides that foreign service suppliers are permitted to take a minority interest in a joint venture (up to 49 per cent) upon accession and to hold a majority equity share within one year after accession. All equity and other restrictions are to be removed from the beginning of the fourth year following accession, at which time warehousing services may be provided by WFOEs.

The impact of these changes in the first three years of accession on warehousing WFOEs in Pudong, GEDA and other special zones is unclear. The Pudong authorities indicated informally that they would wish to continue to approve warehousing WFOEs after China's WTO accession, and, at the time of writing, continue to do so. WFOEs approved prior to accession have presumably been grandfathered.

The most significant benefit to foreign investors arising from China's accession commitments is that there are no specified restrictions on warehousing on an agency basis. Therefore, warehousing FIEs ought to be able to obtain central government approval to store customers' goods. Such approval was difficult to secure under the pre-accession regulatory regime.

Conclusion

China's accession to the WTO is one of the single most significant benchmarks in the process of opening and restructuring China's economy, a process that has been delivering continuous and rapid change since 1978. While this chapter has not examined the historical context of China's accession commitments, nor examined the commitments of other developing jurisdictions by way of comparative analysis, such a contextual framework cannot be ignored in any overall assessment of China's commitments in the distribution and logistics sectors. Nevertheless, many foreign service-oriented companies will be disappointed with the gradual pace of change and by the lengthy timeframe before all substantive restrictions are eliminated in the distribution and logistics sectors. In the wholesale, retail and freight-forwarding sectors, the commitments contained in the Services Schedule rarely represent substantial or dramatic departures from the pre-accession existing regulatory framework, at least not for the first couple of years after accession.

It must also be emphasized that the liberalizations in the distribution and logistics sectors will not flow to all FIEs, only to those who are specifically granted a business scope to engage in the provision of such services. As the chapter showed, liberalizations in each of the sectors discussed here are to be phased in over a period of several years. There is no 'big-bang' elimination of all restrictions. Among the more important of the restrictions that remain, though not necessarily inconsistent with WTO obligations, are business-scope restrictions and government approval requirements. These issues will inevitably impact the implementation of China's commitments, especially if the approval process is used as a mechanism to allow China to delay or 'backslide' from its agreed commitments.

A wide array of other factors will affect the implementation process: transparency of laws, implementation of the non-discrimination and national treatment principles under GATS, corruption, the political effects of continued state-sector reform, and whether Beijing will be able effectively to control dissenting local and provincial authorities are but some of the more difficult issues China will have to face. Notwithstanding that China is now a formal member of the WTO, it still has a great deal of legislative drafting work to do in order to ensure that its laws and regulations impacting on distribution and logistics and other relevant service sectors will be WTO compliant. Much of this legislative work will need to be undertaken at the provincial and local levels, where resources and expertise are most lacking.

Nevertheless, China's WTO accession is the first step on the road leading to full foreign participation in the distribution and logistics sectors and is a significant milestone in the development of China's distribution and logistics industries. Through it all, foreign service suppliers will stay the course. After all, the distribution and logistics sectors are, in a very important sense, the keys to the Promised Land of China's great consumer market.

15

Regulating the new economy: implications of WTO accession for telecommunications and e-commerce in China

IAN MACINTOSH

Introduction

This chapter examines the way in which GATS rules apply to telecommunication services and electronic commerce (e-commerce) in the Chinese context. Rather than list GATS articles, it discusses areas where current Chinese regulation may give rise to inconsistencies with China's WTO accession commitments.

The chapter focuses on the regulation of telecommunications services, including the telecommunications service fundamental to the internet. The chapter treats 'internet services' as composed of both 'carriage' services (the transmission of data over telecommunication networks) and 'content' (the data that are transmitted). It does not discuss internet content regulation. Some consideration, however, will be given to GATS provisions on domestic regulation with implications for e-commerce, focusing on new regulation on telecommunications, internet service providers (ISPs) and internet content providers (ICPs), with a brief discussion of encryption regulation.

The chapter is divided into five sections: the first section describes the priority given to China's telecommunications and internet industry and identifies key regulators; the second section considers the consistency of China's new telecommunications regulation with the WTO Reference Paper on Basic Telecommunications; the third examines the impact of

The opinions expressed are personal and do not necessarily reflect the views of the Australian government.

China's market-access commitments on mobile services as an example of liberalization in a particular sector; the fourth details the debate surrounding the definition of 'internet services' at the WTO and its implications for the regulation of ISP services; and, finally, the fifth section discusses GATS provisions on domestic regulation in relation to recent Chinese encryption regulation.

China's telecommunications sector

The Chinese government has emphasized the importance of the internet and e-commerce to the future development of China's economy. The CCP Central Committee attached great importance to accelerating the development of the IT industry in formulating the Tenth Five-year Plan (2001–5).[1] The IT industry is described as the 'key link' in upgrading China's industrial structure. Since 1993, significant advances have been made in developing the infrastructure for telecommunications and e-commerce, with a fibre-optic grid now in operation.[2] However, the attention given to infrastructure has not been matched by efforts towards regulatory reform, leaving China with an underdeveloped regulatory framework for telecommunications, the internet and e-commerce.

Regulators

The overarching body governing telecommunications and the information industry is the State Council National Information Leading Group, headed by Vice-Premier Wu Bangguo. When established, the leading group had three offices: the State Council Information Office (SCIO), the Network Security Office and the Year 2000 Office.

Within the bureaucracy, the Ministry of Information Industry (MII) has primary responsibility for regulating telecommunications and the internet. MII was formed in March 1998, through the merger of the Ministry of Posts and Telecommunications (MPT) with other agencies including the Ministry of Electronic Industries (MEI). In December 1999, MII Minister Wu Jichuan indicated that ISPs would be regulated by the MII. Although it

[1] AAP Wire Service, 18 October 2000.
[2] 'Wired China: the flies swarm in', *The Economist*, 22 July 2000, p. 22.

has been indicated that ICPs would be regulated by other government agencies (according to the types of content provided),[3] Minister Wu has also said that MII will only allow an ICP to be connected to an ISP after the ICP has obtained its business licence.[4] Furthermore, at other times ICPs have been described as 'value-added' telecommunication service providers,[5] which must by definition obtain a licence from MII.

As many internet firms in China provide both ISP and ICP services, a number of approvals and licences may be required to establish a single operation. This is further complicated by the fact that Minister Wu has signalled that 'more government agencies will have to be involved'[6] for e-commerce. These other agencies could include the Ministry of Foreign Trade and Economic Co-operation (MOFTEC), the State Economic and Trade Commission (SETC), the Ministry of Public Security (MPS), the State Encryption Management Commission (SEMC) and local authorities.[7]

Government agencies involved in regulating the internet all ostensibly seek to improve certainty for users and consumers. Yet there is a strong tendency for regulation to be viewed either as a mechanism for political control, or as a means of bureaucratic 'empire-building'. Despite the oversight role given to the SCIO, inadequate consultation between agencies is an emerging problem.

In October 2001, the State Council gave approval for the restructuring and consolidation of the telecommunications sector into four main providers. The traditional monopoly provider, China Telecom, is to be divided geographically between north and south, and renamed China NetCom in the north. JiTong Network Communications will become part of China Mobile (itself formerly the mobile arm of China Telecom). China

---

[3] *Management Methods on Internet Content and Service Provision*, issued on 1 October 2000.

[4] 'China to rollout new ISP regs by month's end', *China Online*, 3 September 2000. See also 'MII clarifies internet investment ban', www.usembassy-china.org.cn.

[5] 'China to oversee ICPs, ISP Regulations promised by Q1', *China Online*, 1 May 2000. The definition of ISP services will be discussed in the section on 'Electronic commerce', below.

[6] Quoted in *An Overview of China's Internet Market and Its Regulation*, Baker & McKenzie, April 2000, p. 9.

[7] For example, the Beijing Municipal Administration for Industry and Commerce (BMAIC) consumer protection regulation. 'Get the fraud out of the baud: Beijing issues laws to regulate e-commerce', *China Online*, 13 July 2000.

Railway Communications (China Railcom) will become part of China United Telecommunications (China Unicom).[8]

Recent history

China's WTO accession commitments are binding and subject to WTO dispute settlement procedures. WTO accession is likely to help avoid the confusion surrounding the regulation of the telecommunications sector in recent years. An MPT regulation issued in 1993[9] expressly prohibited both wholly foreign owned and joint venture enterprises in the telecommunications sector. Despite this formal ban, between 1994 and 2000, around forty foreign companies invested US$1.4 billion into telecom joint ventures.[10] The investment occurred through 'China-China-Foreign' or 'CCF' arrangements with China Unicom. Under the CCF arrangements, foreign firms invested in other Chinese companies, which in turn formed ventures with regional China Unicom affiliates.[11]

CCF arrangements were approved by relevant officials in MOFTEC, the State Administration of Industry and Commerce (SAIC) and local officials. However, in October 1998, the MII announced that the CCF project contracts were 'irregular' under state policy and regulation. At the request of MII, China Unicom negotiated compensation settlements with all their CCF investors, but some investors remained dissatisfied with the outcome of the compensation offered.[12]

The problems associated with CCF arrangements reflect ideological divisions within the Chinese bureaucracy.[13] MOFTEC took a liberal view in interpreting the regulation to allow investment, whereas MII adopted a conservative approach. By using the term 'irregular' rather than 'illegal', MII was able to avoid directly contradicting MOFTEC and SAIC.[14] The existence of binding WTO commitments may help avoid such problems in the future, although it is likely that there will be difficulties in implementation as a result of resistance both at central and local levels of the bureaucracy.[15]

---

[8] 'State Council approves China Telecom breakup, sector Consolidation', *China Online*, 16 October 2001.

[9] *Opinion on Further Strengthening the Regulation of the Telecommunications Industry*, issued on 3 August 1993. The MPT became part of the MII in 1998.

[10] 'China: will WTO help?' *Business Week Online*, 6 December 1999, www.businessweek.com.

[11] L. Chuang, 'Investing in China's telecommunications market: reflections on the rule of law and foreign investment in China' (2000) 20(3) *Journal of International Law and Business* 519.

[12] Ibid., at 522.   [13] Ibid., at 530.   [14] Ibid., at 529.   [15] Ibid., at 532.

PRC telecommunications regulation and WTO accession commitments

As part of the 'single undertaking' of WTO accession, China has become a party to the General Agreement on Trade in Services (GATS) rules on traded services. This includes general obligations, as well as specific commitments on the provision of market access and national treatment to foreign service providers.[16] China's commitments include undertakings with specific application to telecommunications, which are subject to the obligations on access to networks contained in the GATS Annex on Telecommunications. China's commitments also include a commitment to abide by the Reference Paper on Basic Telecommunications.[17] The Reference Paper, elaborating upon the obligations in the Annex, contains obligations with respect to, *inter alia*, competitive safeguards, interconnection, licensing, the allocation of scarce resources, and universal service obligations.

China's specific commitments on market access and national treatment are the consolidation of the negotiated outcomes reached with members of the China WTO Accession Working Party. For telecommunication services, China has made commitments on all basic and value-added telecommunication services set out in the Services Sectoral Classification List.[18] The commitments include the phased removal of foreign equity and geographic restrictions, and the removal of limitations on the scope of foreign business operations.[19] The phase-in periods for liberalization of the telecommunications market reflect the flexibility given to developing countries under Article IV of the GATS. Nevertheless, China's commitments compare favourably to those made by many Asia Pacific WTO members during the Uruguay Round and the 1998 Basic Telecommunications Agreement.[20] For example, in contrast to China, Thailand has not adopted the

---

[16] China's Services Schedule is contained in WTO Document WT/ACC/CHN/49/Add.2.

[17] During sector-specific WTO negotiations on basic telecom services that entered into force in February 1998 (the Basic Telecommunications Agreement), fifty-seven governments agreed to be bound (either in full or with a few modifications) to the Regulatory Principles of the Reference Paper on Basic Telecommunications (www.wto.org/english/tratop_e/serv_e/telecom_e/telecom_results_e.htm).

[18] WTO Document W/120. The classification of telecommunications services is not always according to W/120 definitions, as noted by a recent EU paper. See S/CSS/W/35.

[19] 'Australia signs big trade deal with China', press release, minister for trade, Australia, 22 May 2000, www.dfat.gov.au.

[20] For an assessment of commitments by regional countries, see Paddy Costanzo, 'Telecommunications liberalisation in the Asia Pacific: impact of WTO' (1999) 49(3) *Telecommunications Journal of Australia* 45–9.

Reference Paper, and neither Malaysia nor the Philippines have adopted it in full.[21]

China's Telecommunications Regulation: consistency with the WTO Reference Paper

In late 2000, the MII began to issue new regulations on the internet and telecommunications.[22] While some of the new rules did not add substantially to existing regulation,[23] the Management Methods for Internet Content and Service Provision require that internet information service providers[24] must obtain approval from MII before they are allowed to list on domestic and overseas markets, or establish joint ventures and partnerships with foreign investors.[25]

Most significant for this chapter was the release of the Regulations on Telecommunications of the PRC introduced in September 2000, and the Regulation on Foreign Invested Telecommunications Enterprises issued in December 2001. The regulations provide the first opportunity to examine the intent of policy-makers to develop regulation consistent with China's WTO commitments.[26] The new regulations are an important step forward in that they address a number of China's obligations under the Reference Paper, as well as commitments on market access and national treatment. Nevertheless, the regulations do contain gaps and flaws, which will need to be addressed before China can implement all of its commitments.

The next section of this chapter, 'Market-access commitments: mobile services', below, considers the consistency of the Regulation on Foreign Invested Telecommunications Enterprises with some of China's scheduled market-access commitments, those relating to mobile services. The rest

[21] This point is not always recognized. See, for example, Paul Budde, 'Special deal for China a mistake', *The Australian*, 6 November 2000.

[22] On 1 October the Management Methods on Internet Content and Service Provision; and on 7 November the Internet Public Information-release Services.

[23] See industry reactions to the Provisional Regulations Regarding Governance of Internet-based News Providers. 'New Net Rules not a Nuisance?', *China Online*, 5 December 2000.

[24] Internet information service (IIS) providers are defined in Article 2 as 'services that provide Internet users with information via the Internet'. This definition would include ICPs and possibly some services provided by ICPs. The definition of ISP services is considered in the section on 'Electronic commerce'.

[25] 'Your list is our command: China unveils new internet, telecom regs', *China Online*, 2 October 2000.

[26] China has not yet announced when it will issue the Telecommunications Law. See ibid.

of the present section examines the extent to which the Regulations on Telecommunications of the PRC meet China's obligations under the WTO Reference Paper. The Annex on Telecommunications, which was adopted by all WTO members in the Uruguay Round, will not be discussed in this chapter, as the Reference Paper expands upon many of the principles contained in the Annex.

Independent regulator

Paragraph 5 of the Reference Paper sets out the requirement for an independent regulator. Article 4 of China's new Regulations on Telecommunications formally provides for an independent regulator for telecommunications with a mandate to encourage competition. The formal separation of the regulator from service providers has significant potential implications, given the historically close relationship between the MII (and previously the MPT) and China Telecom. The very creation of the MII (and demise of the MEI) was the immediate context for the decision to ban contracts that had allowed foreign investment in China Unicom, which had been established by the MEI as the primary competitor to China Telecom. The difficulty of maintaining an effective independent regulator is not a problem unique to China; few regulators in the Asia Pacific are in practice independent.[27] The Reference Paper is itself inadequate in this respect, as paragraph 5 does not specify criteria against which independence can be assessed.

Licensing

Paragraph 4 of the Reference Paper requires that licensing criteria will be made publicly available. MII will issue telecommunication licences and supervise the operations of telecommunication services providers. Under Article 8 of China's Regulations on Telecommunications, it is necessary to obtain a licence as either a category 1 'Proprietory' provider, or a category 2 'Non-proprietory' provider. Article 10 defines general licensing criteria, while Articles 12 and 13 define the criteria an operator must fulfil to obtain a category 1 and 2 licence respectively.[28] Taken together, this publication of criteria would be likely to meet the transparency requirements of paragraph 4 of the Reference Paper. Nevertheless, while most of the criteria are clear, Article 10(6) allows for additional criteria to be added

---

[27] Costanzo, 'Telecommunications liberalisation'.

[28] Article 10 requires that the Chinese shareholding of a category 1 provider shall exceed 51 per cent. Levels of permitted foreign investment are discussed further at pp. 275–6, below.

at a later date. Article 12 requires the regulator to take account of 'competitiveness in the telecommunications market' before issuing a basic telecom licence. These Articles could potentially be applied in a manner inconsistent with the transparency requirements of paragraph 4 of the Reference Paper.

The Regulations on Telecommunications require that a decision on whether to issue a licence will be made within 180 days after receipt of an official application for a category 1 licence, and within 90 days for a category 2 licence.[29] Unsuccessful applications will receive a written response to all applications, which is ostensibly consistent with the transparency requirements of paragraph 4 of the Reference Paper. However, much will depend upon how the procedure operates in practice. For example, a licence denial which simply cited China's 'national interest' as the ground for rejection would be unlikely to meet paragraph 4 obligations.

Article 8 of the Regulations defines category 1 operators as those providing 'basic telecommunications business such as public network infrastructure, public data transmission, and basic voice communication services'. An Annex to the Regulations lists examples of basic telecommunication services.[30] Article 8 defines category 2 providers as those providing value-added services, which are described as 'the provision of telecommunication and information services on the basis of public network infrastructure'.[31] Considered together, the services listed cover those services in which China has made commitments under the terms of WTO accession. It is possible that some foreign firms, such as mobile operators requiring access to existing infrastructure, would only seek to obtain a category 1 licence. Furthermore, foreign firms that have an interest in providing both basic and value-added services are at least initially more likely to enter the market as category 2 companies. Nevertheless, the dual licence system can create problems for foreign firms that need to obtain both types of licences. While not unusual in the region,[32] the implementation of dual licence systems can

---

[29] Articles 11 and 14 respectively.

[30] Telephony, mobile telephone and data business, satellite and international services. Interestingly, it also includes some services provided by ISPs, in particular 'internet and its public data transmission business'. This is discussed further at pp. 279–82, below.

[31] This is further defined in the Regulations on Telecommunications of the PRC (Annex) to include e-mail, voice mail and EDI, as well as 'internet information business' and 'internet access business'.

[32] Singapore and Japan are two examples of WTO members that grant more than one type of licence.

give rise to unnecessarily burdensome regulation, potentially inconsistent with Article VI of the GATS on domestic regulation.[33]

Competitive safeguards

Paragraph 1 of the Reference Paper requires that competitive safeguards be provided to prevent anti-competitive practices. Article 41(1) and (2) of China's Regulations on Telecommunications prohibits any telecommunications operator from engaging in anti-competitive conduct such as restricting the services used by telecommunications subscribers to those which it provides. Furthermore, Article 42 prevents telecommunications operators from restricting the choices of subscribers in respect of other telecommunications services, granting unreasonable cross-subsidies, or providing services below cost, and engaging in activities that constitute unfair competition. These articles not only meet, but are more extensive than the relatively limited competitive safeguard requirements of paragraph 1 of the Reference Paper. If fully implemented, these safeguards should create the conditions for greater competition with China Telecom. To date, however, challenges to the dominance of China Telecom have not been successful, and the practical impact of State Council decisions to break up China Telecom remains to be seen.

Interconnection

Paragraph 2 of the Reference Paper sets out requirements for interconnection with the networks of major telecommunications suppliers. The terms of interconnection have been described as a 'matter of life and death'[34] for telecommunications providers in the China market. For category 2 firms the crucial question is the interconnection rates charged by category 1 companies to complete calls. China's new Regulations[35] specify that these rates will be 'cost-based',[36] which is in accordance with paragraph 2 of the Reference Paper, which requires that the terms of interconnection be 'cost-oriented'. There is no information regarding how rates will be calculated, but this is not a requirement under paragraph 2 of the Reference Paper. Also

---

[33] Article VI requires that regulation be administered in a 'reasonable, objective and impartial manner'.

[34] 'The new PRC Telecommunications Regulations: a first step towards a more level playing field', Linklaters & Alliance, p. 7, www.globalservicesnetwork.com/telecom_regs.pdf.

[35] See the Administration of Interconnection between Telecommunication Networks Tentative Regulations, issued by the MII on 7 September 1999.

[36] 'The New PRC Telecommunications Regulations', Linklaters & Alliance, p. 7.

consistent with obligations under the Reference Paper, where agreement cannot be reached between operators on the terms of interconnection, the MII can mediate, and propose and implement an outcome. Nevertheless, this regulatory framework could be undermined in practice. The Working Party Report on China's accession refers to China's maintenance of price controls, including for the telecommunications sector, although a footnote requires that this government pricing should be applied in a manner consistent with the Reference Paper.[37]

Scarce resources

Paragraph 6 of the Reference Paper builds on the 'reasonable and non-discriminatory' access requirement of the GATS Annex on Telecommunications by requiring that any procedures for the allocation and use of scarce resources, including frequencies, numbers and rights of way, will be carried out in an objective, timely, transparent and non-discriminatory manner. Article 27 of China's Regulations on Telecommunications defines 'telecommunications resources' to include those limited resources ensuring telecommunications functionality such as radio frequency, satellite orbit positions and telecommunications network codes. It provides that the state shall adopt an administrative system for the rational distribution and fee-based utilization of telecommunications resources. This should provide the basis for access to spectrum and other scarce resources by foreign providers, as required under the Reference Paper, although it is uncertain to what extent these regulations will be enforced in practice. It is worth noting that China Unicom subscribers have been prevented from accessing emergency call numbers.[38]

Universal service obligations (USOs)

Paragraph 3 of the Reference Paper requires that universal service obligations (USOs) must be administered in a transparent, non-discriminatory and competitively neutral manner, and not be more burdensome than necessary. China's Regulations on Telecommunications provide that a specific telecommunications company can be delegated with the task of providing a universal service. MII has been directed to work with other agencies to formulate rules on how to compensate telecom companies that

---

[37] WT/ACC/CHN/49, Annex 4, p. 138, note 2.
[38] 'Telecom monopoly set for break-up', *China Daily*, 1 April 2000, www.chinadaily.com.cn.

provide universal service.[39] This uncertainty raises the issue of the consistency of future regulation with paragraph 3 of the Reference Paper. MII and State Development Planning Commission (SDPC) officials have recommended special policies to direct foreign investment toward China's north-west provinces, where telecommunications infrastructure and services are underdeveloped.[40] This raises the possibility that foreign service providers could be subject to substantial USOs to help address the substantial income disparities across China. It will be necessary to monitor potential inconsistencies with paragraph 3 of the Reference Paper.

Market-access commitments: mobile services

In addition to obligations under the Reference Paper, China has made scheduled commitments to phase out geographic and foreign equity restrictions, and to remove limitations on the scope of foreign business operations. The following will consider China's scheduled commitments on mobile services, as an example of how accession commitments will affect a specific telecommunications sector.

China Mobile (formerly the mobile arm of China Telecom) is not only China's largest mobile operator (with 83 per cent of the market),[41] but also Asia Pacific's largest, and the third-largest in the world. High interconnect rates, the lack of transparent regulation,[42] and anti-competitive conduct are barriers to both local and foreign competitors to China Mobile. For example, China Mobile is better placed to gain improved access to the infrastructure through its relations with other, now disaggregated, parts of China Telecom. In this context, foreign investment is an important future source of competition and improved services. The Chinese market at the end of 1999 was penetrated at a mere 3.4 per cent,[43] although there has been substantial investment in China Mobile and China Unicom.[44] China has made significant commitments to liberalize its mobile services market,

---

[39] 'The New PRC Telecommunications Regulations', Linklaters & Alliance, p. 11.

[40] Xing Fan, 'China's WTO accession and its telecom liberalization', International Communications Study Program, Center for Strategic and International Studies, Washington, D.C., p. 8.

[41] 'China Mobile on Telstra guest list', *The Australian*, 2 September 2000, p. 34.

[42] See, for example, the uncertainty surrounding the regulation of mobile billing services. 'Wu weighs in: China's telecom regulator urges need to better "manage" internet', *China Online*, 5 December 2000.

[43] 'Vodafone steals a march on Telstra', *Financial Review*, 6 October 2000, p. 57.

[44] See ibid.

although the market-access commitments were not as comprehensive as those which the United States announced unilaterally in April 1999.[45] In some areas, the EU–China Agreement accelerated the implementation of commitments to liberalize mobile services.

Upon accession, foreign suppliers will be permitted to establish joint venture enterprises, without quantitative restrictions, and provide services in and between[46] the cities of Shanghai, Guangzhou and Beijing. Foreign investment in the joint venture shall be no more than 25 per cent. Within one year[47] of accession, the areas will be expanded to include fourteen major cities,[48] and foreign investment shall be no more than 35 per cent. Within three years[49] of accession, foreign investment shall be no more than 49 per cent. Within five years of accession, there will be no geographic restrictions.

An indication of the likely difficulties of implementing these commitments can be obtained by an examination of China's Regulation on Foreign Invested Telecommunications Enterprises, issued in December 2001. The Regulation expressly permits foreign investment in China's telecommunications sector for the first time.[50] However, under Article 5, joint venture basic telecommunication companies will be required to have RMB 2 billion (US$241 million), and value-added companies RMB 10 million (US$1.2 million), in registered capital. These additional licence conditions are not inscribed in China's scheduled commitments, and are therefore inconsistent with China's accession obligations.[51] Furthermore, while it is encouraging that the maximum foreign investment levels scheduled for basic and value added services are set out in Article 6 (49 per cent and 50 per cent respectively), the phase-in periods are left for the MII to determine 'according to related regulations'.[52] The same phrase is used with respect

---

[45] The April 1999 US–China bilateral 'deal', published on the internet by the United States but denied by China, permitted up to 51 per cent foreign equity participation in basic telecommunications services. The November 1999 deal only permits 49 per cent foreign equity participation.

[46] The EU–China Agreement included operations 'between cities'. See 'Highlights of EU China Agreement on WTO' (www.europa.eu.int). This addressed the problem that the November 1999 US–China Agreement had allowed foreign companies to operate 'within' certain cities but not 'between' those cities.

[47] The EU–China Agreement improved on the US–China phase-in period of three years.

[48] Chengdu, Chongqing, Dalian, Fuzhou, Hangzhou, Nanjing, Ningbo, Qingdao, Shenyang, Shenzen, Xiamen, Xian, Taiyuan and Wuhan.

[49] The EU–China Agreement improved on the US–China phase-in period of five years.

[50] See 'Full text of regs on foreign-invested telecom enterprises', China Online, 21 December 2001.

[51] In contrast, capital requirements for insurance companies are inscribed. See WT/ACC/CHN/49/Add.2, p. 33.

[52] 'Full text of regs on foreign-invested telecom enterprises', China Online, 21 December 2001.

to the phased removal of geographic restrictions under Article 4. As these 'related regulations' are not specified in either article, it is unclear whether implementation will be in accordance with the timeframes in China's Services Schedule. Commentators have noted that 'the regulations seem to be designed to add as much ambiguity and complexity to the process as possible'.[53]

Electronic commerce (e-commerce): internet service providers (ISPs)

E-commerce is simply a particular means of conducting commerce, and existing WTO rules should continue to apply to commerce conducted over telecommunication networks.[54] Concepts such as 'e-commerce', 'internet services' and the 'global information economy' blur the basic distinction between 'carriage' and 'content'. Carriage refers to the service of transmitting a product (good or service), whereas content refers to the product that is transmitted. As with a postal, maritime or air transport service, in an internet transaction a product can be transported from point A to B without undergoing a transformation. It is submitted that an 'internet service' is therefore made up of several components or layers of services, which can include:

- basic telecommunications service: the delivery of packet-switched data;[55]
- value-added services: for example, e-mail hosting, and search engines;[56]
- content services: for example audiovisual, advertising and professional services delivered electronically.[57]

---

[53] 'Foreign investors unhappy with new telecom regs', *China Online*, 20 December 2001.

[54] This is the premise of the WTO Work Programme on Electronic Commerce, announced by WTO ministers in May 1998, WT/MIN(98)/DEC/2.

[55] In contrast to the 'circuit-switched' traditional telephone network, which establishes a dedicated pathway between caller and receiver, the internet is based on 'packet-switched' technology. Digital data (text, graphic, video or voice) is broken into discrete packets, each of which is addressed (internet protocol) and travels to the destination over its own path, where it is reassembled with the other packets in the correct order (transmission control protocol). See definition of 'TCP/IP' at www.whatis.com.

[56] The WTO Secretariat defines value-added services to 'involve enhancement of the form or content of information by providing, for example, storage or retrieval'. In contrast, basic services 'such as voice telephony and data transport services' involve 'no change in form': M. Bachetta, P. Low, A. Mattoo, L. Schuknecht, H. Wagner and M. Wehrens, *Electronic Commerce and the Role of the WTO* (Geneva, 1998), p. 47.

[57] This approach is in accordance with the principle of 'technology neutrality'. It is the 'general view' of WTO members that the GATS is technologically neutral in that it does not contain any provisions that distinguish between the different technological means through which a service may be supplied. WTO Document S/L/74, p. 1.

WTO members have yet to reach a formal decision on the definition of services provided by ISPs. As a result, significant differences exist with respect
to both the definition of the services provided by ISPs and the application
of GATS rules to such services.[58] Only ten members have made express
commitments on the supply of internet 'access' services (as distinct from
the supply of other services that use the internet as a medium of delivery).[59]
As noted by the WTO Secretariat, however, commitments on internet 'access' services may already exist 'implicitly in the broader definition of basic
telecommunication services'.[60] A key unresolved issue is whether WTO
members will define internet delivery services (as distinct from the content
delivered) as a 'basic' or 'value-added' telecommunications service.[61]

Australia considers that the delivery of data over the internet is a 'packet-
switched data transmission service'.[62] As WTO members agree that the
provision of 'packet-switched data services' is a basic telecommunications
service,[63] then internet delivery services should be considered a basic service. However, the United States has not yet clarified whether it considers
internet delivery services a packet-switched data transmission service. A
US paper submitted to the WTO Services Council refers to 'internet services' and 'internet-based' services, but does not define these terms. The
paper states that the line between basic and value-added services should
be drawn 'as narrowly as possible', but does not define what, if any, internet services are basic telecommunications services.[64] Some indication of
possible US approaches can be found in domestic US regulation. Under
the US Communications Act, a basic telecommunications service is subject
to regulation. In contrast, ISPs are currently considered to only provide
'value-added' or enhanced services, and are therefore not subject to basic
telecommunications regulation.[65]

---

[58] Content providers (ICPs) would not be considered to provide a data-transmission service
(www.usembassy-china.org.cn).

[59] Bachetta et al., *Electronic Commerce and the Role of the WTO*, p. 47. For example, the United
States has expressly scheduled 'Transmission control protocol and internet protocol', whereas
the European Union, Australia and China have not.

[60] Bachetta et al., *Electronic Commerce and the Role of the WTO*, p. 47.

[61] WTO Documents S/L/74, p. 4, and S/C/M/35, pp. 3–4.

[62] Australian Negotiating Proposal, WTO Document S/CSS/W/17.

[63] See WTO Secretariat commentary on classification of telecommunications services:
www.wto.org/english/tratop_e/serv_e/ telecom_e/telecom_coverage_e.htm#basic.

[64] S/CSS/W/30, p. 4.

[65] J. Oxman, *The FCC and the Unregulation of the Internet* (Office of Plans and Policy Working
Paper 31, July 1999), p. 13 (www.fcc.gov). Oxman's paper suggests that even large ISPs do
not provide basic telecommunications delivery services, despite the fact that they transport
packet-switched data over their own networks.

China's domestic approach to the regulation of services provided by ISPs remains unclear. It has been claimed that in China 'internet service provision is to be classified in the same way as value-added'[66] services. Minister Wu himself has previously indicated in interviews that both ICPs and ISPs provide value-added telecommunications services.[67] However, under China's new Regulations on telecommunications, 'internet and its public data transmission business' is defined as a basic telecommunications service (supplied by category 1 providers). An ISP providing data-transmission services would therefore prima facie be required to obtain a category 1 licence. If it was, in addition, providing value-added services[68] it would presumably also be required to obtain a category 2 licence.

The definition of ISP services has important implications for (a) the application of the WTO Reference Paper to internet delivery services; (b) permitted levels of foreign investment in ISPs; and (c) regulation in the context of convergent technologies. If WTO members were to agree that internet delivery services are basic telecommunications services, then China would be required to meet associated obligations with regard to treatment of foreign ISPs.

Application of the Reference Paper

If internet delivery services are defined as a basic telecommunications service (packet-switched data transmission service), the Reference Paper would apply to such services. WTO members including the United States, the European Union, ASEAN economies, Australia and China (as part of WTO accession) have made commitments on packet-switched data services.

If all ISP services were to be classified as 'value-added' services, as maintained by the United States in the domestic context, the Reference Paper would not apply to internet delivery services. This would mean that any ISP supplying delivery services would have no obligations under the Reference Paper, regardless of what commitments that member had made on packet-switched data services. US claims that China had made commitments on

---

[66] *An Overview*, Baker & McKenzie, p. 17.

[67] Minister Wu is reported to have told *Caijing Zazhi* [Financial Magazine] that 'Just above basic telecommunications services is a layer of telecom value-added services including internet services. That layer can be divided into ISPs and ICPs.' 'China to oversee ICPs, ISP regulations promised by Q1', *China Online*, 1 May 2000.

[68] The definition of 'value-added' services under the Regulations on Telecommunications of the PRC (Annex) includes 'internet services' such as 'e-mail', 'internet access business' and 'internet information business'.

internet services would be invalid to the extent that the service provided by the ISP was a delivery of packet-switched data. Most ISP services in China are controlled by a few backbone service operators, such as China Telecom and China Unicom. Under the US definition, China Telecom would not be subject to the Reference Paper obligations to act in a way consistent with competitive safeguards or to provide 'cost-oriented' interconnection terms.

In the United States, where ISPs are not subject to basic telecommunications regulation, the market has become 'highly concentrated'.[69] A similar outcome in China would mean that a small number of Chinese firms would dominate the market, effectively undermining China's market-access commitments. This could become a significant problem, given that foreign firms are already cautious that China Telecom could move to deny bandwidth access.[70]

It should also be noted that if WTO members were in future to agree to define internet delivery services as a basic telecommunications service, China would be required to apply the principles of the Reference Paper to such services, regardless of how such services were defined within China's domestic laws and regulation.

Permitted levels of foreign investment

Until the December 2001 release of the new Regulation on Foreign Invested Telecommunications Enterprises, foreign investment in the internet sector (in either ISPs or ICPs) was not formally permitted. Yet the MII had not enforced the ban on the grounds that when the earliest telecommunications investment laws were drafted, the concept of ICPs (and ISPs) did not exist in China.[71] As a result, as much as US$100 million in foreign investment has poured into China's internet sector and more than 50 per cent of ICPs have foreign funding, including the major companies Sina.com, Netease.com and Sohu.com.[72]

MII officials have since said that these foreign investments in internet services were contrary to policy, and that the Chinese government would

---

[69] This was the view of the US Department of Justice in filing against the WorldCom–Sprint merger. See, for example, the speech by the director of operations and merger enforcement, 'Network effects in telecommunications markets', 13 August 1999, www.usdoj.gov.

[70] 'Data firm gains clients in China', *Wall Street Journal*, 28 August 2000. Cited in www.ft.com.

[71] 'MII clarifies internet investment ban', www.usembassy-china.org.cn, 28 September 1999.

[72] *An Overview*, Baker & McKenzie, p. 17.

take 'appropriate, logical and reasonable' procedures to solve the problem.[73] It remains controversial whether, and to what extent, foreign firms may now need to divest. However, China has undertaken, in horizontal commitments on services, not to make conditions of ownership, operations and scope of activities in licences or agreements authorizing the supply of services more restrictive 'than they exist as of the date of China's accession'.[74] In contrast to CCF arrangements discussed previously, foreign investment in ISPs/ICPs were in place at the time of accession, and should therefore be grandfathered.

In addition, China's scheduled market-access commitments will allow foreign investment in China-based internet companies. The extent of foreign investment permitted depends, however, on the definition of the service supplied by internet companies. Under China's commitments on value-added services, foreign suppliers may hold 30 per cent foreign equity share upon accession, 49 per cent after one year and 50 per cent after two years. Yet if ISPs are recognized as also supplying basic telecommunications services, ISPs will be subject to commitments on basic telecommunications; that is, foreign investment will be permitted up to 25 per cent within three years of accession, 35 per cent after five years and 49 per cent after six years.

In the short term, foreign investors may prefer all ISP services to be defined as value-added services. This would permit foreign equity participation up to 50 per cent within two years, rather than 49 per cent within six years. It may also avoid the need for foreign firms to obtain a category 1 licence. It is unclear, however, whether all ISP services will be classified as value-added services, given that Chinese regulators have yet precisely to define all ISP services. Furthermore, in the long term, foreign operators may find that their interests are better served if internet delivery services are defined as basic telecommunications services, and the Reference Paper is considered to apply to such services.

Convergence

The Tenth Five-year Plan describes the eventual convergence of telecommunications, television and internet networks into a 'seamless cloud' of information.[75] Minister Wu has recognized that the merging of cable and telecom services in China is inevitable. 'In future, voice, data, and

73 'MII clarifies internet investment ban', www.usembassy-china.org.cn.
74 WT/ACC/CHN/49/Add.2, p. 3.
75 'Information highway to become data cloud', *China Online*, 19 October 2000.

video will converge, and that is an irreversible trend.'[76] A pilot project in Shanghai has already integrated cable and television, computer networks and a phone system into a single platform. A cable-television station in Shanghai provides telecom services, internet services and internet protocol telephony.[77]

Nevertheless, Minister Wu has announced that cable-television companies would not be allowed to enter the telecommunications market to provide internet services.[78] MII officials have clarified that this restriction only applies to foreign companies as 'mutual access between telecom and cable-TV networks applies to domestic operators'.[79] This restriction would not be consistent with China's WTO commitments, to the extent that 'internet services' includes a basic telecommunications service. China has not scheduled a derogation from national treatment under Article XVII and market access under Article XVI of the GATS. China has adopted the *Chairman's Note on the Scheduling of Basic Telecommunication Services*,[80] which requires that basic telecommunications services can be provided through any means of technology, unless expressly excluded. China has not expressly excluded cable services (or other platforms) in its scheduled commitments. China has therefore undertaken to permit foreign operators to provide basic telecommunications services (consistent with scheduled market-access commitments) over cable networks.

Encryption regulation

A further example of how GATS rules can be applied to address problems in Chinese regulation of e-commerce has arisen in relation to encryption. Article VI of the GATS gives WTO members the flexibility to develop domestic regulation to achieve legitimate public-policy objectives such as privacy and consumer protection, and authentication. This kind of regulation is already under consideration by Chinese authorities, including at the sub-regional level.[81] As discussed in relation to licensing arrangements for telecommunications services, Article VI:1 requires

---

[76] 'Wu weighs in', *China Online*, 5 December 2000.
[77] 'Information highway to become data cloud', *China Online*, 19 October 2000.
[78] 'TV the key to Chinese puzzle', *Australian Financial Review*, 24 October 2000.
[79] 'MII pushes integration of telecom, cable networks', *China Online*, 18 December 2001.
[80] S/GBT/W/2/Rev.1.
[81] GATS also applies to measures taken by regional or local governments and authorities: GATS, Art. 1:3(a)(i).

that regulation be administered in a 'reasonable, objective and impartial manner'.

In October 1999, the State Encryption Management Commission published new regulations governing the use of encryption in China.[82] The regulations required all users of encryption in China to register their products, personal details of the users and users' e-mail addresses. Foreign encryption products could only be used by foreigners and only when registered.[83] The regulation would have been unlikely to have met the requirements that a measure be 'reasonable, objective and impartial'. Vice-minister for MOFTEC, Zhang Xiang, 'clarified' that the encryption regulations exempted software where encryption was part of a wider package (for example, Windows 2000, Lotus).[84] Zhang expressly stated that the encryption rules could be further modified, if necessary, in light of China's WTO commitments.

Conclusion

US and EU negotiators have highlighted the significant advantages of China's accession to the WTO for both foreign service providers and China's future economic growth. This chapter concurs with the view that China's undertakings provide a key framework of rules for trade in telecommunications services, and a commitment to improve substantially market access for foreign suppliers.

The chapter has, nevertheless, also considered China's commitments in light of the next stage of Chinese regulation of telecommunications and e-commerce. In particular, it has identified a number of problems that are likely to arise on the ground, given the gaps and flaws in China's new telecommunications regulation, as well as areas of uncertainty in the regulation of convergence, ISPs and encryption. It is also submitted that the more optimistic claims, such as that by former USTR Barshefsky that internet investment in China was 'no longer an issue',[85] should be treated with some scepticism.

The most significant factor in determining future regulatory structures will be domestic political judgements concerning the appropriate pace of

---

[82] Regulation of Commercial Encryption Codes, October 1999.
[83] 'China's new encryption rules take effect Monday', *China Online*, 28 January 2000.
[84] 'China softens encryption rules', *China Online*, 14 March 2000.
[85] 15 November 1999, www.ustr.gov.

China's economic reform. Telecommunications is likely to be a particular area of contention, where there is substantial resistance to change at all levels of the administration. The power of the MII was a considerable factor in the end-game negotiations, with telecommunications the major stumbling block in concluding bilateral negotiations with both the United States and European Union. Minister Wu's likely future approach has already been indicated in his statement that entry to the WTO 'would not have a significant impact on China's information industry'.[86]

Over the long term, there is likely to be greater recognition of the role that foreign suppliers can play in providing the key elements for the next stage of economic growth: investment, competition and technology transfers. Consumer demand for new and improved services will give further momentum to this change. In this transition period, however, many barriers will remain to an open and competitive market for telecommunications and e-commerce in China.

[86] 'China's net czar downplays WTO effect on high tech industry', *China Online*, 19 November 1999.

16

Segregation and convergence: the Chinese dilemma for financial services sectors

RICHARD WU

'Financial segregation' can refer either to 'business segregation' or 'regulatory segregation'. Business segregation' means financial sectors operating along distinct business lines. Generally speaking, the distinct sectors are banking, securities and insurance. 'Regulatory segregation', on the other hand, refers to separate regulators regulating different financial sectors. For instance, the banking regulators usually regulate banks while securities regulators usually regulate securities markets. For the purpose of this chapter, the term 'financial segregation' is confined to the first meaning, namely 'business segregation'.

In the past, financial segregation was common in western countries, the United States being the leading example. In the United States, the Glass–Steagall Act was adopted in 1933 to impose legal barriers between investment and commercial banking activities.[1] Other countries, such as Japan, also adopted financial segregation as they modelled their financial regulations on the United States.[2] In recent years, however, 'financial convergence' has become increasingly popular. Under financial convergence, institutions in one financial sector can engage in businesses in other sectors. At the end of 1999, the United States adopted the Gramm–Leach–Bliley Act. This largely removed the legal separation between businesses of investment and commercial banks, and created the necessary legal framework for financial convergence in the United States.[3] In China, these alternative

---

[1] The Glass–Steagall Act referred to sections 16, 20, 21 and 32 of the Banking Act 1933: see George J. Benston, *The Separation of Commercial and Investment Banking – the Glass–Steagall Act Revisited and Reconsidered* (London, 1990).

[2] Richard Dale, *Risk and Regulation in Global Securities Markets* (West Sussex, 1996), pp. 104–34.

[3] Jonathan R. Macey, 'The business of banking: before and after Gramm–Leach–Bliley' (2000) 22 *Journal of Corporation Law* 691.

policies have generated attention and discussion in academic and government circles. The debates became more intense after China signed agreements with the European Union[4] and the United States[5] in 2000, paving
the way for its accession to the WTO.

In China, the concept of financial segregation is called 'fen ye jing ying',
which means the separation of businesses into different financial sectors, including the banking, securities and insurance sectors. Conversely, financial
convergence is called 'he ye jing ying', which refers to the 'merger' of businesses into different financial sectors. At present, China is adopting a policy
of financial segregation. Now that China is acceding to the WTO, there are
pressures for China to shift its policy from one of financial segregation to
one of financial convergence.

The first part of this chapter sets out the historical background to China's
adoption of financial segregation. It also outlines the policy document
and legislation that enshrine this financial segregation policy and assess
its merits and demerits. The second part deals with factors that are leading some Chinese academics and financial institutions to pressurize the
government to change the financial segregation policy, including factors
brought about by accession to the WTO; it also deals with the problems
of implementing a financial convergence policy in China. The third part
of this chapter gives some examples of *de facto* financial convergence in
China. In conclusion, the Chinese dilemma in choosing between financial
segregation and convergence is highlighted.

Policy documents and legislation setting out financial segregation in China

The adoption of financial segregation can be traced back to 1993. On 25
December 1993, the State Council of China promulgated an important policy document called 'Decisions on the Reform of the Financial System' ('the
Decisions'),[6] which officially marked the beginning of the financial segregation policy in China. In the Decisions, the financial segregation policy
was set out as follows: 'The state-owned commercial banks shall separate

---

[4] http://www.chinalegalchange.com/subs/2000-10/10eu-wto.html.
[5] See Jing Zhou Tao, 'US trade deal opens China on WTO accession' (1999) 18 *International Financial Law Review* 9–11.
[6] For a full Chinese text of the Decisions, see *Law Yearbook of China* (Beijing, 1994), pp. 640–3.

their connections with the insurance, trust and securities businesses, in terms of human, financial and physical resources. They shall implement the principle of financial segregation.'[7]

Financial segregation was enshrined in subsequent regulations adopted by China. For example, the Commercial Banking Law of 1995 stipulated that 'commercial banks shall not be permitted to engage in trust investment and stock operations and invest in immovable property within the territory of the People's Republic of China that is not for their own use'.[8] The Securities Law of 1998 stipulated that 'securities businesses must be operated and regulated separately from banking, trust and insurance businesses. Securities companies must be established separately from banking, trust and insurance companies.'[9]

At first sight, financial segregation seems to be pervasive throughout Chinese financial regulation. However, a deeper probe into these regulations shows that the segregation policy is not absolute. For example, commercial banks may engage in certain businesses that, strictly, belong to the securities and insurance sectors. Under the Commercial Banking Law, commercial banks are allowed to issue financial bonds, buy and sell government bonds and act as agent for insurance businesses.[10] Moreover, while Chinese commercial banks are prohibited from carrying on investment and securities businesses on trust within China, the Commercial Banking Law leaves open the question of whether they can engage in such businesses outside China. In other words, while Chinese financial regulations strongly favour financial segregation, the policy is not as absolute as many people perceive.

Further, even under the present segregation policy, there are a few financial institutions in China that operate on a *de facto* financial convergence basis. For example, the China Everbright Group (Everbright) owns banks, securities companies and trust companies. Similarly, the China International Trust & Investment Corporation (CITIC) also owns banks, securities companies and insurance companies. Both Everbright and CITIC achieve *de facto* financial convergence by way of financial holding companies. It is interesting to note that there is no separate law or regulation governing such financial holding companies in China.

---

[7] Ibid., p. 642.   [8] Commercial Banking Law, Art. 43.   [9] Securities Law, Art. 6.
[10] Commercial Banking Law, Art. 3.

Historical background to the adoption of financial segregation in China

Why did China adopt a financial segregation policy? To answer this, one needs to trace recent political and economic developments of China. On 4 June 1989, China shocked the world with the Tiananmen Massacre. After this, many western countries imposed sanctions on China. Consequently, the Chinese economy suffered a setback in the early 1990s. In 1992, the Chinese paramount leader, Deng Xiaoping, called for faster economic and financial reforms in his tour of the southern provinces of China. This historical tour of Deng was subsequently known as *nanxun*.[11]

The Chinese economy has since then entered a new phase of rapid development. At the same time, however, speculation on the securities market and real-estate market was getting out of control. Many state-owned banks in China participated, directly or indirectly, in these speculative activities as they generated huge profits for the banks themselves. As a result, large sums flowed from Chinese state-owned banks to the securities and property markets. For example, it was estimated that during the four months from January to April 1993 alone, a total of RMB 50 billion was raised from direct and indirect financing, of which 80 per cent was used for property and securities speculation. Moreover, those involved in property and securities speculation were willing to pay an interest rate as high as 40 per cent per year, much higher than the rates charged for normal business operations. The reserves of many Chinese banks fell to less than 5 per cent of their assets, some even less than 1 per cent.[12] The financial system of China, as a whole, became highly unstable and chaotic.

In June 1993, Zhu Rongji, the then vice-premier, started to tackle the chaos and advocated his concept of 'regulating financial order and strengthening macro-adjustment of the economy', imposing what he called 'the three commitments' and 'the four tasks'.[13]

---

[11] For a full account of *nanxun*, see Willy Wo Lap Lam, *China after Deng Xiaoping* (Hong Kong, 1995), pp. 75–83.

[12] Qin Chijiang, *Change and Liberalization in the Financial System* (in Chinese) (Beijing, 1993), pp. 169–70.

[13] The 'three commitments' and 'four tasks' were used by Zhu to summarize his strategy of tackling the financial chaos in a series of government meetings chaired by Zhu himself in July 1993. For a full account of the 'three commitments' and 'four tasks', see Zheng Yongnian, *New Reign under Zhu* (in Chinese) (Hong Kong, 1999), pp. 121–2.

The three commitments were:

- restricting unlawful lending by state-owned banks;
- prohibiting banks from advancing loans to business-unrelated entities; and
- compelling banks to sever their links with other businesses owned by them.

The 'four tasks' were

- restoring financial order;
- imposing financial discipline;
- continuing financial reform; and
- strengthening macroeconomic adjustment.

The measures implemented by Zhu were aimed at segregating financial sectors by products, markets and institutions. This formed the core of the financial segregation policy. State-owned banks were required to separate or divest themselves from such businesses as trust and securities companies. The banks were prohibited from lending to these companies. Insurance companies were also prohibited from investing in government bonds and bank deposits. These measures were enshrined in the regulations subsequently adopted, including the Commercial Banking Law discussed above.

It is interesting to compare what happened in China in the early 1990s and what happened in the United States in the late 1920s and early 1930s. At that time, American banks had invested heavily in equity and bonds issued by non-financial companies. When the securities markets collapsed in October 1929, a large number of banks failed. In fact, the number of bank failures in the United States increased from 642 in 1929 to 1,345 in 1930 and 2,298 in 1931.[14] To stop bank failures escalating further, the US Congress adopted the Glass–Steagall Act in 1933.

While no similar bank failures occurred in China during the mid-1990s, Chinese policy-makers at that time had the same concerns as the US Congress had in the 1930s. Their concerns were wholly justified, as the banking system plays an even more important role in China than its counterpart did in the pre-Depression United States. For example, the four major state-owned commercial banks in China[15] owned 84 per cent of financial

---

[14] See Benston, *The Separation of Commercial and Investment Banking*, p. 218.

[15] Bank of China, Construction Bank of China, Agricultural Bank of China and Industrial and Commercial Bank of China.

assets in China.[16] Any failure in these four major state-owned commercial banks would have disastrous consequences for the Chinese financial system.

Consequences of China's adoption of a financial segregation policy

The policy of financial segregation was highly successful. The Chinese financial system stabilized and the 'overheated' economy cooled down in a short span of two years. The cool-down can be illustrated by changes in China's annual inflation rates: inflation rose from 13.2 per cent in 1993 to 21.7 per cent in 1994. It then fell to 14.8 per cent in 1995 and to 6.1 per cent in 1996.[17] These figures demonstrate that China's economic policy-makers succeeded in giving the economy a 'soft landing' only two years after the implementation of its financial segregation policy. The success of the financial segregation policy contributed to the subsequent rise of Zhu Rongji to the Chinese premiership.

Financial segregation created a stable environment for the growth and development of Chinese financial sectors. In the past few years, the banking, securities and insurance markets of China have steadily progressed. In particular, China's securities markets have grown in an impressive manner; the total value of the securities markets has risen from RMB 369.1 billion in 1994 to RMB 984.2 billion in 1996 and RMB 1,752.9 billion in 1997.[18]

Financial segregation also strengthened the overall stability of the financial system. This explains, to a certain extent, why China weathered the Asian financial crisis that destroyed the economies of many other Asian countries in 1997 and 1998. A root cause of the financial crisis in Thailand was the flow of money from the banking system into the property market. When the property bubble burst, the banking system also collapsed.[19] Thus, Chinese policy-makers were even more convinced of the merits of the financial segregation policy after the Asian financial crisis.

---

[16] See Zheng Wei, Peng Hui and Zhao Rong, *The Future Direction of China's Financial System* (in Chinese) (Beijing, 1999), p. 109.
[17] Ibid., p. 50.
[18] Zhao Kaikuan and Guo Tianyong, *The 20 Years of Chinese Financial System Reform* (in Chinese) (Beijing, 1998), p. 92.
[19] See Tull Traisorat, *Thailand: Financial Sector Reform and the East Asian Crises* (London, 2000), pp. 119–134.

Problems with the financial segregation policy

Despite the success of financial segregation, many Chinese academics and financial institutions have challenged it in recent years. They put up several arguments to support their position. First, under the present segregation policy, Chinese financial institutions are restricted as to what services they can offer. Under the Commercial Banking Law, commercial banks are allowed to engage in such businesses as taking deposits, granting loans, interbank lending and providing letter-of-credit services.[20] Most of these are 'traditional' banking services within the banking sector. Many new banking products and services, however, are 'cross-sectoral' in nature. They are either prohibited or discouraged under financial segregation. It was therefore argued that the financial segregation policy unduly constrains financial innovations and development of new financial products and services in China.

The second argument against financial segregation is that it hampers the ability of Chinese financial institutions to develop into financial 'supermarkets' offering 'cross-sectoral' financial services to their customers. It was argued that such a policy does not serve the best interests of Chinese customers, because consumers must go to different financial institutions to obtain the different financial services they need.

Thirdly, it was argued that the financial segregation policy restricts the competitive strength of Chinese financial institutions. When Chinese financial institutions develop their business in overseas markets, they find that they have to compete with much larger financial conglomerates that offer a wide range of financial services. As financial markets are increasingly globalized, it is felt to be indispensable for Chinese financial institutions to be able to offer a wider array of financial services, so that they can face the increased competition with these foreign conglomerates.

Impact of accession to the WTO on the financial segregation policy

The accession of China to the WTO added urgency to the debate. Under agreements with the European Union and the United States, upon accession to the WTO China will allow foreign financial institutions access to key financial sectors such as banking, securities and insurance. In the banking sector, foreign banks will be allowed to provide services using renmimbi to Chinese companies and individuals. In the insurance sector, foreign

---

[20] Commercial Banking Law, Art. 3.

insurance companies will be allowed to offer group, health and pension insurance. In the securities sector, foreign companies will be permitted to hold minority shares in mutual funds companies. All these developments will occur within three to five years of accession.[21]

Chinese financial institutions will therefore face fierce competition from foreign competitors within a prescribed time after Chinese accession to the WTO. It is argued that if China maintains financial segregation, it will constrain the competitive strength of Chinese financial institutions. Because the competitive strength of Chinese financial institutions is inherently weak, such 'competitive inequality' will only worsen after accession to the WTO.

Therefore, it is argued that China should change its financial segregation policy to a policy of financial convergence. A financial convergence policy would allow Chinese financial institutions to engage in businesses outside the narrow scope of their own sectors. Moreover, under such new policy, some Chinese financial institutions will be able to develop into financial supermarkets offering a wide range of financial services to consumers, or in Chinese terms, 'yi tiao lung' service (meaning 'one-stop' service). This will enhance the competitive strength of Chinese financial institutions. In this view, Chinese institutions will have a better chance of survival against their foreign competitors if China adopts a financial convergence policy.

These arguments appear justified. Foreign financial institutions have a huge competitive advantage over their Chinese counterparts. Their advantages range from their size, product sophistication and expertise to their capital – for instance, the asset value of Citigroup alone is about US$700 billion and equal to the total asset value of the four major state-owned banks in China.[22] Moreover, the total number of bank staff employed by Chinese banks is three times the number employed by their US counterparts. Further, the ratio of returns to assets of Chinese banks is only 0.2 per cent, while its western counterpart is about 2.2 per cent.[23] These figures exemplify the mismatch in competitive strength between Chinese financial institutions and their western counterparts.

In addition, if Chinese financial institutions cannot provide a comprehensive range of financial services like their foreign counterparts, it

[21] See http://www.chinalegalchange.com/subs/2000-10/10eu-wto.html and Tao, 'US trade deal'.

[22] Shi Yong, 'WTO and electronic development of Chinese banks' (in Chinese), *Guoji shangye bao* [International Commercial News], 24 December 2000.

[23] Wang Jingyi, 'The development trend of Chinese banks after accession to WTO' (in Chinese), *Guoji jinrongbao* [International Finance News], 28 September 2000.

is possible that many quality customers of Chinese institutions will shift to foreign institutions after China's accession to the WTO. In China, most quality customers are concentrated in coastal cities and in big cities such as Beijing, Shanghai and Guangzhou. If a large number of these quality customers were to shift their business to foreign financial institutions, it would seriously affect the profit margins of Chinese financial institutions. This would in turn affect the overall stability of the Chinese financial system.[24]

This worry is justified. In the past, the amount of deposits in the Chinese banking system rose steadily. For example, the total amount of deposits rose from RMB 3,852 billion in 1996 to RMB 4,627.9 billion in 1997, then to RMB 5,340.8 billion in 1998. On average, total deposits rose by RMB 800 billion per year. However, there are signs that the rate of increase in bank deposits has recently been slowing. For example, the amount of the deposit increase was reduced to RMB 500 billion in 2000.[25] If a large amount of money flows from Chinese financial institutions to their foreign competitors after Chinese accession to the WTO, it will jeopardize the financial health of Chinese financial institutions and affect the overall stability of Chinese financial system. Therefore, it is imperative to maintain the competitiveness of Chinese financial institutions so that they can retain their customers' and depositors' money after China's accession to the WTO.

Problems of implementing a financial convergence policy in China

While China has good reasons to shift to financial convergence, there are many policy and practical problems that hinder implementation. To begin with, China needs to maintain confidence in the banking system, which is vital to resolving its non-performing loan problem. Any change to the present financial segregation policy may affect the necessary confidence. At the end of June 2000, the total amount of 'non-performing loans' of Chinese banks amounted to RMB 1,300 billion.[26] The Chinese government spends RMB 30 to 40 billion every year to tackle the non-performing loan problem,[27] and the percentage of non-performing loans is expected to drop

---

[24] Yang Guangsheng, 'Recent developments in private commercial banks in China' (in Chinese), *Xin jingji* [New Economy], 1 December 2000.

[25] Ibid.

[26] Zheng Fengxi, 'The Chinese financial industry develops new industrial pattern in 2000' (in Chinese), *Zhongguo jingyingbao* [Chinese Management News], 26 December 2000.

[27] Song Shihong, 'Chinese economy should avoid the lesson of Japan' (in Chinese), *Zhongguo gongshang shibao* [Chinese Management News], 30 May 2000.

by between 2 and 3 per cent annually in the years to come.[28] Despite the existence of such a huge amount of non-performing loans, Chinese people still have confidence in their banking system and continue to deposit their money.

However, confidence is fragile. It could be shattered if Chinese banks are allowed to engage in riskier businesses, such as securities trading, under a financial convergence policy. As the bank crisis of the 1990s exemplified for the western world, banks suffer heavier losses when they engage in activities that do not fall within traditional commercial banking activities. Thus, before adopting financial convergence, Chinese policy-makers need to assess carefully whether by allowing Chinese banks to engage in other financial businesses, in particular securities, they will substantially increase business and systemic risks to Chinese banks. They will also have to assess the effect that such change would have on public confidence in the Chinese banking system.

The second challenge to full implementation of financial convergence is the uneven development of Chinese financial sectors. The banking system is well established and has a long history. By contrast, the securities markets are relatively 'young' and only started to develop in the 1990s. Unlike their western counterparts, market participants in Chinese securities markets are primarily individual investors. This makes the markets highly volatile and unstable. At present, financial segregation serves to insulate the banking system from any possible crisis in the securities markets. If China were to shift to financial convergence, the contagious effects of a crisis in one financial sector on other sectors will be immensely increased. It remains doubtful whether Chinese policy-makers will risk this, particularly before the Chinese securities markets become more mature and stable.

Thirdly, a common argument against financial convergence in the West is the potential for conflicts of interest. If financial institutions are allowed to carry on banking and other financial activities, they may use information obtained from clients in one activity for the benefit of clients in another activity. In countries that have adopted financial convergence, 'firewalls' were built into the system to prevent or minimize such potential conflicts. It is, however, doubtful whether such firewalls would be effective in China. In China, the officers of major financial institutions are either current or

---

[28] Peng Xiaohong and Ma Luyao, 'The president of PBOC, Dai Xianglong, elaborated on the focus of Chinese finance' (in Chinese), *Zhongguo gongshang shibao* [China Industrial and Commercial Times], 18 January 2001.

former government officials, and corruption is still rampant in many parts of the financial system. As one senior Chinese banker pointed out, the four major state-owned commercial banks operated under a centrally planned economy for a long time. Many of their officers still regard themselves more as government officers than as commercial bank officers.[29] In other words, the western style of market operation is not yet fully in place in China. If China shifts to financial convergence abruptly, it may only be providing another seedbed for corruption.

In recent years, Chinese banks have strengthened their internal control systems, and have introduced practices developed by western banks to deal with corruption. However, many of these measures were only introduced after the Asian financial crisis. It will take time to build up a culture of credit and integrity in Chinese banks. Thus, any abrupt change from financial segregation to convergence could potentially lead to more systemic corruption within the Chinese financial system.

Fourthly, the problem of concentration of financial power has been a common concern in the West when adopting financial convergence. This is particularly relevant in China. The four major state-owned commercial banks enjoy enormous competitive advantage in the Chinese financial system: they own 84 per cent of the financial assets and employ 90 per cent of the finance professionals in China.[30] If Chinese banks are allowed to enter other financial sectors, the Big Four (the People's Bank of China, the Agricultural Bank of China, the Industrial and Commercial Bank of China and the Bank of China) are likely to dominate other Chinese financial businesses. As Chinese securities markets are still at an infant stage of development, it is doubtful whether policy-makers would prefer this to allowing Chinese securities firms to develop. Moreover, it is not in the public interest for too much power to be concentrated in the four major state-owned commercial banks. A crisis in any one of them would cause many financial and social problems in China.

Fifthly, many vested interests in China, including the financial regulators themselves, are opposed to an abrupt shift to financial convergence. They maintain that before China adopts financial convergence, financial institutions in different sectors must improve their performance and become more competitive within their own sectors. Apparently, they have agreed to

---

[29] Peggy Sito, 'Time not ripe for big four to join market listing rush', *South China Morning Post*, 10 October 2000, p. 5.
[30] Wei et al., *The Future Direction of China's Financial System*.

remove the restrictions on scope of businesses in different financial sectors only gradually after Chinese accession to the WTO.[31]

Sixthly, many western countries shifted to financial convergence because of competition between commercial banks and securities companies. In fact, bank financing represented 60 per cent of financing in western countries in the early 1980s, but that has dropped to 20 per cent in recent years.[32] This sharp drop in bank financing forced commercial banks in western countries to diversify and pushed their governments to adopt financial convergence. No similar pattern of competition exists in China. Commercial banks in China still play a dominant role in its financial system. Securities companies, on the other hand, have but a short history in China. They lack the resources and capacity to compete with banks, unlike their counterparts in the West. Chinese securities markets are still in their infant stage of development and Chinese securities companies lack the resources and scale of operations to compete with Chinese commercial banks for business. Therefore, neither commercial banks nor securities companies in China have incentives to push for financial convergence.

Moreover, both the regulatory framework and expertise in China are inadequate for financial convergence. Such a policy would bring up a host of questions about the current regulatory framework and regulators themselves. For instance, what would be the respective jurisdictions of different regulators? Should the different regulators merge into one single regulatory body, as in the United Kingdom? Is there adequate regulatory expertise in China to supervise financial conglomerates? As China only established its present regulatory structure for financial segregation a few years ago, it remains doubtful whether its regulatory organizations have the flexibility and expertise to adapt to changes brought about by adoption of financial convergence.

Financial convergence will create political issues for regulators as well. China can easily change its legal framework for financial segregation but defining the powers of financial regulators remains a political issue that needs to be resolved by the political system. Until China can reconcile the interests of its different financial regulators, its transition to financial convergence is unlikely to be smooth.

---

[31] Stephen M. Harner, 'China watch: Beijing blocks the banks', *The Asian Wall Street Journal*, 20 July 2000, p. 10.

[32] See Shi, 'WTO and electronic development'.

Examples of *de facto* financial convergence in China

While debate about financial segregation and convergence continues in China, many Chinese financial institutions have already responded to the emerging trend of convergence. Apart from Everbright and CITIC, a number of developments in the last few years indicate that the process of *de facto* financial convergence has already taken place in China, despite an official stance on financial segregation. Some institutions achieve *de facto* financial convergence by purchasing controlling shares in financial institutions in other sectors. For example, Everbright bought a controlling 18.67 per cent share in a Shanghai-based securities company, Shenyin and Wangguo Securities Co., in March 2000. These two companies then controlled 7.17 per cent of the total securities-market transactions on the Chinese securities market.[33]

As competition intensifies, some Chinese financial institutions strengthen co-operation with financial institutions in other sectors to achieve *de facto* financial convergence. Such 'inter-sectoral' co-operation enables Chinese financial institutions to provide one-stop service to their customers for a wide range of financial services and products, thereby providing value-added services to their clients. For instance, Shanghai Pudong Development Bank signed a co-operative agreement with the Guangda Securities Ltd. Under this, the two companies co-operated by providing priority services to each other and by sharing information. The agreement marked a strengthening of the working relationship between the banks, securities firms and insurance firms in Shanghai.[34]

Other examples include China Construction Bank (CCB) signing a co-operative partnership agreement with Shandong Securities Co. Ltd to co-operate in such fields as securities-based mortgage loans and investment banking.[35] In addition, the Industrial and Commercial Bank of China (ICB) signed a co-operative agreement with Guotai Junan Securities, a top Chinese securities firm. Under the agreement between ICB and Guotai, their clients were allowed to transfer funds from deposit accounts of ICB to securities trading accounts of Guotai and vice versa. The main purpose was to facilitate stock trading, as Guotai could make use of the wide branch

---

[33] 'Everbright buys into Wangguo Securities', *Asianfo Daily News*, 15 March 2000, p. 7.

[34] 'Shanghai bank, securities firm sign cooperative agreement', *World News Connection, PRC*, 11 October 2000.

[35] 'CCB joins hands with Shandong Securities firm', *Xinhua News Agency*, 6 July 2000.

network of ICB.[36] CCB also signed a co-operative agreement on stock hy-
pothecation with Xiangcai Securities Co. Ltd, the first of its kind between a
state-owned commercial bank and a securities firm in China. Under their
agreement, Xiangcai could obtain short-term loans by pledging stocks to
CCB as securities.[37]

Other Chinese financial institutions achieve *de facto* financial convergence by innovative use of information technology. For example, Everbright, through a subsidiary, started to operate the first 'internet financial platform' in China in August 2000. This was a new medium that
offered on-line securities, banking and insurance services to its customers.[38]
Chinaweb, a Sino-foreign joint venture company, started an on-line stock-
trading platform called Trading On-line Platform with CITIC. This allowed
existing customers of CITIC to buy and sell stock over the internet. They
also planned to expand into other businesses, such as on-line trading of
bonds and foreign exchange, and insurance brokerage.

It is foreseeable that more Chinese financial institutions will follow these
examples because of competitive pressures in the market before China formally adopts financial convergence.

The accession of China to the WTO has also imbued Chinese policy-
makers with a sense of urgency. Behind Chinese policy-makers' anxiety are
perceptions that all major countries around the world have adopted financial convergence and that China cannot afford to fall behind in this global
trend of financial regulation; so it is likely that China will only gradually
shift from its present financial segregation policy to a financial convergence
policy. In fact, experts from the Chinese Academy of Social Sciences, a high-
level Chinese government think-tank, recommended last year that China
should take about six years to shift from segregation to convergence.[39]

In recent years, the Chinese government has been paving the way for
financial convergence. In August 1999, China promulgated the Regulations
on Securities Companies Accessing Inter-bank Markets and Regulations
on Fund Management Companies Accessing Inter-bank Markets. These allowed Chinese securities and fund-management companies to access the

[36] 'China's biggest banking, securities firms forge alliance', *Dow Jones International News*, 29 September, 2000.
[37] 'Chinese banks sign agreement with securities firm', *World News Connection*, 2 March, 2000.
[38] 'China – Everbright subsidiary launches country's first internet financial platform', China On-line, 12 September 2000.
[39] 'Experts advocate Chinese financial institutions adopting financial convergence', *China News Agency*, 23 December 2000.

Chinese inter-bank markets. In February 2000, China promulgated the Measures on Securities Companies Pledging Shares as Bank Collateral. This enables securities companies to pledge shares to Chinese commercial banks. As a result, Chinese banks and insurance companies are now able to participate indirectly in the securities markets. In the long run, these regulations serve to link up capital in the three sectors, thereby facilitating financial convergence in China.

Conclusion

In conclusion, the issue of financial segregation and convergence is an issue of policy choice between financial stability on the one hand and enhanced competition and financial innovation on the other. In western countries, the choice is relatively easy, as their financial markets are mature and sophisticated. Their financial institutions have a long history of development and a track record of surviving financial crises. They need fear financial instability less than Chinese financial institutions. It is therefore logical that these countries shift to a financial convergence policy to enhance competition and innovation in their financial markets.

In China, the situation is different and the policy choice is, at least for the time being, the other way round. The Chinese financial markets have only a short history. They are relatively unstable compared to their western counterparts. They are also more fragile, as they suffer from problems not found in their western counterparts – for example, Chinese banks are plagued by the problem of non-performing loans, and securities markets are rendered highly unstable by the high percentage of individual investors. Moreover, as recent history in China and other developing countries exemplifies, financial instability can lead to social unrest or even change in political power. It is therefore logical that Chinese policy-makers are more concerned about financial stability than competition and financial innovation. Judged from this standpoint, it is not difficult to understand why Chinese policy-makers have favoured a policy of financial segregation over one of financial convergence.

As one can see, China is put in a dilemma in choosing between financial segregation and convergence. On the one hand, the present policy stifles competition and innovation, which hinders the healthy growth and development of the Chinese financial system. On the other hand, shifting to financial convergence will increase the systemic risk in the Chinese financial system, which can lead to financial chaos and crisis. It is difficult for Chinese policy-makers to decide whether and when to shift from financial segregation to financial convergence. 'To change, or not to change?' This will be a big question with no easy answer for Chinese policy-makers in the years to come.

17

Adopting a competition law in China

MARK WILLIAMS

Introduction

Competition law in China is a developing subject. As part of the government's policy of restructuring the planned economy of the past into a 'socialist market' economy,[1] a mechanism to obtain an efficient allocation of economic goods is a key policy goal. At present a patchwork of laws and regulations seeks to prevent the most damaging anti-competitive activities found in the transitional economy, but a strong theoretical foundation for the competitive mechanism is currently lacking, as is a comprehensive legal code to set market rules.

However, since at least 1994 central government has been considering its options. State organs have been studying competition regimes around the world, seeking to gain insight into how governments police free-market systems. The help of multilateral organizations, particularly the OECD, has been sought and an outline competition law for China has been prepared for comment.[2]

China's imminent entry into the WTO has increased pressure on senior government officials. A comprehensive anti-monopoly law is needed to strengthen domestic industries in the face of foreseeable ferocious foreign competition in the hitherto-protected Chinese domestic market. However, not all government factions are favourably disposed to an effective competition regime that would inevitably reduce their power and prestige.

---

[1] This term is used in Article 15 of the Constitution of the People's Republic of China, adopted on 29 March 1993, but not defined or explained. There are inherent contradictions within the phrase 'socialist market', but the policy of restructuring of Chinese economy has progressed without interruption since the inception of the open door policy at the Third Plenum of the Eleventh Communist Party Congress in 1978.

[2] Outline of the Anti-Monopoly Law of the People's Republic of China, 30 November 1999. This is an internal government document and has not been officially published.

Existing economic and political conditions in China

Prior to 1978, China was a classical socialist state. The government took a supreme role in economic policy and management. The economic system was based upon the state plan formulated, implemented and monitored by the state agencies. The state controlled all productive resources in China and competition between economic actors was seen as wasteful.

However, in 1978 Deng Xiaoping assumed power. His vision was to modernize China by encouraging foreign investment and by the implementation of the 'responsibility system' for agricultural production to replace the Maoist collectivized farm unit.

Over the last quarter century, the state plan has been consigned to history and private enterprise has received formal legal recognition as part of China's Constitution.[3] The state, however, continues to dominate and 'own' significant industries – steel, coal, railways, airlines, petrochemicals, electricity generation and supply, gas, water, shipping, automotive, banks, insurance, and many others. These continue in the state-controlled sector and are little troubled by internal or external competition. However, it should not be assumed that state control is monolithic.

A common misapprehension is that the Chinese state is highly centralized and that economic command and control is exercised by ministries in Beijing whose every diktat is heard and implemented by local organs of government. This is far from the truth.

Legal ownership and control of state assets in China is complex. In the past, ownership was not important as assets did not have a market value as they were not bought or sold in a market. 'Ownership' in the legal sense had little meaning. Control of assets, however, was important and China's structure of government confused that issue. Whilst authority for national economic matters rests squarely with the State Council in Beijing, each province and municipality in which a productive asset is situated also has considerable influence over how it is operated, staffed and financed. Conflicting priorities and policies originate from different government bodies, for example 'corporatization' on the one hand and maintenance of former social-welfare obligations on the other, so making effective demarcation of 'ownership and control' almost impossible.[4]

---

[3] Article 11 of the PRC Constitution, adopted 15 March 1999, states: 'The non-public ownership sector comprising the individual economy and the private economy within the domain stipulated by law is an important component of the country's socialist market economy. The state protects the lawful rights and interests of the individual economy and the private economy.'

[4] See E. Steinfield, *Forging Reform in China: The Fate of State Owned Industry* (Cambridge, 1998).

Administrative monopoly

This government structure generates another widespread Chinese phenomenon – administrative monopoly. This is the use by government, at
all levels, of administrative powers, both legal and extra-legal, to promote, manipulate, impede or prevent economic activities, especially those
deemed to be inimical to a sector of the economy that requires promotion
or protection. Administrative monopoly has been criticized by Chinese
academic writers as creating waste and inefficiency.[5] Examples of administrative monopoly include differential taxation applied to goods from
outside the 'home' territory, outright boycotts of 'foreign' goods, physical blockades at provincial or municipal boundaries, the use of administrative permits in a discriminatory fashion, orders to all state business
answerable to local government only to purchase supplies from local manufacturers and forced tie-in sales of unrelated goods to benefit favoured
producers.[6]

Administrative monopoly can also be found in the service sector. The
national telephony and gas providers had policies of requiring new subscribers to purchase equipment from them before they would connect the
customer to the system. These tie-in sales were outside the monopoly that
central government had granted. Interestingly in this case, the municipal
government intervened on behalf of the consumer and sought to enforce the
current Anti-Unfair Competition Law. The consumers won because these
two monopolists are nationally accountable and the municipal government
had no vested interest to protect. Perhaps the political kudos of protecting
local consumers and the promotion of local equipment suppliers trumped
the political influence of national monopolists.

These are mere examples of common practices that have had serious
consequences. The system:

- props up local uneconomic industries that generally produce low-quality
  and high-priced goods;
- prevents economies of scale as larger and more productive units cannot
  easily expand outside their local area;

[5] Zhang Shufang, 'Analysis of administrative monopoly and legal measures that can be taken
to counter it' (1999) 4 *CASS Journal Of Law* 34–9; Shi JiChun, 'Definition and regulation of
administrative monopoly in China' (1999) 3 *Frontiers of Jurisprudence* 137; Wang Xiaoye, *Studies
in Competition Law* (Beijing, 1999).

[6] Further examples of local protectionism can be found in Trish Saywell, 'China's city limits', *Far
Eastern Economic Review*, 14 October 1999.

- prevents the establishment of nationally recognized brands, to the detriment of efficient companies seeking national market penetration;
- by encouraging over-capacity, prevents the restructuring of state-owned enterprises. Local governments may superficially comply with central government orders to close a local production unit but as soon as the government inspectors leave the area production is recommenced. Such local policies are at odds with national economic policy and inhibit restructuring. They drain state bank funds to loss-making, inefficient, publicly owned businesses, in turn creating a shortage of funds for productive enterprises and insolvency problems for the banks themselves.[7]

The duplication of industrial capacity[8] is a direct consequence of the Maoist policy of regional domestic self-sufficiency. Defence also played a part in the dispersal of industry – the so-called Third Front policy, whereby each region should be able to supply itself with the matériel needed for a defensive war.

The local governments' 'beggar-thy-neighbour' policies in China are reminiscent of the activities of the former colonies of America, which led to the inclusion of inter-state commerce provisions in the US Constitution to prevent internal protectionism. Another comparator is the European Union. It, too, had an overriding economic objective in the founding European Community (EC) Treaty, to create a single, common market for goods, services, capital and labour.[9] However, national rules and policies initially inhibited the creation of a single market. It required the removal of official barriers to trade, vigorous implementation of competition law and more active enforcement of the rules on public procurement and state aids, to complete the single market. The effect of the single market has been assessed by the EU Commission as increased employment, increased economic growth and reduced inflation.[10] These are benefits that China would seek to emulate.

Thus, administrative monopoly is the use of government power to prevent the creation of a single internal market in China. It is a single market

---

[7] For a detailed account of the situation of China's banks, see N. Lardy, *China's Unfinished Economic Revolution* (Washington, D.C, 1998).

[8] In 1987, 80 factories in 21 provinces produced refrigerators, over 100 factories in 26 provinces produced televisions, and 300 factories in 28 provinces produced washing machines. See World Bank, *China: Internal Market Development and Regulation* (Washington, D.C., 1994), p. 36.

[9] Arts. 2 and 3 EC Treaty as amended at Amsterdam, OJ 1997 No. C340, 10 November 1997.

[10] *Impact and Effectiveness of the Single Market*, http://europa.eu.int/comm/dg15/en/update/impact/smsumen.htm.

issue, not a competition matter. The relevance of the European example has not been lost on the Chinese government. As will be seen below, the jurisprudence and policies of EU market integration have had a major influence on Chinese policy-making.

Thus, China's challenges are not unique but they may be more intractable due to the nature of political structures and an official ambivalence to the notion of the rule of law as opposed to rule by law. The Chinese judicial system can offer little assistance in overcoming administrative monopoly, whereas in the European Union the Court of Justice has taken a leading role in creating the single market. In China the court system is organized by local governments; they provide the finance, the buildings and personnel. The local Communist Party secretary oversees appointments and promotions. Individual decisions involving economically important local industries can be subject to extraneous pressure.

Administrative monopoly also demonstrates that China should not be viewed as a monolithic whole but rather as a loose confederation of economically separate fiefdoms. The central apparatus is outwardly strong but its actual internal power is limited. As the old proverb from China's imperial past puts it, 'The mountains are high and the emperor far away.'

Given its size and population, China was historically governed by imperially sanctioned administrators who were able to achieve a high degree of autonomy, whilst maintaining outward loyalty to the centre. This historical model based on interventionist state-mediated outcomes may now be breaking down under the influence of several new factors:

• the growth of the private sector, where the state has less opportunity to meddle;
• central government has realized that stern measures need to be taken to curb local protectionism, as this severely impairs the overall economic welfare of the nation. A World Bank report in 1994 found that between 1985 and 1992 retail goods 'exports' from one province to another declined from 36.6 per cent to 27.6 per cent.[11] This shrinkage of internal trade is a worrying trend for central government and seems to confirm the existence of severe impediments to internal trade, which conspire to pauperize many regions of China. There is no evidence to suggest that this trend has reversed in the last decade;

[11] World Bank, *China*, p. 35.

- the government is anxious to encourage enterprise mergers to produce 'national champions'. Administratively sponsored amalgamations have proved either difficult to achieve or of dubious economic value, so competition and market forces may be allowed to do what the state cannot;
- China's entry into the WTO will lead to market opening in many closed sectors of the domestic economy. Competitive pressure on domestic firms will increase. The government is worried that many domestic businesses will be too weak to compete effectively with foreign transnational corporations' promotional budgets, streamlined production and distribution channels, goods of international quality and pockets deep enough to sustain loss leaders.

For these reasons China's government has apparently come to a consensus that competition policy is a legislative priority.

Current competition law provisions

The competitive process is not entirely neglected in Chinese law. The principal statute is the 1993 Anti-Unfair Competition Law enacted by the Standing Committee of the National People's Congress.[12] This statute is primarily a consumer protection law. It is not a complete competition code but it does prohibit:

- predatory pricing policies to destroy embryonic competitors (Articles 6 and 11);
- tic-in sales of unrelated goods (Article 12). This was the provision used by the Shanghai authorities against the gas and telephony suppliers mentioned above;
- bid rigging (Article 15);
- administrative monopoly conduct (Article 7); and
- government organs are enjoined against restricting freedom of choice of suppliers of products, restricting arbitrarily the business freedom of operators and abusing administrative powers to prevent or restrict the marketing of non-local products within their administrative area.

So administrative monopoly was already identified as a pressing problem some ten years ago. However, in China there is a world of difference between the expression of legislative will and execution in practice. If Article 7 had

---

[12] For an English translation, see *China Law and Practice*, 18 November 1993, pp. 31–9.

been effectively enforced, this issue would not be important today. Whilst the national legislative will is apparent, the mechanisms of enforcement provided by the statute are weak and incapable of overcoming the realities of local political power.

Enforcement of the 1993 Law is provided for in Articles 16 to 19, which include powers of investigation, and requirements for the subjects of the investigation to co-operate and provide information and records to inspectors. Penalties, set out in Articles 20 to 29, include financial penalties and injunctive powers to prevent reoccurrence. Article 30 provides for higher levels of government to supervise lower levels – for example, for provincial governments to supervise municipal authorities.

The usual enforcement authority is the State Administration of Industry and Commerce (SAIC), a national organization answerable to the State Council, the permanent executive arm of the Chinese government. The SAIC is a central government ministry but has local branches. The branches are financed and staffed by the local government administrative unit, not by the central government. Therefore, branch offices are dependent upon local government patrons for funding and tend to respond to local, in preference to national, policies especially if there is strong local political interest in a particular subject. Uniformity of administration is therefore all but impossible. The municipal branch of the SAIC is responsible, in the first instance, for investigating its sponsoring local authority or local businesses. Needless to say, few investigations are pursued with vigour, when the subjects of their potential investigations or their allies control the pay, promotion and privileges of local SAIC staff.

Enforcement against private businesses is also weak for similar reasons. Businesses in the private sector often have a formal or informal link, such as part ownership or a familial relationship, between local officials and the owner of the specific firm, leading to favourable treatment by the local authority.

The statute is also incapable of dealing with many commonly found competition problems – abusive conduct by monopolists, cartel operations, oligopoly situations, vertical restraints or mergers.

Competition policy-making, 1994–2000

In early 1994 central government set up an interdepartmental working group to study the need for China to adopt a comprehensive competition

policy as part of its economic reform programme. The stated aims were
to consider the necessity for a competition law and then, if appropriate, to
proceed to draft a statute. The group was led jointly by two departments of
the State Council: the State Economic and Trade Commission (SETC) and
the SAIC.

The SETC has several roles, including the amalgamation of state-owned
industries into more viable organizations, economic-policy advice to central government and promoting competition policy as part of wholesale
restructuring of the economy into a 'socialist market economy'. The SAIC
grants business-licences to enterprises and enforces business-related laws.
The working group also comprised additional members co-opted from
various industrial ministries and members of the NPC legislative affairs
committee. The first public outline draft appeared four years late in 1999
(referred to below as the 1999 draft).

Many industrial ministries made a case for special treatment or exemption, citing the national interest, the need for economies of scale, and the
consequences of cut-throat price competition. Industry lobbies were also
consulted. They were worried about regional blockades, demarcation between permissible and impermissible competition, the need for a clear distinction between acceptable economies of scale and monopolization, and
that the mere size of an undertaking might be considered impermissible,
rather than its behaviour in the marketplace.

Academics' views were also sought. They worried that distinguishing
between economic monopoly and abuse of administrative powers of governmental organs would not be an easy task, given China's singular governmental structures and practices. Information was sought on a number
of countries' monopoly-control regimes, translations of laws were carried
out and summaries of individual regimes prepared.

Economic analysis of important Chinese industries was carried out,
which showed, interestingly, that most of them were not unduly concentrated, save for explicit utility monopolists such as telecommunications,
railways, power generation and petrochemicals. However, the actual scale
of some of the business units was enormous in absolute terms due to China's
size and population. Each producer tends to operate regionally and may well
have absolute dominance in a province or region that might contain 50–100
million consumers.

Such large-scale operations with regional dominance cannot be subject
to effective competition, given rampant regional protectionism. Further, the

difficulties of transport and distribution over such large distances provide considerable barriers to entry. The working group's national perspective and eye to industrial consolidation, economies of scale and the industrial policy of promoting national champions may have caused it to lose sight of the need to promote economic efficiency by competition at consumer level.

Significant battles have yet to be fought over the scope and coverage of the legislation, its definitions and thresholds for triggering action and the powers, organization, control and penalty provisions that will be granted to the enforcement agency. The role of the State Council and whether it will be competent to grant appeals from decisions of the enforcement body or provide exemptions from the law's provisions is also a major issue, as yet unresolved.[13]

For several years, WTO entry seemed a distant prospect as talks with the United States and European Union ran into the sand. However, with accession, by 2005 China may be facing intense foreign encroachment on its previously protected home ground. This may well be the crucial factor that speeds up the progress of legislation. Concern about foreign domination of Chinese markets is a real spur to competition legislation. The impetus to legislate still appears mired in bureaucratic infighting. An amended draft law appeared in autumn 2001 and further internationally sponsored discussion forums are scheduled to be held in the latter part of 2002. Thus, for the time being, there is no final version of the law and legislation now seems unlikely before the second half of 2003 or even 2004.

The draft Anti-Monopoly Law 1999

Objectives and definitions

This section analyses the proposals currently tabled, looking at the substantive provisions: Part I (definitions), Part II (abuse of dominant position), Part III (restrictive agreements), Part IV (merger control) and Part V (administrative monopoly). Other important issues contained in Part VI (administration and enforcement) and Part VII (penalties and enforcement) will not be discussed for reasons of space.

---

[13] This information was obtained as a result of personal interviews with several members of the working group and with senior Chinese academics involved in the process.

The 1999 draft adopts the EU approach to competition law. Articles 81 and 82 (ex Articles 85 and 86) of the EC Treaty are adopted almost verbatim and merger control by reference to turnover thresholds is established. An additional Chinese element is the prohibition of administrative monopoly practices. Further, an independent regulator is envisaged with effective enforcement powers including investigatory procedures and administrative powers of prohibition of condemned conduct and financial penalties. As with the substantive law, this is a strikingly similar regime to that of the European Union.

Article 1 of the 1999 draft states that the law's purpose is to prevent monopoly behaviour, defend the competitive process, protect the legitimate interests of consumers and operators and promote the healthy development of the socialist market economy. Some of these objectives seem in conflict or even mutually exclusive, particularly the protection of competitors as opposed to the protection of the process. But the interests of protected competitors must be 'legitimate' and so, one might argue, they have a legitimate interest in the preservation of the competitive process, rather than in intervention to protect market players.

Broad aims for competition policy that are not always compatible are nothing unusual.[14] If the provisions, when enacted, are used solely to promote efficiency, then another goal of the Chinese government, that of integrating the national market, may suffer. However, market integration may not be as powerful a political objective as it was in the case of the European Union, where rigid market segmentation along Member State boundaries was to be extirpated at all costs. Even in Europe this approach may well now have been softened as a result of the single-market policies of the last two decades, which have substantially improved market integration.

In China, removing administrative barriers to inter-regional trade may provoke consolidation within industries that are more exposed to competition and less able to seek the protection of the local authorities. Thus, market integration and economic efficiency may be complementary objectives in China; but if consolidation were to go too far, problems of dominance would be a concern. Attaining a balance between consolidation and competition should be the ultimate goal of Chinese policy-makers. But that will be difficult to achieve and in the final analysis depends on political factors not the primary concern of competition policy-makers and enforcers. However,

---

[14] On EU competition policy, see J. Steiner and L. Woods, *Textbook on EC Law* (7th edn, London, 2000), pp. 208–86.

given China's political environment and governmental structures, ignoring the political dimension of competition policy would be naïve in the extreme.

Article 2 contains definitions. The law regulates 'operators' who are legal persons, organizations and individuals engaged in commodity operations (presumably production, distribution or sale of manufactured goods, raw materials or agricultural products at a profit). The provision of services at a profit is included in the definition of commodity. Presumably, non-profit governmental functions such as education or health services would not be included, but private enterprises in these sectors would be. Difficulties of definition and coverage are potentially serious in an economy where the army and government departments run businesses of every sort.

Monopoly behaviour is also defined in terms of 'abuse of market domination status' alone or in collusion, whereby competition in a given market is excluded or restricted. This definition is in line with EU law in Article 82 (ex Article 86) of the EC Treaty.

The term 'given market' is also defined both by reference to geographical area and to a particular commodity. Substitutability and cross-elasticities of demand must be taken into account in deciding what amounts to a market share of a particular commodity. This problem is familiar in EU law and has spawned many leading cases[15] and substantial official guidance as to how the EU Commission arrives at a definition of the relevant market in specific cases.[16] If the draft Chinese law is enacted, reference to the relevant principles of EU law would be instructive.

Article 4 expressly instructs government departments at all levels to promote competition and desist from abuse of administrative powers to restrict competition.

Abuse of dominance

Part II turns to substantive prohibitions. Article 7 prohibits abuse of 'market dominance', defined in Article 8 as a sole operator in a given commodity market, or where an operator has an 'overwhelming position' in a given market 'which is difficult to enter' (presumably with significant barriers to entry). As is explained below, utilities are exempted from the ambit of the law but the telecoms and banking sectors are not.

---

[15] E.g. Case 27/76 *United Brands v. Commission* [1978] ECR 207.

[16] *Commission Notice on the Definition of the Relevant Market for the Purposes of Community Competition Law*, OJ 1997 No. C372.

Article 8(4) states that market domination can be assumed when a single operator has 50 per cent of a given market or two operators together have 66 per cent, or three operators together have 75 per cent.

Under Article 9, operators with dominance shall not unjustifiably set, adjust or maintain prices or supplies of commodities, impede access to the market of competitors, prevent or obstruct the entrance of new operators to the market or harm consumers.

Other activities are also outlawed:

- price discrimination or the imposition of differential terms of supply (Article 10);
- incitement of intimidatory conduct by other operators against competitors (Article 11);
- forced tie-in sales (Article 12);
- predatory pricing (Article 13); and
- monopolization of distribution channels (Article 14).

Restrictive agreements

Part III deals with restrictive agreements, both horizontal and vertical. Article 15 prohibits agreements, of whatever nature, between competitors that restrict competition. Examples provided of prohibited conduct include price fixing or price maintenance, bid rigging, restrictions on quantities or the quality of goods supplied, exclusive territoriality, exclusive dealing with suppliers or customers, restrictions on utilization of new techniques or equipment and collusion to exclude or remove competitors.

Article 16 specifically bans resale price maintenance. However, just as in Article 81(3) (ex Article 85(3)) of the EC Treaty, Article 17 provides for exemptions from the prohibitions on condition that they are conducive to overall economic development and the public interest, competition is not thereby eliminated and that the regulatory authority grants an exemption.

Examples provided of the types of agreement that might be favourably received by the regulator include: agreements to adopt new technology, improve product quality, raise economic efficiency, reduce costs, standardize specifications and to undertake research and development. Small and medium-sized businesses that co-operate to improve efficiency are granted favourable consideration (presumably a *de minimis* exemption). Crisis cartels are also potentially permissible.

Article 18 provides for offending agreements to be notified to the regulator, which may grant exemption, condemn the agreement or make it subject to conditions. However, agreements that create or reinforce market dominance or relating to price fixing or price maintenance cannot be exempted.

Horizontal agreements of the most blatant type, production limitations and price fixing, are common in China[17] and vertical restraints are equally prevalent.[18] Consequently, the number of restrictive agreements must be great. The administrative system to adjudicate exemptions will break down, unless a system of block exemption or even the non-application of the provision to most vertical agreements occurs. Presumably, these matters could be dealt with in subordinate legislation, which the draft law provides power for the regulatory body to make, in similar fashion to the EU Commission.

Merger control

Part IV turns to merger control. Article 20 defines a merger situation and Article 21 envisages control of mergers by requiring application for ratification of a merger proposal be submitted to the regulator. The thresholds for notification are:

(1) the merged enterprise has more than a 50 per cent market share of a given commodity market; or
(2) one of the potential merger partners has a 25 per cent market share of a given commodity market prior to the merger; or
(3) one of the potential merger partners has a turnover volume in excess of an administratively defined amount, which is not specified in the draft.

Under Article 22 the application for ratification must contain relevant information on the enterprise's business, assets, employees, sales volume, profit margins and taxes paid. Company annual reports and financial statements, production and operational costs, prices, an assessment of the

---

[17] For example, on 20 January 2000 the Chinese Automobile Industry Association announced a decision by the ten domestic automobile manufacturers that they would not compete with each other on price and would agree on a tariff of automobile prices: *China Daily*, 3 March 2000. In June 2000 nine television manufacturers formed a price alliance to co-ordinate the sale prices of televisions: *China Daily*, 31 July 2000.

[18] For example, in July 2000 a television manufacturer, Changhong, announced that it had suspended supplies of its television sets to Guomei, a large Beijing retailer, as a result of the store reducing the retail price of its products without the manufacturer's agreement.

effects of the merger relative to the overall economic social and public interest and the rationale for the merger must be provided by the
applicant.

This appears to be an *ex post facto* notification system rather than a preliminary approval procedure. However, where enterprises are about to sign
a merger agreement they could make the validity of the contract conditional
on approval from the regulator.[19]

There is a presumption against any merger that creates or strengthens market dominance or even one that merely restricts competition.
Mergers must improve market competition before they can be ratified
under Article 24, but there is an overriding power under Article 25 for
the State Council to approve a merger that promotes the national economic, social or public interest. No further clarification of this provision is
offered.

Clearly, there is tension between Articles 24 and 25. Article 24 seems
unrealistically pro-competition. Mergers between substantial competitors
must reduce competition to some extent. But if the merger promotes other
sorts of economic or technical progress or creates new products and competition is not eliminated, mergers can be beneficial. Article 24 needs
to reflect a more realistic approach to merger control. Article 25 proceeds to
drive a coach and horses through this policy. This is, unashamedly, a tool to
promote a national champion policy. There are no countervailing requirements of technical improvements or even that any competition remains
at all within a given market. Article 25 could allow the creation of new
monopolists. If enacted in this form, the integrity of the merger-control
regime could easily be undermined, given the traditional interventionism
of industrial ministries.

If ratification is refused or not sought, the regulator may, under Article 26,
prohibit the merger or require divestiture or reinstatement of the status quo
ante or impose a financial penalty.

Administrative monopoly

Part V deals with the Chinese peculiarity of a monolithic, single-party,
non-democratic government having to issue a legal prohibition to prevent

---

[19] PRC Contract Law 1999, Art. 45, states 'The parties may agree to attach conditions to the
effectiveness of the contract.'

other parts of the same government from breaking or abusing its own administrative powers.

Article 28 prohibits government organs from obtaining supplies of commodities from a single supplier or from using administrative measures against legitimate competition. Article 29 deals with regional protectionism and forbids the use of administrative powers to restrict the inflow or outflow of commodities to or from a particular locality. Article 30 prohibits forced mergers and forced association agreements; compulsory alignment of prices; forced purchase or sale of commodities by operators; and administrative orders requiring operators to desist from competing or to set output limits or to limit product ranges.

The prohibition of compulsory mergers is perplexing. Clearly, mergers in the state-owned enterprise sector are a pressing issue. If industries such as automotive and steel are to have a chance of competing in the more open trading environment that should eventuate after the transitional phase of WTO accession has passed, consolidation is required. Perhaps the provision is aimed at purely localized forced mergers to form uneconomic conglomerates that reflect local political factors rather than commercial logic. Presumably, central government-sponsored mergers of state-owned industries would not be affected or would be exempted by the State Council under Article 25.

At present administratively sponsored prohibitions against competition are common. A recent example has been in the airline industry. Once freed from the shackles of the China National Aviation Corporation (CNAC), new operating companies began to compete on previously monopolized routes, offering discounted fares. In 1998 some airlines began to suffer losses but, instead of withdrawing from the market, they complained to CNAC, which ordered a cessation of 'malignant competition' and imposed regulations in 1999 to establish a uniform national tariff.[20] However, the travelling public was irate[21] and passenger traffic fell precipitately by some 3 million in 1999.[22] In July 2000 the CNAC announced that the operating airlines would be reorganized into three major groups and the new entities would once again be allowed to compete on price.

The draft provisions may be aimed at curbing such behaviour.

---

[20] See *China Eastern Airlines Today Magazine*, July 2000, p. 18, citing Li Zhongming, president of China Eastern Airlines.
[21] See *China Daily*, 17 November 1999, 27 April 2000 and 24 May 2000.
[22] See *China Daily*, 30 July 2000.

Exemptions

Parts VII and VIII (administration and enforcement) are not discussed in this chapter, apart from considering the question of exclusions.

Part VIII contains miscellaneous provisions. It provides for the enactment of detailed implementation and enforcement rules, and the complete exclusion from the scope of the law of the exercise of intellectual property rights and various utility services – post office, railways, the electricity, gas and water industries. The exclusion for the utility sectors is for five years from the implementation date. Arguably, the exclusion of a significant block of industries from the application of the law is damaging to the integrity of the system envisaged by the draft law, but at least the exclusion is limited to a fixed period.

Telecommunications is not excluded. This sector is dominated by China Telecom, which holds over 90 per cent of the vast Chinese telecommunications market. China Telecom's charges verge on confiscation, rather than a fee for service, and the cost of long-distance and international calls is prohibitive.[23] It appears that this state leviathan was not politically favoured enough to be excluded. The government may consider that the sector should be subject to the rigours of market competition to force the pace of modernization of infrastructure. China Unicom, the only licensed competitor at present, has faced massive interconnection problems and other impediments from the incumbent.[24]

The sector would undoubtedly benefit from foreign investment, which would increase consumer welfare by providing choice and, at the same time, lower prices. Under China's WTO accession agreements, foreign interests will be able to own up to half of Chinese telecommunications businesses and liberalization of the industry is now gathering pace.[25]

Implementation

Competition law has been on the Chinese government's agenda for over ten years. Significant progress has been made but the government has,

---

[23] In 1998 20,000 complaints were made to the Chinese Consumer Association concerning low quality and high prices in the telecommunications sector: *China Daily*, 15 March 1999.

[24] *China Daily*, 15 January 1999.

[25] Announcement of new regulations on foreign involvement in telecoms by the telecommunications minister, Wu Jichuan: *China Daily*, 26 September 2000. For further discussion, see Ian Macintosh's chapter in this volume (chapter 15).

nevertheless, tried a number of more interventionist policies, such as officially sponsored industry associations to ensure an 'orderly market'. These have failed to solve chronic problems such as the oversupply of certain commodities. Cartel action has similarly failed to set minimum prices or restrict supply. Chronic oversupply and deflation continue to afflict the Chinese economy.

State-owned enterprises do not go out of business as state banks continue to support local politically sponsored producers. Industrial ministries still try to force mergers of enterprises to create 'national champions', which are unlikely to be economically successful unless state banks continue their uncommercial lending policies, as equivalents once did in Thailand, Indonesia, Korea and Japan.

Monopolies continue to thrive as a result of government fiat and abuse of administrative power. The national market continues to be artificially compartmentalized, so impeding the growth of internal trade and the process of specialization so badly needed in the Chinese economy.

Adding to the pressure on Chinese policy-makers is the entry of China to the WTO, which will lead to a steady increase in the presence of foreign corporations in the domestic Chinese market. That pressure began on accession and will become even more intense five years later when the transitional period ends.

Conservative forces have managed to restrain a full-blooded commitment to competition by waving the shrouds of economic, social and political instability, but WTO entry and the failure of the current policies are likely to force the government to legislate and enforce a competition statute. However, the more conservative forces and regional cadres in the Chinese government may still seek to continue to prevent or restrict access to domestic markets and so make them less genuinely contestable, even after WTO accession. Official action to undermine market-access agreements by non-national treatment of foreign products or discriminatory licensing or technical standards would be amenable to complaint to the WTO dispute settlement procedures. This would include the case where a provincial authority was the culprit.

Without an enforceable domestic competition law, however, monopolistic or collaborative behaviour of private actors would not be touched by WTO commitments made by the Chinese government. They could continue to divide or dominate markets and exploit consumers and receive higher than market returns. A further complication is the opacity of the ownership of many businesses. Are they private sector, public sector or collective? Is the government able to utilize business vehicles in a way to disguise governmental activities and state domination of an industry? It can be hard to prove mixed government/private-sector actions of a market-exclusionary kind and thus for foreign entities to utilize WTO remedies – see the *Kodak* v. *Fuji* case.[26]

Another issue is whether the draft law is overly ambitious. It laudably seeks to overcome all the issues that a comprehensive competition policy should seek to address – monopoly power, restrictive agreements, mergers and an internal free market – but is it realistic for China to attempt to take on all these complex and contentious issues at once? Would an incremental approach be better?

China's administration and the skills of its public servants may be insufficient to handle the complex issues arising out of the adoption of a comprehensive competition policy. Consequently, if the draft law is enacted in substantially its current form, selective and phased implementation may be needed. The prohibition of cartels might be the easiest aspect to implement first. This would allow the regulators to gain experience of implementation and to overcome problems on a smaller scale before being faced with the great complexities of fact finding and economic analysis required in other competition situations.

If this is correct, the weaknesses of the draft law need to be rectified to have a properly functioning, rational structure. Even if these legal technicalities are overcome and a coherent law is enacted by the NPC in 2003, major issues of implementation will remain outstanding.

A national body capable of enforcing a comprehensive competition law in a country the size of China will need a small army of highly qualified accountants, economists and lawyers ideologically committed to competition policy. China does not, at present, have a sufficient pool of such professionals, and even if sufficient personnel could be trained they would be most unlikely to be attracted by the very low civil-service salaries currently offered. Additionally, the prestige, job security and fringe benefits of government service are diminishing in value, whilst the demand for skilled commercial lawyers in China is about to explode. WTO entry will undoubtedly cause an exponential growth in demand for well-qualified lawyers to handle all aspects of trade-related liberalization.

---

[26] WTO Panel Report, *Japan – Measures Affecting Consumer Photographic Film and Paper*, WT/DS44/R, adopted 22 April 1998.

Given the shortage of lawyers,[27] it is improbable that sufficient high-quality personnel can be found to staff the competition regulatory body. If this is so, the implementation of a comprehensive law may prove impossible to achieve, even with the full political backing of central government.

Conclusion

China has made remarkable progress in economic restructuring in the last twenty-five years. However, a great deal remains to be done. Competition law is one of the major policy tasks necessary if China is to complete its transformation from a centrally planned economy to a market-focused one. The adoption and proper implementation of a comprehensive competition law will be a key test of the level of political support for the marketization of the Chinese economy. It will also test the commitment of the government to advancing the cause of the rule of law and to honour the spirit and the letter of its market-opening commitments made in the bilateral trade agreements with the United States and the European Union and in the WTO Accession Protocol.

This chapter has discussed some of the major problems in the draft competition law and suggested remedies for those defects. Unless the wider economic issues are resolved, a workable set of competition rules adopted and a genuine internal market developed, greater economic efficiency will not be achieved and the ability of many Chinese domestic businesses to survive market opening will be threatened.

The central government seeks to achieve four principal objectives in pushing the Chinese economy in a more market-oriented direction:

- to complete a genuine internal market;
- to promote more rational and efficient distribution of scarce economic resources;
- to encourage the growth of more market-oriented, larger and viable firms; and
- to provide a mechanism to regulate the activities of new market entrants from abroad.

---

[27] In a recent speech, Jia Wuguong of the PRC Ministry of Justice stated that in 1979 China had 212 qualified lawyers and in 1999 had 110,000, only 50 per cent of whom had a bachelor's degree in law and only 4,000 of whom were qualified to deal with foreign-related work. Most law firms had fewer than twenty employees.

Protecting the consumer from exploitation is not one of the principal objectives.

The old structure of a fragmented, protected, domestic market is no longer viable. Change is inevitable. Therefore, the likely adoption of a competition law in China has been catalysed, though not principally caused, by China's WTO accession.

Whether the economic reformers in the Chinese government who support an active competition policy will prevail cannot, at present, be predicted with certainty. The balance of advantage seems to be in their favour, especially when the post-accession clock starts to tick away the time that remains to the current economic structures. The reality of increased imports and the ever more urgent need to tackle the structural imperfections of the Chinese domestic economy will militate in favour of an active competition policy.

PART VI

Intellectual property

18

Chinese trademark law and the TRIPs Agreement – Confucius meets the WTO

ANGELA GREGORY

Is it necessary for a steel worker to put his name on a steel ingot that he produces in the course of his duty? If not, why should a member of the intelligentsia enjoy the privilege of putting his name on what he produces?

> Popular saying in China during the Cultural Revolution (1966–76), cited in W. Alford, *To Steal a Book is an Elegant Offense* (Stanford, 1995), p. 56.

Introduction

One of the most frequently aired concerns about China's accession to the WTO has been that China will not be able to implement the Agreement on Trade-related Aspects of Intellectual Property Rights (TRIPs)[1] so as to ensure that foreign IP right holders will be able to enforce their rights effectively. While those concerns relate to most of the areas of intellectual property covered by the TRIPs Agreement, one of the biggest areas of concern continues to be whether the Chinese government will be able to reduce the pervasive practice of copyright and trademark counterfeiting that exists in China.[2] This chapter deals with the Chinese government's implementation of those provisions of the TRIPs Agreement that relate to trademarks and to the problem of trademark counterfeiting.

Trademark laws, like other intellectual property laws, are relevant to international trade because of the effect that uneven or inadequate

---

[1] See Final Act Embodying the Results of the Uruguay Round of Multilateral Trade Negotiations, Annex 1C: Agreement on Trade-related Aspects of Intellectual Property Rights, GATT, Doc. MTN/FA/Add.1, 15 December 1993.

[2] E.g. see Report of the Working Party on the Accession of China to the WTO, WT/ACC/CHN/49, para. 288.

protection has on competition.[3] In a market with effective IP protection, manufacturers compete against each other on the basis of quality and price.[4] Manufacturers may invest in quality control, good materials, research and development, and marketing so that consumers will associate their brand with particular characteristics, such as quality. Counterfeiters, on the other hand, avoid the costs of establishing a reputation. They have no interest in investing in good-quality materials, quality control, research and development, advertising or marketing. Thus, a counterfeiter's overall costs are low, creating barriers to entry for the producers of genuine products.[5] More specifically, the goodwill attached to a trade mark, in particular to well-known trade marks such as Coca-Cola, Microsoft or Levis, can amount to billions of dollars in commercial value. Counterfeit trade diminishes the value of trade marks and is detrimental to business reputations.[6] The consumer may receive poor-quality goods at inflated prices and can be exposed to health and safety risks.[7]

For these reasons, coupled with the advent of new technologies that make piracy and counterfeiting all the more easy, industrialized countries insisted on bringing the TRIPs Agreement to the Uruguay Round. An additional attraction for bringing intellectual property to the GATT forum was for the strong enforcement and dispute settlement mechanisms, which are not offered under other international IP agreements.[8] Combining IP rights with the GATT allows Member States to impose trade sanctions on countries that do not provide TRIPs-consistent legal and administrative structures for the civil and criminal enforcement of intellectual property.[9]

---

[3] J. McKeough and A. Stewart, *Intellectual Property in Australia* (2nd edn, North Ryde, 1997), p. 478.

[4] Centre for Economic and Business Research, *The Economic Impact of Counterfeiting*, commissioned by the Global Anti-Counterfeiting Group, p. 3: http://www.a-cg.com/index2.htm, last updated 23 November 1999.

[5] OECD, *The Economic Impact of Counterfeiting*, prepared for the ICC Counterfeiting Intelligence Bureau, for the Industry Division of the OECD's Directorate for Science, Technology and Industry 1998, p. 22: http://www.oecd.org//dsti/sti/industry/indcomp/prod/fa/fakes.htm, last updated 26 November 1998.

[6] J. Keon, 'Intellectual property rules for trademarks and geographical indications: important parts of the new world trade order', in C. Correa and A. Yusuf (eds.), *Intellectual Property and International Trade: The TRIPs Agreement* (London, 1998), pp. 165–78, at p. 173.

[7] OECD, *Economic Impact*, 23.

[8] A. Yusuf, 'TRIPs: background, principles and general provisions', in Correa and Yusuf (eds.), *Intellectual Property and International Trade*, pp. 3–20, at p. 10.

[9] P. Drahos, 'Global property rights in information: the story of TRIPs at the GATT' (1995) 19 *Prometheus* 6.

Although the People's Republic of China was not a party to the GATT[10] at the time of the negotiation of the TRIPs Agreement, it was negotiating its accession (or resumption of party status) to the GATT[11] and it did participate in the Uruguay Round. China co-operated with other nations of similar economic development in drafting a joint proposal for the TRIPs negotiations.[12] Chinese officials insisted they should be admitted to the proposed new TRIPs Agreement as a developing country, receiving such benefits as delayed implementation. In contrast, the United States maintained that China was capable of curtailing IP rights violations and should be admitted with developed-country status.[13] Accordingly, the Contracting Parties and China could not agree. Major trading nations, including the United States, cited China's IP rights violations as one of the reasons (along with dissatisfaction with China's market-access offers) for challenging the application.[14]

Now that China has acceded to the WTO it will need to comply with all facets of the TRIPs Agreement.[15] In China, commercial counterfeiting has reached epidemic proportions, expanding beyond TAG watches and Gucci bags into the realms of medical devices and aeronautical parts.[16] In the first six months of 2000, 665 cases involving the improper use of foreign trade marks were uncovered.[17] The United States has been particularly concerned about the misuse of IP rights in China, and has instigated four Sino-American IP-related trade agreements since 1979,[18] including

[10] W. Cai, 'China's membership in the GATT/WTO: historical and legal issues', in W. Cai, M. Smith and X. Xu (eds.), *China and the World Trade Organization: Requirements, Realities, and Resolution* (Centre for Trade Policy and Law, Carleton University, Canada, 1996), pp. 10–32, at p. 10.

[11] See the application to resume status, GATT Doc. L/6017 (Geneva, GATT, 10 July 1986) and the establishment of the WP in GATT *Focus*, No. 44 (Geneva, GATT, March 1987) cited in Cai, 'China's membership', 12–13.

[12] *Communication from Argentina, Brazil, Chile, China, Colombia, Cuba, Egypt, India, Nigeria, Peru, Tanzania, Uruguay and Pakistan*, MTN.GNG/NG11/W/71, 14 May 1990, p. 441.

[13] A. Beam, 'Piracy of American intellectual property in China' (1995) 4 *Journal of International Law and Practice* 335, at 356.

[14] Ibid.

[15] Protocol of Accession of the People's Republic of China, WT/L/432, 23 November 2001.

[16] For statistics see Global Anti-Counterfeiting Group: 'What is counterfeiting?', http://www.a-cg.com, last updated 17 April 2000.

[17] 'China uncovers 665 cases involving violations of foreign trademarks in the first half of 2000', http://www.chinaonline/commentary_analysis/issues/econ_news/currentnews/secure/c00080415.asp, last updated 7 August 2000 (reported from the *Zhongguo Xin She* [China News Service] 3 August).

[18] The four trade agreements were in 1979, 1992, 1995 and 1996. S. Tiefenbrun, 'Piracy of intellectual property in China and the former Soviet Union and its effects upon international trade:

a unilaterally enforceable Section 301 provision.[19] Section 301 under the US Trade Act of 1974 gives the US president unilateral power to penalize countries that either deny adequate and effective protection of IP rights or fair and equitable market access for US persons.[20] In the face of voter pressure, it is likely that the United States will invoke every mechanism to ensure China fully complies with the TRIPs Agreement.

This chapter examines whether the minimum standards of protection afforded to trade marks (Articles 15–21) and the remedies and procedures for enforcing violations or unauthorized use of IP rights (Articles 41–61) set by the TRIPs Agreement are satisfied by the recently amended Chinese Trademark Law (revised as at 27 October 2001).[21] The first section of the chapter explores the historical background and development of Chinese trade marks. The second section explores some of the cultural, political and economic realities that limit the success of the trademark legislation. The third and fourth sections analyse and compare the Chinese trademark provisions with the TRIPs Agreement and highlight the similarities and deficiencies. The next section discusses the prospects for sanction-based retaliation for non-compliance and the final section offers alternatives for foreign mark holders to protect their IP rights.

Recent history of trademark law in China

The intellectual property laws of imperial China were far from the contemporary capitalist ideal. In fact, IP rights are something foreign to Chinese culture. Confucian teachings encourage learning by copying, in stark contrast to contemporary principles of intellectual property rights.[22] This philosophy resounds throughout Chinese culture. The ancient art form of calligraphy is taught by copying the style of the great masters. It is not until a person has perfected the style of another that they are ready to

---

a comparison' (1998) 46 *Buffalo Law Review* 1, at 27 and A. McCall, 'Copyright and trademark enforcement in China', (1996) 9 *Transnational Law* 587, at 593.

[19] J. Simons, 'Cooperation and coercion: the protection of intellectual property in developing countries', (1999) 11 *Bond Law Review* 59, at 71.

[20] Ibid.

[21] Trademark Law of the PRC (1982) as amended on 27 October 2001, in force 1 December 2001. The Implementing Rules of the Trademark Law of the PRC (1988) as amended on 23 April 1995.

[22] B. O'Connor and D. Lowe, 'Comparative analysis of intellectual property dispute resolution processes in mainland China, Taiwan and the United States', in P. Liu and A. Sun (eds.), *Intellectual Property Protection in the Asian-Pacific Region: A Comparative Study* (Occasional Papers/Reprint Series in Contemporary Asian Studies 4, 1996), p. 63.

develop their own unique style.[23] Andrew McCall noted that in China 'the greatest compliment that authors can receive is having someone copy their works'.[24] Whilst this is true for most creators, this attitude makes intellectual property enforcement in China all the more difficult.

International influence encouraged the formal adoption of the Chinese Trademark Law by the Nationalist government in 1931.[25] With the establishment of the People's Republic of China in 1949, the Chinese Communist Party promulgated the Procedures for Dealing with Trademarks Registered at the Trademark Office of the Former Guomingdang Government and the Provisional Regulations on Trademark Registration, which in effect, invalidated all registration made under the Nationalist government.[26] A new 'first to file' system based heavily on Soviet socialist ideology was implemented. The Soviet model instructed that all property, including intellectual property, should be collectively owned by the state to eliminate class inequalities. All creations and inventions were for the benefit of the state.[27] Accordingly, because registration was not required, intellectual property law remained unfamiliar. Fear of political repercussions of asserting such property rights also prevented many individuals from registering their marks.[28]

The adoption of the open door policy[29] in 1979 marked the start of a fundamental shift not only in Chinese economic policy, but also in individual rights. There was a shift away from collectivism to promoting productivity through individual rewards. The importance of foreign investment was realized and, at the substantial urging of international trading partners, China began implementing new IP-related legal protection.[30] A Chinese Trademark Law was promulgated on 23 August 1982 and became effective on 1 March 1983. This law, however, failed to appease leaders of the international community, in particular the United States.[31] In April 1991, the US trade

---

[23] K. Wang, *Chinese Commercial Law* (Melbourne, 2000), p. 205.

[24] McCall, 'Copyright and trademark enforcement', at 590.

[25] C. Paglee, 'Chinese trademark law revised: new regulations protect well-known trademarks' (1997) 5 *University of Baltimore Intellectual Property Journal* 37, at 38.

[26] W. Alford, *To Steal a Book is an Elegant Offense* (Stanford, Calif., 1995), p. 56.

[27] Ibid., at 57.   [28] Tiefenbrun, 'Piracy of intellectual property', at 12.

[29] Generally, on the open door policy of economic liberalization, see C. Dietrich, *People's China: A Brief History* (New York, 1986), p. 257.

[30] O'Connor and Lowe, 'Comparative analysis', p. 64.

[31] R. Feaver, 'China's copyright law and the TRIPs Agreement' (1996) 5 *Journal of Transnational Law and Policy* 431, at 435.

representative placed China on a Priority Watchlist for failing to protect
IP rights adequately. After lengthy negotiations, and just hours before US
retaliatory measures were to be implemented, the United States and China
signed a Memorandum of Understanding (MOU) on the Protection of Intellectual Property in January 1992.[32] Pursuant to the MOU, China revised
much of its substantive law, including the Trademark Law, in an attempt to
bring the Chinese intellectual property system into line with international
standards.[33] During the reform process, China also improved its administrative and judicial systems by establishing special tribunals, such as the
Intellectual Property Court and national IP offices, to deal with matters
arising under the new legislation.[34]

Despite China's progress in implementing the 1992 MOU, widespread
piracy violations continued unabated.[35] In 1994, due to the continued lack
of enforcement, the US trade representative determined that China had
'failed to create an effective intellectual property rights enforcement regime'
and placed it on the Priority Watchlist once again.[36] China responded by
raiding and closing illegal factories, seizing pirated goods and arresting
over 7,000 people.[37] This was, however, insufficient for the US officials,
who insisted on improved enforcement measures. The Chinese refused the
additional demands and the United States threatened China with trade
sanctions on more than US$1.8 billion worth of Chinese imports. On 26
February 1995, the day of the deadline, China and the United States averted
the mutually threatened trade war by reaching the 1995 US–China Intellectual Property Agreement.[38] The Agreement is primarily an accord outlining
the steps that the Chinese government must take to curb counterfeiting and
to ensure an improved IP rights-enforcement system.[39]

China's accession to the WTO and the most recent amendments to the
Chinese Trademark Law, which came into force just before the accession
became effective, mark the beginning of a new era in Chinese trademark

[32] See ibid.   [33] Ibid.
[34] W. Long, 'Intellectual property in China' (1999) 31 St Mary's Law Journal 63, at 69.
[35] McCall, 'Copyright and trademark enforcement', at 593.
[36] United States Trade Representative, 'Identification of foreign countries that deny adequate and
     effective intellectual property protection' (1994) 59 Federal Regulations, p. 26, 341, cited in
     P. Hu, ' "Mickey Mouse" in China: legal and cultural implications in protecting US copyrights'
     (1996) 14 Boston University International Law Journal 81, at 90.
[37] Simons, 'Cooperation and coercion', 84.   [38] Ibid.
[39] McCall, 'Copyright and trademark enforcement', 595.

law.[40] This may afford the opportunity to break the cycle of the threatening of trade sanctions followed by highly publicized raids and promises to improve enforcement.

Cultural and social impediments to IP protection

The Chinese government has made significant efforts to meet the requirements of international agreements and to reform domestic law. Its efforts at policing counterfeiting, however, have been less than adequate.[41] Government statistics indicate that the number of trademark-infringing cases continues to increase whilst the number involving criminal punishment and compensation for economic losses declines.[42] This section attempts to glean some explanation for China's inadequate protection of IP from an examination of Chinese enforcement practices, and Chinese cultural and economic factors.

Social and cultural influences – Confucianism

Despite China's attempts to move closer to a western-style rule of law, traditional Confucian political philosophies still govern much of Chinese thought. At the heart of Confucian thought is the concept of *li*. In essence, *li* is the notion of a moral or social order guiding interpersonal relationships. Integrity and benevolence are to direct people in their interaction with others and, in particular, within the five defined roles of ruler/subject, father/son, husband/wife, elder brother/younger brother and friend/friend.[43] Confucius believed that if society was ordered to these principles, the state would be harmonious and strong.[44]

It is also largely due to these principles of political, social and familial relationships that litigation and the promotion of individual rights are

[40] Protocol of Accession of the People's Republic of China, dated 10 November 2001, in force 10 December 2001 (WT/L/432, 23 November 2001).
[41] China adheres to at least twelve international Conventions including the Convention Establishing the World Intellectual Property Organization and the Paris Convention for the Protection of Industrial Property, 14 July 1967 ('Paris Convention'). C. Zheng, 'TRIPs and intellectual property protection in China' (1997) 5 *European Intellectual Property Review* 243.
[42] 'China uncovers 665 cases', 1.
[43] Yu-Chien Kuan, *Magnificent China: A Guide to its Cultural Treasures* (Hong Kong, 1983), p. 58.
[44] F. Dernberger, K. DeWoskin, S. Goldstein, R. Murphey and M. Whyte (eds.), *The Chinese: Adapting the Past, Facing the Future* (Centre for Chinese Studies, The University of Michigan, Ann Arbor, 1991), p. 152.

avoided.[45] Even today, Chinese justice is geared towards dispute settlement, rather than upholding individual rights.[46]

It is for these cultural and social reasons that the Confucian relationships, known as *guanxi*, frequently have more influence in interpersonal, bureaucratic and commercial dealings than the use of law.[47] However, the flexibility of dealings has translated into endemic corruption and opportunism in state industries and administrative bureaucracies.[48] Consequently, the Chinese have a distrust for formal law and individual rights is not a concept to which the general population is accustomed.

The Constitution

Chinese citizens are only granted the rights offered under the Constitution if they 'perform the duties prescribed by the Constitution and the law'.[49] As a result, counter-revolutionaries in the Cultural Revolution were not included as 'people' protected under the Constitution as they did not fulfil their 'duties'. In fact, the Constitution considers them enemies of the 'people'.[50] Evidently, individual rights and compensation to individuals for the violation of these rights are enforceable only when the citizen is first serving the interests of the state.

Courts and judges

The judicial system offers a further impediment to the enforcement of intellectual property rights. First, many judges lack the necessary education, largely due to the Cultural Revolution, which prevented many children attending school between the 1960s and the late 1970s. As recently as the early 1990s large numbers of army officers were assigned to the courts to perform as judges.[51] Moreover, in some jurisdictions, there has been (at best) very little case reporting to allow judges to see how other judges decide similar cases.[52]

---

[45] G. Butterton, 'Pirates, dragons and U.S. intellectual property rights in China: problems and prospects of Chinese enforcement' (1996) 38 *Arizona Law Review* 1100, at 1109.

[46] J. Fung, 'Can Mickey Mouse prevail in the court of the Monkey King? Enforcing intellectual property rights in the People's Republic of China' (1996) 18 *Loyola of Los Angeles International and Comparative Law Journal* 613, at 620. See also the PRC Trademark Law, Art. 53.

[47] Butterton, 'Pirates, dragons', 1113.   [48] Ibid.

[49] Art. 33 of the Chinese Constitution.   [50] Fung, 'Can Mickey Mouse prevail?', 621.

[51] D. Clarke, 'Dispute resolution in China' (1991) 5 *Journal of Chinese Law* 245, at 257.

[52] Ibid., 259.

Secondly, Chinese judges have no security of tenure and their poor salaries render them highly susceptible to bribery and corruption.[53] The expenditures of the courts, including salaries of judicial personnel and their families, are the responsibility of local governments.[54] Thus, it is not uncommon for the judiciary to believe that they should decide a case in a certain manner.[55] Obviously, in the absence of reliable empirical data, the extent of any corruption is unquantifiable; however, it is well documented that official corruption is a serious problem in China.[56] Even high officials are unable to resist the temptation, and corruption undoubtedly extends to the judiciary.[57]

The opaqueness and arbitrariness of the Chinese administrative process is also of concern. Under international pressure, China has published most of its trade laws and regulations.[58] However, in addition to the officially published legislation, China still maintains a system of so-called internal regulations, or *neibu*, which, although enforceable, are not available to the public.[59] (Time will tell whether WTO membership changes this practice.) As aptly put by a Chinese proverb, 'Of ten reasons by which a magistrate may decide a case, nine are unknown to the public'.[60] Together, these factors create a general lack of faith in the legal system that makes knowing the grounds upon which a decision has been made difficult to determine.

Enforcement – IP rights cases

In recent years, the Chinese IP courts have seen numerous actions brought by both domestic and foreign parties. However, due to the lack of judicial expertise and independence, the unpredictability of trial outcomes and the

[53] S. Biddulph, 'The legal structure of decision making in Chinese police enforcement powers: some preliminary issues', in V. Taylor (ed.), *Asian Laws Through Australian Eyes* (Sydney 1997), pp. 207–38, at p. 223.

[54] Wang, *Chinese Commercial Law*, p. 26.   [55] Ibid.

[56] J. Cohen, 'Enforcement of intellectual property rights in Asia: the case of China', in H. Hansen (ed.), *International Intellectual Property Law and Policy* (New York, 1996), pp. 63–8, at p. 65; Clarke, 'Dispute resolution', 259.

[57] L. O'Donnell, 'Only the small fry to face real punishment', *The Australian*, 11 October 2000, p. 9.

[58] S. Kho, *The Impact of the World Trade Organization of the Lack of Transparency in the People's Republic of China* (Occasional Papers/Reprints Series in Contemporary Asian Studies 2, 1998), p. 53.

[59] Ibid., p. 12.

[60] Cited in D. Bodde and C. Morris, *Law in Imperial China* (Harvard, 1967), p. 334.

lack of known IP enforcement policies, litigation in Chinese courts remains an expensive and risky exercise.[61]

In March 1992, the Shenzhen Reflective Materials Institute was found to have copied 650,000 Microsoft Corporation trademark holograms.[62] Nearly two years later the Chinese authorities found that the Institute had infringed Microsoft's trademark and fined the Institute approximately US$252.[63] In contrast, Chinese courts have imposed the death penalty for those who have traded in famous Chinese liquor and cigarettes[64] – in this case, the trademark holder was awarded compensation of US$115,000.[65] Most of the IP cases appear to reflect a bias towards Chinese nationals. However, there are cases where foreigners have been awarded substantial amounts, although at somewhat convenient times. For example, in June 2000, a Chinese court gave the first ruling on cybersquatting,[66] when a well-known foreign trademark,[67] IKEA, was victorious over Cinet, which registered the domain name in bad faith. Some of China's commentators will see this as a sign of China's commitment to protecting IP rights; however, the decision was made at a politically convenient time when the US Congress was debating whether to grant China permanent normal trade relations.[68]

Even in the instance where both parties – the trademark holder and the infringer – are Chinese there is evidence of a general lack of recognition of the value of IP rights. In one trademark infringement case, Qingdao No. 3 Pharmaceutical Factory was only compensated for its losses to the extent of RMB 20,000, although it cost them more than RMB 50,000 in travel expenses alone to pursue the action.[69] In the Microsoft case, the losses for the company have been estimated as being near to US$30 million and could possibly have been as high as US$180 million if the standing order for

---

[61] Ibid.   [62] Feaver, 'China's copyright law', 450.   [63] Ibid.   [64] Ibid.

[65] Ibid., citing *China: New Laws Fail to Bite: (Micro)soft on Offenders*, 2/21/1994, available in LEXIS.

[66] Cybersquatters are those who register someone else's trade name as a domain name.

[67] P. Torbert, 'Cyber-squatters beware: IKEA case a telling one', http://www.chinaonline.com/comment/secure/currentnews/a00039483, last updated 5 July 2000.

[68] Permanent normal trade relation status was previously known as 'most favoured nation' status under US trade law. The change in terminology occurred in 1998. B. Bacon, 'The People's Republic of China and the World Trade Organization: anticipating a United States congressional dilemma' (2000) 9 *Minnesota Journal of Global Trade* 369, at 372.

[69] W. Huang, 'China's accession to the WTO and its intellectual property rights protection', in Cai, Smith and Xu (eds.), *China and the World Trade Organization*, pp. 204–53, at p. 237.

3 million holograms had not been intercepted.[70] The fine of US$252 against the defendant is absurd in comparison to the loss suffered.

Criminal liabilities have also been inadequate. The administrative enforcement bodies are more likely to impose fines than a prison term. Rather than discouraging counterfeiting, such enforcement measures are, in fact, encouraging violators to return to counterfeiting to recoup the losses incurred from the fine.[71] There is also concern that even where fines are awarded, there is a lack of enforcement measures to ensure that the fines are actually paid. For example, in the province of Liaoning, one violator should have been fined a total of RMB 18 million, but was only ordered to pay RMB 7 million. Of this amount, only RMB 3.15 million was collected.[72]

Foreign parties who have been awarded damages are finding it increasingly difficult to have their judgements enforced.[73] Much of China's IP enforcement occurs at the provincial or local levels, and the national government lacks the resources to monitor and enforce national IP enforcement policies.[74] Investigating counterfeiting cases also poses problems, requiring extensive resources even to identify the infringing parties.[75]

Economic factors

China's swift transfer from a socialist economy to a market economy has further exacerbated the problem of intellectual property counterfeiting.[76] Young Chinese people are tasting the fruits of a capitalist market economy. Girls want to be seen in Christian Dior clothing and boys want to wear Ralph Lauren shirts and TAG watches.[77] Counterfeiters are making the most of the opportunities offered by the huge increase in purchasing power and desire for brand names.[78] Further, counterfeit goods are making foreign goods – once beyond the reach of the average Chinese person – affordable.

---

[70] Butterton, 'Pirates, dragons', 1099 citing 'Observers expect Taiwan to be cited by USTR for intellectual property rights' (1992) *Patent Trademark & Copyright Law Daily*, 28 April.
[71] Huang, 'China's accession', p. 237.
[72] Ibid.   [73] Hu, ' "Mickey Mouse" ', 88.
[74] J. Spierer, 'Intellectual property in China: prospectus for new market entrants' (2000) *Harvard Asia Quarterly* 3: http://www.fas.harvard.edu/~asiactr/haq/199902/9902a010.html, last updated 2 April 2000.
[75] Ibid., 4.   [76] Hu, ' "Mickey Mouse" ', 93.   [77] Ibid.   [78] Ibid., 94.

Counterfeit goods, however, not only appeal to the average citizen but also to officialdom. Even government departments have been known to use or be involved in the production of pirated goods.[79] Whilst most of China's state-run enterprises are running at a loss, the economic benefits of using counterfeit goods or turning a blind eye to their production outweigh the costs involved in enforcing intellectual property rights.[80]

It appears that, in the eyes of the Chinese government, the short-term economic advantages of counterfeiting in China outweigh the costs of enforcement. However, as more and more Chinese citizens acquire IP rights, government officials will come to value the long-term economic benefits of their enforcement, such as increased consumer confidence and foreign direct investment. It is the threat of trade sanctions, however, that will remain persuasive now that China has joined the WTO.[81]

China's trademark protection and the TRIPs Agreement

China's inability or lack of desire properly to protect IP frustrated its attempts to accede to the WTO. Now that the country has acceded to the WTO, the question remains as to whether the 1993 revisions and the recent October 2001 amendments to the Chinese Trademark Law bring China's protection up to international standards and the requirements outlined in the TRIPs Agreement.[82] The TRIPs negotiations extended international rules protecting trade in products relying heavily on trademark protection with seven detailed articles (Articles 15–21).[83]

This section of the chapter addresses the consistency of the Chinese Trademark Law with those six provisions, and also with the TRIPs Intellectual Property Conventions clause[84] and the National Treatment clause.[85] In particular, it discusses the subject-matter, grounds for refusal, rights of trademark owners, the use requirement, publishing and opposing, exceptions, term of protection and licensing.

---

[79] Alford, *To Steal a Book*, p. 58.   [80] Bacon, 'The PRC and the WTO', 421.

[81] TRIPs, Art. 64.

[82] An English version of the amended law is available at www.cpahkltd.com/Newsletter/NewTrademarkLaw.html.

[83] E.g. the Paris Convention and the Trademark Registration Treaty, at Vienna, 12 June 1973, as in force 7 August 1980.

[84] TRIPs, Art. 2: 'In respect of Parts II, III, and IV of this Agreement, Members shall comply with Articles 1 through 12, and Article 19, of the Paris Convention (1967).'

[85] TRIPs, Art. 3.

Intellectual property Conventions

Certain obligations of the Paris Convention are incorporated into TRIPs pursuant to Article 2 of the TRIPs Agreement. One of these obligations is the 'right of priority'.[86] The 'right of priority' offers all members of the Paris Convention a six-month priority period from the date of their first application in a Convention country during which they may apply for registration in another Convention country.[87] Where an application is made within this period, the date of the registration in the first Convention country is deemed to be the date of first application in the subsequent Convention country.

The revised Article 24 of Chinese Trademark Law now expressly states that a six-month right of priority exists in accordance with any international agreement or treaty that China is party to. Further, the new amendments extend the right of priority to trade marks that have been first used for goods in an international exhibition sponsored or recognized by the Chinese government.[88]

National treatment

Article 3 of the TRIPs Agreement is a general provision, applicable to all forms of intellectual property protection covered by the Agreement, concerned with the national treatment of foreigner individuals. National treatment requires Member States to give nationals of other Member States no less favourable treatment than they give their own residents. Article 18 of the Chinese Trademark Law compels foreigners to appoint a Chinese government-designated agent for any trademark-related activity.[89] This provision cannot be reconciled with the national treatment principle and should be amended.

Protectable subject-matter

Article 15(1) of the TRIPs Agreement provides that all signs and combination of signs that are capable of being distinguished from other goods or services are eligible for registration as trade marks. Such signs are defined as including words, personal names, letters, numerals, figurative elements and combinations of colours, as well as any combination thereof. Registration

---

[86] Paris Convention, Art. 4C(1).   [87] Ibid.   [88] Art. 25.   [89] Former Art. 10.

of marks that are not 'visually perceptible', such as those pertaining to sound or smell, are generally excluded. Before the recent amendments, the Chinese Trademark Law protected 'any word or design' or combination with 'distinctive characteristics so as to facilitate identification'.[90] This definition was not as prescriptive as the one offered under the TRIPs Agreement in that there was no mention of signs, colour, shapes, numerals or names. The revised Chinese law now extends to any 'word, design, letters of an alphabet, numerals, three-dimensional symbol, combination of colours, and any combination of the above'.[91] The Chinese Trademark Law does not expressly cover names as required under the TRIPs Agreement.

It is noteworthy that protection now also extends to collective marks, certification marks and marks held by natural persons.[92] Previously only enterprises, institutions, individual producers or traders were allowed to register a mark.[93]

Grounds for refusal

According to Article 15.2 of the TRIPs Agreement, a member may deny registration provided that they do not derogate from the provisions of the Paris Convention.[94] Article 6ter(1)(a) of the Paris Convention prohibits official signs and 'hallmarks indicating control and warranty', 'and any imitation from a heraldic point of view' from being used as trade marks. Article 10 (formerly Article 8) of the Trademark Law prohibits various types of trade marks from being registered. Neither words nor designs that are identical or similar to the military medals of China or the national name, national flag, national emblem, or military flag of China or any foreign country are permissible. This provision is in conformity with Article 6ter(1)(a) of the Paris Convention. Similar protection is offered to international intergovernmental organizations under Article 6ter(1)(b) of the Paris Convention, which is also reflected in Article 10 of the Chinese Trademark Law.

The use of trade marks indicating the kind, quality, intended purpose, value or other characteristics of the goods may be denied registration under Article 6quinquiesB(2) of the Paris Convention. Similar wording and exceptions apply under the Chinese Trademark Law.[95] Trade marks that are contrary to morality or public order and, in particular, of such a nature as to

---

[90] Former Art. 7.   [91] Art. 8.   [92] Art. 4, now Art. 3.   [93] Former Art. 4.
[94] China became a signatory to the Paris Convention on 19 March 1985.
[95] Formerly Art. 8(5) and (6), now Art. 11.

deceive the public, may be denied or invalidated according to Article 6*quin-quies*B(3) of the Paris Convention. The Chinese Trademark Law prohibits the registration of marks that discriminate against any nationality (Article 10(6)),[96] exaggerate or are fraudulent (Article 10(7))[97] or impact negatively with socialist morality and customs (Article 10(8)).[98] These exceptions are within the ambit of the Paris Convention provision.

Rights of trademark owners

Article 16.1 of the TRIPs Agreement states that the proprietor of a registered trade mark has the exclusive right to prevent others from using the trade mark on goods or services that are identical or similar to those they have registered. In conformity with this provision, the Chinese Trademark Law provides that to sell or make counterfeit products without authorization, to use an identical or similar mark on the same kind of goods without authority or to cause prejudice to the exclusive right of the registered mark owner amount to an infringement of the right to exclusive use of a registered trade mark.[99]

Article 16.1 of the TRIPs Agreement further provides that the granting of a new exclusive right must not prejudice any existing priority right. The TRIPs Agreement does not define the term 'existing prior rights'.[100] Zheng Chengsi suggests, in light of the model laws of the World Intellectual Property Organization and general international opinion, that 'existing prior rights' could be trademarks that have acquired market reputation.[101] Article 6*bis*(1) of the Paris Convention compels members to protect well-known marks, whether registered or unregistered, against the unlawful registration or the unauthorized use in connection with identical or similar goods. Article 16.2 and 16.3 of the TRIPs Agreement qualify this provision. Article 16.2 requires protection of service marks that are well known 'in the relevant sector of the public'; Article 16.3 requires protection of any *registered* well-known mark, irrespective of the type of goods or service, if the interests of the owner of the registered trade mark are likely to be damaged. The second paragraph in Article 13 of the Chinese Trademark Law now prohibits the registration of reproductions, imitations or translations of already registered well-known marks if it is likely to mislead the

[96] Formerly Art. 8(7).   [97] Formerly Art. 8(8).   [98] Formerly Art. 8(9).
[99] Formerly Art. 38(1), now Art. 52.
[100] Zheng, 'TRIPs and intellectual property protection', 3.   [101] Ibid.

public. This provision satisfies the requirements of Article 16.3 of the TRIPs Agreement.

Article 13 of the Chinese Trademark Law also prevents the registration of a trade mark for identical or similar goods that is a reproduction, imitation or translation of another person's mark *not* registered in China if the registration is likely to cause confusion. This provision is broad enough to include unregistered well-known trade marks. However, unregistered well-known service marks that are not of similar goods are not afforded any protection under the Chinese law as required by Article 16.2 of the TRIPs Agreement.

In regard to Article 16.2 of the TRIPs Agreement, there is debate as to whether the 'relevant sector of the public' refers to the public in the country of origin or in the country where protection is being sought.[102] However, the general view, and the view expressed by China, is that 'well-known status' refers to the reputation in the relevant public in the country where protection is desired.[103] Accordingly, China's definition of well-known mark is in conformity with general international opinion.

Although an owner of a well-known trade mark may also be offered protection under the Product Quality Law[104] or the *Unfair Competition Law*,[105] China will need to offer greater protection for unregistered well-known service marks, if it wishes to comply with the TRIPs Agreement.

Use requirements

In China, and indeed in most countries,[106] the only way to ensure exclusive use of an ordinary trade mark is through registration.[107] In the United States, registration is not required to establish rights in a mark; trademark rights can arise from actual use of a mark. Registration of unused marks is only

---

[102] A. Kur, 'TRIPs and trademark law', in F. Beier and G. Schricker (eds.), *Studies in Industrial Property and Copyright Law* (Munich, 1996), pp. 93–116, at p. 107.

[103] Ibid. Also see Art. 14.

[104] Law of the PRC on Product Quality (1993) effective as of 1 September 1993. Paglee, 'Chinese trademark law revised', 45.

[105] Law of the PRC Against Unfair Competition (1993) as effective 1 December 1993. K. Pun, 'Protection of well-known goods in China' (1996) 10 *European Intellectual Property Review* 537, at 537.

[106] e.g. Article 25 of the Japanese Trademark Act 1959; Article 34(b) of the Malaysian Trademarks Act 1976. See D. Campbell and S. Cotter (eds.), *International Intellectual Property Law: Global Jurisdictions* (West Sussex, 1996). Article 20 of the Australian Trademarks Act 1995.

[107] Art. 3; Zheng, 'TRIPs and IP protection', 3.

permitted if the application is accompanied by an assurance of an intent to use.[108] The TRIPs Agreement allows the absence of use to be a consideration when rejecting an application for registration; however, it must not be the sole reason for rejecting a mark.[109] In addition, an application is not to be cancelled on the basis that the intended use of a mark has not taken place within three years from the date of application without a valid reason.[110] Article 44 of the Chinese Trademark Law states that registered trade marks that have not been used for three consecutive years may be cancelled. This provision basically falls within the parameters of the TRIPs Agreement, however, it does not provide for situations where the registered owner has not used the mark for a valid reason. The TRIPs Agreement suggests that a valid reason may include situations beyond the control of the trademark owner, such as import restrictions.[111] China must recognize valid reasons for non-use now it has acceded to the WTO.

Publishing and opposing

Article 15(5) of the TRIPs Agreement requires members to publish each trade mark either before or immediately after registration and afford a 'reasonable opportunity for petitions to cancel the registration'. In brief, the Chinese laws require the Trademark Office to publish a trade mark upon preliminary approval.[112] If no opposition is filed within three months of publication then the registration is granted.[113] The TRIPs Agreement does not specify what is a 'reasonable opportunity' – however, the state practice of many TRIPs signatories are comparable to that of China. Australia[114] and South Africa[115] allow objections to be raised within three months after the publication of the application. Canada,[116] Japan[117] and Malaysia[118] permit

---

[108] § 1115 Lanham Act, US Patent and Trademark Office, *Basic Facts About Registering a Trademark*, http://www.uspto.gov/web/offices/tac/doc/basic/basic_facts.html last updated 31 July 1995.
[109] TRIPs, Art. 15.3.   [110] Ibid., Art. 19.1.   [111] Ibid., Art. 19.1.
[112] Chinese Trademark Law, Art. 27.   [113] Art. 30.
[114] Regulation 5.1 of the Trade Marks Regulations 1995.
[115] Trademark Act, promulgated 5 January 1995, cited in J. Cullabine, 'South Africa', in Campbell and Cotter (eds.), *International Intellectual Property Law*, p. 298.
[116] Trademarks Act, RSC 1985, c. T-13 cited in V. Prince, 'Canada', in Campbell and Cotter (eds.), *International Intellectual Property Law*, p. 7.
[117] Art. 17, Trademark Act, Law No. 127 of 1959: T. Doi, 'Japan', in Campbell and Cotter (eds.), *International Intellectual Property Law*, p. 135.
[118] Art. 28(1), Trademark Act: D. Kandan, 'Trademark law in Malaysia', in Hansen (ed.), *International Intellectual Property Law*, pp. 89–100, at p. 92.

a two-month period, and the Dominican Republic[119] a thirty-day interval to oppose trademark applications.

A trademark owner also has five years to file a request with the Trademark Review and Adjudication Board (TRAB) to cancel a registered trade mark where the registration prejudices the petitioner's prior rights.[120] Owners of well-known marks are not restricted by the five-year limitation.[121]

Exceptions

According to Article 17 of the TRIPs Agreement, limited exceptions to the rights conferred by a trade mark are permissible as long as they take into account the legitimate interests of the owner of the trade mark and of third parties. This provision is not applicable to the Chinese Trademark Law as there is no express exception to the exclusive rights of trademark owners.

Term of protection, licensing and assignment

The minimum term of protection of a registered trade mark prescribed by the TRIPs Agreement is seven years – a compromise between industrialized countries that wanted a ten-year period and developing and threshold countries that wanted to reserve the setting of a minimum term to the national legislature.[122] In compliance, the period of validity of a registered trade mark in China is ten years from the date of approval.[123]

Licensing, renewal and assignment of trade marks is permitted under Chapter IV, Articles 38 to 40[124] of the Chinese Trademark Law, and is in compliance with Article 21 of the TRIPs Agreement.

Enforcement provisions of the TRIPs Agreement

One of the key initiatives of the TRIPs Agreement was to resolve the enforcement issues left by the existing IP protection regimes. As a result,

[119] Law No. 1450 on Trademarks and Commercial and Industrial Names of 4 January 1938: O. Mera, 'Dominican Republic', in Campbell and Cotter (eds.), *International Intellectual Property Law*, p. 38.
[120] Art. 41, Chinese Trademark Law.
[121] Formerly petitioners had to lodge an application within one year of the registration (refer to former Article 27).
[122] Kur, 'TRIPs and trademark law', p. 109.   [123] Formerly Art. 23, now Art. 38.
[124] Formerly Arts. 23–6

Part III (Articles 41–62) of the TRIPs Agreement contains provisions pertaining to the enforcement of IP rights. Essentially, members must provide civil, judicial or administrative procedures to enable foreign and national IP rights holders to enforce their rights.[125] Enforcement measures are to be 'fair and equitable' and provide 'expeditious remedies to prevent infringements and remedies which constitute a deterrent to further infringements'.[126] Requirements include provisions on evidence,[127] injunctions,[128] damages,[129] destruction of infringing goods[130] and criminal procedures.[131] There is no obligation to establish a specific judicial system or provide additional resources for the enforcement of rights.[132] Hence, the effectiveness of the enforcement measures depends on the prevailing national legislature and practice, which is not subject to scrutiny.[133]

The Chinese Trademark Law addresses these issues. Article 53 of the Trademark Law encourages the parties to mediate a settlement, including the quantum of damages, before exercising their right to institute legal proceedings. This provision also authorizes the administrations for industry and commerce (AICs) and the People's Court to order injunctions and to confiscate and destroy infringing products, trade marks and the manufacturing equipment. The former power of the AICs to order compensation has been recently removed, so parties unable to negotiate a settlement will need to seek compensation from the People's Court.[134]

Under the new amendments, compensation is defined to include either an account of profits or 'the losses incurred' by the party during the period of infringement.[135] It is debatable whether this provision is 'adequate', as required under Article 45 of the TRIPs Agreement. Neither exemplary, consequential nor non-pecuniary damages are mentioned, nor is any consideration given to the lack of resources of the infringing entities to satisfy the deterrent obligation in Article 41.1 of the TRIPs Agreement.[136] However, in cases where the amount of compensation is difficult to determine, Article 56 of the Trademark Law allows statutory damages of no

---

[125] TRIPs, Arts. 41, 42 and 49.   [126] Ibid., Art. 41.1.
[127] Ibid., Art. 43.   [128] Ibid., Art. 44.   [129] Ibid., Art. 45.
[130] Ibid., Art. 46.   [131] Ibid., Art. 61.   [132] Ibid., Art. 41.5.
[133] A. Pacon, 'What will TRIPs do for developing countries?', in F. Beier and G. Schricker (eds.), *From GATT to TRIPs – the Agreement on Trade-Related Aspects of Intellectual Property* (Munich, 1996), pp. 329–56, at p. 351 citing Rehbinder and Staehelin, 'Das Urheberrecht im TRIPs-Abkommen – Entwicklungsschub durch die New Economic World Order' (1995) 127 *UFITA* 13, p. 26.
[134] Formerly Art. 39.   [135] Art. 56.   [136] Art. 45 specifies that damages must be 'adequate'.

more than RMB 500,000 to be awarded.[137] Interestingly, vendors who have been caught selling infringing goods will avoid liability if they are able to identify the supplier and prove that they obtained their infringing items legitimately.[138]

Under Article 61 of the TRIPs Agreement, members must also provide criminal procedures and penalties that will apply in cases of 'wilful trademark counterfeiting or copyright piracy on a commercial scale'. The nature of the penalties and other sanctions is not expressly provided for, but imprisonment and monetary fines must be 'sufficient to provide a deterrent'.[139] Article 54 of the Trademark Law requires AICs to transfer cases of a criminal nature to the judicial authority for handling.

Some members of the Working Party on the Accession of China are of the opinion that Chinese criminal procedures cannot be used effectively to address piracy and counterfeiting, as the 'monetary thresholds' for bringing a criminal action are very high. The Chinese representative confirmed that the judicial authority would be advised to make the necessary adjustments to lower the cost involved.[140]

Article 62.4 and 62.5 of the TRIPs Agreement requires the opportunity for judicial or quasi-judicial review for final administrative decisions in respect of opposition, revocation or cancellation of intellectual property rights. As a result of the recent amendments, decisions made by the TRAB are no longer final.[141] Any interested party who is not satisfied with a decision by the TRAB may institute proceedings in the People's Court.[142] Preliminary injunctions and measures to preserve relevant evidence are now provided for under Articles 57 and 58 of the Trademark Law in conformity with Article 50 of the TRIPs Agreement.

The recent amendments to the Chinese Trademark Law have greatly improved the trademark protection offered by China. Only in a few key areas, such as national treatment, the lack of protection of names and unregistered well-known service marks, does China not conform with the protection required under the TRIPs Agreement. None the less, China confirmed that it will fully apply the provisions of the TRIPs Agreement, giving full

---

[137] Art. 56.   [138] Art. 56.

[139] The second sentence of Article 61 states: 'Remedies available shall include imprisonment and/or monetary fines sufficient to provide deterrent, consistently with the level of penalties applied for crimes of a corresponding nature.'

[140] Protocol of Accession, p. 304.   [141] Formerly Arts. 21, 22 and 29.

[142] Arts. 32, 33, 43 and 49.

attention to IP right cases in the courts, strengthening anti-piracy work in the administrative authorities and educating the general public.[143]

Are sanctions likely to be used for non-compliance?

WTO members are committed to abide by the dispute settlement process when seeking redress for the violation of the TRIPs Agreement. No member may issue a determination that another government has violated a provision unless a Panel or Appellate Body has first reached that conclusion.[144] Furthermore, members specifically commit themselves not to retaliate except in accordance with authorization from the Dispute Settlement Body.[145] Accordingly, if a Member State were to initiate an investigation against China for its inadequate trademark provisions, the Member State would need to go through the formal dispute settlement procedures, rather than resort to bilateral IP enforcement agreements.[146]

A quick glance at the action taken by the United States in the last twenty years shows that the United States is more than willing to apply pressure and impose sanctions against countries that are not offering sufficient protection to American IP.[147] Australia and the European Union have not escaped US pressure; both appear regularly on the US Priority Watchlist. In particular, in 1999 the US trade representative stated that the US government

---

[143] Protocol of Accession, pp. 288 and 305.

[144] Final Act Embodying the Results of the Uruguay Round of Multilateral Trade Negotiations, Annex 2: Understanding on Rules and Procedures Governing the Settlement of Disputes (DSU), Art. 23.

[145] Ibid. The issue of whether the United States Special 301 is in compliance with Article 23 of the DSU is highly contentious and beyond the scope of this chapter: Simons, 'Cooperation and coercion', 76.

[146] e.g. the United States and China have signed several bilateral IP-related agreements: Tiefenbrun, 'Piracy of intellectual property'.

[147] e.g. against Vietnam, P. Heald, 'Viet Nam or bust: why trademark pirates are leaving China for better opportunities in Viet Nam' (1996) 14 *Dickinson Journal of International Law* 291, at 291; against India, *India – Patent Protection for Pharmaceutical and Agricultural Chemical Products*, WT/DS50/AB/R, complaint by the United States, adopted 16 January 1988; against Indonesia, *Indonesia – Certain Measures Affecting the Automobile Industry*, WT/DS55/R, adopted 23 July 1998, complaint by the United States; against Pakistan, *Pakistan – Patent Protection for Pharmaceutical and Agricultural Chemical Products*, WT/DS36/4, mutually agreed solution with the United States; against Portugal, *Portugal – Patent Protection under the Industrial Property Act*, WT/DS37/2/Corr.1, mutually agreed solution with the United States; and against Denmark, *Denmark – Measures Affecting the Enforcement of Intellectual Property Rights*, WT/DS83/1, request for consultations by the United States.

was 'seriously concerned with the minimalist approach Australia has taken towards intellectual property protection in recent years'.[148] While the United States has never been shy in making threats to China, it has been slower in taking further action.[149] Now that China is a WTO member, one can expect that, under pressure from IP rights holders at home, the United States will continue to threaten to invoke trade sanctions to protect US intellectual property. It will probably use WTO consultations to make the threats real. It is harder to predict whether the United States will request adjudication by WTO panels. There may be a greater willingness to use WTO dispute settlement in situations of deficiencies in substantive law rather than in cases in which the substantive law meets TRIPs requirements but enforcement is lacking. In the latter situations, other strategies may be more effective than WTO dispute settlement, as suggested below.

Alternatives

Although the Chinese Trademark Law is now largely in conformity with the TRIPs Agreement, the benefits of protection may not be realized for some time. At ground level there is a general culture of acceptance of counterfeit goods, partly because it makes previously unobtainable foreign goods affordable and partly because there is a lack of interest in enforcing IP rights that are largely owned by foreign companies. In this environment, counterfeiting will always seem attractive as it allows those involved to access an already existing market with low entry costs. In the meantime, however, foreign entities could take an active role in furthering the protection of their rights.

Licensing of IP rights to Chinese nationals and establishing joint ventures would be advantageous. The foreign party would have the benefit of local assistance in navigating legal red tape, and the Chinese party would be encouraged to protect its IP rights through economic incentive. Increased Chinese ownership of IP rights or licences would not only increase public awareness, but also compel enforcement agencies to be more vigilant in carrying out searches. The Microsoft Corporation has been investing in joint ventures involved in building manufacturing enterprises, research

---

[148] USTR, Executive Office of the President, *USTR Announces Results of Special 301 Annual Review*, Official Press Release (30 April 1999), p. 3, cited in Simons, 'Cooperation and coercion', 74 .

[149] 'China uncovers 665 cases', 1.

and development projects and training programmes at universities for this reason.[150] The Corporation's strategy is that by building friendships with the Chinese ministries and local computer manufacturers, these entities will become more committed to working with Microsoft in the future and protecting its products.[151]

Similarly, courtesy calls on customs officials and IP enforcement agencies are also an effective way of ensuring greater protection.[152] If officials are given descriptions of the trademarked goods, details of the particular counterfeiting problems and are informed of the 'broader implications such as the potential harm to human safety from fake goods'[153] and damage to the international reputation of China from IP right violations, then the IP right-holders have a greater chance of preserving their rights.[154]

An interdisciplinary network of experts to assist officials at the provincial level in developing concrete programmes to combat counterfeiting, or perhaps establishing a mobile working group of legal experts, would be extremely useful in protecting IP rights. Organization and support for regional and international symposia that bring together representatives of non-government organizations, policy-makers and others to discuss contemporary IP issues would increase awareness of IP problems. Even the TRIPs Agreement recognizes that effective enforcement cannot be achieved in isolation. Article 69 indicates that countries should 'be ready to exchange information on trade in infringing goods, and should promote the exchange of information with regard to trade in counterfeit trademark goods and pirated copyright'.[155] 'Sharing "difficulties", "successes", general implementation strategies and practical steps that each jurisdiction has undergone will assist in improving the enforcement environment'[156] and alert each state to practical issues that they must tackle. Nevertheless, it would appear that any of the above-mentioned measures require a backbone of enforceable legal rights to offer any real protection to IP rights.

---

[150] Butterton, 'Pirates, dragons', 1122 citing D. Lee, 'Microsoft to open US$100m China window', *The South China Morning Post*, 9 November 1994, at Business 1.
[151] Ibid.
[152] M. Leung, 'Counterfeit Beanie Babies: customs to the rescue', *The China Business Review*, January–February 1999, p. 18.
[153] Ibid.   [154] Ibid.
[155] This stemmed from APEC IPEG X, *Enforcement of Intellectual Property Rights: Discussion Paper From Australia*, 3; http://www.apecsec.org.sg/ipr/ipr_enforce.html.
[156] Ibid., 4.

Conclusion

In the past decade China has made great progress in reforming its economy and becoming a major player in the world economy. It has also made advances in adopting and enforcing intellectual property rights in a short period of time. The Chinese Trademark Law, in substance, is not far from meeting its obligations under the TRIPs Agreement, although certain provisions, including criminal and civil penalties, need to be expanded. At the same time, foreign trademark owners must accept the challenge of defending their rights in China. The difficulty is that in China statutes and regulations sit alongside social, cultural and economic norms specific to China, and do not clearly prove determinative in a given case.

Despite the growth in counterfeiting and deep-rooted cynicism about law in China, there is reason for optimism. The creation and ongoing development of the Chinese intellectual property system has seen the acquisition of IP rights by ordinary Chinese citizens. The assertion of these rights in court and in the world market will then pave the way for an effective intellectual property system. As the great Chinese scholar Ying Shaowu once said, 'Whatever is rushed to maturity will surely break down early. Whatever is accomplished in a hurry will surely be easily destroyed.'[157]

[157] Cited in Paglee, 'Chinese trademark law revisited', 81.

19

TRIPs goes east: China's interests and international trade in intellectual property

ANTONY S. TAUBMAN

Introduction

China's implementation of the WTO Agreement on Trade-related Aspects of Intellectual Property Rights (TRIPs) is generally characterized as reluctant compliance with externally imposed standards. China seemingly goes against the cultural grain and impairs its own economic interests to introduce 'strong' protection of intellectual property rights (IPRs), only to safeguard its real trade interests (access to developed-country markets, principally the United States, and WTO membership).

This chapter first sets 'TRIPs implementation' in the broader context of China's underlying economic interests, by considering the emerging status of China as a producer, beneficiary and exporter of intellectual property. It then considers how 'TRIPs implementation' has been undertaken within the framework of a longstanding programme of domestic legal development, that has been shaped just as much by domestic social and economic imperatives as by reactive compliance with external demands.

Background: IP as a trade issue

The extensive literature on protection of IPRs in China is outweighed by writing on the lack of IPR protection. The issue takes a high profile in China's trade relations. IPR infringement is unquestionably widespread in China. A senior patent office official acknowledges that patent infringement

The views expressed are the author's own and do not necessarily reflect any Australian Government or any other official position.

is 'rather rampant'.[1] The International Intellectual Property Alliance (IIPA), a US-based industry body, claims that:

> Despite efforts made by the Chinese government to crack down on massive domestic piracy of all types of copyrighted products earlier in 2000, including raids netting hundreds of thousands of pirate optical media products, piracy rates in China continue to hover at the 90% level.[2]

The IIPA estimates losses on business software of US$659 million in 2000, a piracy rate of 93 per cent and total estimated losses of over $2 billion. Such estimates may only count as rough approximations. Trade problems on this general scale do, however, challenge the view that IP protection is an unassimilated alien in the world of trade rules, and that TRIPs is not a 'market-access' agreement. Saturation of a domestic market by infringing copies of entertainment software, reducing the available market for original products to the order of 1 per cent, for example, functions as a barrier to market access as effective as any tariff, quota or national treatment constraint on services trade. Quite apart from trade in IP-related products, and despite widespread infringement, reported international transactions in royalty and licence fees alone (for the commercial use of IPRs and similar non-tangible assets) exceeded $67 billion in 1999.[3] Trade tensions arising over international commercial interests on this scale will inevitably be resolved by unilateralist or pragmatic means,[4] if multilateral trade rules like the TRIPs Agreement are not available.

The growing value of IPR licensing and IP-dependent trade will ensure that claims of inadequate enforcement remain a vexed market-access issue in international trade. The TRIPs Agreement was negotiated as a multilateral means of managing this issue in a transparent, rules-based manner, as an alternative to ad hoc bilateral arrangements driven by unilateral leverage. Hence, the TRIPs Agreement established standards for the recognition, grant and exercise of IPRs, and mandated specific legal remedies to enforce those rights, international obligations on domestic legal processes that are

---

[1] Yin Xintian, 'On the second amendment of the Patent Law,' *Legal Forum*, 2001, at www.chinalawinfo.com.

[2] International Intellectual Property Alliance, *2001 Special 301 Report: PRC* (Washington, 2001), www.iipa.com.

[3] 1999 figures, *Balance of Payments Statistics Yearbook* (International Monetary Fund, Washington, 1999), code 266.

[4] J. Bhagwati, 'Aggressive unilateralism: an overview', in J. Bhagwati and H. Patrick (eds.), *Aggressive Unilateralism: America's 301 Trade Policy and the World Trading System*, pp. 1–45 (Ann Arbor, 1990).

unprecedented in their scope and detail. Yet TRIPs implementation is still no guarantee that infringing activity will be effectively eradicated. Concerns about enforcement may indeed reach a new pitch following China's WTO accession, given the prospect of formal dispute settlement proceedings making an objective determination on the efficacy of enforcement measures.

Management of IPR enforcement as a trade issue is hampered by its sheer complexity, and by continuing legal uncertainty about IPRs in trade law: what is the extent of a government's obligations to deliver actual enforcement outcomes; can the United States claim nullification and impairment of benefits[5] on the basis of industry's claimed losses? In practice, it is irreducibly difficult to meet expectations that infringement be reduced to *de minimis* levels: far from the world of tariff bindings and non-discriminatory application of regulatory standards, actual implementation of TRIPs obligations can involve hazardous crackdowns on criminal activities.[6]

Analysis differs on whether large-scale infringement is good or bad for the Chinese economy, whether it is transitional and accidental, or planned, whether it is due to deep-seated cultural reasons or short-term commercial expediency. The causes of IPR infringement, and the policy mechanisms for dealing with it, are deeper and broader than the market-access concerns of foreign IPR interests. Locating IPR enforcement in the context of trade relations, and conceiving of the solution as ostensive servicing of foreign right-holders' interests, is unlikely to lead to sustained public-sector investment in the IP system and acceptance of enforcement as a social good. Considering IPR enforcement solely in the context of bilateral trade relations[7] can indeed lead to 'a pattern of ineffectiveness and futility'.[8]

Analysis of IPRs in China often points to cultural differences that make the notion of exclusive IPRs an alien concept, difficult to comprehend for Chinese society.[9] Western interests are described as seeking to 'convert' the

---

[5] GATT, Art. XXIII and TRIPs, Art. 64.1.

[6] Tang Anming, head of the Shuanghe village tobacco bureau in Chongqing municipality, was killed in November 2000 while arresting a person suspected of selling counterfeit foreign-brand cigarettes (Agence France Presse, 5 December 2000).

[7] Alisa M. Wrase, 'US bilateral agreements in the protection of intellectual property rights in foreign countries: effective for US intellectual property interests or a way out of addressing the issue?' (2001) 19(1) *Dickinson Journal of International Law* 245.

[8] Peter Yu, 'From pirates to partners: protecting intellectual property in China in the twenty-first century' (1990) 50 *American University Law Review* 131, at 134.

[9] William P. Alford, *To Steal a Book is an Elegant Offense: Intellectual Property Law in Chinese Civilization* (Stanford, 1994).

Chinese people to a rights-conscious approach to IP.[10] Exasperation with the scale of infringement tempts some to infer that failure to enforce IPRs is a conscious part of economic planning: 'No nation has ever built a healthy, modern economy without protecting intellectual-property rights. But it's hard to escape the conclusion that China's rulers may be gambling on an exception.'[11] The dominant perception seems to be of foreign IPR holders pursuing their interests, either justifiably or insensitively, and of China grudgingly and reactively taking whatever minimal action is required to safeguard its real trade interests, with no conviction that it has an inherent interest in a better-functioning IP system. Equally, China's implementation of the TRIPs Agreement is viewed from the perspective of formalist rules-compliance, of undertaking a set of legislative steps, unwillingly or at least diffidently, to meet rigorous international standards laid down in the TRIPs Agreement and insisted on by western economies. Indeed, during the accession process, China's trading partners voiced concerns about high levels of copyright piracy and trademark counterfeiting; systemic difficulties in getting and enforcing judicial decisions on IPR infringements; and conformity with TRIPs standards. TRIPs implementation reduces to an unwelcome chore. Overhauling the IP system becomes a burden borne only as a necessary evil to gain WTO accession and to relieve bilateral trade and political pressure, thus ensuring continued access for non-IP Chinese trade.

The historical record bears this out. China has been under diplomatic and trade pressure since the late 1970s to improve IP protection. Major reforms to IPR laws from 1992 to 1994 directly followed bilateral agreement with the United States, in the face of threatened trade sanctions to the tune of $1.5 billion under the 'Special 301' provisions of the US Trade Act 1974.[12] This cycle repeated in 1994–5, and in 1996, with especial attention to concerns about shortcomings in the enforcement of IPRs. The legislative reform process appears to be motivated more by external coercion than domestic interests.

---

[10] Peter Yu, 'Piracy, prejudice, and perspectives: an attempt to use Shakespeare to reconfigure the US–China intellectual property debate' (2001) *Boston University International Law Journal* 1–16.

[11] Richard Behar, 'Beijing's phony war on fakes', *Fortune Magazine*, 30 October 2000, p. 188.

[12] Wayne M. Morrison, *Report for Congress: China–U.S. Trade Agreements: Compliance Issues*, Congressional Research Service, RL30555, updated 1 September 2000, http://www.cnie.org/nle.

Domestic IP reform and voluntary external commitments

The limited focus on the inelegant use of bilateral trade leverage and on implementation of the TRIPs Agreement as a new breed of humiliating 'unequal treaty' – indeed, the abstraction of the issue as a case study in the clash of civilizations – overlooks the organic development of the domestic Chinese IP system within the context of evolving technology and innovation policies. It discounts the energetic use of the IP system domestically, as a means of accessing new technology and increasingly as a safeguard for new indigenous technology, and also overlooks how the progressive privatization of IP rights accords with the general trend away from state-owned and directed economic activity to the socialist market economy. Whether conceived in Confucian or individualistic terms, the steady accumulation of a quantum of domestic interest in the IP system is the most plausible guarantee of effective and equitable IPR protection.

China has been progressively establishing IP laws broadly in line with TRIPs standards since well before the Uruguay Round commenced. China's interests are increasingly aligned with both the letter and spirit of the TRIPs Agreement, as its exports grow in IP-rich goods and IPRs per se. China's experience illustrates that 'TRIPs implementation' is not an isolated process, and TRIPs-consistent measures can be introduced with a view equally to promoting productive domestic interests and to meeting trading partners' expectations. It is more likely that China's extensive investments in creating an IPR system follow from calculations about its own longer-term interests, including growing domestic IP interests.

In institutional and substantive legal terms, China's voluntary engagement in the international IP system eclipses any specific bilateral concessions and any steps taken during WTO accession – between 1980 and 1999, it adhered to twelve multilateral treaties covering a broad spectrum of IP protection.[13] Some of these accessions served to ease political and

---

[13] In chronological order of accession: the WIPO Convention in 1980; the Madrid Agreement (international trademark registration) in 1989 and Protocol in 1995; the Paris Convention (Industrial Property) in 1985; the Berne Convention (Protection of Literary and Artistic Works) and the Universal Copyright Convention in 1992; the Geneva Convention (Unauthorized Duplication of Phonograms) in 1993; the Patent Co-operation Treaty and the Nice Agreement (International Classification of Goods and Services) in 1994; the Budapest Treaty (Deposit of Micro-organisms) in 1995; the Locarno Agreement (International Classification for Industrial Designs) in 1996; the Strasbourg Agreement (International Patent Classification) in 1997; and the UPOV Convention (Plant Variety Protection) in 1999.

350 ANTONY S. TAUBMAN

trade pressure, and in the case of the Berne and Geneva Conventions were precipitated by an explicit bilateral deal.[14] They entail substantive obligations and evidence an inherent interest in engaging in the international legal infrastructure for IP protection beyond the scope of the TRIPs Agreement. These accessions support TRIPs implementation, legally and practically. China's accession to the Berne Convention, and to a lesser extent the Paris Convention and the UPOV Convention, anticipated the application of some key substantive standards of the TRIPs Agreement. China's engagement in 'facilitation' treaties (PCT, Madrid and Budapest) and classification treaties (Nice, Locarno, IPC) give practical effect to the TRIPs Agreement obligation that acquiring and maintaining IPRs not be 'unnecessarily complicated or costly'.[15] Participation in the PCT, Madrid and UPOV systems promotes the practical application of international substantive norms in the grant of patent, trademark and plant-variety rights.

Chinese municipal law gives direct effect to these treaties, with implications for IPR administration and enforcement:

> Wherever the international treaty contains provisions differing from those in civil laws, the provisions of the international treaty shall apply according to Article 142 of the *General Principles of Civil Law*. For instance, the Chinese *Regulations for the Protection of Computer Software* stipulate that registration of computer software is a condition precedent to initiation of any administrative dispute resolution or legal proceedings in China. Obviously, this is not in conformity with the Berne Convention's requirement. In this case... foreigners may obtain protection for their computer software works without registration.[16]

This interpretation was made explicit in the 1992 bilateral agreement with the United States.[17] Similarly, the Paris Convention has been applied to protect a Hong Kong business name not registered in the PRC, and the Bejing People's High Court ruled in *Walt Disney Company v. Beijing Publishing*

---

[14] Article 3 of the Memorandum of Understanding Between the Government of the PRC and the Government of the USA on the Protection of Intellectual Property, 17 January 1992.

[15] Art. 62.4.

[16] Guo Lulin, 'China's intellectual property protection system in progress', in Frederick M. Abbott (ed.), *China in the World Trading System – Defining the Principles of Engagement* (1998), pp. 127–37, at p. 130.

[17] Art. 3.3, Memorandum of Understanding, above.

Company that the bilateral Memorandum of Understanding with the United States helped establish enforceable rights for a US plaintiff.[18]

IPR protection in China is arguably not a mere external legal or cultural artefact. Article 19 of the Constitution requires the state to reward 'scientific research as well as technological innovations and inventions'. China has strong technological and indigenous research capacities. Its cultural richness has long found diverse forms of commercial expression. China has a long history as a trader keen to preserve a comparative advantage through the careful management of technological know-how. China's ambition to become a major export-focused technological economy and to maintain cultural autonomy sits uneasily with the assumption that its long-term economic, cultural and developmental interests lie in the imitation of imported products and the dissemination of foreign cultural works subsidized by infringement. IP protection may, over time, become less a perfunctory exercise in reactively complying with external demands and more a straightforward application of domestic economic and cultural policy.

The self-defeating characteristic of IPR infringement as an instrument of economic development is becoming increasingly apparent for China. A highly permissive approach to IPR infringement can serve paradoxically to entrench foreign technological monopolies and a dependence on imported technology. Reportedly, 'a nation-wide survey over the period 1995–7 of Chinese software enterprises, conducted in mid-2000 by a research entity under the Ministry of Information Industry, found that the number one barrier to their development was the widespread piracy of their products'.[19]

During the WTO accession process, China's unique economic circumstances led to debate about its status as a developing country. Although per capita incomes remain at a low level, China is a major international economy – the World Bank estimates its GDP at $991.2 billion in 1999, double the South Korean economy, and more than double that of Russia. It is a significant producer of technology – high-technology exports (generally embodying IPRs[20]) were at the high level of 15 per cent of manufactured

---

[18] Cited in Guoqiang Lu, 'Advances in the protection of intellectual property rights in China' (1998) 1(1) *Harvard China Review*, on-line at http://www.harvardchina.org/magazine/article/intell-property1.html.

[19] Cited in IIPA Report for 2001, www.iipa.com/rbc/2001/2001SPEC301CHINA.pdf.

[20] World Bank, *2000 World Development Indicators* (from www.worldbank.org) define these as 'products with high R&D intensity. They include high technology products such as in aerospace, computers, pharmaceuticals, scientific instruments, and electrical machinery.'

exports in 1998, squarely between Germany at 14 per cent and Switzerland at 16 per cent, at a total value of US$23,308 million.[21] 53 per cent of tertiary students were engaged in scientific disciplines over 1995–7[22] – the highest reported level for *any* country but for two low-population Caribbean islands. There were 787,000 full-time personnel engaged in research and development in 1996, rivalling Japan (891,783) and the United States (962,700, in 1993).[23] This suggests a potential for the generation of indigenous IP that is now being borne out by patent statistics.[24]

Its Patent Law came into force only in 1985, but China is already a leading patent jurisdiction. In 1997, Chinese nationals filed 12,786 patent applications with their national patent office, three times the corresponding rate in Canada, and more than any European country but for France, Germany, the United Kingdom and Russia. More foreign patent applications were lodged in China in 1997 than domestic filings – but this was so everywhere but for the United States, Japan and the Republic of Korea. In fact, at 21 per cent, the proportion of applications filed in China by domestic applicants was higher than the corresponding rate in Australia (19 per cent), Canada (8 per cent), France (17 per cent) and the United Kingdom (18 per cent).

While the rate of applications is a useful measure of patenting activity, granted patents constitute the true legal and economic impact of the patent system. Significantly fewer patents are granted than are applied for, a pattern accentuated in a rapidly growing system such as that of China. Many applications are abandoned prior to grant due to refusal by the examiner, lack of technical or commercial feasibility, financial constraints or strategic decisions to concentrate on other markets. The Patent Cooperation Treaty system accentuates the statistical gulf between applications and grants. At the initial stage, once five countries have been designated, there is no additional cost to designate all 115 PCT countries. This encourages a wide spread of initial designations which are not normally all pursued when specific investments are needed to prosecute individual applications at the national level. The chronic backlog in processing applications in many patent administrations can also lead to a significant lag in

---

[21] World Bank, *2000 World Development Indicators.*

[22] UNDP Human Development Report, 2000 (www.undp.org).

[23] UNESCO Statistical Yearbook 1999.

[24] All industrial property statistics quoted in this chapter are derived from published WIPO statistics at www.wipo.int.

grant of patents when applications are pursued. The surge of patent activity in China (from 34,741 applications in 1994 to 82,289 in 1998) will take time to work through the system. All these factors may explain why the number of patents China granted in 1997 was only 6 per cent of the number of applications received that year.

Patents will normally be granted to a higher proportion of domestic applicants than the proportion of domestic applications filed. Portfolio management considerations, legal differences and transaction costs are more likely to lead to the abandonment of applications in foreign markets than in the applicant's home country, and the PCT system will particularly accentuate the rate of foreign applications not pursued to grant. This skew in patent grants is especially pronounced in China: in 1997, 44 per cent of patents granted went to domestic applicants, a proportion exceeded only in a handful of leading developed economies. The decline in interest between application and grant on the part of foreigners may be partly due to lack of confidence in the Chinese patent system and particularly the enforceability of rights, issues addressed in recent amendments to the Patent Law.

The dominance of domestic interests is more pronounced for other forms of industrial property. China was the second most active trademark jurisdiction in 1998 (153,692 applications) after the United States, and 84 per cent of these were domestic filings – well ahead of corresponding figures in Canada (51 per cent) and Australia (63 per cent), and comparable with France (75 per cent), the United States (84 per cent) and Japan (86 per cent). In the same year, China was the second most active industrial design jurisdiction, second only to Japan, and over 90 per cent of applicants were domestic.

So, on the face of it, in so far as 'TRIPs implementation' favours individual right-holders' interests, China's trading partners seem to be calling on China to improve a system with the potential to benefit its domestic interests to a proportion greater than in almost all other WTO members. Implementation of the TRIPs Agreement – in contrast to other WTO rules – produces direct benefits for domestic interests, less abstracted than the economic benefits flowing from reductions in tariffs and other forms of domestic protection. The nature of the IP system is that any benefit accruing to foreign right-holders – such as broader scope of IPRs, or better administration and enforcement – would normally be available to domestic right-holders.

Chinese IP activity abroad

Use of the PCT is a good, if general, indicator of the export focus of a country's patent activity. Having joined the PCT system in 1994, China became its twelfth largest user by 2001, ahead of Finland, Italy, Israel and Denmark, and three times Russia's use. PCT applications from China tripled in 2001, having doubled in 2000. This recent surge in international activity builds on the high underlying rate of domestic patent activity, and should in coming years translate into extensive use of foreign patent systems. China may follow the examples of Japan and the Republic of Korea, which built on intensive, initially domestically focused patent activity, to build extensive foreign patent portfolios. China's international focus should be enhanced by the recent easing of legal constraints on state-owned enterprises (SOEs) assigning patent rights and the strengthening of the legal basis for PCT applications.[25]

China currently receives modest levels of royalty and licence fees[26] from the exploitation of its IPRs overseas – receiving $75 million in 1999,[27] comparable with South Africa ($71 million) and Hungary ($62 million). By contrast, China paid $792 million in foreign royalties and licence fees. Such deficits were common, with only the United States, Finland and Sweden reporting a surplus. But the value of this income is still low, and close to negligible on a per capita basis for China (the United States received $36 billion the same year). It may be explained by China's recent shift in focus towards foreign IP systems, its lack of IPR commercialization capacity in foreign markets, and the time lag of commercialization, income from patented inventions typically only beginning to flow several years after applications are filed. The income level does represent an increase of 19 per cent over the previous year, suggesting a trend towards commercialization overseas.

China's royalty and licence payments for incoming technology also increased more dramatically in 1999 than in previous years, rising by 88 per cent. This may in part be a measure of more effective enforcement of foreign IPRs. Yet one of the incentives for IPR compliance is that it opens up export markets. China's royalty payments should be set in the context of its

[25] Repeal of Article 10(2) of the Patent Law by the Decision Regarding the Revision of the Patent Law of the PRC.

[26] Defined as 'payments and receipts . . . for the authorized use of intangible, nonproduced, nonfinancial assets and proprietary rights': World Bank, *2001 World Development Indicators*, p. 313, from www.worldbank.org.

[27] *2001 World Development Indicators*, p. 310.

high-tech exports, which rose 27 per cent to $29.6 billion in 1999. Given China's status as a major manufacturing economy, the value of Chinese-owned IPRs is more likely to be captured in domestic production for the export market, rather than licensed externally. China's outlay of $792 million in royalty and licence fees in 1999 could be seen partly as an investment in high-tech industries with an export focus, and is eclipsed (at 2.6 per cent) by the scale of high-tech exports, and even by the increase in such exports over 1999 ($6.3 billion increase). This investment in foreign IP is also likely to boost export in low-tech, high-IP products such as branded clothing and footwear.

Seeking the social and economic benefits of TRIPs implementation

China's IP trade interests are steadily increasing, as domestic IP use grows, its right-holders look increasingly overseas, and foreign and domestic IP are built into its manufacturing exports. Benefits from TRIPs Agreement implementation should therefore flow increasingly to Chinese interests over time. But a TRIPs-compliant IP system does not exist solely for the benefit of the patent applicant, or, more broadly, the IP right-holder. IP protection is intended, according to the objective of the TRIPs Agreement (Article 7), to promote innovation, transfer of technology, and a balance of rights and obligations conducive to social and economic development. China's Patent Law[28] and its use of the patent system illustrate how this balance of interests can be achieved under the TRIPs Agreement, and how a major shift in national economic and innovation policy has been effected within the general TRIPs framework.

Technology transfer through patent disclosure

The TRIPs Agreement (Article 29) requires that a patented invention be disclosed in a way 'sufficiently clear and complete for the invention to be carried out by a person skilled in the art' – an obligation fundamental in national patent law, which had lacked explicit recognition in international law. This mandates the transfer of practical knowledge about new technology

---

[28] This reading is based on the text available on the MOFTEC website (http://www.moftec.gov.cn/moftec/official/html/laws_and_regulations/trade21.html) and does not take account of potential translation issues, supplemented by briefings on the 25 August 2000 Decision regarding the Revision of the Patent Law of the PRC, which introduced thirty-five changes.

into the public domain, normally before the applicant is assured of securing patent rights. Increasing access to information technology and reduced official charges have recently made the resulting patent information readily available and easier to search and utilize. The obligation of disclosure and the dissemination of information technology operate decisively to tilt the balance of interests towards the user of technology, for those willing to make use of patent information. China has promoted the use of patent information resources,[29] and has used them adeptly to leap-frog existing technologies and to create improvement technologies that are licensed back to the patentee of the original invention.

Public-policy exceptions

Exceptions to patent rights serve as the fulcrum for balancing private and public interests in the patent system, typically permitting certain non-commercial use of patented inventions, such as research and educational use. Article 30 of the TRIPs Agreement provides for such exceptions but in very general terms, so it is unsurprising that they were soon tested in the WTO dispute settlement mechanism. The Panel in *Canada – Pharmaceutical Patents*[30] found that the patent right was not confined to actual sales of the patented product, but extended to any use of the patent undertaken for commercial purposes, and that an exception that allowed for commercial-scale use of the patent but fell short of actual sales was not permissible.

China's Patent Law expresses these exceptions indirectly: the patent right can restrain infringing acts that are 'for production or business purposes'.[31] Prima facie, this leaves open the possibility of research and educational exceptions, but not production on a commercial scale or use of the patented invention in preparing for commercial production, nor importation for production or business purposes. This provision may permit importation that is clearly not 'for production or business purposes' – this might, for instance, allow the unauthorized importation and distribution of generic drugs for non-commercial humanitarian purposes, such as for free distribution, despite the existence of a patent. Depending on the strict judicial

---

[29] e.g. 'China launches agricultural IP rights information center', *People's Daily*, 5 November 2001.
[30] WTO Panel Report, *Canada – Patent Protection of Pharmaceutical Products*, WT/DS114/R, adopted 7 April 2000.
[31] Art. 11.

interpretation made of this provision, there may be a wide degree of latitude for non-commercial public policy use of patented material, potentially challenging the TRIPs Agreement requirement that such exceptions be 'limited'.

Patents and the state-owned economy

China's experience with the patent system led to a conclusion that SOEs, especially, were failing to make effective use of it to create innovative products for the market. The Constitution provides that the state-owned economy should be the leading force in the national economy.[32] Along with the shift towards a more atomized socialist market economy came recognition of the need for more effective innovation and IP management, expressed in particular in the Central Committee's 1999 decision on SOE reform.[33] This called on SOEs to 'develop products with their independently owned IPRs', and set the objectives of 'separating administrative and enterprise functions' and exploring 'effective ways for management of state assets'.

These policy settings led to some of the most significant elements of the Patent Law amendments in 2001. SOEs do not now merely 'hold' but actually 'own' patents on inventions produced in their service, putting them on an equal footing with private enterprises and helping them to 'play a dominant role in the national economy'.[34] Restrictions on the entitlement of SOEs to assign patent rights were eased, because it was considered 'neither necessary nor appropriate' for government agencies to intervene in matters which 'fall into the scope of the decision-making power'[35] of individual SOEs. These TRIPs-neutral[36] provisions illustrate a decisive shift away from centrally planned and collective direction of IP portfolios in the state sector.

Yet against this trend, the Patent Law retains a distinctive form of public ownership and equitable reward for public-sector innovations. Article 14 empowers certain government agencies to exploit SOEs' patented inventions, subject to payment of an exploitation fee – in effect, a compulsory

---

[32] Art. 7 of the 1993 Constitution: Chinalaw translation at http://www.qis.net/chinalaw/lawtran1.htm.

[33] Decision of the Central Committee of the Communist Party of China on Major Issues concerning the Reform and Development of State-owned Enterprises, 22 September 1999.

[34] Yin, 'On the second amendment'.   [35] Ibid.

[36] Article 28.2 confirms the patent-holder's right to assign patent rights, although this could arguably be limited in the case of a domestic, state-owned enterprise.

licence system for government use of SOE-owned patents. Compensated government use of patented technology is in principle consistent with the TRIPs Agreement (Articles 31(h) and 44.2). Given the difficult transition of SOEs to the market environment, and the emerging competitive pressures, this form of collective entitlement to patented inventions may deprive the patentee of strategic opportunities through selective access to the technology, and erode leverage in licensing negotiations, also removing the possibility of exclusive licences. In effect, it sets limits to the privatization of SOE IPRs and the transition to a full market orientation for IPR management.

Compulsory licensing and availability of patented technology

The 2001 amendments tightened the requirements for compulsory licensing of dependent patents, introducing the requirement that the second patent include 'an important technical advance of considerable economic significance' in line with Article 31(l)(i) of the TRIPs Agreement.[37] Yet the general compulsory licensing provisions remain quite powerful, on paper at least, and leave considerable scope for discretion. Refusal of a request for the patentee to license the invention 'on reasonable terms' is sufficient grounds for a possible compulsory licence. In principle, this creates an assumption that a patentee cannot deny access to the patented technology to any party, since no reasonable offer can in effect be refused. The prospect of a presumption of availability would limit the patent-holder's strategic options and its leverage in licensing negotiations, still within a TRIPs framework. (The Patent Law gives effect to TRIPs safeguards of the patentee's interests in compulsory licensing, such as the patentee's entitlement to compensation, domestic market focus and non-exclusivity.)

Incentives for patenting

The SOE reform process identified the need for an incentives programme 'to attract talents and kindle the enthusiasm of technological personnel' and to protect IPRs.[38] While China's rate of domestic patent activity is very high by international standards, it is still not commensurate with the

[37] As opposed to 'technically more advanced' in the earlier Article 53.
[38] Part X of the Decision of the Central Committee.

reported levels of research. The Patent Law already provided for individual rewards to inventors in a service relationship, according with the Civil Law provision that 'citizens who make inventions or other achievements in scientific and technological research shall have the right to apply for and receive certificates of honour, bonuses or other awards' (Article 97). Yet in practice this arrangement was considered 'trivial' by many entities, so that inventors did not 'practically ensure their interests'.[39] To stimulate better use of the patent system, the Patent Law was amended to increase the remuneration due to the inventor 'based on the extent of exploitation and application and the economic benefits yielded'. This entitlement was further clarified in the revised implementing rules that went into force in 2001.[40]

Scope of patentability and public-policy objectives

A contested area of policy flexibility under the TRIPs Agreement concerns the scope of patentable subject-matter and the exclusion of certain kinds of technology for broader policy reasons; this overlaps in an uncertain way with the definition of 'invention' itself. Article 27 of the TRIPs Agreement stipulates that patents be available, in principle, to any eligible 'invention' without discrimination as to the field of technology, and sets out several exceptions to this general principle. China's Patent Law (Article 25) appears to mix a restrictive definition of 'invention' with exclusions of specific tech- nologies, with the result that scientific discoveries and rules and methods for mental activities are excluded for want of inherent patentability. In prac- tice, this serves as a limiting interpretation of the word 'invention'. Other exceptions apply to what might otherwise qualify as inherently patentable inventions – such as methods for diagnosis and treatment of diseases, ani- mal and plant varieties.

The Patent Law (Article 5) proscribes the grant of a patent for an in- vention that is 'contrary to the laws of the State or social morality or that is detrimental to public interest'. The TRIPs Agreement (Article 27) allows patents to be denied to inventions when it is necessary to prohibit their com- mercial exploitation 'to protect *ordre public* or morality... provided that such exclusion is not made merely because the exploitation is prohibited

---

[39] Yin, 'On the second amendment'.
[40] Implementing Rules of the Patent Law of the PRC, approved by the State Council on 15 June 2001, summarized by the State Intellectual Property Office, Press Conference, 26 June 2001.

by [members'] law'. On the face of it, these provisions are in conflict. Does the Patent Law's exclusion of inventions that are 'contrary to the laws of the state' allow for a patent to be refused solely because its exploitation would be technically illegal, even when this was not contrary to social morality or detrimental to the public interest? One line of argument advanced during China's accession was that this provision is TRIPs-consistent because the laws simply codify and define social morality and the public interest, in effect that law and public morality and interest are coextensive. But some technology does fall between these two positions: for example, when a new pharmaceutical or a genetically modified organism is at the stage of a pending patent application, it would almost certainly be illegal to exploit it – it is unlikely to have been approved for market release by the regulatory authorities. In practice, it appears that the TRIPs consistency of this provision would depend on its actual application. Because of this uncertainty, the new Implementing Rules stipulate that the Article 5 exclusion 'shall not include inventions whose exploitation is merely prohibited by the laws of the state'.[41]

The legal issue – how to justify an exception to a TRIPs rule on the basis of *ordre public* – has an interesting resonance with the exceptions under Article XX of the GATT for measures that are 'necessary to protect public morals' and 'necessary to protect human, animal or plant life or health'. To what extent does the precautionary principle apply in relation to exclusion of patentable subject-matter? What considerations might a patent examiner apply in determining whether exploitation of a subject invention might contravene social order or prejudice environmental or health interests? Clearly this is an area of considerable potential controversy, but equally one where a distinctive cultural perspective can be argued to apply.

Enforcement

China's legal system exceeds TRIPs standards, on paper at least, for enforcement of patent rights. The TRIPs Agreement reflects western countries' general reliance on civil remedies for patent matters, and does not require criminal sanctions or border-control measures for patent infringement. China's Criminal Code defines patent infringement as a 'crime undermining

---

[41] Implementing Rules, Art. 9.

the order of the socialist market economy',[42] and provides for prison terms
and fines. The Customs Law[43] provides both export and import border-
control measures for patent infringements. These remedies mean that the
patentee enjoys in principle a higher degree of legal support from the state
than in most other jurisdictions.

Recent Patent Law amendments focused especially on clarifying the scope
of the patent right, enforcement and simplification of patent administration, in some cases to accord with TRIPs Agreement standards on substance
(eliminating the defence of innocent infringement, extending patent rights
to 'offer for sale') and procedure (provisional measures including injunctions, and clearer damages in civil cases); in other cases, the amendments
concern streamlining of patent administration and examination (such as
the elimination of an automatic obligation to furnish foreign search and
examination documentation). This reform process is illustrative of a mature patent system in which domestic-oriented reform and adherence to
international standards become increasingly intertwined.

These enforcement mechanisms will not immediately curb the pattern
of endemic infringement; yet the growing quantum of domestic interest in effective enforcement is arguably having effect. Chinese patentees
are becoming increasingly active in defending their interests, including
taking legal action against major foreign companies such as Wal-Mart[44]
(including the application of the TRIPs-plus border-control measures to
suspend exports of alleged infringing goods to the United States), Ericsson[45]
and Motorola,[46] and taking action against infringers for demonstration and
precedent-setting effect.

Conclusion

Intellectual property rights are inseparable from trade. There is little
prospect of divorcing IP protection from trade negotiations, yet negotiators

---

[42] Art. 216, Part II, Chapter III of the Criminal Law of the PRC (adopted 2nd Session of the 5th
NPC, 1 July 1979, and amended by the 5th Session of the 8th NPC, 14 March 1997).

[43] The Regulations of the PRC on the Customs Protection of Intellectual Property (Decree 179 of
the State Council of the PRC, 5 July 1995).

[44] 'Wal-Mart sued in patent case', *China Daily*, 21 September 2001.

[45] 'Motorola, Ericsson in hot water', *People's Daily*, 21 August 2000, http://english.peopledaily.com.
cn/200008/21/eng20000821_48621.html.

[46] 'Motorola sued over patent infringement', *Cellular News*, 11 January 2001, http://www.cellular-
news.com/story/2635.shtml.

and analysts alike need to address the complexities of IPRs and their domestic economic and policy context. Linear, polarized models – North–South, technology producer or consumer – and the assumptions that underly them – fixed centres of technological innovation, absolutist conceptions of the patent right – can give way to an empirically better based and conceptually more supple understanding of IPRs in international trade.

China's implementation of the TRIPs Agreement and bilateral agreements is inevitably seen from the historical perspective of the 'unequal treaties'. But 'TRIPs implementation' is consonant with the progressive development of IPR systems in China as an instrument of domestic economic policy, and the decision to atomize, decentralize and promote innovation and product development. China's success in promoting patent activity – from a standing start – suggests that the enhanced IPR protection associated with TRIPs implementation will in time assist proportionately more domestic right-holders in China than almost anywhere else. Apart from the scale of use, the way the patent right is conceived and applied in China, within the overall TRIPs framework, will also illustrate the scope for policy flexibility and diversity of policy values that the framework can accommodate. The tendency is to consider 'TRIPs implementation' somewhat reductively, essentially as a grudging process of conceding to external commercial interests and externally imposed standards. Yet this may overlook the domestic perspectives that apply during the development and operationalization of IP laws, whatever the external impulse and international influences may be. In turn this may divert attention from the positive opportunities to adapt and apply the IPR system to meet evolving domestic needs. These opportunities include making use of the impetus provided by TRIPs implementation both to use the IP system as a more effective tool of national economic development, and to clarify and redefine IP-related external trade interests.

20

The impact of China's WTO membership on the review of the TRIPs Agreement

DANIEL STEWART AND BRETT G. WILLIAMS

Introduction

The high-profile negotiations for the accession of China to the WTO have focused attention on how China may implement the obligations binding WTO members. Now attention is turning to the question of what impact China will have upon the WTO itself and upon WTO treaty law.[1] This chapter asks that question specifically in the field of intellectual property, considering the impact that China's membership might have upon the evolution of the Agreement on Trade-related Aspects of Intellectual Property Rights (the TRIPs Agreement).[2]

The TRIPs Agreement contains provisions that require WTO members to negotiate on possible changes or amendments to certain parts of the TRIPs Agreement. There are also matters that were the subject of negotiation in the Uruguay Round but which were left unresolved by the TRIPs Agreement as well as other matters that have arisen in the last five years that the TRIPs Agreement has been in force. The recent Ministerial Conference in Doha has emphasized the need for continued examination and reform of the TRIPs Agreement, and highlighted the role of the TRIPs Agreement in

This work was substantially completed while Dr Williams was employed by the China and WTO Project at the Faculty of Law, Australian National University. The authors are grateful to Dr Antony Taubman, then of the Australian Department of Foreign Affairs and Trade, now of the Faculty of Law, Australian National University, for valuable advice.

[1] e.g. see William A. Kerr and Anna L. Hobbs, 'Taming the dragon: the WTO after the accession of China' (2001) 2(1) *The Estey Centre Journal of International Law and Trade Policy* 1–9 (www.esteyjournal.com).

[2] Agreement on Trade-related Aspects of Intellectual Property Rights, Annex 1C to the Agreement Establishing the World Trade Organization, done at Marrakesh, 15 April 1994, [1995] *Aust. Treaty Series* No. 8, (1994) 33 *ILM* 1144; also in WTO, *The Result of the Uruguay Round of Multilateral Trade Negotiations – The Legal Texts* (Geneva, 1994), pp. 365–403.

the protection of public health. This chapter reviews all of the subject-matter of mandatory WTO negotiations and the issues surrounding the Doha Declaration on the TRIPs Agreement and Public Health and offers some thoughts on how they may be affected by China's entry into the WTO.

China has only recently begun to regard intellectual property law as an important part of its legal infrastructure. For example, the Patent Law was only introduced in 1984 and the Copyright Law in 1990. It was also only as the WTO accession negotiation reached its latter stages that the Chinese government began to accord any priority to enforcement of IP law. However, this reticence does not necessarily suggest that China should be viewed merely as an importer or user of IP. As time passes, China will have more of an interest in ensuring that Chinese owners of IP receive protection in other countries.

The TRIPs review agenda and beyond

Negotiations mandated under the TRIPs Agreement

The TRIPs Agreement's provisions require members either individually or through the TRIPs Council to engage in further negotiations:

- to increase protection of individual geographic indications under Article 23 (Article 24.1);
- concerning establishment of a multilateral system of notification and registration of geographical indications for wines (Article 23.4);
- to review the system which permits members to exclude plant varieties from patentability provided that they maintain an effective *sui generis* system for protection of plant varieties (Article 27.3(b));
- on the 'scope and modalities' for non-violation and situation complaints in dispute settlement under the TRIPs Agreement (Article 64);
- to review the implementation of the TRIPs Agreement no later than 1 January 2000 and each two years after that (Article 71).

Other matters under consideration

The Ministerial Conference in Doha in November 2001 discussed various matters needing examination in the review of the TRIPs Agreement.

Foremost among these is the relationship between the TRIPs Agreement and access to medicines, particularly in relation to less-developed countries. The Declaration on the TRIPs Agreement and Public Health included instructions to the TRIPs Council to examine the difficulties faced by WTO members with insufficient or no manufacturing capacities in the pharmaceutical sector in making effective use of compulsory licensing under the TRIPs Agreement.[3] However, the issues involved with public health are related to other issues likely to be faced by the TRIPs review, such as:

- the detailed elaboration of some of the exceptions to IP rights;
- the question of exhaustion of rights and parallel importation; and
- the grounds for compulsory licensing of patents.

The Ministerial Declaration for the Doha Ministerial Conference[4] committed the TRIPs Council to include 'the relationship between the TRIPs Agreement and the Convention on Biological Diversity, the protection of traditional knowledge and folklore, and other relevant new developments raised by Members pursuant to Article 71.1' in the review of the TRIPs Agreement. Some discussion of these issues is included below in discussing the mandated negotiations but their breadth and complexity largely take them outside the scope of this chapter. This chapter will therefore consider the mandated discussions and the issues surrounding the recent Ministerial Declaration.

Mandated negotiations

Non-violation disputes – Article 64

Article XXIII of the GATT provided for complaints to be brought in at least two cases. A non-violation complaint could be brought when a party's measure nullified or impaired a benefit accruing to another party under the Agreement, whether or not the measure conflicted with any provision of the Agreement (paragraph 1(b)), and when any other situation led to nullification or impairment (paragraph 1(c)). Over the fifty-year life of the GATT,

---

[3] Declaration on the TRIPs Agreement and Public Health, adopted 14 November 2001 (WT/MIN(01)/DEC/2, dated 20 November 2001), Art. 6.

[4] Doha 'Ministerial Declaration', adopted on 14 November 2001 (WT/MIN(01)/DEC/1, dated 20 November 2001), Art. 19.

the Contracting Parties treated these provisions with caution. No dispute decision has ever been made upon the basis of the situation complaints provision of Article XXIII:1(c) and only a few fairly narrow decisions have been made upon the basis of the non-violation provision in Article XXIII:1(b).

The rationale for Article XXIII:1(b) is that the objective of the GATT is to balance the obligations and benefits that have been achieved in tariff negotiations rather than to protect any particular tariff obligation. Therefore, arguably, the purpose of the non-violation provision is to help restore the balance of obligations where that balance has been upset by a party's measure that is not strictly a violation of the Agreement.

The TRIPs Agreement incorporated Article XXIII of the GATT into Article 64 of the TRIPs[5] but added two qualifications:

(1) that Article 64.2 excludes non-violation complaints under Article XXIII:1(b) from the TRIPs Agreement for the first five years of the WTO;
(2) that Article 64.3 asks the TRIPs Council to make recommendations to the Ministerial Council on the scope and modalities of non-violation and situation complaints of the type provided for under paragraphs 1(b) and 1(c) of Article XXIII of the GATT.

The five-year period expired on 1 January 2001 without the TRIPs Council having made a recommendation to the Ministerial Council on this point.

There are different views about the current legal position, but the matter continues to be under discussion in the TRIPs Council.[6] The United States has been alone in arguing that the non violation provisions are now in force and that the TRIPs Council should step back from the matter and leave the detailed operation of non-violation complaints under the TRIPs Agreement to be resolved through the dispute settlement process.[7] A number of developing countries have been arguing that the moratorium on non-violation complaints should be extended indefinitely and other countries have been arguing that the moratorium should be extended at least until further time is allowed for the TRIPs Council to make submissions on the

---

[5] TRIPs, Art. 64.1: 'The provisions of Articles XXII and XXIII of GATT 1994 as elaborated and applied by the Dispute Settlement Understanding shall apply to consultations and the settlement of disputes under this Agreement except as otherwise specifically provided herein.'

[6] The three positions argued before the TRIPs Council are drawn from Australian Department of Foreign Affairs, *TRIPs Update, Edition 1: March 2001* (Canberra, 2001), pp. 5–6.

[7] See, e.g., TRIPs Council Minutes for November–December 2000, IP/C/M/29, dated 6 March 2001, para. 229.

scope and modalities of non-violation complaints. A large number of countries have taken the view that the Council should try to reach agreement on the occasions in which non-violation or situation complaints might be possible. Some of those countries seek a formal extension of the period under Article 64.2 during which these types of complaints were suspended.

Reaching agreement on the scope and modalities of non-violation and situation complaints has not been and is unlikely to be easy. Many matters that might be considered non-violation complaints might also be regarded as falling within the category of ordinary violation complaints. Possible non-violation arguments might relate to administration or enforcement of intellectual property law. In Part III of the TRIPs Agreement, dealing with enforcement of intellectual property rights, a number of the obligations are expressed in terms of what procedures members must make available or what powers judicial authorities must have. It is possible that, even where the formal law does provide certain rights and the judicial authorities do have the required powers, the remedies may be insufficient for IP owners to stop or prevent infringements. Perhaps some might be tempted to class this as an appropriate subject-matter for non-violation complaints. However, even here, one can argue fairly strongly that provisions in Article 41.1 and 41.2 already create a possible violation complaint to deal with such a situation.

Although the legality of a non-violation claim relating to enforcement of IP rights is doubtful, this is probably the area where it is most likely that another member might attempt to make a non-violation complaint against China. Concerns have been expressed over the enforcement of Chinese intellectual property law, including the problem of counterfeiting, and also over the difficulty of obtaining remedies from Chinese courts. Were a precedent to be set for such situations by a non-violation case, then China might find itself subject to quite a number of such complaints.

On the basis of the possibility of claims on enforcement issues, one may expect that China will join those countries which seek an extension of the moratorium on non-violation complaints. China may even join with those countries that seek an indefinite moratorium on application of the non-violation provisions to the TRIPs Agreement. However, in the longer term, China may have a greater interest as an exporter of intellectual property. Therefore, one should not assume that China is likely to join those countries that seek an indefinite extension of the moratorium.

*Review of Article 27.3(b) – protection of plants, animals and the
biological processes for their production*

Article 27.3(b) of the TRIPs Agreement allows members to exclude from
patentability plants, animals and the essentially biological processes for
their production. Non-biological and microbiological processes cannot be
excluded. Where plant varieties are not patentable they have to be protected
by a *sui generis* system. Article 27.3(b) also provides for its review within
four years after the commencement of the TRIPs Agreement. Below, the
issues involved in review of the whole clause are discussed, followed by a
more specific discussion of plant-breeders' rights.

Review of the exclusion under Article 27.3(b)

The review of this article commenced in 1999. There remain considerable
difficulties in establishing the scope and purpose of review, with discussions
presently concentrating on the form of the review process.[8] The wide range
of issues being discussed and the potential scope of the review have so
far inhibited consensus. The impact that China's accession to the TRIPs
Agreement may have is difficult to establish. However, this chapter examines
China's possible impact on the resolution of some of the more distinct
issues.

The scope of the exception   The exception in Article 27(3) of the TRIPs
Agreement reflects the exception to patentability included in Article 53(b)
of the European Patent Convention. The 1998 Biotechnology Directive[9]
suggests that this exception be interpreted narrowly. Biomolecular or other
technologies that go beyond the narrow taxonomical limits of an individual
plant variety[10] or a particular animal variety can generally be patented. This
includes plant or animal cells, or, indeed, plant groupings characterized
by a particular gene rather than its whole genome. Essentially biological
processes have been distinguished from technical processes in which the
course of events is influenced by a means other than those which occur
in nature. Therefore procedures for extracting, transforming and using

---

[8]   See WTO, IP/C/22 *Annual Report (2000) of the Council for TRIPs*, 6 December 2000.

[9]   Directive 98/44/EC, adopted on 6 July 1998, OJ 1998 No. L213, 30 July 1998, p. 13.

[10]   It has been generally accepted that a plant variety is defined as in the Act of the Union for the
Protection of New Varieties of Plants (UPOV) revised in 1991 by characteristics that result from
a given genotype or combination of genotypes, distinguished by expression of at least one of the
said characteristics, and considered as a unit with regard to its suitability for being propagated
unchanged. See further the discussion of protection of plant varieties below.

micro-organisms, developments in the fields of cell and molecular biology, and inventions relating to genes or proteins can also be patented as not falling with the exception.

However, other countries have taken a more restrictive interpretation. Developing countries such as Brazil and Argentina prohibit the patenting of naturally occurring substances, even when isolated. Because of the potential variation in interpreting the scope of the exception in Article 27.3(b), to facilitate the review, the TRIPs Council is collating information on the various interpretations employed, particularly by developing countries.[11]

China's Patent Law provides for an exclusion from patentability of plant and animal varieties.[12] While there has been little indication of the scope of the exception, it is clear that biological material and biotechnology has been patented in China,[13] suggesting that China will not wish to exclude biological matter that forms part of a plant or animal variety from potentially being patented.

Encouragement of innovation The expense and complexity of biotechnological innovation limits the capacity of many countries to provide sufficient public funding for research and development. Patent or plant-breeders' rights have largely provided the incentive for the substantial private investment needed.

Countries with no capacity to engage in biological innovation are therefore dependent on the ability to utilize foreign innovation. Without intellectual property protection, there will be less incentive for the private provision of new products. However, for countries, including China, that may have the capacity for a significant biotechnological industry,[14] a

---

[11] WTO, IP/C/23 *Annual Report (2001) of the Council for TRIPs*, 5 October 2001, para. 34.

[12] Article 25(4) of the Patent Law of the PRC, adopted 12 March 1984, Second Amendment and Re-promulgation 25 August 2000, effective 1 July 2000. Previous amendments also included this exception.

[13] In 1990–5 there were 173 patents relating to biotechnology that originated in China: CEFI, *The Challenges of Biotechnology* (Madrid, 1997).

[14] China, along with a number of other countries in Asia and Latin America, has a relatively high level of plant biotechnological capacity, especially in early generation biotechnology areas: Charles Spillane, 'Recent developments in biotechnology as they relate to plant genetic resources for food and agriculture', Commission on Genetic Resources for Food and Agriculture, Background Study Paper No. 9 (1999), available at ftp://ext-ftp.fao.org/ag/cgrfa/BSP/bsp9E.pdf, p. 8, citing J. Komen and G. Persley, *Agricultural Biotechnology in Developing Countries: A Cross-country Review* (ISNAR–IBS Research Report No. 2, The Hague, 1998). China has developed micropropagation technology for more than 100, largely indigenous, crop species: A. Sasson, 'Biotechnology and food production: relevance to developing countries', in A. Altman (ed.), *Agricultural Biotechnology* (New York, 1998), p. 693.

trade-off is required. The provision of protection may require paying more for foreign technology that could perhaps have been produced locally in order to provide sufficient incentive to encourage domestic innovation or the development of products better suited to domestic conditions.[15]

Access to biological material   A further issue in providing for patent protection of biological material relates to the allocation of benefits among the various contributors to the invention. Developing countries have much to contribute to the development of biotechnological innovations, such as indigenous flora and fauna, and knowledge of their characteristics and properties.[16] The Convention on Biological Diversity facilitates access to genetic resources, subject to the prior informed consent of the state providing the resources.[17] Measures should be adopted with the aim of sharing in a fair and equitable way the benefits arising from the commercial and other utilization of genetic resources with the state that has provided such resources. This is to be on 'mutually agreed terms which recognize and are consistent with the adequate and effective protection of intellectual property rights'.[18] Similarly, provision is made for the protection of indigenous knowledge and the sharing of benefits with indigenous knowledge providers.[19]

Various countries[20] have enacted legislation in line with the Convention on Biological Diversity. This has included legislation requiring that the interests of states or indigenous communities who contribute biological material or information be recorded in patent registrations.[21] Similar proposals have been put forward by the Commission on Genetic Resources

---

[15] See F. M. Scherer, 'The pharmaceutical industry and world intellectual property standards' (2000) 53 *Vanderbilt Law Review* 2245, at 2249–50.

[16] Carolyn Oddie, 'Bio-prospecting' (1998) 9 *Australian Intellectual Property Journal* 6, at 6–7. See also WIPO, 'Intellectual property and genetic resources – an overview', WIPO/IP/GR/00/2, 24 March 2000, p. 9: 'Many types of biological inventions draw from and build on information and characteristics of naturally occurring plants, animals and other living organisms.'

[17] Article 15 of the Convention on Biological Diversity, opened for signature June 1992, (1994) 31(4) *ILM* 818.

[18] WIPO, 'Intellectual property and genetic resources', 8.

[19] Convention on Biological Diversity, Art. 8(j).

[20] Peter Drahos 'Indigenous knowledge, intellectual property and biopiracy: is a global collecting society the answer?' (2000) *European Intellectual Property Review* 245, at 245–6.

[21] South Africa has also at least introduced a Bill on the Protection and Promotion of South African Indigenous Knowledge which provides for acknowledgement of community and geographic place from where knowledge is obtained in all printed publications: WIPO, 'Intellectual property and genetic resources', 10.

for Food and Agriculture[22] and the Food and Agriculture Organization and are being considered in the review of Article 27.3(b). Questions over what degree of dependence on the biological material sourced from particular countries is necessary before requiring acknowledgement, the operation of private agreements and the consequences of non-fulfilment of the requirements on the validity of the patent are just some of the considerations that will have to be addressed if such a proposal is to be accepted.

A registration system might help identify relevant interests and the enforcement of access and benefit-sharing requirements. However, the parties are yet to overcome divergent views on the possible distorting effects of a decentralized system of protecting access to, exploitation and protection of biological resources, both from the view of international trade and the environment.

China, along with a number of developing countries, has played a significant role in developing proposals in this area in other forums, calling in particular for the sharing of benefits derived from genetic resources being applied to the conservation and sustainable use of crops in developing countries.[23] It is therefore likely that China will continue to take an active role in relation to these issues.

Sui generis protection for plant-breeders' rights

The review of Article 27.3(b) necessarily involves consideration of what level of protection of plant varieties is sufficient to meet the existing provisions and of whether some change to that level of protection is appropriate. In a legal adjudication of what is an effective *sui generis* system, consideration would be given to 'subsequent practice of the parties in the application of the treaty which [might establish] the agreement of the parties regarding its interpretation'.[24] This emphasizes the importance of the TRIPs Council's collection of information on state practice in this area.[25]

---

[22] See, for example, Commission on Genetic Resources for Food and Agriculture, 'Chairman's simplified text', CGRFA/Ex-6/01/2, Item 2 of the Provisional Agenda, 6th Extraordinary Session, Rome 24–30 June 2001.

[23] See, for example, Commission on Genetic Resources for Food and Agriculture, ibid., Appendix 5, 'Proposal by the G77 and China for Article 15 – *ex situ* collections of plant genetic resources for food and agriculture held by the international agricultural research centres of the consultative group on international agricultural research and other international institutions . . .'.

[24] Vienna Convention on the Law of Treaties, done 23 May 1969, in force 27 January 1980, 1155 UNTS 331; (1969) 8 *ILM* 679, Art. 31(3)(b).

[25] Australia, DFAT, *Intellectual Property – A Vital Asset for Australia, a Background Briefing Paper on the Review of the TRIPs Agreement* (Canberra, March 2000), p. 7.

One important indicator of state practice is the number of states that have adjusted their law to meet the requirements of the International Convention for the Protection of New Varieties of Plants 1961 (the UPOV Convention), first in force in 1961 and revised by subsequent Acts in 1972, 1978 and 1991, which increased the level of protection(b) given to owners of plant-breeders' rights.[26] In April 1994, when the Agreement Establishing the WTO was signed by the original WTO members, twenty-three states were parties to either the 1961/72 Act of the treaty or the 1978 Act. At that time, no state had ratified the 1991 Act. Since then (up to 7 February 2002),[27] five of those twenty-three parties have ratified the 1991 Act, eighteen additional states have become parties to the 1978 Act of the treaty and nine additional states have become parties to the 1991 Act, bringing the total number of states applying one of the versions of the treaty to fifty. WTO membership has risen from just below 100 to just over 140 in the same period, so there remain over ninety WTO members which are not a party to any of the versions of the UPOV Convention. However, the greater number of those ninety or so states did not become bound by Article 27 of the TRIPs Agreement until 1 January 2000 when the transition periods ended and the review of the TRIPs commenced, which means that almost all countries bound by Article 27 for a reasonable period of time have ratified one of the versions of the UPOV Convention.

The importance of the standards applying under the UPOV Conventions has been reflected in the work of the WTO Council on TRIPs, which, in collecting information about members' protection of plant varieties, issued a questionnaire with a number of questions about whether members applied standards contained in the UPOV Conventions.[28] In submissions to the TRIPs Council, a number of members have expressed the view that since their domestic legislation conformed to the 1978 Act of the UPOV Convention, then it also conformed to the requirement in Article 27.3(b) to have an effective *sui generis* system of protection for plant varieties.[29] A

---

[26] International Convention for the Protection of New Varieties of Plants, done 2 December 1961 ('UPOV Convention'). 'UPOV 1961/72' refers to the 1961 treaty as amended by the additional Act of 10 November 1972. 'UPOV 1978' refers to the Act of the Convention of 23 October 1978. 'UPOV 1991' refers to the Act of the Convention of 19 March 1991.

[27] The statistics are taken from 'States Party to the International Convention for the Protection of New Varieties of Plants' on the UPOV website at http://www.upov.org/eng/ratif/pdf/ratifmem.pdf.

[28] See, 'Review of the provisions of Art 27.3(b), illustrative list of questions prepared by the Secretariat', IP/C/W/122, 22 December 1998.

[29] e.g., see the statements by Brazil at para. 61 and by Mexico at para. 76 in 'Minutes of the Council for TRIPs', IP/C/M/26, 24 May 2000.

number of other countries have raised broader issues relating to ownership of genetic material and to movement of genetically modified material. The attempt to include such matters in the review of Article 27.2(b) may mean that little progress is achieved in reaching an agreement.

The Chinese Patent Law excludes plants from the scope of subject-matter over which patents may be granted.[30] However, in October 1997, China introduced a separate system of protection for owners of plant varieties when it passed the Regulations for the Protection of New Varieties of Plants.[31] The regulations contain an exception for planting of 'farmer-saved seed'[32] and do not give variety right-holders any authority to prevent the sale of the crop grown from the planting of farmer-saved seed.

China became a party to the 1978 Act of UPOV in April 1999. Under UPOV 1978, China does not need to give variety right-owners the right to negotiate a royalty at the time of planting the seed they have grown themselves nor must it give them the right to prevent farmers from selling their crops in situations in which the owners have not had an opportunity to negotiate a royalty at the time of planting. However, the position is different for parties to the 1991 Act, who must provide for a right to collect a royalty either at the time of planting farmer-saved seed or at the time of harvest.

It seems likely that China would agree with those states that have argued that compliance with UPOV 1978 should be regarded as compliance with the existing Article 27.3(b) of the TRIPs Agreement. Further, it seems fairly certain that China would oppose any proposals to incorporate into Article 27 a level of protection based on the 1991 Act.

Negotiations relating to the protection of geographical indications

Existing protection of geographical indications under the TRIPs Agreement

Articles 22 to 24 of the TRIPs Agreement require WTO members to provide legal protection to enable interested parties to prevent the misuse of geographical indications (GIs) as to the source of goods. These articles also

---

[30] See Article 25(4) of the Patent Law of the PRC.

[31] Regulations of the PRC on the Protection of New Varieties of Plants. Article 46 of the Regulations provides that they come into force on 1 October 1997. References in this chapter to the Regulations are to the translation on the UPOV website, which is described as being the Regulations published in *PVP Gazette*, Issue No. 85, October 1999.

[32] Article 6 sets out the rights of the variety right-holder and Article 10 contains the 'farmer-saved seed' exception.

require members to provide an even higher level of legal protection in relation to GIs that relate to the source of wines and spirits. GIs are defined as indications of the geographic origin of a product, 'where a given quality, reputation or other characteristic of the good is essentially attributable to its geographic origin'.[33] There is an exception for generic words, which provides that the provisions do not require members to provide protection in relation to GIs identical to the commonly used name of the product in the territory of the relevant member.[34] Nor do members have to protect a GI if the country in which the geographic area is located does not protect the use of the GI.[35]

Existing TRIPs provisions on geographical indications relating to all goods   In relation to goods generally, Article 22 requires members to:

- provide legal means for the prevention of use of GIs where the use misleads the public as to the geographical origin of the goods for sale;[36]
- provide legal means for the prevention of uses of GIs which are contrary to honest practices including any such uses which 'create confusion... with the establishment, the goods or the [business] of a competitor';[37]
- at the request of an interested party, refuse or invalidate registration of a trade mark which contains a GI in respect of goods not originating in the territory indicated if the use of the GI would mislead the public about the place of origin of the goods.[38]

The result is that a company in country A who sells goods that genuinely come from a particular geographic region X, can prevent certain sales in three situations:

- within country A, it can prevent sale of imports that bear a name that could make people think the imported product is from region X ('home-country rights');
- when exporting to country B, it can prevent local producers in country B from selling a product that consumers in country B might think comes from region X in country A ('export-country rights');

---

[33] TRIPs, Art. 22.1.   [34] Ibid., Art. 24.6.   [35] Ibid., Art. 24.9.   [36] Ibid., Art. 22.2(a).
[37] See Paris Convention for the Protection of Industrial Property of 1883, Stockholm Act of 14 July 1967 as revised on 28 September 1979, Art. 10*bis*(1) and (3), which is incorporated by TRIPs, Art. 22.2(b).
[38] TRIPs, Art. 22.3.

- when exporting to country B, it can prevent an exporter in country C
  from selling goods in country B if it might make consumers in country
  B think that country C's product originates in region X in country A
  ('third-country rights').

These provisions apply even if there is a town or region in country B that
shares the name of geographic region X.

**Existing TRIPs provisions on geographical indications relating to wine
and spirits**   In relation to wine and spirits, the level of protection is higher.
The difference between the obligations on wine and spirits and the above-
described obligations that apply to any products is that the obligation to
provide legal means to prevent the use of the GIs in connection with wine
and spirits cannot be made subject to any test of whether the use of the
GI misleads the public as to the origin of the goods, is dishonest or creates
confusion with the goods or businesses in the named geographic area.
Indeed, the right to prevent the use of the GI must be available even if the
label makes it clear that the goods do not come from the named geographical
area but from another named place.

The same definitions and general provisions apply, so these rules only apply to indications of the geographic origin of a product 'where a given quality, reputation or other characteristic of the good is essentially attributable
to its geographic origin' and they do not apply to GIs which are identical
to the commonly used name of the product in the territory of the relevant
member.[39]

Negotiations under the TRIPs Agreement on
geographical indications

There are three separate parts of the provisions on geographical indications
that have been under review by the TRIPs Council:

(1) under Article 24.1, members are required to 'enter into negotiations
    aimed at increasing the protection of individual geographical indica-
    tions under Article 23';
(2) under Article 23.4, members are required to enter into negotiations
    'concerning the establishment of a multilateral system of notification

---

[39] Ibid., Art. 24.6, which also contains an exception for GIs that are the customary names of grape
varieties.

and registration of geographical indications for wines eligible for protection in those Members participating in the system'; and

(3) under Article 24.2, the TRIPs Council is required to 'keep under review the application of the provisions of' all of the provisions relating to GIs.

There has been some disagreement over the scope of Article 24.1 and whether it obliges members to negotiate to extend protection given by Article 23 to products other than wine and spirits,[40] or only obliges members to negotiate on strengthening the protection given to GIs on wine and spirits.[41] On the second view, the negotiation would only involve discussing the various limitations in Article 24 – such as those which permit use of generic words, of one's own name or of the names of grape varieties. However, on the first view, the negotiation would be broader, based on the argument that if wine and spirits can be protected then why not also Kalamata olives and Basmati rice.

Similarly, members have different views about the purpose of the negotiation under Article 23.4 to establish a multilateral register. Some have argued that the register should only give information about protection that is accorded and that no new legal obligations should flow from the entries in the register. Others argue that the entry of a name in the register should create an obligation to protect that name. The crux seems to be the uncertainty that arises from the fact that it is domestic courts that decide whether a GI is the same as the generic word – that is, whether the GI is the 'term customary in common language as the common name for such goods or services in the territory of that Member'. If the listing in a register created an obligation to protect, then there would be a violation if the courts in the relevant Member State decided not to protect the GI because it was the generic name for the product. There has also been disagreement about the scope of products to which such a register might apply. Hong Kong has expressed the view that the mandated negotiation should only deal with a register for GIs on wine as is specified in Article 23.4. Others have been happy to extend this to wine and spirits, and a larger group has argued that proposals for a multilateral register should be considered in the context of proposed negotiations to extend the protection under Article 23 to

---

[40] See 'Communication from Bulgaria, the Czech Republic, Egypt, Iceland, India, Kenya, Liechtenstein, Pakistan, Slovenia, Sri Lanka, Switzerland and Turkey, *Revision*', IP/C/W/204/Rev.1, dated 2 October 2000, at paras. 11–12.

[41] e.g., see 'Communication from New Zealand', IP/C/W/205, 18 September 2000, para. 22.

products other than wine and spirits so that a register could perform the same function for GIs on any products.

Whilst the specific issues covered by Articles 24.1 and 23.4 could be seen as separate issues from each other and from the more general review under Article 24.2, in practice it seems that the three processes have begun to merge into one linked negotiation. There will be two main themes to the broader negotiation: whether to require members to protect GIs on all agricultural products (or even all products) without any test of their use being misleading or confusing; and whether to set up a register so that obligations flow from it or merely to give information about existing protection.

China's possible position

Chinese law does prevent the use of false, misleading or confusing use of names of products, names of enterprises, labels, and indications of quality.

The provisions of Article 5 of the Law Against Unfair Competition of 1993 are similar to provisions against false and misleading statements that are present in many countries' laws.[42] These provisions appear to satisfy the requirements of Article 22.2 of the TRIPs Agreement, provided that Chinese civil procedures provide a mechanism for interested parties to stop those in breach of the law from continuing their infringing activity. Some observers are sceptical of the ability of the Chinese legal system to provide appropriate remedies.[43]

Article 8 of the Trademark Law of the PRC 1993[44] provides that 'foreign geographic names known to the public shall not be used as trade marks, with the exception, however, of those geographic names having other meanings'. Therefore, only those foreign GIs that are known to the public in China as a foreign GI are protected against registration. This may often, in practice,

---

[42] Law of the PRC Against Unfair Competition, adopted by the Standing Committee of the Eighth National People's Congress on 2 September 1993, promulgated 1 December 1993. See Mark Williams' chapter in this volume (chapter 19).

[43] See, e.g., Richard Behar, 'Beijing's phony war on fakes', *Fortune Magazine*, 30 October 2000, p. 161.

[44] In Trademark Law of the PRC adopted by the 24th meeting of the Standing Committee of the Fifth National People's Congress on 23 August 1982, as amended by Decision of the 30th meeting of Standing Committee of the Seventh National People's Congress of 22 February 1993. Following an amendment in October 2001, in force December 2001, Article 8 is now Article 10 of the Trademark Law. It appears from an unofficial translation (available from the website of China Patent Agents (H.K.) Ltd at http://www.cpahkltd.com/home.html) that this text has not substantively changed.

be equivalent to establishing that the use of the trade mark was misleading. However, on the face of it Article 8 allows registration of GIs with more than one possible meaning where there might be confusion as to the origin of the product. On that basis it is arguable that the Chinese law does not comply with Article 22.3.[45] The lack of any special provision for wine and spirits means that neither of these provisions would meet the requirements of Article 23.[46]

What can one expect from China? While China would have an interest in protecting certain names of spirits, it is unlikely that it has occurred to Chinese politicians or legislators that there is public benefit from according a higher level of protection to those GIs that relate to wine and spirits. Secondly, there are various Chinese geographical indications that are commonly attached as a sign of quality to meat products, fruits and vegetables – for example, certain types of ham, or tea. Therefore, if China becomes obliged to pass laws protecting GIs on wine and spirits from other WTO members, China might join such countries as Pakistan and India which have argued that similar protection should be extended to other agricultural products.

Would China have an interest in the certainty of protection that could be offered by the multilateral register or would it prefer the issue of whether GIs are generic to remain a decision for domestic courts in each case? China might see it as onerous to register foreign GIs and to protect them in circumstances where the words are used by Chinese people who have no knowledge that the word is the name of a foreign place. In respect of Chinese GIs, China may not have any need of the clarity of obligations that a register could provide because few Chinese names would tend to become generic names in other countries.

Future negotiations on patent protection

Limitations to patent protection and access to medicines

The Doha Ministerial Declaration on TRIPs and Public Health confirmed that the TRIPs Agreement is not intended to prevent members from taking

---

[45] The exception in the Chinese provision being broader than what is permitted by TRIPs, Art. 24.6.

[46] There is also a Regulation on the Protection of Place of Origin Products (State Bureau of Quality and Technical Supervision, No. 6, 1999) but to date we have not been able to obtain an English translation.

action to protect public health. It does this through provisions for exclusions from patentable subject-matter where necessary to protect health (Article 27.2), compulsory licensing (Article 31) and, indirectly, the exhaustion of rights allowing parallel importation (Article 6).

Compulsory licences

The ability of patent-holders to prevent access to patented technology, particularly where a subsequent inventor has made substantial improvements or wishes to utilize the invention in an unintended way, has led to most countries adopting some form of compulsory licensing regime.[47] These allow for the unauthorized use of the patented invention, provided that some form of compensation is paid.

Article 31 of the TRIPs Agreement provides for the compulsory licensing of patented inventions.[48] It does not limit the grounds for such a licence, but instead sets out various conditions under which the grant of the licence may take place. These conditions include:

> (b) ... the proposed user has made efforts to obtain authorization from the right holder on reasonable commercial terms and conditions and that such efforts have not been successful within a reasonable period of time. This requirement may be waived by a Member in the case of a national emergency or other circumstances of extreme urgency or in cases of public non-commercial use ...
> (f) any such use shall be authorized predominantly for the supply of the domestic market of the Member authorizing such use ...
> (h) the right holder shall be paid adequate remuneration in the circumstances of each case, taking into account the economic value of the authorisation.

Paragraphs 31(b) and (f) do not apply where the licence is to remedy anti-competitive behaviour. Where the licence is being granted to allow a subsequent invention to be exploited without infringing a prior invention, the subsequent invention must be an 'important technical advance of

---

[47] Carlos Correa, 'Access to plant genetic resources and intellectual property rights', Commission on Genetic Resources for Food and Agriculture, Background Study Paper No. 8 available at ftp://ext-ftp.fao.org/ag/cgrfa/BSP/bsp8E.pdf, p. 15; Spillane, 'Recent developments', pp. 46–7.

[48] Article 5(2) of the Paris Convention, which is incorporated into the TRIPs Agreement, also provides for compulsory licences: 'Each country of the Union shall have the right to take legislative measures providing for the grant of compulsory licenses to prevent the abuses which might result from the exercise of the exclusive rights conferred by the patent, for example, failure to work.'

considerable economic significance in relation to' the prior invention and the owner of the first patent shall be entitled to a cross-licence on reasonable terms to use the second patent.[49]

The Doha Declaration recognized that 'Each Member has the right to determine what constitutes a national emergency or other circumstances of extreme urgency, it being understood that public health crises . . . can represent a national emergency or other circumstances of extreme urgency.'[50] However, how far this extends to permit compulsory licensing in other situations where it is perceived to be in the interests of providing developing countries with access to technology is not clear.

China's recent amendments to its patent laws involved changes to compulsory licensing which substantially accord with the requirements under Article 31 of the TRIPs Agreement. However, there is no restriction of the compulsory licence for use within China.[51] There is also provision in Article 14 of the Chinese Patent Law for a form of compulsory licence where a patent of a state-owned enterprise, government institution, collectively owned units or an individual is of great significance to the interests of the state or to the public interest and where there is a need to promote its application. In these cases, government departments can allow designated units to exploit the invention upon the payment of a fee according to the provisions of the state.[52]

New implementation rules of the Patent Law may restrict the operation of the compulsory licensing laws in China,[53] and indeed a possible ambiguity in the English translation may suggest that it is intended to apply Article 14 only to patents owned by Chinese nationals. However, China's adoption of an apparent extension to the compulsory licensing regime and the potential importance of compulsory licences in providing access to new forms of innovation at a price affordable to developing countries, suggests that broadening the compulsory licence regime may be considered after China's accession.

---

[49] TRIPs, Art. 31.1.

[50] Article 5(c) of the Declaration on the TRIPs Agreements and Public Health.

[51] There is also no special provision for the licensing of semi-conductor technology that is required under Article 31(c), which restricts such licences to public non-commercial use or as determined by a court to remedy anti-competitive behaviour.

[52] Patent Law of the PRC, Art. 14.

[53] Elizabeth Chaien-Hale, 'China overhauls compulsory licensing', *Managing Intellectual Property*, www.legalmediagroup.com/mip, May 2001.

Parallel importation and segmenting markets

The owner of a patent is able to exclude others from exploiting the patented invention. In many countries, however, this right extends only to the first sale of the invention. After the first sale by the owner or licensee of the patent owner, the rights to exclude further sales may be 'exhausted'. In this way, patented goods may be 'parallel imported' into a country without infringing the patent owner's rights in that country after their legitimate purchase overseas.

Parallel importation may therefore prevent the segmentation of markets to reflect the differing market conditions. In particular, it has been argued that developing countries may be prevented from negotiating preferential access to patented technologies due to the possibility of products being exported to other, more commercially attractive, markets. This would prevent exploitation of the patented product in developing countries or in relation to research and development for markets not seen as commercially lucrative.[54]

Under Article 6 of the TRIPs Agreement, countries are allowed to determine for themselves whether to provide for the exhaustion of intellectual property rights. The European Union is moving towards permitting parallel importation within the European Union to prevent price differentials that disadvantage domestic consumers.[55] Many countries have moved to remove or limit parallel importation restrictions.[56] The Doha Declaration on the TRIPs Agreement and Public Health made it clear that each member is free to establish their own regime for exhaustion.[57]

There are other factors that can lead to price differentials among countries.[58] Other differences in intellectual property rules, and market conditions, in particular the degree of competition among producers, may

---

[54] Spillane, 'Recent developments', p. 45.

[55] This follows the decision in ECJ Case C–355/96 *Silhouette International Schmied GmbH & Co. KG v. Hartlauer Handelsgesellschaft GmbH* [1998] ECR I-4799 which held that the Trade Mark Directive had harmonized trademark rules within the European Union.

[56] See, for example, Australia's recent introduction of the Copyright Amendment (Parallel Importation) Bill 2001. Australia has long recognized the exhaustion of rights in patent law: see Intellectual Property and Competition Review Committee, *Interim Report* (Canberra, 2000), p. 9.

[57] Declaration on the TRIPs Agreement and Public Health, Art. 5(d).

[58] See Margaret Duckett, 'Compulsory licensing and parallel importing, What do they mean? Will they improve access to essential drugs for people living with HIV/AIDS?', Background Paper, International Council of AIDS Service Organizations (ICASO) (July 1999), available at http://www.icaso.org/compulsory_english.htm.

enable considerable limitations being placed on licensing and distribution agreements that may also result in geographical segmentation of the market for a patented product. Technology transfer agreements providing access to patented technology may also include restrictions preventing non-domestic use or sale.[59] Parallel importation at least enables access to patented technology at the lowest possible price available in overseas markets.

It is an infringement of Article 11 of China's Patent Law to import the patented product without the authorization of the patentee. China's Patent Law only provides for domestic exhaustion. Under Article 63(1), it is not an infringement of the patent 'Where, after the sale of a patented product that was made or imported by the patentee, or made or imported with the authorization of the patentee, or of a product derived directly from a patented process, any other person uses, promises to sell or sells that product.'[60] Therefore, parallel importation of a product may require the authorization of the holder of the patent *in China*. If this is maintained in the rules implementing the Patent Law, then China may not encourage the abolition of parallel importation restrictions as part of the TRIPs agenda.

Conclusions

This chapter has engaged in some speculation of the possible views of China, though the speculation is grounded, as far as possible, on the available information. It seems that China will not support the use of non-violation complaints, nor would it support the adoption of obligations on plant-breeders' rights that would implement the 1991 version of the UPOV Convention. On geographical indication, the Chinese position is difficult to predict – but it seems unlikely that China will rally to support EU positions without injecting some demands of its own. It is likely that China will take an active role in any further developments in patent protection.

However, regardless of these specifics, the chapter has drawn attention to the important role that China is likely to play in the deliberations of the TRIPs Council and, through that, in determining the future boundaries of international intellectual property law. Intellectual property law is always a balance between encouraging innovators and making the benefits of innovation available to the public, including those who will innovate

---

[59] See examples given in Spillane, 'Recent developments', p. 46.
[60] Patent Law of the People's Republic of China (see n. 12, above).

further. International trade law under the WTO always has the dual character of being both an attempt to create beneficial constraints on domestic policy-making by governments and the outcome of a mercantile bargain between competing export interests. China's input into the TRIPs Agreement (like that of other countries) will reflect both aspects of this dual character. China's participation will be partly a product of Chinese history and culture and its leaders' attitudes to what is optimal for intellectual property regulation. At the same time, one can expect Chinese commercial interests to play a role in shaping the outward Chinese position just as they shape positions in other countries. Whatever the Chinese influence will be, it will not be insignificant. Negotiators and policy-makers will need to have an awareness of the Chinese perspective just as they now need to have an awareness of the US or EU perspective. Perhaps the speculation in this chapter will encourage others to dig further.

PART VII

Dispute settlement

21

Interpeting China's Accession Protocol:
a case study in anti-dumping

MICHAEL LENNARD

Introduction

This chapter considers some of the treaty interpretation issues that may arise in relation to China's Accession Protocol,[1] from a public international law perspective. It uses the provisions of the Protocol relating to anti-dumping measures as a case study to bring those issues into relief.

WTO treaty interpretation rules

The Vienna Convention

In a recently published article,[2] I considered the methodologies used by the WTO Appellate Body in interpreting WTO agreements generally. I noted that the WTO Panels and the Appellate Body rely on the treaty interpretation rules expressed in the Vienna Convention on the Law of Treaties[3] (the 'Vienna Convention') as the basic rules for interpreting WTO instruments. This is because those rules represent the 'customary rules of interpretation of public international law', which Article 3.2 of the Understanding on Rules and Procedures Governing the Settlement of Disputes[4] (the 'Dispute

---

The views expressed in this chapter are not intended to reflect those of the Australian Tax Office or the Australian government.

[1] WTO Document WT/MIN(01)/3, 10 November 2001, pp. 74 ff. (available at http://www.wto.org/english/thewto_e/acc_e/protocols_acc_membership_e.htm).

[2] Michael Lennard, 'Navigating by the stars: interpreting the WTO agreements' (2002) 5(1) *Journal of International Economic Law* 17–89.

[3] Done at Vienna, 23 May 1969, in force 27 January 1980, 1155 UNTS 331; (1969) 8 *ILM* 679.

[4] Annex 2 to the Agreement Establishing the World Trade Organization; World Trade Organization, *The Results of the Uruguay Round of the Multilateral Trade Negotiations* (Geneva, 1994), p. 404.

Settlement Understanding') requires Panels and the Appellate Body to apply.[5]

The Accession Protocol as a treaty

The same Vienna Convention rules would apply to an Accession Protocol, which is in essence an agreement, binding both on China and on current and future WTO members, as to the modified terms of China's accession to the WTO.[6] Those terms of accession include any paragraphs of an Accession Working Party Report that are specifically picked up by the Protocol, as well as the member schedules that are annexed to the Accession Protocol.[7]

China's Accession Protocol does, in fact, pick up such Working Party Report paragraphs as reflect China's commitments made in the Working Party process. The mechanism for achieving this is provided at section 1.2 of the Protocol: 'This Protocol, which shall include the commitments referred to in paragraph 342 of the Working Party Report, shall be an integral part of the WTO Agreement.' In turn, paragraph 342 of the Working Party Report incorporates the specific commitments of China (recorded at various other paragraphs of the Report) when it provides that:

> The Working Party took note of the explanations and statements of China concerning its foreign trade regime, as reflected in this Report. The Working Party took note of the commitments given by China in relation to certain specific matters which are reproduced in paragraphs 18–19 ... 339 and 341 of this Report and noted that these commitments are incorporated in paragraph 1.2 of the Draft Protocol. [Various paragraph numbers omitted]

In summary, then, certain Chinese commitments have become part of China's WTO accession terms, binding in international law. The Accession Protocol does not, in contrast, render binding as part of the terms of

---

[5] See, for example: WTO Appellate Body Report, *United States – Standards for Reformulated and Conventional Gasoline*, WT/DS2/AB/R, adopted 20 May 1996, p. 17; WTO Appellate Body Report, *Japan – Taxes on Alcoholic Beverages*, WT/DS8/AB/R, WT/DS10/AB/R, WT/DS11/AB/R, adopted 1 November 1996, p. 10.

[6] See, for example, section 1.2 of China's Accession Protocol: 'The WTO Agreement to which China accedes shall be the WTO Agreement as rectified, amended or otherwise modified by such legal instruments as may have entered into force before the date of accession. This Protocol, which shall include the commitments referred to in para. 342 of the Working Party Report, shall be an integral part of the WTO Agreement.'

[7] See, e.g., WTO Appellate Body Report, *European Communities – Measures Affecting the Importation of Certain Poultry Products*, WT/DS69/AB/R, adopted 23 July 1998, para. 79.

China's WTO obligations, what ostensibly appear to be just as much the apparent 'commitments' or 'confirmations' by the Working Party members as to what WTO members will do in meeting their obligations to China. An example is found at paragraph 246 of the Working Party Report:

> Members of the Working Party noted that the Draft Protocol included specific requirements that WTO Members needed to follow in connection with an action under that Section. Members of the Working Party confirmed that in implementing the provisions on market disruption, WTO Members would comply with those provisions and the following...

A specific procedural *modus operandi* is then provided. Because that *modus operandi* is not picked up in the Accession Protocol, the 'commitments' made *to* China do not operate directly as part of the terms of China's entry. Whether such an 'unimplemented undertaking' may have some indirect significance, and the nature of any such significance, is considered in the third section of this chapter, below, when the Accession Protocol anti-dumping provisions to which the *modus operandi* relates are specifically addressed.

With this background as to what does and does not constitute part of China's Accession 'package', with its attendant rights and obligations, the rules for interpreting that 'package' can be considered in more detail.

Relevant Vienna Convention provisions

The provisions of the Vienna Convention on the Law of Treaties directly relevant to interpreting China's Accession Protocol are Articles 31 and 32, which read as follows:

Article 31: General rule of interpretation

1. A treaty shall be interpreted in good faith in accordance with the ordinary meaning to be given to the terms of the treaty in their context and in the light of its object and purpose.
2. The context for the purpose of the interpretation of a treaty shall comprise, in addition to the text, including its preamble and annexes:
   (a) any agreement relating to the treaty which was made between all the parties in connexion with the conclusion of the treaty;
   (b) any instrument which was made by one or more parties in connexion with the conclusion of the treaty and accepted by the other parties as an instrument related to the treaty.

3. There shall be taken into account, together with the context:
   (a) any subsequent agreement between the parties regarding the interpre-
       tation of the treaty or the application of its provisions;
   (b) any subsequent practice in the application of the treaty which estab-
       lishes the agreement of the parties regarding its interpretation;
   (c) any relevant rules of international law applicable in the relations
       between the parties.
4. A special meaning shall be given to a term if it is established that the parties
   so intended.

Article 32: Supplementary means of interpretation
Recourse may be had to supplementary means of interpretation, including
the preparatory work of the treaty and the circumstances of its conclusion, in
order to confirm the meaning resulting from the application of Article 31, or
to determine the meaning when the interpretation according to Article 31:

(a) leaves the meaning ambiguous or obscure; or
(b) leads to a result which is manifestly absurd or unreasonable.

The 'textual' approach

The Vienna Convention rules, reflecting customary international law, take
an essentially 'textual' approach to treaty interpretation, focusing primarily
on the treaty text, which is presumed to be the final, authentic and most
reliable expression of the negotiators' intent.[8] Those rules only look beyond
the text in limited circumstances, such as where the text leaves the question
unanswered. The Vienna Convention rules, in other words, seek to discover
the objectively ascertained intention of the parties as manifested in the text
of the agreements, the 'expressed intent' rather than the 'subjective intent'
of the parties.[9]

Maxims and principles not expressly mentioned in the Vienna Convention – 'good faith' aspects of interpretation

WTO Panels and the Appellate Body have relied on several interpretative
'maxims' or 'principles' in interpreting WTO obligations. These are not

---

[8] Ian Sinclair, *The Vienna Convention and the Law of Treaties* (2nd edn, Manchester, 1984), p. 115.
[9] See, for example, 'International Law Commission Commentary on the Draft Vienna Convention', *Yearbook of the International Law Commission*, Vol. II (New York, 1966), p. 220. The 'ILC
Commentary' has often been relied on by the Appellate Body: see, for example, Appellate Body
Report, *US – Gasoline*, p. 23, fn. 45; Appellate Body Report, *Japan – Alcohol*, pp. 11–12.

explicitly referred to in the Vienna Convention, but they have been treated by the Appellate Body and Panels as emerging naturally from those principles explicitly mentioned. In particular, they are generally seen as deriving from the requirement to *interpret* treaties in 'good faith',[10] which represents an interpretative principle, and the substantive customary international law obligation, separately reflected in the Vienna Convention, that 'every treaty in force is binding upon the parties to it and must be *performed* by them in good faith'[11] (emphasis added).

The main maxims and principles relied on in WTO jurisprudence, and potentially relevant to the interpretation of the China Accession Protocol, are:

- *'expressio unius est exclusio alterius'*: this means that because of the relationship of two or more objects or ideas, the explicit indication that a certain situation exists or certain rules apply for one of the objects or ideas implies that the same situation does *not* exist, or the same rules do *not* apply, for the other objects or ideas, about which there is no such indication;[12]
- 'presumption of consistency': this presumes that the choice and use of different words in different places in an agreement are deliberate, and that different words are designed to convey different meanings. The Appellate Body has indicated that a treaty interpreter is not entitled to assume that such usage was merely inadvertent on the part of the negotiators of that agreement;[13]
- 'effectiveness': this provides that 'an interpreter is not free to adopt a reading that would result in reducing whole clauses or paragraphs of a treaty to redundancy or inutility'.[14] It has been expressed most broadly in the WTO context to the effect that it is the duty of any treaty interpreter to read all applicable provisions of a treaty in a way that gives meaning to all of them, harmoniously;[15]

---

[10] Vienna Convention, Art. 31(1).   [11] Ibid., Art. 26.

[12] See, e.g., WTO Panel Report, *United States – Tax Treatment for 'Foreign Sales Corporations'*, WT/DS108/R, adopted (as modified) 20 March 2000, para. 7.118.

[13] See, e.g., WTO Appellate Body Report, *European Communities – Measures Affecting Meat and Meat Products*, WT/DS26/AB/R and WT/DS48/AB/R, adopted 13 February 1998, para. 164, citing WTO Appellate Body Report, *United States – Restrictions on Imports of Cotton and Manmade Fibre Underwear*, WT/DS24/AB/R, adopted (as modified) 25 February 1997, p. 17.

[14] Appellate Body Report, *US – Gasoline*, p. 23.

[15] See, e.g., WTO Appellate Body Report, *Korea – Definitive Safeguard Measure on Imports of Certain Dairy Products*, WT/DS98/AB/R, adopted 12 January 2000, para. 81.

- *'in dubio mitius'*: this is to the effect that it cannot be lightly assumed that sovereign states intended to impose upon themselves the more oner- ous, rather than the less burdensome, obligation.[16] In deference to the sovereignty of states, if the meaning of a term is ambiguous, that meaning is to be preferred which is less onerous to the party assuming an obliga- tion, or which interferes less with the territorial and personal supremacy of a party, or involves fewer general restrictions upon the parties;[17]
- *'abus de droit'*: this provides that an abusive exercise of a state's treaty rights is prohibited and that whenever the assertion of a right 'impinges on the field covered by [a] treaty obligation, it must be exercised bona fide, that is to say, reasonably'.[18] An abusive exercise by a member of its own treaty right thus results in a breach of the treaty rights of the other members and, additionally, in a violation of the treaty obligation of the member so acting;[19] and
- *'lex specialis generalia specialibus non derogant'*: this provides that more specific treaties or provisions generally take precedence over more general treaties or provisions dealing with the same subject-matter. There is a somewhat mixed practice in the WTO on this 'principle'.[20]

Acquiescence and estoppel

There is also increasing reference in WTO jurisprudence to principles of 'acquiescence' and 'estoppel', to the effect that the practice of the two parties to a dispute (or the practice of one with express or implied acceptance by the other) might in certain cases be relevant to determining that dispute between them. This can be the case even where the practice or acquiescence

[16] See, e.g., Appellate Body Report, *EC – Hormones*, para. 165 and fn 154.
[17] Ibid., at fn 154, citing, *inter alia*: Robert Jennings and Arthur Watts (eds.), *Oppenheim's International Law* (9th edn, London, 1992), Vol. I, p. 1278; *Nuclear Tests* case (*Australia* v. *France*) [1974] *ICJ Reports* 253, at 267; *Access of Polish War Vessels to the Port of Danzig* [1931] *PCIJ Reports*, Series A/B, No. 43.
[18] WTO Appellate Body Report, *United States – Import Prohibition of Certain Shrimp and Shrimp Products*, WT/DS58/AB/R, adopted 6 November 1998, para. 158, fn 156.
[19] Ibid., para. 158.
[20] WTO Panel Report, *United States – Tax Treatment for 'Foreign Sales Corporations'*, para. 4.468: 'This principle is not mentioned in the Vienna Convention and its application to the WTO is not without difficulty in the light of the general interpretative note to Annex 1A of the WTO.' More recently, one WTO Panel expressed the view that the Appellate Body in *EC – Bananas* was applying *lex specialis*: Panel Report, *United States – Anti-Dumping Act of 1916 – Complaint by Japan*, WT/DS162/R, adopted 26 September 2000, para. 6.269. The Panel did not, however, address the issue raised by the *US – Foreign Sales Corporations Panel*.

in it is not widespread enough to constitute 'subsequent practice' of WTO members as a group, and is therefore insufficient substantively to affect the interpretation of the WTO agreements generally.[21] Because the principles of acquiescence and estoppel do not affect the general interpretation, they are more correctly regarded as principles of procedure or substantive law than of interpretation, but their operation is closely related to the interpretative task, and therefore needs to be borne in mind.

Most of the principles outlined above, when applied cautiously, are un-controversial, although whether '*in dubio mitius*' and '*abus de droit*' have a legitimate place in WTO jurisprudence can be questioned,[22] and the place of acquiescence and estoppel in WTO jurisprudence is still somewhat uncertain.[23]

A Vienna Convention flowchart

The general WTO approach to interpreting accession protocols and other WTO agreements is diagrammatically expressed in figure 21.1. It should be noted that there is no particular sequence in which aspects of the inter-pretative task must be undertaken; the ordering of the flowchart expresses, instead, the relationships between the different elements of the interpreta-tive task.[24]

Interpretation of China's Accession Protocol: a case study

How the Appellate Body might interpret China's Accession Protocol, in the light of the approaches noted above, can best be analysed by looking at a particular provision in detail. The following analysis is based on the anti-dumping provisions of the Protocol.

Price comparison in anti-dumping cases – 'general' rules and 'special' rules

The Protocol language for price comparability in anti-dumping cases is a direct transposition of the wording from the US–China bilateral accession

---

[21] As noted by the Panel in *Guatemala – Definitive Anti-dumping Measures on Grey Portland Cement from Mexico*, WT/DS156/R, adopted 17 November 2000, paras. 8.23 ff.

[22] Lennard, 'Navigating by the stars', 61–6 and 67–70.

[23] Ibid., 76 ff.   [24] Ibid., 23.

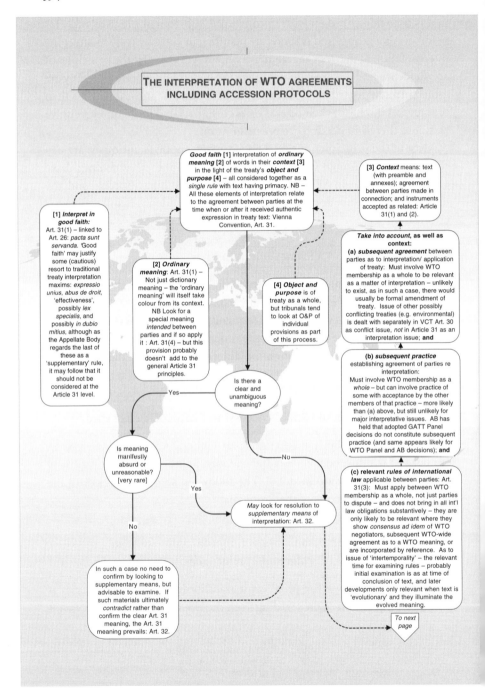

Figure 21.1 The interpretation of WTO agreements including accession protocols.

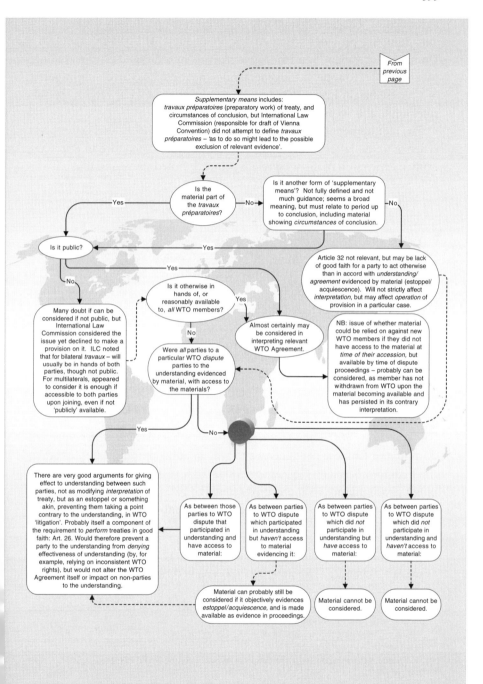

Figure 21.1 (*cont.*)

agreement.[25] The head paragraph to the Protocol provisions dealing with anti-dumping provides[26] that Article VI of the GATT 1994,[27] the Anti-Dumping Agreement[28] and the Agreement on Subsidies and Countervailing Measures[29] are to apply as the general rules in proceedings involving imports of Chinese origin into a WTO member – 'consistent with' certain special rules applicable to price comparability in such cases.

The requirement of 'consistency' with the special rules clearly gives precedence to the latter in the event of a conflict. It is therefore in effect an explicit expression of the *lex specialis* principle noted above and that is itself reflected in Article 1.2 of the WTO Dispute Settlement Understanding. To the extent that the special rules are clear, any potential conflict is resolved in their favour.

Where the special rules do not clearly displace the normally applicable WTO rules, the mirroring aspect of the Accession Protocol comes into play – namely the fact that it provides, positively, for the general WTO rules to apply, in the absence of a conflict with the special rules. That sort of relationship between the special and general rules has the makings of some difficult interpretational decisions in the more 'borderline' cases, even though the supremacy of the former (or special) rules is, in principle, clear.

The special Protocol rules on anti-dumping price methodologies

Under section 15(a) of the Protocol, WTO members dealing with suspected dumping of Chinese products are to use, in anti-dumping cases, either a methodology based on Chinese prices or costs, or else a different methodology, in accordance with specified rules. The rules, which are taken word-for-word from the US–China bilateral agreement on China's accession,[30] are as follows:

> In determining price comparability under Article VI of the GATT 1994 and the Anti-Dumping Agreement, the importing WTO Member shall use either

---

[25] US–China bilateral agreement, previously publicly available at http://www.uschina.org/public – copy held by author.
[26] Section 15, following the wording of domestic US legislation.
[27] *Results of the Uruguay Round*, p. 21.
[28] That is, the Agreement on Implementation of Article VI of the GATT 1994, ibid., p. 168.
[29] Ibid., p. 264.
[30] Sub-paragraph 1 of proposed protocol wording in US–China bilateral agreement.

Chinese prices or costs for the industry under investigation or a methodology that is not based on a strict comparison with domestic prices or costs in China based on the following rules:

(i) If the producers under investigation can clearly show that market economy conditions prevail in the industry producing the like product with regard to the manufacture, production and sale of that product, the importing WTO Member shall use Chinese prices or costs for the industry under investigation in determining price comparability;

(ii) The importing WTO Member may use a methodology that is not based on a strict comparison with domestic prices or costs in China if the producers under investigation cannot clearly show that market economy conditions prevail in the industry producing the like product with regard to manufacture, production and sale of that product.

The special provision in sub-paragraph (ii) will expire after fifteen years, but the whole of section 15(a) may expire before then in certain cases, in relation to particular WTO members. If China is able to establish that it is a market economy either for the relevant industry or sector, or else generally, under the other member's laws, the provisions will then expire either for that industry or sector, or more generally, as applicable. A requirement that the member's national law contains market-economy criteria as of the date of China's accession seems to apply in both cases.[31]

Are there special rules for interpreting anti-dumping provisions?

The Vienna Convention rules on interpretation are representative of customary international law, but, as such, they would yield to specific interpretative rules in a treaty itself. The first issue is therefore whether there are specific rules to the contrary in the terms of China's accession, whether as part of the special terms or under the general WTO agreement provisions.

Generally, this is not the case, and the Vienna Convention rules apply unmodified in the WTO context, in accordance with Article 3.2 of the Dispute Settlement Understanding, but there is a question as to whether Article 17.6 of the Anti-Dumping Agreement modifies this position in respect of anti-dumping actions. It provides that when the matter comes before a Panel for review:

---

[31] Protocol, section 15(d).

(i) in its assessment of the facts of the matter, the panel shall determine whether the authorities' establishment of the facts was proper and whether their evaluation of those facts was unbiased and objective. If the establishment of the facts was proper and the evaluation was unbiased and objective, even though the panel might have reached a different conclusion, the evaluation shall not be overturned;

(ii) the panel shall interpret the relevant provisions of the Agreement in accordance with customary rules of interpretation of public international law. Where the panel finds that a relevant provision of the Agreement admits of more than one permissible interpretation, the panel shall find the authorities' measure to be in conformity with the Agreement if it rests upon one of those permissible interpretations.

The supremacy of the Article 17.6 rules over the normal rules of interpretation, in the event of a conflict, is specifically confirmed by Article 1.2 of the Dispute Settlement Understanding, read with Appendix 2 of that Understanding.

Article 17.6(i) is really dealing with factual determinations, so that it does not bear upon the immediate issue of treaty interpretation. It gives what may be termed a 'margin of deference' to the importing member on review by a Panel of that member's treatment of *factual* issues.[32] That margin of deference is designed 'to prevent a panel from "second-guessing" a determination of a national authority when the establishment of the facts is proper and the evaluation of those facts is unbiased and objective'.[33]

Article 17.6(ii) addresses the treaty interpretation issue directly and, as I have considered its operation elsewhere,[34] it suffices to say that its second sentence, which again gives some margin of deference to the domestic decision, seems only to apply where there are two permissible legal interpretations after a full examination of relevant interpretative materials, in accordance with the first sentence. It forms a 'tie-breaker' when the Vienna Convention rules have been applied but still leave open two permissible interpretations, and it therefore addresses a situation not expressly dealt with in those rules, rather than displacing them.

In effect, then, the normal Vienna Convention rules should apply to antidumping with, in 'administrative review' of an investigating authority's

---

[32] See WTO Appellate Body Report, *Thailand – Anti-dumping Duties on Angles, Shapes and Sections of Iron or Non-alloy Steel and H-Beams from Poland*, WT/DS122/1/AB/R, adopted 5 April 2001, para. 117.

[33] Ibid., para. 117.   [34] Lennard, 'Navigating by the stars', 80 ff.

decision, a special 'tie-breaker rule' giving some deference to the importing member in the event of an ultimate ambiguity, one not resolved by those rules. The tie-breaker does not give complete freedom: the interpretation of the importing Member's authority must be one of the permissible ones left open by a Vienna Convention analysis.

This limitation on the margin of deference would be most consistent with the role of the panels, as expressed in Article 11 of the Dispute Settlement Understanding: 'a panel should make an objective assessment of the matter before it, including an objective assessment of the facts of the case and the applicability of and conformity with the relevant covered agreements...'.

The analysis favoured in this chapter accords with the approach of the Panel in *US – Steel Plate from Korea*,[35] as well as those of the Appellate Body in *Thailand – Steel*[36] and in *European Communities – Bed Linen*.[37] The Appellate Body Report in *US – Steel from Japan* considered the issue in more detail and referred to both its earlier reports in concluding that 'a permissible interpretation is one which is found to be appropriate *after* application of the pertinent rules of the *Vienna Convention*'.[38]

Proving that market conditions prevail

Having established that the Vienna Convention rules still apply to interpreting the anti-dumping provisions, the Protocol wording itself should be examined in that light. The key factor in the choice of methodologies under the Protocol wording is, according to section 15(a)(i), whether producers of the Chinese product under investigation can or cannot 'clearly show that market economy conditions prevail in the industry producing the... product'.

---

[35] WTO Panel Report, *United States – Anti-dumping Measures on Stainless Steel Plate in Coils and Stainless Steel Sheet and Strip from Korea*, WT/DS179/R, adopted 1 February 2001, para. 6.4; cf. WTO Panel Report, *United States – Anti-dumping Duty on Dynamic Random Access Memory Semiconductors (DRAMs) of One Megabit or Above from Korea*, WT/DS99/R, adopted 19 March 1999, para. 6.54, fn. 499.

[36] In *Thailand – Steel*, paras. 125–7, the Appellate Body, while not dealing with the issue in detail, fully supported the Panel's normal application of the Vienna Convention rules in an anti-dumping case, without any suggestion that they were in any significant sense curtailed.

[37] WTO Appellate Body Report, *European Communities – Anti-dumping Duties on Imports of Cotton-type Bed Linen from India*, WT/DS141/AB/R, adopted 12 March 2001, paras. 63–5.

[38] Appellate Body Report, *United States – Anti-dumping Measures on Certain Hot-rolled Steel Products from Japan*, WT/DS184/AB/R, adopted 23 August 2001, para. 60.

Whether or not the subjective intention on the US side (when this provision was first drafted in the US–China bilateral agreement) was to leave completely to the domestic law of the importing country the question of what is necessary to show that market-economy conditions prevail, the real issue for the Appellate Body would be whether a *consensus ad idem* between the parties to the WTO Accession Protocol had been objectively expressed to that effect. If it was not, the question in effect becomes: what *was* the level of obligation upon which the text demonstrates a *consensus ad idem*, even if one or more of the WTO members anticipated that more would be required?

The treaty terms in their context

Applying the Vienna Convention rules, then, the question arises of whether the words 'clearly show' in the Protocol wording may set some *objective standard*, which might possibly be less onerous (for the Chinese producer) than may be provided for in the domestic law and administrative practices of the United States or some other importing WTO member. In such a case, the very existence of those laws or other measures,[39] let alone their application, may therefore breach that member's WTO obligations to China. Alternatively, is the test that of proof that market-economy conditions prevail, under the prevailing domestic law standard of the importing country, *whatever* that standard?

The WTO Appellate Body and Panels regularly look to dictionary meanings, but a dictionary definition of 'show' is of no real assistance in answering this question, because it does not itself indicate what constitutes the thing to be shown. The 'context' of the terms and the 'object and purpose' of the Accession Protocol therefore become highly relevant.

Looking to the immediate context of the Protocol wording, one point stands out. In a case where the domestic law standard is meant to entirely govern an issue, that position is explicitly stated. Section 15(d) of the Protocol wording on anti-dumping, which deals with the duration of the non-market-economy methodologies, states: 'Once China has established, *under the national law of the importing WTO Member*, that it is a market economy...' (emphasis added).

---

[39] See, e.g., the discussion in Appellate Body Report, *United States – Anti-Dumping Act of 1916*, WT/DS136/AB/R–WT/DS162/AB/R, adopted 26 September 2000, paras. 60 ff., and decisions cited therein.

Expressio unius

Looked at through the lens of the maxim *expressio unius est exclusio alterius,* the absence in section 15(a)(i) of the wording used in section 15(d) ('under the national law of the importing WTO Member') suggests, prima facie, the lack of an expressed *consensus ad idem* between parties to the Accession Protocol that the importing member's law is in every respect the reference point as to whether market-economy conditions prevail, for the purposes of section 15(a)(i).

The fact that these words are so closely placed together in a single section (and perhaps also that they are both derived directly from the same US–China bilateral agreement) appears to give special force to such an implication.

Effectiveness

The Appellate Body has relied on more than one interpretative maxim, however, and there is a potential issue of 'effectiveness' here, a reminder that the different maxims relied on by the WTO might sometimes appear to compete, as well as a further caution that they should not be followed blindly or unhesitatingly.[40]

The issue is this – if the domestic law of the importing member does not prevail, what is the appropriate test, and, without one, can the provision be properly regarded as 'effective'? If there was intended to be some objective minimum test, why was it left unstated? The argument would then be that the term must be given the importing member's domestic law meaning to render the text 'effective', as well as to provide some symmetry with section 15(d) on market conditions.

In fact, recognizing some objective minimum standard does not lead to the 'inutility' referred to in *US – Gasoline,* and thereby does not run contrary to an 'effective' reading of the text of section 15(a)(i) *in its context.* Remembering that the Anti-Dumping Agreement is stated by the Protocol to apply in proceedings involving imports of Chinese origin into a WTO Member State consistent with the special rules then elaborated, the Anti-Dumping Agreement is part of the text or context, and its provisions may be highly relevant for interpretation purposes.

---

[40] See, for example, Sinclair, *Vienna Convention,* p. 153.

'Proper' comparisons

While not specifically addressing this question, Article 2.2 of the Anti-Dumping Agreement provides that:

> When, because of the particular market situation . . . such sales do not permit a proper comparison, the margin of dumping shall be determined by comparison with a comparable price of the like product when exported to an appropriate third country provided that this price is representative, or with the cost of production in the country of origin plus a reasonable amount for administrative, selling and any other costs and for profits.

In this 'fall-back' rule for issues not dealt with in the special rules, there is, then, a similarly broad (or perhaps even broader) concept of whether the market situation prevents a 'proper comparison', a concept that is not dealt with in any detail by the agreements.[41] It was derived from the GATT Tokyo Round Anti-Dumping Code,[42] but neither the Code and its jurisprudence nor the Uruguay Round negotiating documents throws much light upon its meaning. While there is some vagueness about when a comparison is 'proper', it appears to set a minimum objective standard, so that the Working Party Report paragraphs picked up in the Accession Protocol do not render, specifically or by necessary implication, any domestic law, by its very nature, a 'proper comparison'.

In dubio mitius

As noted above, the Appellate Body in *EC – Hormones* has applied the interpretative principle of *in dubio mitius* as a 'supplementary means of interpretation'. Apart from the problematic issue of the status of *in dubio mitius* in modern treaty interpretation practice,[43] there are particular issues about how this principle applies to an agreement such as an Accession Protocol, which is inherently one-sided in that it imposes special burdens on one side (China) as the 'price of admission' to the WTO. It is not

---

[41] The footnote to this provision in the WTO texts addresses cases where low sales volumes prevent a proper comparison, but the text itself contemplates other cases where the 'particular market situation' may prevent a 'proper comparison', revealing a broad meaning for the term.

[42] Kenneth R. Simmonds and Brian H. W. Hill, *Law and Practice Under the GATT* (New York, 1994), Vol. I, p. 33; the Tokyo Round Anti-Dumping Code is also available at http://www.worldtradelaw.net/tokyoround/antidumpingcode.pdf.

[43] I have considered this elsewhere: Lennard, 'Navigating by the stars', 61 ff.

completely one-sided, of course; China gains the rights of a WTO member, but only subject to the specific modifications provided for in the Accession Protocol, and the special terms of the China Protocol are almost always less advantageous to China than if it had been an original member of the WTO.

It can therefore be argued that too blindly following maxims such as *in dubio mitius*, and construing ambiguities in favour of the WTO aspirant, could dilute the accession requirements and inadvertently reduce the 'price of admission' to the WTO.

Let us assume that the principle of *in dubio mitius* is nevertheless applied. If that is the case, one might assert that any doubt should in fact be construed in favour of China's position, since requiring an *objective* minimum standard of whether market conditions apply is the interpretation least intrusive on China's sovereignty. It would not leave the decision on a key and public economic evaluation completely up to the laws of another country, unconstrained by the requirement that it be objectively based.

The *in dubio mitius* principle may actually support the importing member's position, however. This would be on the basis that while *in dubio mitius* seeks an outcome that least intrudes upon the sovereignty of a *country*, it is the interest of a producer, not China as a country, that is directly affected here. Further, the importing member's sovereignty might itself be intruded on by an objective standard being overlaid on its domestic legislation when dealing with Chinese producers. Ultimately, the principle of *in dubio mitius* appears too problematical to make a major contribution on interpreting this aspect of the Protocol.

Object and purpose

The Vienna Convention rules require the text at issue to be examined in its context and in the light of the treaty's object and purpose. The Appellate Body in *Japan – Alcohol* noted that: 'the treaty's "object and purpose" is to be referred to in determining the meaning of the "terms of the treaty" and not as an independent basis for interpretation'.[44] It was therefore clearly rejecting a teleological approach to interpretation.

---

[44] Appellate Body Report, *Japan – Alcohol*, p. 12, fn 20.

The 'object and purpose', in the case considered here, seems to add nothing of substance, because while the object and purpose of the special provisions in section 15 of the Accession Protocol is to provide importing members greater latitude than normal, it does not indicate the limits, if any, of such latitude. On the other hand the underlying object and purpose of the Anti-Dumping Agreement gives little illumination as to what constitutes a 'proper comparison', much less what is 'consistent with' the special Accession Protocol provisions.

Looking at these primary materials, then, it seems likely that if a Chinese producer can objectively demonstrate that the market situation is such as to allow a 'proper comparison' of prices on normal WTO rules, yet the domestic law of an importing country nevertheless refuses to treat the market-economy status as proven, China's WTO rights, even as modified by the Protocol, have been breached by the importing member.

The more obvious aspects of 'context' – the rest of the Accession Protocol and the other WTO agreements – appear at least consistent with this reading, but an important issue will be whether such aspects of the Working Party Report cast any further light on the issue.

The Working Party Report as part of the context

There are two potentially relevant aspects of the Working Party Report. The first is those provisions of the Report that are specifically incorporated into the Protocol and therefore into the WTO agreements as they apply in relation to China's membership. They would form part of the relevant text of the Accession Protocol in any WTO dispute.

The Working Party Report is quite detailed in dealing with non-market-economy methodologies. It provides, at paragraphs 150–1, as already noted, a *modus operandi* designed to promote a fair hearing and a transparent procedure when applying such a methodology to Chinese imports.[45] However, as paragraphs 150–1 are not commitments by China, they are not picked up in the Protocol. These procedural 'requirements' therefore do not form part of the text of the China Accession Protocol (as the adopted provisions do) and at most may form part of the context. This possible contextual relevance forms the second aspect of the Working Party Report's potential relevance.

[45] At paras. 150–1.

Related agreements and instruments

The first type of contextual material referred to under the Vienna Convention rules is 'any agreement relating to the treaty which was made between all the parties in connexion with the conclusion of the treaty'.[46] The second is 'any instrument which was made by one or more parties in connexion with the conclusion of the treaty and accepted by the other parties as an instrument related to the treaty'.[47] In *United States – Copyright Act*, the Panel gave rare WTO consideration to these aspects of Article 31, when it said:[48]

> It is essential that the agreement or instrument should be related to the treaty. It must be concerned with the substance of the treaty and clarify certain concepts in the treaty or limit its field of application. It must equally be drawn up on the occasion of the conclusion of the treaty.

The Panel also expressed the view that 'uncontested interpretations given at a conference, e.g., by a chairman of a drafting committee, may constitute an "agreement" forming part of the "context" '.[49] While the latter may be doubted,[50] the Panel's very inclusive approach suggests that in the WTO the Working Party Report would probably be considered as part of the 'context' of the Protocol; most likely as an 'instrument' accepted by all WTO members as bearing on the Protocol terms, rather than as an 'agreement' between all WTO members, and of course it was in any case made 'in connexion with the conclusion of the treaty'. Arguably it might also be 'any agreement… made between all parties' if one considers the Working Party membership as agents or delegates of the whole body of WTO membership, as the wording of the Report sometimes suggests.[51]

Matters to be taken into account, together with the context

Article 31(3) of the Vienna Convention specifically requires that reference be made to certain matters, where they exist, even though they are not treated as part of the text or context. These are: (a) subsequent agreements

---

[46] Vienna Convention, Art. 31(2)(a).   [47] Ibid., Art. 31(2)(b).

[48] WTO Panel Report, *United States – Section 110 (5) of the US Copyright Act*, WT/DS160/R, adopted 27 July 2000, paras. 6.45 ff.

[49] Ibid., para. 6.46.   [50] Lennard, 'Navigating by the stars', 25.

[51] Such as at para. 246 of the Working Party Report: 'Members of the Working Party confirmed that in implementing the provisions on market disruption, WTO Members would…'.

between the parties on interpretation or application, (b) subsequent practice establishing an agreement on interpretation between the parties and
(c) relevant rules of international law applicable between the parties.

No part of the Working Party Report could constitute a 'subsequent'
agreement or practice – not being subsequent to the Protocol itself. If abided
by, a *modus operandi* indicated in the Report could itself develop into subsequent practice, however. Such paragraphs are most unlikely to be regarded
as representing 'relevant rules of international law applicable in the relations
between the parties', however. Paragraph 151 (as to the *modus operandi* that
'should' be followed) would, in particular, appear to lack the inherently
binding character that is needed before the *Nuclear Tests* cases approach to
unilateral declarations made by states could apply.[52]

Supplementary means

The text of the Protocol is nevertheless sufficiently ambiguous to allow
consideration of any 'supplementary means' of interpretation, and such
supplementary means could be decisive. In any case, they can always be
used to test the reading given under Article 31. The only difficulty would
be if they contradicted a clear Article 31 reading, in which case they would
have to be rejected as being less 'authentic' than the clear reading under
Article 31.[53]

The 'fair' comparison

In summary, no relevant materials appear likely to displace the implication
arising from the ordinary meaning of the terms of the Accession Protocol
in their context, interpreted in the light of relevant treaty objects and
purposes – namely, that there is some objective standard as to what must be
proven in 'clearly showing' that market conditions prevail, rather than the
matter being left entirely to the importing member's domestic law. Such a
standard would reflect the basic requirements of the Anti-Dumping Agreement that where a 'proper' or 'strict' comparison of Chinese prices or costs
and prices or costs in the importing member is not possible, there should

---

[52] *Nuclear Tests* case (*Australia* v. *France*), at 267; *New Zealand* v. *France* [1974] *ICJ Reports* 457,
at 472.
[53] Art. 32(a). They could override a clear meaning if that was manifestly absurd or unreasonable
(Art. 32(b)), but there is no possibility of such a rare situation occurring here.

nevertheless be a 'fair' comparison under the methodologies allowed by section 15(a) of the Accession Protocol.

As its opening words indicate, section 15(a) is about 'determining price comparability' and in *EC – Bed Linen*[54] the Appellate Body relied on the concept of a 'fair comparison' to inform, as part of the context, the meaning of 'comparable' in Article 2.4 of the WTO Anti-Dumping Agreement, noting that:

> Article 2.4 sets forth a general obligation to make a 'fair comparison' between export price and normal value. This is a general obligation that, in our view, informs all of Article 2, but applies, in particular, to Article 2.4.2 which is specifically made 'subject to the provisions governing fair comparison in [Article 2.4]'. [Original parenthesis]

The GATT Panel in *United States – Fresh and Chilled Atlantic Salmon from Norway*[55] considered that:

> . . . it was possible to interpret the first sentence [of Article 2.6 of the Anti-Dumping Code] to reflect a requirement of a 'fair comparison' which applied generally to any aspect of the comparison of normal values and export prices. The Panel considered, however, that this interpretation of Article 2.6 would not permit a conclusion that a method whereby average normal values were compared to individual export prices was per se inconsistent with Article 2.6. Rather, the 'fairness' of such a method would have to be evaluated in the light of the circumstances of each case.

This would suggest that the overall fairness of the comparison can be scrutinized, on a case-by-case basis, the matter not depending entirely on the requirements of the importing member's domestic law.

'Strict' comparison not required

Further support for such a minimum objective standard can be found in the fact that section 15(a)(ii) of the Accession Protocol provides that 'the importing WTO member may use a methodology that is *not based on a strict*

---

[54] *EC – Bed Linen*, para. 59.

[55] GATT Panel Report, *United States – Imposition of Anti-dumping duties on Imports of Fresh and Chilled Atlantic Salmon from Norway*, ADP/87, adopted by the Committee on Anti-Dumping Practices, 27 April 1994, para. 481. See also GATT Panel Report, *European Commission – Anti-dumping Duties on Audio Tapes in Cassettes Originating in Japan*, ADP/136, circulated 28 April 1995 but unadopted, para. 352.

comparison with domestic prices or costs in China' (emphasis added) if the producers under investigation cannot clearly show that market-economy conditions prevail in a specified situation.

An examination of dictionary meanings shows that 'strict' when used in this sense usually means something like 'rigid' or 'absolute',[56] and the word in its context does seem to have some function in expressing that concept. Here the provision, in stating that a 'strict' comparison is not required, seems to 'loosen the reins' on the importing country, but not totally to throw those reins away. When 'strict' compliance is said to be unnecessary, it is generally meant to imply that 'basic' compliance is still obligatory.

The wording therefore seems to affirm that in not requiring a 'strict comparison' it nevertheless requires something that objectively passes the test as a genuine, good-faith, comparison – or a 'fair comparison', to use the language of the Anti-Dumping Agreement.

To take account of this when interpreting the Protocol wording is in accord with the good-faith approach to treaty interpretation and the related 'effectiveness' principle, consistent with two points. First, the rules relating to China's participation in the WTO will be the normal WTO anti-dumping rules 'consistent with' the special rules provided in the Protocol language and, secondly, the more ambiguously the special rules are expressed, the more likely it would be that a Panel or the Appellate Body will have recourse to the general rules in the linked agreements, namely Article VI of the GATT 1994 and the Anti-Dumping Agreement.

Assume that under section 15(a) of the Protocol, a producer fails to show that market-economy conditions apply, so that a methodology not involving a strict comparison is allowed. In such a case there is much to be said for the view that the Accession Protocol, when read in accordance with the Vienna Convention rules, requires that the United States, or any other WTO member, must base its assessment on what objectively (in the circumstances of the particular case) constitutes a comparable and representative price of the like product when exported to an appropriate third country. Alternatively, it may look to the objectively ascertained cost of production in the

---

[56] 'Of correspondence, agreement, or connexion between facts, ideas etc: Close, exactly fitting... With defining word: restricted to the exact use or definition indicated by the word... Of a law, ordinance, etc or its execution: Stringent and rigorous in its demands or provisions, allowing no evasion... Of a quality or condition, an attitude or line of action: Maintained to the full, admitting no deviation or abatement; absolute, entire, complete, perfect': *The Compact Oxford English Dictionary* (2nd edn, Oxford, 1991).

country of origin plus a reasonable amount for administrative, selling and any other costs and for profits.

Beyond that, there is obviously a great deal of latitude given to the domestic law of an importing member, although it is unclear whether, if a WTO member did not apply the *modus operandi* outlined in paragraph 151 of the Protocol, that, *by itself, and apart from the issue of whether there was a fair comparison*, would have any practical effect in a WTO dispute proceeding. To find that it did so would probably require some recourse to the concept of '*abus de droit*' sometimes referred to in WTO jurisprudence and noted above, or to the more general good-faith aspects of treaty application and interpretation. The exact wording of the *modus operandi* in paragraph 151 of the Protocol first needs to be closely examined in this light, however.

'*Would*' versus '*should*' – the wording of the modus operandi

Paragraph 151 of the Working Party Report states that in implementing section 15(a)(ii) of the Protocol, WTO members 'would' (which is generally used in international practice for the language of obligation) 'comply with the following', but then uses the term 'should' (which is *not* normally used for the language of obligation, and usually reflects something more in the nature of an aspiration) when referring to adoption of the specific *modus operandi* provided for.

A WTO member not 'complying' with the *modus operandi* provided for in paragraph 151 would therefore probably argue that it does not comprise an interpretational gloss on section 15(a)(ii) of the Protocol, but rather represents merely a statement of the way a member 'should', but not necessarily *must*, 'implement' the section.

Such a member could note that, generally, in an agreement between countries that mixes the language of obligation and language of aspiration as to a particular obligation, the 'lowest common denominator' (the non-binding language of aspiration, rather than the language of obligation) will be the operative language in practical terms. A contrast (in *expressio unius* terms) can be made to the confirmation by the Working Party of what WTO members would do in respect of market disruption.[57] That is expressed, even as to the specifics, in the language of what 'would' be

---

[57] At paras. 246 ff. of the Report.

done, although of course the Protocol does not specifically pick up even that *modus operandi* as a treaty obligation towards China.

Against such an approach, the failure to implement section 15(a)(ii) in a manner consistent with such a publicly expressed position, could be regarded as contrary to the 'good faith' interpretation (so often stressed by the Appellate Body) of the provision. Whatever may be thought of the Appellate Body's legal basis for relying upon the principle of '*abus de droit*', there would appear to be clear grounds for China to argue that a failure to operate in accordance with the agreed and published *modus operandi* would clearly be contrary to the application of that principle as set out by the Appellate Body in the *United States – Shrimp* Report.[58]

In a non-violation complaint case, such 'legitimate expectations' of China may even have a formal legal significance, since the Appellate Body Report in *EC – Computer Equipment*, when concluding that legitimate expectations could only ever be relevant in relation to a non-violation complaint, thereby recognized their potential significance in such cases.[59]

Conclusion on the nature of the required comparison

Assuming there is nothing in the supplementary means to interpretation, which can be referred to according to the Vienna Convention, that can be relied on to the contrary, the best 'textual' reading of the Protocol provisions seems to be that section 15(a)(ii) requires a genuine and good-faith comparison, even though it need not be a strict or exact comparison. The importing member's domestic law will need to meet that requirement. Once the objective standard is set, the issue is whether the test has been met on the facts of a particular case.

This takes us back to Article 17.6(i) of the Anti-Dumping Agreement and the (limited) margin of deference on factual issues. The investigating authority would be expected to apply the correct legal test, and under that test its factual conclusions would still need to be such that an unbiased and objective investigating authority, evaluating that evidence, could properly have determined that sufficient evidence of price comparability existed.[60]

[58] Appellate Body Report, *US – Shrimp*, para. 158.
[59] WTO Appellate Body Report, *European Communities – Customs Classification of Certain Computer Equipment*, WT/DS62/AB/R, WT/DS67/AB/R, WT/DS68/AB/R, adopted 22 June 1998, para. 80.
[60] Appellate Body Report, *Thailand – Steel*, para. 117.

Relevance of bilateral antecedents to accession provisions?

While the terms of China's Accession Protocol, including the attached Schedules, are the products of a multilateral process and must be read in that light, there is an issue as to what extent the Protocol's bilateral antecedents, such as the US–China bilateral agreement and the European Union–China bilateral agreement, might be considered in a WTO dispute.[61]

A treaty between state A and state B, even if it forms the basis of state A's treaty with state C, does not for that reason form part of the *travaux préparatoires* of the later treaty.[62] It is possible that the existence of the former treaty may sometimes be taken into account in interpreting that later treaty where the third state was aware of it,[63] but if that occurred, it should only be in extremely rare cases, because of the Vienna Convention rule against two states binding a third state without its consent.[64]

There is even less likelihood that the *travaux* of the US–China bilateral agreement would become *generally* relevant to interpretation of China's Accession Protocol; it would only become relevant if picked up in the *travaux* to the Accession Protocol, and its entire relevance would then solely be by virtue of that incorporation or restatement.

It does seem possible, however, that the Appellate Body might take account of such bilateral *travaux* in proceedings between parties to the *consensus ad idem* that may be expressed by the *travaux* – not as being directly relevant to the meaning of the Accession Protocol itself, but as denying China or the United States, for example, from taking a point, in disputes between them, that contradicts that consensus, even if the view taken represents the accepted interpretation applicable between WTO members generally.[65] This can be seen as a form of estoppel and an expression of the good faith required in interpreting and implementing treaties.

The WTO Panel in *EC – Asbestos*[66] restated the requirements for an estoppel, but also indicated the fairly narrow range of operation in practice in

---

[61] Lennard, 'Navigating by the stars', 48.

[62] Jennings and Watts (eds.), *Oppenheim's International Law*, p. 1278, fn 14.

[63] Ibid., citing *Italy – United States Air Transport Arbitration* [1965] *ILR* 45, at 393, 417.

[64] Vienna Convention, Arts. 34 and 35.

[65] See, e.g., Lennard, 'Navigating by the stars', 76 ff; WTO Appellate Body Report, *United States – Tax Treatment for Foreign Sales Corporations*, WT/DS108/AB/R, adopted 20 March 2000, para. 165.

[66] WTO Panel Report, *European Communities – Measures Affecting Asbestos and Asbestos-containing Products*, WT/DS135/R, adopted (as modified) 5 April 2001, para. 8.60. The matter was not addressed in the Appellate Body Report, WT/DS135/AB/R, adopted 5 April 2001.

denying that a notification to the Committee on Technical Barriers to Trade could form the basis of an estoppel.[67] Estoppel may still be a possibility, however, for agreements with such a distinct bilateral aspect as accession protocols – where the two parties to the bilateral agreement are in dispute on the multilateral agreement. Such concepts of acquiescence and estoppel can take genuine account of the special characteristics of the bilateral international law relationship between disputing countries, without modifying the underlying WTO rights and obligations operating as between members generally, *as* WTO members.

Where the multilateral agreement picks up the bilateral wording exactly, as in the current case, there might be a special importance in recognizing that bilateral consensus, but the Appellate Body would have to assure itself that it was not superseded by the multilateral consensus (which would be the almost inevitable conclusion if there was a clear consensus to the contrary in the Accession Working Party Report) or had not simply lapsed. Any such estoppel would not operate against other WTO members, presumably even those joining a dispute between the two members subject to the bilateral agreement and the 'side-consensus'.

Conclusion

The rules applicable to interpreting China's Accession Protocol are those that apply to the WTO agreements generally, and are in turn reflections of customary international law rules of interpretation. They are essentially focused on the text of the Protocol itself, in its context, including reference to other relevant WTO agreements, and to those aspects of the Working Party Report picked up in the accession terms.

As the anti-dumping case study illustrates, this can make for some delicate and nuanced judgements, which will not always reflect the subjective understanding of some negotiators. However, in seeking the *consensus ad idem* as objectively expressed in the Protocol text, the interpretative quest can reveal a meaning of deeper significance to those not participating in the negotiations: to a wider constituency, distant in time. This may provide a clearer and more enduring snapshot of what the Protocol achieves than the one that holds in the memories of individual negotiators.

---

[67] At para. 8.60. This was expressed to be on the basis that they are made for reasons of transparency, and are recognized as not having legal effects.

22

WTO dispute settlement and sub-national entities in China

RAVI P. KEWALRAM

Introduction

The focus of this chapter is on China's WTO obligations with regard to the activities of its sub-national entities. In particular, the chapter examines whether the WTO Agreement requires China to remove inconsistent sub-national measures, or whether China's obligation stops at taking available 'reasonable measures' to ensure compliance. If the latter is correct, the chapter provides an opinion as to what would constitute 'reasonable measures'.

China's sub-national entities – why are they relevant?

In the process of acceding to the WTO, and in its economic reforms until this point, China has undergone a significant liberalization process. However, given the scale of the change taking place, it may be that not all parts of China reach the end-goal at the same time.

Clearly, the Chinese central government will seek to implement China's WTO obligations in a uniform manner across the nation, and intends to fulfil its obligations in good faith.[1] This chapter does not question China's commitment to act in good faith. Rather, it seeks precisely to define China's

The views expressed in this chapter are the author's and do not necessarily reflect the view of the government of Australia or the Department of Foreign Affairs and Trade. The author wishes to thank John Stroop, Philippa Kelly, Joan Hird, Damien Miller and the team in the DFAT Library for access to their written work, helpful suggestions and/or research assistance, but is solely responsible for any errors or omissions.

[1] An example of this intent can be found in the Report of the Working Party on the Accession of China (WT/ACC/CHN/49), para. 67, where the representative from China is said to have noted that China has consistently performed its international obligations and would do so with regard to WTO obligations as well.

obligations with regard to sub-national entities, and what the legal consequences of not being able to meet these obligations would be, from a WTO
perspective.

A constitutional construction

According to the Constitution of the People's Republic of China, China is
a 'unitary, multinational' state.[2] Article 30 notes that the administrative
division of China consists of provinces, autonomous regions and municipalities directly under the central government.

Article 2 of the Constitution provides for both the National People's
Congress and local people's congresses. However, the legislative power of
the state, according to Article 58, resides in the National People's Congress
and its Standing Committee.[3]

The State Council, by virtue of Article 85, is the highest level of the state
administration. Local governments at the provincial, city and county levels
can issue local regulations and rules within their respective constitutional
powers and functions with application at that local level.[4] However, the
National People's Congress and its Standing Committee have the power to
annul administrative or local regulations that contradict the Chinese Constitution, laws and administrative regulations.[5] In any case, sub-national
governments do not, according to the Chinese government, have autonomous authority over issues of trade policy to the extent these are related to
the WTO Agreement.[6]

Accession to the WTO

The WTO Secretariat has noted that the entire package of Report, Protocol
of Accession and Schedules of Concessions and Commitments in Goods and
Services constitute the conditions under which the acceding government
is permitted to join the WTO Agreement.[7] But what if the Protocol and
pre-existing terms of the WTO Agreement are in conflict? To answer this,
it should first be noted that the Protocol becomes an integral part of the
WTO Agreement. Further, the Appellate Body has noted that the WTO

---

[2] http://www.qis.net/chinalaw/prccon5.htm.
[3] See Qingjian Kong, chapter 9, above, for a description of the Chinese legal system.
[4] Working Party Report, para. 74.   [5] Ibid., para. 66.   [6] Ibid., para. 70.
[7] http://www.wto.org/english/thewto_e/acc_e/tn_4accprocess_d_e.htm.

Agreement is a single treaty instrument – accepted by WTO members as a 'single undertaking'.[8]

If there is a conflict, whereby the Protocol states that a particular commitment is to apply as opposed to the relevant provision in the pre-existing WTO Agreement, the terms of the Protocol prevail. This flows from Article XII of the Marrakesh Agreement Establishing the WTO, which states that new members accede on terms to be agreed between that member and the WTO – obviously, such terms can extend or derogate from pre-existing WTO obligations which are amenable to extensions or derogations.[9]

This approach is also consistent with the various conflict rules contained in the WTO Agreement where a rule for an issue that is specifically addressed prevails over a rule in general terms. For example, the 'General interpretative note' on Annex 1A to the WTO Agreement provides that where there is conflict between the GATT 1994 and a provision of another agreement in Annex 1A, the provision of the latter prevails. Similarly, Article 1.2 of the Understanding on Rules and Procedures Governing the Settlement of Disputes (DSU) states that the rules and procedures in that agreement apply subject to special or additional rules contained in the covered agreements.

Consequently, applying this approach: the Protocol is the specific agreement relating to the acceding country, and where it cannot be read consistently with other parts of the WTO Agreement, either by design or inadvertently, the terms of the Protocol prevail.

China's Protocol of Accession

In China's Protocol of Accession, China has committed that its WTO obligations will be applied uniformly across China, and the Working Party has taken 'note' of this.[10] Further, the Chinese government's commitment includes not just ensuring that local rules and regulations are WTO consistent, but also local measures.[11] With the use of the word 'measures', the

---

[8] WTO Appellate Body Report, *Brazil – Measures Affecting Desiccated Coconut*, WT/DS22/AB/R, 21 February 1997; see text after footnote 15 of the Report. See also WTO Appellate Body Report, *Argentina – Safeguard Measures on Imports of Footwear*, WT/DS121/AB/R, 14 December 1999, para. 81.

[9] Note that according to Article XVI:5 of the Marrakesh Agreement Establishing the World Trade Organization, no reservations may be made in respect of any provision of the Marrakesh Agreement itself. Reservations to any of the agreements annexed to the Marrakesh Agreement can only be to the extent provided for in those annexed agreements.

[10] Working Party Report, para. 73.   [11] Ibid., para. 70.

commitment is therefore not just that the rules will be consistent with China's obligations, but that all activities taken under those rules or related to them will be consistent. China has also committed to setting up a mechanism whereby the central authorities can be alerted to any non-uniform application of China's trade regime.[12]

The WTO agreements

In addition to the text in the Protocol, a WTO member's obligations with regard to sub-national entities are addressed by a number of WTO provisions. For example, Article XXIV:12 of the GATT requires that each member 'take such reasonable measures as may be available to it' to ensure observance with the Agreement of all levels of government within that member. The General Agreement on Trade in Services (Article I:3), the Understanding on Rules and Procedures Governing the Settlement of Disputes (Article 22.9) and the Agreement on Sanitary and Phytosanitary Measures (Article 13) have similar references, as do a range of the multilateral trade agreements.[13]

These provisions demonstrate that there is some textual variety in the way that this issue is dealt with in the agreements, which may have been partly a result of the manner in which the separate agreements were negotiated. Nevertheless, the provisions support the following statements:

- China bears responsibility in WTO terms for the trade-related measures of its sub-national entities – this means that it bears the cost for non-compliance, if any.[14]
- In some cases, for example the SPS Agreement, China has to take positive steps to support compliance with the relevant agreement by the sub-national entity.

Further, there is one common thread: where the measure is not a national measure, a WTO member is to take such 'reasonable measures as may be available' to the national government to ensure compliance with its

---

[12] Ibid., para. 75.

[13] See, for example, paragraph 3, Annex 3 of the Agreement on Agriculture; Article 3 of the Agreement on Technical Barriers to Trade; Article 1 (definition of subsidy includes contribution by a government or any public body) and paragraph 6 of Annex IV of the Agreement on Subsidies and Countervailing Measures.

[14] In WTO terms, and following a finding of inconsistency, Article 22 of the DSU would apply. This envisages compensation provided by China to the WTO members that have successfully challenged the sub-national measure, or the suspension of concessions extended to China by these members. Compensation or suspension of concessions are meant to be temporary measures.

WTO obligations. The obligation is *not* that a member must remove a sub-national measure found to be inconsistent with that member's WTO obligations, but to try to seek its removal.

Given that China is not a federal system, does it have to remove an inconsistent measure, or does it have to take reasonable measures to seek the removal of the measure? If the latter is correct, what would a potential WTO dispute settlement panel assess as reasonable measures in the context of the Chinese system?

GATT / WTO jurisprudence

Paragraph 12 of Article XXIV of the GATT 1947 was clearly a carefully worded compromise between federal and unitary GATT Contracting Parties, and has been interpreted in a manner reflecting that compromise.[15] For example, the Panel in the (unadopted) 1985 report on *Canada – Measures Affecting the Sale of Gold Coins*[16] noted that Article XXIV:12 granted a special right to federal states not granted to unitary states.[17] This, in the Panel's opinion, meant that Article XXIV:12 applied to federal states, but that it limited the obligations with regard to securing implementation.

Subsequent GATT panels have followed this approach by applying GATT provisions to the sub-national measures at issue, but distinguishing this from the obligation of the national government to bring the measure into conformity.[18] One of these reports notes from the drafting history of Article XXIV:12 that it was meant to apply to measures outside the constitutional powers of the central government.[19]

---

[15] WTO, *Guide to GATT Law and Practice* (Geneva, 1995), pp. 830–8.

[16] GATT Document L/5863 (unadopted, dated 17 September 1985) extracted in relevant part in WTO, *Guide to GATT Law and Practice*, pp. 830–1.

[17] Note that unadopted panels have no legal status in the WTO but can provide useful guidance to the work of panels: WTO Appellate Body Report, *Japan – Taxes on Alcoholic Beverages*, WT/DS8/AB/R, at text around fn 30.

[18] GATT Panel Report, *Canada – Import, Distribution and Sale of Alcoholic Drinks by Canadian Provincial Marketing Agencies*, 35S/37, adopted 22 March 1988; GATT Panel Report, *Canada – Import, Distribution and Sale of Certain Alcoholic Drinks by Provincial Marketing Agencies* 39S/27, adopted 18 February 1992; GATT Panel Report, *United States – Measures Affecting Alcoholic and Malt Beverages*, 39S/206, adopted 19 June 1992.

[19] GATT Panel Report, *United States – Alcoholic and Malt Beverages*, para. 5.79. No formal negotiating history has been issued for the WTO agreements: see the US arguments as reported by the WTO Panel in *United States – Section 301–310 of the Trade Act of 1974*, WT/DS152/R, paras. 4.450–4.451.

Perhaps reflecting some of these developments, paragraph 13 of the Understanding on the Interpretation of Article XXIV of the General Agreement on Tariffs and Trade 1994 notes that each member is fully[20] responsible, but then repeats the obligation as requiring members to take 'reasonable measures as may be available'.

In *Australia – Measures Affecting Importation of Salmon – Recourse to Article 21.5 by Canada*, with regard to certain actions by the Australian state of Tasmania, the Panel concluded that the Tasmanian measures fall under the responsibility of Australia when it comes to observance of SPS obligations.[21] However, the Panel concluded that Canada had not substantiated a claim under Article 13 of the SPS Agreement and that it therefore did not have to decide whether Australia met this obligation. It is submitted that the Article 21.5 Panel in *Australia – Salmon* maintained the distinction between the responsibility for a sub-national measure, as opposed to the obligation to address the measure.

However, in none of the provisions cited above from the GATT 1994, the SPS Agreement, the GATS or the DSU is it apparent from the *text* of those provisions that they are limited in application to federal WTO members only. For example, the obligation in Article 13 of the SPS Agreement quite clearly applies to all WTO members regardless of constitutional divisions by virtue of its reference to non-governmental entities within members. All members, federal and unitary, can have non-governmental entities that play a role in that member's activities related to SPS issues.

Similarly, it is submitted that the use of the word 'authorities' in the phrase 'regional or local governments or authorities' suggests that these provisions are meant to include all entities within a member which have the effective power to regulate, control or supervise individuals through the exercise of lawful authority.[22] It is irrelevant whether such lawful authority derives from constitutional divisions of power, or through constitutionally valid delegation of authority.

Even though China is not a federal state with a division of powers allocated by its constitution, measures put in place by the administrative

---

[20] The use of the word 'fully' engendered some debate during the Uruguay Round negotiations, with some arguing that it did not add anything to the word 'responsible'. See MTN.GNG/NG7/22, para. 14.

[21] WT/DS18/RW, para. 7.13.

[22] This analysis borrows from the WTO Appellate Body's reasoning in *Canada – Measures Affecting the Importation of Milk and the Exportation of Dairy Products*, WT/DS103/AB/R.

divisions of provinces, special administrative regions or municipalities are legally valid within China. Therefore, for the purposes of the WTO Agreement, measures by these administrative divisions of China are measures of 'regional or local governments or authorities', as opposed to measures of the central government.

This may be a controversial conclusion given that Article XXIV:12 of the GATT 1947 was seen as the 'federal' clause.[23] However, even though it may have been the case for the equivalent provision in the GATT 1947, there is nothing in the text of the current agreements to suggest that the provisions discussed above are applicable only to federal systems.[24] However, because it is not a federal state by a constitutional division of powers, the 'reasonable measures as may be available' to it may be different in China's case, as compared to that of a federal state.

'Reasonable measures as may be available'

Again, pre-WTO GATT cases are useful in providing a framework for what might constitute 'reasonable measures'. These cases are useful notwithstanding they were predicated on Article XXIV:12 of the GATT applying only to federal states.

The first point to note from these decisions is that the Contracting Party within which the inconsistent measure had taken place did not have the sole authority to judge whether all reasonable measures had been taken. Rather, the Contracting Party in question had to demonstrate to the GATT 1947 Contracting Parties that it had taken all reasonable measures, and it would then be up to the Contracting Parties to decide whether that member had met its obligations under Article XXIV:12.[25]

---

[23] WTO, *Guide to GATT Law and Practice*, p. 830.

[24] There is no formal negotiating history for the WTO Agreement (for discussion on this point, see the Panel Report on *United States – Sections 301–310 of the Trade Act of 1974*, paras. 4.450–4.451). However, it is clear from discussions around the time of the Uruguay Round negotiations that this conclusion accords with the views of some of the negotiators at that time. See, for example, the views attributed to Canada in 'Negotiating Group on GATT Articles: Note on Meeting of 1, 15, and 19 October 1990', MTN.GNG.NG7/22, para. 13. See also MTN.GNG/NG7/20, para. 15. Further, these discussions make clear that Article XXIV:12 also applies to supranational organizations such as (at that time) the EEC. See the reference to Canada's comment above, and also the chairman's comment at para. 25 confirming this.

[25] GATT Panel Report, *Canada – Import, Distribution and Sale of Alcoholic Drinks by Canadian Provincial Marketing Agencies*, 35S/37, adopted 22 March 1988, para. 4.35.

Secondly, to demonstrate that a Contracting Party has taken all reasonable measures, it would have to show that it had 'made a serious, persistent and convincing effort to secure compliance' with the provisions of the General Agreement.[26]

Thirdly, it would be harder to avoid a Contracting Party's obligations when GATT law is part of the federal law of the Contracting Party, and as such is superior to GATT-inconsistent state (regional or local government) law.[27]

In the light of these factors, it is submitted that in the case of a *unitary* state such as China, where the central government has the power to override local government acts, 'reasonable measures' would be likely to be held to mean the removal of the offending sub-national measure. The central government would have to remove, administratively or legislatively as appropriate, the offending measure, or, through administrative or legislative means, ensure that the offending measure does not have any legal effect and cannot be enforced at the sub-national level.

Conclusion: China's obligations with regard to sub-national entities

Based on the above analysis, it is submitted that the pre-accession WTO text makes clear that China, like any other WTO member, is responsible for the actions of its sub-national entities. China has confirmed this in the Protocol of Accession.

Leaving aside the issue of responsibility, in federal WTO members the central government must take all reasonable measures to seek the removal of the sub-national WTO-inconsistent measure, which is a different obligation from removing the measure itself. However, in China's case, because of the nature of its unitary system, where there are few legal limits on the central government's power in relation to the regions, as set out in its Constitution, the end result is that it may be *unreasonable* for China *not* to remove the measure. In any case, China's commitments in its Protocol of Accession confirm that China's obligation is to remove any sub-national measure that is inconsistent with its WTO obligations.

---

[26] GATT Panel Report, *Canada – Import, Distribution and Sale of Alcoholic Drinks by Canadian Provincial Marketing Agencies*, 39S/27, adopted 18 February 1992, para. 5.37.

[27] GATT Panel Report, *United States – Alcoholic and Malt Beverages*.

SELECT BIBLIOGRAPHY

Books and book chapters

Abbott, Frederick M. (ed.), *China in the World Trading System – Defining the Principles of Engagement* (Kluwer, The Hague, 1998).

Alford, William P., *To Steal a Book is an Elegant Offense: Intellectual Property Law in Chinese Civilization* (Stanford University Press, Stanford, 1994).

Anderson, K. and Hayami, Y., *The Political Economy of Agricultural Protection: East Asia in International Perspective* (Allen and Unwin, Sydney, 1986).

Bhagwati, J. and Patrick, H. (eds.), *Aggressive Unilateralism: America's 301 Trade Policy and the World Trading System* (University of Michigan Press, Ann Arbor, Mich., 1990).

Biddulph, S., 'The legal structure of decision making in Chinese police enforcement powers: some preliminary issues', in V. Taylor (ed.), *Asian Laws Through Australian Eyes* (Law Book Company, Sydney, 1997), pp. 207–38.

Bodde, D. and Morris, C., 'Basic concepts of Chinese law' in *Law in Imperial China: Exemplified in 190 Ch'ing Dynasty Cases* (Harvard University Press, Cambridge, Mass.,1967), pp. 1–39.

Cai, W., 'China's membership in the GATT/WTO: historical and legal issues', in W. Cai, M. Smith and X. Xu (eds.), *China and the World Trade Organization: Requirements, Realities, and Resolution* (Centre for Trade Policy and Law, Carleton University, Canada, 1996), pp. 10–32.

Chen, J., *Chinese Law* (Kluwer Law International, The Hague, 1999).

Chinese Yearbook of International Law (in Chinese) (China Foreign Translation and Publication Company, Beijing, 1993).

Cohen, J., 'Enforcement of intellectual property rights in Asia: the case of China', in H. Hansen (ed.), *International Intellectual Property Law and Policy* (Juris, New York, 1996), pp. 63–8.

Dernberger, F., DeWoskin, K., Goldstein, S., Murphey R. and Whyte, M. (eds.), *The Chinese: Adapting the Past, Facing the Future* (Centre for Chinese Studies, University of Michigan, Ann Arbor, 1991).

Dietrich, C., *People's China: A Brief History* (Oxford University Press, New York, 1986).

Drysdale, Peter and Song, Ligang (eds.), *China's Entry to the WTO: Strategic Issues and Quantitative Assessments* (Routledge, London, 2000).

Findlay, C., Martin, W. and Watson, A., *Policy Reform, Economic Growth and China's Agriculture* (Development Centre Studies, OECD, 1993).

Garnaut, Ross and Song, Ligang (eds.), *China: Twenty Years of Reform* (Asia Pacific Press, Canberra, 1999).

Garnaut, Ross, Song, Ligang, Yao, Yang and Wang, Xiaolu, *Private Enterprise in China* (Asia Pacific Press, Canberra, 2001).

Gillis, M., Perkins, D. H., Roemer, M. and Snodgrass, D. R., *Economics of Development* (4th edn, New York, Oxford University Press, 1996).

Gray, J., *False Dawn: The Delusions of Global Capitalism* (Granta, London, 1999), ch. 7.

Gregory, Neil, Stoyan, Tenev and Wagle, Dileep, *China's Emerging Private Enterprises: Prospects for the New Century* (International Finance Corporation, Washington D.C., 2000).

Groombridge, Mark A., and Barfield, Claude, *Tiger by the Tail: China and the World Trade Organization* (The AEI Press, Washington, D.C., 1999).

Krishna, K. M. and Tan, L., *Rags and Riches: Implementing Apparel Quotas under the Multi-Fibre Arrangement* (University of Michigan Press, Ann Arbor, 1998).

Kueh, Y., 'Economic decentralization and foreign trade expansion in China', in J. Chai and C. K. Leung (eds.), *China's Economic Reforms* (University of Hong Kong, Hong Kong, 1997).

Kur, A., 'TRIPs and trademark law', in F. Beier and G. Schricker (eds.), *Studies in Industrial Property and Copyright Law* (Max Planck Institut, Munich, 1996), pp. 92–116.

Lam, Willy Wo Lap, *China after Deng Xiaoping* (P. A. Professional Consultants Ltd, Hong Kong, 1995).

Lardy, N., *China's Unfinished Economic Revolution* (Brookings Institution Press, Washington, D.C., 1998).

Lardy, N., *Foreign Trade and Economic Reform in China, 1978–1990* (Cambridge University Press, Cambridge, 1991).

Law Yearbook of China (Press of Law Yearbook of China, Beijing, 1994).

Leeung Mei-fun, Priscilla (ed.), *China Law Report*, 1991, Vol. III (Butterworths Asia, Singapore, Malaysia and Hong Kong, 1995).

Lubman, S., *Bird in a Cage: Legal Reform in China After Mao* (Stanford University Press, Stanford, 1999).

Lulin, Guo, 'China's intellectual property protection system in progress', in Frederick M. Abbott (ed.), *China in the World Trading System –*

Defining the Principles of Engagement (Kluwer, The Hague, 1998), pp. 127–37.

Ostry, Sylvia, 'Coherence in global policy-making: is this possible?', in *Asia and the Future of the World Economic System* (mimeo, Chatham House, London, March 1999).

Qin, Chijiang, *Jinrong tizhi bianqian yu songjin zhuanhuan* [Change and liberalization in the financial system] (China Finance and Economics Press, Beijing, 1993).

Steinfield, E., *Forging Reform in China: The Fate of State Owned Industry*, (Cambridge University Press, Cambridge, 1998).

Tay, Alice E. S., 'From Confucianism to the socialist market economy: the rule of man vs the rule of law', in Alice E. S. Tay and Günther Doeker-Mach (eds.), *Asia-Pacific Handbook, Volume I: People's Republic of China* (Baden-Baden, 1998), pp. 81–142.

Tay, Alice E. S., and Doeker-Mach, Günther, 'Twenty years of law-making', in Alice E. S. Tay and Günther Doeker-Mach (eds.) *Asia Pacific Handbook – PRC Legislation* (Nomos Verlagsgesellschaft, Baden-Baden, forthcoming).

Thomson, G., 'Market disturbances and the Multifibre Arrangement: comment', in R. H. Snape (ed.), *Issues in World Trade Policy: GATT at the Crossroads* (St Martin's Press, New York, 1986), pp. 88–92.

Tull, Traisorat, *Thailand: Financial Sector Reform and the East Asian Crises* (Kluwer, London, 2000).

Wang, K., *Chinese Commercial Law* (Oxford University Press, Melbourne, 2000).

Wang Xiaoye, *Studies in Competition Law* (China Legal System Press, Beijing, 1999).

Xing, Fan, 'China's WTO Accession and its telecom liberalization', International Communications Study Program (Center for Strategic and International Studies, Washington D.C.).

Zhao, Kaikuan and Guo, Tianyong, *Zhongguo jinrong tizhi gaige ershinian* [The twenty years of Chinese financial system reform] (China Old Books Press, Beijing).

Zheng, Wei, Peng, Hui and Zhao, Rong, *Zhongguo jinrong zouxiang* [The future direction of the China financial system] (China Finance Press, Beijing, 1999).

Zheng, Yongnian, *Zhi Rongji ji xinzheng* [New reign under Zhu Rongji] (Global Publishing Co., Hong Kong, 1999).

Articles in journals

Alford, W., 'Tasselled loafers for barefoot lawyers: transformation and tension in the world of Chinese legal workers' (1995) 141 *The China Quarterly* 22.

Arup, C., 'Lawyers for China' (2001) 4 *Journal of World Intellectual Property* 741.

Bach, C., Martin, W. and Stevens, J., 'China and the WTO: tariff offers, exemptions and welfare implications' (1996) 132(3) *Weltwirtschaftliches Archiv* 409.

Baucus, Max, 'Re-assessing U.S.–China policy' (2001) 21(1) *SAIS Review* 303.

Baughman, L., Mirus, R., Morkre, M. E. and Spinanger, D., 'Of tyre cords, ties and tents: window dressing in the ATC?' (1997) 20(4) *World Economy* 407.

Beam, A., 'Piracy of American intellectual property in China' (1995) 4 *Journal of International Law and Practice* 335.

Bhala, R., 'Marxist origins of the "anti-Third World" claim' (2001) 24 *Fordham International Law Journal* 132.

Bloom, D. and Williamson, J. G., 'Demographic transitions and economic miracles in emerging Asia' (1998) 12(3) *World Bank Economic Review* 419.

Burke, M., 'China's stock markets and the World Trade Organization' (1999) 30 *Law and Policy in International Business* 361.

Butterton, G., 'Pirates, dragons and U.S. intellectual property rights in China: problems and prospects of Chinese enforcement' (1996) 38 *Arizona Law Review* 1100.

Chen, J., 'The development and conception of administrative law in China' (1998) 16(2) *Law in Context* 72.

Chuang, L., 'Investing in China's telecommunications market: reflections on the rule of law and foreign investment in China' (2000) 20(3) *Journal of International Law and Business* 519.

Clarke, D., 'Dispute resolution in China' (1991) 5 *Journal of Chinese Law* 245.

Clarke, Donald C., 'Power and politics in the Chinese court system: the enforcement of civil judgments' (1996) 10 *Columbia Journal of Asian Law* 1.

Cooper, J., 'Lawyers in China and the rule of law' (1999) 6 *International Journal of the Sociology of Law* 71.

Costanzo, Paddy, 'Telecommunications liberalisation in the Asia Pacific: impact of WTO' (1999) 49(3) *Telecommunications Journal of Australia* 45.

Drucker, Peter F., 'Trade lessons from the world economy' (1994) 73(1) *Foreign Affairs* 99.

Feaver, R., 'China's copyright law and the TRIPs Agreement' (1996) 5 *Journal of Transnational Law and Policy* 431.

Fung, J., 'Can Mickey Mouse prevail in the court of the Monkey King? Enforcing intellectual property rights in the People's Republic of China' (1996) 18 *Loyola of Los Angeles International and Comparative Law Journal* 613.

Gehlhar, M., Hertel, T. and Martin, W., 'Economic growth and the changing structure of trade and production in the Pacific Rim' (1994) 76 *American Journal of Agricultural Economics* 1101.

Hongming, Xiao, 'The internationalisation of China's legal services market' (2000) 1(6) *Perspectives* (available at www.oycf.org/perspectives/law.htm).

Hu, Patrick, ' "Mickey Mouse" in China: legal and cultural implications in protecting US copyrights' (1996) 14 *Boston University International Law Journal* 81.

Jones, C., 'Capitalism, globalization and the rule of law: an alternative trajectory of legal change' (1994) 3 *Social and Legal Studies* 195.

Keller, Perry, 'Sources of order in Chinese law' (1995) 42 *The American Journal of Comparative Law* 711.

Kerr, William A. and Hobbs, Anna L., 'Taming the dragon: the WTO after the accession of China' (2001) 2(1) *The Estey Centre Journal of International Law and Trade Policy* 1.

Krishna, K., Erzan, R. and Tan, L. 'Rent sharing in the Multi-Fibre Arrangement: theory and evidence from US apparel imports from Hong Kong' (1994) 2(1) *Review of International Economics* 62.

Lapres, J., 'The EU–China WTO deal compared' (2000) 27(4) *The China Business Review* 8.

Li, Donglü, 'The trend of economic decentralizing and its impact on foreign policies' [in Chinese] (1996) 6 *Strategy and Management* 44.

Liu, P. and Sun, A. (eds.), 'Intellectual property protection in the Asian-Pacific region: a comparative study' (1996) 4 *Occasional Papers/Reprint Series in Contemporary Asian Studies* 63.

Long, W., 'Intellectual property in China' (1999) *St Mary's Law Journal* 63.

Lou, Jianbo, 'China's bank non-performing loan problem: seriousness and causes' (2000) 34 *The International Lawyer* 1185.

Lu, Guoqiang, 'Advances in the protection of intellectual property rights in China' (1998) 1(1) *Harvard China Review*, on-line at http://www.harvardchina.org/magazine/article/intell-property1.html.

Martin, W., 'Modeling the post-reform Chinese economy' (1993) 15(5&6) *Journal of Policy Modeling* 545.

McCall, A., 'Copyright and trademark enforcement in China' (1996) 9 *Transnational Lawyer* 587.

Ostry, Sylvia, 'China and the WTO: the transparency issue' (1998) 3(1) *UCLA Journal of International Law and Foreign Affairs* 1.

Paglee, C., 'Chinese trademark law revised: new regulations protect well-known trademarks' (1997) 5 *University of Baltimore Intellectual Property Law Journal* 37.

Shi JiChun, 'Definition and regulation of administrative monopoly in China' (1999) 3 *Frontiers of Jurisprudence* 137.

Simons, J., 'Cooperation and coercion: the protection of intellectual property in developing countries' (1999) 11 *Bond Law Review* 59.

Spinanger, D., 'Textiles beyond the MFA quota phase-out' (1999) 22(4) *World Economy* 455.

Tanzer, A., 'The great quota hustle' (2000) 165(6) *Forbes* 118.

Tao, Jing Zhou, 'US trade deal opens China on WTO accession' (1999) 18 *International Financial Law Review* 9.

Thorn, Craig and Carlson, Marinn, 'The Agreement on the Application of Sanitary and Phytosanitary Measures and the Agreement on Technical Barriers to Trade' (2000) 31(3) *Law and Policy in International Business* 841.

Tiefenbrun, S., 'Piracy of intellectual property in China and the former Soviet Union and its effects upon international trade: a comparison' (1998) 46 *Buffalo Law Review* 1.

Wang, Zhi and Fan, Zhai, 'Tariff reduction, tax replacement, and implications for income distribution in China' (1998) 26 *Journal of Comparative Economics* 358.

Wrase, Alisa M., 'US bilateral agreements in the protection of intellectual property rights in foreign countries: effective for US intellectual property interests or a way out of addressing the issue?' (2000) 19 *Dickinson Journal of International Law* 245.

Yang, Y., 'The impact of MFA phasing out on world clothing and textile markets' (1994) 30(3) *Journal of Development Studies* 892.

Yu, Peter, 'From pirates to partners: protecting intellectual property in China in the twenty-first century' (1990) 50 *American University Law Review* 131.

Yu, Peter, 'Piracy, prejudice, and perspectives: an attempt to use Shakespeare to reconfigure the US–China intellectual property debate' (2001) *Boston University International Law Journal* 1.

Yu, Xingzhong, 'Legal pragmatism in the People's Republic of China' (1980) 3 *Journal of Chinese Law* 28.

Zhang Shufang, 'Analysis of administrative monopoly and legal measures that can be taken to counter it' (1999) 4 *CASS Journal Of Law* 34–9.

Reports

'Background on China's Logistics Industry', report issued by UN Development Program on opening of the International Conference on Modern Logistics and E-commerce, Beijing, 29 October 2000 (available at www.unchina.org/undp/news/html/bk001029.htm).

Bachetta, M., Low, P., Mattoo, A., Schuknecht, L., Wagner, H. and Wehrens, M. *Electronic Commerce and the Role of the WTO* (World Trade Organization, Geneva, 1998).

Baker & McKenzie, *An Overview of China's Internet Market and Its Regulation*, April 2000.

Ben-David, Dan and Winters, L. Alan, *Trade, Income Disparity and Poverty* (WTO Special Studies No. 5, 1999) (www.wto.org)

CIE (Centre for International Economics), *Barriers to Wool Fibre Products Trade: Costs to US Consumers and Australian Woolgrowers* (commissioned by Wool Council of Australia, Canberra, 1999).

CITA (Committee for Implementation of Textile Agreements), *New Transhipment Charges for Certain Cotton, Wool, Man-made Fibre, Silk Blend and other Vegetable Fibre Textiles and Textile Products produced or Manufactured in the People's Republic of China*, 6 December 2000 (http://otexa. ita.doc.gov/fr000/china3.htm).

EU Commission, *Comparative Analysis on Applied and Bound Tariff Rates in the Textile Sector* (1999) (http://europa.eu.int/comm/trade/goods/textile/texttarif.htm).

EU Commission, *The Council of the European Union Authorises the Commission to open Bilateral Negotiations with WTO Members to Improve Market Access for Textile and Clothing Products* (2000) (http://europa.eu.int/comm/trade/goods/textile/whatson02b.htm).

EU Commission, *China: Agreement on Trade in Textile Products* (2000) (http:/europa. eu.int/comm/trade/goods/textile/legitext2.hm, links to main and silk agreements with China).

EU Commission, *Textile Liberalisation Measures – Background* (2000) (http://europa.eu.int/comm/trade/pdf/tlm.pdf).

Industrial Structure Council, *Report on the WTO Consistency of Trade Policies by Major Trading Partners* (2000) (available from the website of the Ministry of Economy, Trade and Industry at http://www.meti.go.jp/english/report/index.html).

International Intellectual Property Alliance, *2001 Special 301 Report: PRC* (www.iipa.com/rbc/2001/2001SPEC301CHINA.pdf).

Komen, J. and Persley, G., 'Agricultural biotechnology in developing countries: a cross-country review' (ISNAR – IBS Research Report No. 2, The Hague, 1998).

Morrison, Wayne M., Report for Congress: China–U.S. Trade Agreements: Compliance Issues, Congressional Research Service, RL 30555, updated 1 September 2000, at http://www.cnie.org/nle.

'The new PRC Telecommunications Regulations: a first step towards a more level playing field', Linklaters & Alliance, p. 7 (www.globalservicesnetwork.com/telecom_regs.pdf).

OECD, *International Trade in Professional Services: Assessing Barriers and Encouraging Reform* (OECD, Paris, 1997).

OECD, *The Economic Impact of Counterfeiting*, prepared for the ICC Counterfeiting Intelligence Bureau, for the Industry Division of the OECD's Directorate for Science, Technology and Industry, 1998 (http://www1.oecd.org/dsti/sti/industry/indcomp/prod/fakes.htm).

Office of the United States Trade Representative, *2000 National Trade Estimate Report on Foreign Trade Barriers* (available from the USTR website, http://www.ustr.gov/reports/nte/2000/contents.html).

SCER, 'A comprehensive investigation report of local officials in China' [in Chinese] (1996) 2 *Management World* 197.

US Department of Commerce, *Expired Performance Reports (China)*, provided by US Information Service, Canberra.

US International Trade Commission, *Assessment of the Economic Effects on the United States of China's Accession to the WTO* (Publication 3229, Washington, D.C., 1999).

Wei, Shang-Jin, 'Local corruption and global capital flows' (Brookings Paper on Economic Activity 2, Washington, D.C., 2000), pp. 303–46.

World Bank, *China: Foreign Trade Reform* (World Bank, Washington, D.C., 1994).

World Bank, *China: Internal Market Development and Regulation* (World Bank, Washington, D.C., 1994).

World Bank, *China Engaged: Integration with the World Economy* (World Bank, Washington, D.C., 1997).

World Bank, *China: Long-term Food Security* (World Bank, Washington, D.C., 1997).

International agreements

Doha Ministerial Declaration, adopted 14 November 2001 (WT/MIN(01)DEC/1, dated 20 November 2001).

European Union, *The Sino–EU Agreement on China's Accession to the WTO: Results of the Bilateral Negotiations* (2000) (http://europa.eu.int/comm/trade/bilateral/china/wto.htm).

Protocol on the Accession of The People's Republic of China, 10 November 2001, Doha (published in Ministerial Decision of 10 November 2001, 'Accession of the People's Republic of China', WT/L/432, dated 23 December 2001) (available at http://www.wto.org/english/thewto_e/acc_e/completeacc_e.htm).

Report of the Working Party on the Accession of China, WT/ACC/CHN/49, 1 October 2001 or WT/MIN(01)/3, 10 November 2001. Schedule of concessions and commitments on goods, WT/ACC/CHN/49. Add.1 or WT/MIN(01)/3 Add. 1; Schedule of specific commitments on services and List of Article II MFN Exemptions, WT/ACC/CHN/49.Add.2 or WT/MIN(01)/3 Add 2. (Available at http://www.wto.org/english/thewto_e/acc_e/completeacc_e.htm.)

US–China bilateral agreement, previously publicly available at http://www.uschina.org/public and on *Inside U.S. Trade* website.

WTO Agreement – Marrakesh Agreement Establishing the World Trade Organization, done at Marrakesh, 15 April 1994, in Force 1 January 1995, (1994) 33 *ILM* 1144.

Miscellaneous works

Anderson, K., Francois, J., Hertel, T., Hoekman, B. and Martin, W., 'Potential gains from trade reform in the new millennium', paper presented at Third Annual Conference on Global Economic Analysis, Monash University, Australia, 27–30 June 2000.

Baucus, Max, 'The contours of a bipartisan China policy', speech given at the Nixon Center, Washington, D.C., 27 February 2001 (http://www.senate.gov/~baucus/td52.html).

Carter, C., *China's Trade Integration and Impacts on Factor Markets* (mimeo, University of California at Davis, 2001).

Carter, C., Chen, J. and Rozelle, S., *China's State Trading in Grains: an Institutional Overview*, mimeo, University of California at Davis, 1998.

Carter, C. and Huang, Jikun, *China's Agricultural Trade: Patterns and Prospects*, mimeo, University of California, Davis, 1998.

Chaien-Hale, Elizabeth, 'China overhauls compulsory licensing', *Managing Intellectual Property* (on-line magazine), May 2001 accessed at www.legalmediagruop.com/mip.

Chen, Xiwen, 'The WTO and the Sino-US agricultural agreement', Symposium on WTO and the Chinese Economy, sponsored by the State Information Center, Beijing, 22–3 May 1999.

Dehousse, F., Ghemar, K. and Iotsova, T., *Market Access Analysis to Identify Barriers in China and Russia Affecting the EU Textiles Industry: Final Report* (Centre d'Etudes Economiques et Institutionnelles, Brussels, 2000).

Fan, Ming-tai and Zheng, Yu-xin, 'China's trade liberalization for WTO accession and its effects on China – a computable general equilibrium analysis', paper presented at Third Annual Conference on Global Economic Analysis, Monash University, Australia, 27–30 June 2000.

Fan Zhai and Li Shantong, 'The implications of accession to WTO on China's economy', paper presented at Third Annual Conference on Global Economic Analysis, Monash University, 27–30 June 2000.

Gilbert, J. and Wahl, T., *Applied General Equilibrium Assessments of Trade Liberalization in China*, mimeo, Washington State University, 2001.

Ianchovichina, E. and Martin, W., *Comparative Study of Trade Liberalization Regimes: The Case of China's Accession to the WTO*, mimeo, World Bank, 2001.

Martin, W., *Trade policy Reform in the East Asian Transition Economies* (World Bank Policy Research Working Paper No. 2535, World Bank, Washington, D.C., 2001).

Martin, W., Dimaranan, B., Hertel, T. and Ianchovichina, E., *Trade Policy, Structural Change and China's Trade Growth* (Working Paper No. 64, Stanford Institute for Economic Policy Research, Stanford University, 2000).

OTEXA (1997), *Visa Arrangement Between the People's Republic of China and the United States of America Concerning Textiles and Textile products* (http://otexa.ita.doc.gov/).

Rozelle, S., Park, A., Huang, Jikun and Hehui, Jin, *Bureaucrat to Entrepreneur: The Changing Role of the State in China's Transitional Commodity Economy*, mimeo, Stanford University, Stanford, 1996.

Song, Ligang, 'Interest rate liberalization in China and the implications for non-state banking', paper presented at the International Conference on Financial Sector Reform in China, John F. Kennedy School of Government, Harvard University, 11–13 September 2001.

Walmsley, T. and Hertel, T., 'China's accession to the WTO: timing is everything', paper presented at the Third Annual Conference on Global Economic Modelling (Melbourne, 2000).

Williams, B. and Cass, D., *Legal Implications for Regulation of Trade in Services of China's Accession to the WTO* (Working Paper No. 2 of the China and the WTO Project, School of Law, Australian National University, Canberra, 2000) (http//law.anu.edu.au/china-wto/index-html).

Xintian, Yin, 'On the Second amendment of the Patent Law,' *Legal Forum*, 2001 (www.chinalawinfo.com).

Yang, Y., *China's WTO Accession: Why has it Taken so Long?* (Working Paper 00–2, Asia Pacific School of Economics and Management, Australian National University, Canberra, 2000).

Yang, Y., *China's Textile and Clothing Exports: Changing International Comparative Advantage and its Policy Implications* (Working Paper 99–3, Asia Pacific School of Economics and Management, Australian National University, Canberra, 1999).

Zhonghua Renmin Gongheguo Falü Quanshu [The Complete Laws of the PRC] (Jilin Renmin, 1989).

For Chinese legal materials in translation see http://www.qis.net/chinalaw/lawtran1.htm.

INDEX

Some agreements and conventions have been abbreviated. Acronyms are generally used. *See Abbreviations and Acronyms.*